A Wrong Life:
Studies in Lifeworld-Grounded
Critical Theory

SOCIAL AND CULTURAL THEORIES, Volume 1

Edited by: **Ben Agger**, *Office of the Dean, University of Texas at Arlington*

A Wrong Life:
Studies in Lifeworld-Grounded Critical Theory

by STEVEN P. DANDANEAU
*Department of Sociology, Anthropology
and Social Work
The University of Dayton*

and

MAUDE FALCONE
Dayton, Ohio

 JAI PRESS INC.

Stamford, Connecticut   *London, England*

Library of Congress Cataloging-in-Publication Data

Dandaneau, Steven P.
  A wrong life : studies in lifeworld–grounded critical theory / by
Steven P. Dandaneau and Maude Falcone.
     p.   cm. — (Social and cultural theories : v. 1)
  Includes bibliographical references and index.
  ISBN 0-7623-0478-2 (hardcover : alk. paper)
  1. Sociology—Moral and ethical aspects.   2. Critical theory.
3. Postmodernism—Social aspects. I. Falcone, Maude.   II. Title.
III. Series.
HM216.D257   1998
301—dc21   98-28055
                                                     CIP

Dedicated to
Maurice R. Stein and Richard T. Peterson

CONTENTS

LIST OF PHOTOGRAPHS

Preface

The splinter in your eye is the best magnifying-glass.
—Theodor W. Adorno, *Minima Moralia* ([1951]1974, p. 50)

This book is conceived as a contribution to the development of an empirically oriented critical theory of postmodern society.[1] In particular, we address what J.M. Bernstein (1995) has called the project of "recovering ethical life" via the methodology of "lifeworld-grounded critical theory," as named and developed by Ben Agger (1992b). In this book, as in Bernstein and Agger, the unique if unfinished critical theory of Theodor W. Adorno looms large.[2] It is our conviction that a meaningful critical theory of postmodern society must necessarily emerge from "damaged life," and that, furthermore, it must address itself to the theoretical and empirical work that death prevented Adorno from completing: the work of developing a sociology, not *of*, but *as* postmodern ethics.[3] We, too, then, are concerned with the paradoxical "actuality of Adorno."[4]

Whatever else one can say about the state of ethical life in postmodern times, the question of the possibility of ethical and moral judgement is a compelling one. It requires for an answer not so much more philosophy but a phenomenological, reflexive, philosophically sensitive sociology attuned to the empirical experience of the contemporary lifeworld.[5] This is because it is against embodied experience that ethics must prove itself. As a strictly philosophical question, ethics refers to the task of developing a stable and generalizable code capable of regulating and orienting judgements concerning the behavior of individuals. Ethics necessarily involves the positing of an ideal order as the context for judging activity. And yet, humans can not live in that order. They are instead compelled to work out their lives in a historically specific (dis)order. This social fact, which cannot be denied, renders any philosophical judgement, no matter how fair or lenient, a harsh one.

A culture reflexively aware of its constitutive activity understands that there is no pure realm immune to social and historical process. In such a culture, ethics must self-consciously reflect its origins. If it is to remain true to its own orientation towards the right and the good, it must give up its claim to judgment in search of the experience of the embodied individual. In short, ethics must transform itself into sociology. Sociology *as* ethics means that any ethics responsible to the conditions of human existence here and now must include within itself a social and historical understanding of the experience of living in a postmodern, late capitalist, increasingly integrated global social order of complex organizations and myriad institutions perpetually regulating and limiting individual behavior. Working within this always already existing context, which is *experienced* as *sui generis* even if we demure from the reification therein once so steadfastly held to, we contend that ethics must attend to and take the perspective of the embodied acting individual, the traditional focus of judgement, if it is to be anything more than one more discourse regime or one more matrix of knowledge/power, further diminishing the already trapped individual.

An ethics responsive to the perspective of the embodied individual, in all its limitations and frailties, becomes, then, a study of the impossibility of ethics, whose only conclusion is, following Adorno, "wrong life cannot be lived rightly." Such an ethics will take as its starting point the irresolvable contradictions and unwinnable negotiations of one's own experience if it is to avoid the tautological coherence of a grand, philosophical system. More than this, it should seek to understand one's own experience as neither private nor idiosyncratic, but in its systematic determination by objective contexts of disempowerment and illusion. Thus, in attending to the demands of the embodied subject, sociology *qua* ethics gives primacy to the objective conditions which threaten the subject's dissolution. It thus studies power from the bottom up.

To encapsulate our perspective, the only ethical principle true to its own impulse refers directly to the impossibility of ethics. That our life cannot be lived rightly, that the "ethical life" is a luxury afforded only through denying the material facts of late twentieth-century experience, is our first principle and guiding assumption. What is at stake is clear: confrontation with the conditions of catastrophe, domination, and mystification that threaten to suffocate not just humans, but humanity. Needless to say, such an ethical principle requires for its fulfillment the critical analysis of the prevailing hegemonic conditions that undermine the ethical life.

Our assumption is that ethics as the philosophical articulation of normative principles cannot sustain itself. In our view, almost as soon as the possibility of ethics is posited, it is forced to choose sides: either form an alliance with power or become a nullity. As such, the philosophical problem of ethics breaks apart into three analytically distinct but empirically entwined fields of explication. These fields are ethics as an aid to domination in the context of public administration, ethics as the burden of individual moral subjects in the context of objective powerlessness, and finally, ethics as the negation of historical consciousness in the context of twentieth-century human catastrophe.

Regarding the first field of explication, the practical negation of ethics in a fragmented and fragmenting social order—an order where the positing of universals (the common good, the interests of society) becomes a force of domination—results in a situation where similarities are posited and suppressed according to institutionalized social logics that operate independent of any particular individual's interest or control. This field loosely corresponds to the areas of policy administration and social engineering, which, in the interests of social order, seeks both to adequately represent the concerns of various statistical categories and fairly distribute public goods and services. Thus, we are divided into demographic groups according to various criteria (e.g., race, ethnicity, income, gender, sexual orientation, age, disability, where we live and what we do for a living) in the pursuit of efficient administration. Our differences are institutionalized accordingly, transformed into legal categories and objectified into conflicting interests.

From this perspective, ethics refers to the principles according to which competing demands for public goods and services are managed. These principles are shortcuts taken on behalf of administrative efficiency through which the responsibility for difficult decisions is displaced onto policies and procedures. In essence, such an ethics tends toward nothing other than the evasion of ethical responsibility. At best, this evasion ameliorates the bad conscience of administrators charged with the trying task of administering public policies in a contradiction-ridden social order. At worst, it legitimates and justifies indifference concerning the consequences of public administration and provides ideological support for the status quo.

At this point, and turning our attention to the second field of explication, it can be said that ethics as a social problem further fragments into the dilemma of the individual moral subject whose agency is severely limited by objective contexts of powerlessness. Even with certainty concerning right and wrong, the problem of acting in accordance with such certainty appears insurmountable, given that agency is increasingly centralized in "global" institutions. The fact that our individual actions are irrelevant to the global totality must be denied so that we might work ourselves up to the effort of doing anything at all. Recycling, for example, has no impact on the trash pile growing skyward. Strict adherence to a vegetarian diet does nothing to alter the global system of food production that demands that countless animals be granted life only so that they can be slaughtered to feed a gluttonous humanity. Such facts as these must be ignored, a bit of bad faith perhaps justifiable in its own right, but which does not change anything of historical/spatial consequence.

Ethics thus becomes a way of compensating for powerlessness. It is but an expression of complacency. We do what right we can and, having done so, take therapeutic comfort in this fact. That the totality remains the same, no matter how selflessly we take on our responsibilities, does not disturb a conscience at peace with its own compromise, for its only goal, its only ambition, is to preserve its restfulness.

In this context, an ethics responsive to its own inability to effect consequential social change insists that its own judgements must be false. The totality requires its victims to be superhuman in order to consistently live up to the most minimal moral standard, and judges them harshly, to be less than human, for failing to do so. The demands placed on the embodied, frail, limited individual who is expected through their own ingenuity to make ends meet and bear fully and by themselves the stresses of a contradictory existence, renders suspect all moral judgments, save only those directed at ethics itself.

Finally, and perhaps most significantly, there is the undeniable fact of an undeniable history which, in Karl Marx's ([1852] 1963, p. 15) memorable words, "weighs like a nightmare on the brain of the living." The disasters of the twentieth century render null and void the question of an ethical life. What has been done is done, and nothing we can do will ever right the scales of justice. Even the very act of positing the possibility of ethical conduct is, for us, morally dubious; it would demand forgetting the actuality of the unthinkable: the preponderant empirical history of the twentieth century. Such a positing would bear the stamp of mind without remembrance, the events of a well-nigh hundred years gone down the memory hole.

And yet, mindfulness of this history carries the danger of destroying the pre-theoretical sensitivity, the openness to moral impulse, that underwrites the possibility of ethics. The question remains open: how much of this wretched, mirror-of-mirrors, hyperreal, nightmare-of-a-world can humanity stand without becoming immune to its own desperation and closing itself to moral experience altogether? At stake then, are the empirical limits to moral consciousness within the historically specific nature of our human nature at the latest *fin de siecle*.

The inescapable conclusion that emerges from this orienting consideration of the possibility of ethics and the ethical life refers immediately to a paradox: an empirically committed, historically informed, and socially situated understanding of the complexities of our shared global situation underwrites the conclusion that it would be wrong, on ethical grounds, to posit the possibility of an ethically and morally responsible life. Ethics, in the present, must incorporate into its own consciousness its origins in its own failed project. The problem of recovering ethical life seems, therefore, like Jean-Paul Sartre's ([1943]1966, p. 784) vision of man as "a useless passion." This futility of ethics is not so much a consequence of our "anguish" before our ontological "freedom," as in Sartre's early existentialism, but, rather, is a historical consequence of our human praxis in-the-world. It is a result of our history-making, nation-building, society-erecting, all-too-phallocentric power. Thus, it is not so much what we *are* that renders ethics futile as what we have *done*.

An ethics which includes within its consciousness the experience of its own failure and futility refuses judgement and demands laws which prohibit their own enforcement. This Great Refusal must be undertaken without sliding into a cynical false consciousness; such a consciousness hardened against the impossibility of a moral life, takes the impossibility of ethics as a license to deny the reality or relevance of the moral impulse. This ethics situates itself between the nauseating panic-inducing awareness of the catastrophes humans have enacted on our own accord and under our own authority and the cynical appreciation of the facts of life. Moreover, such an ethics recognizes that even a free fall into the alternative poles of panic and cynicism is not entirely unproductive of enlightenment and emancipation, the final intention of any critical theory of the postmodern moment, for existence precedes essence like life precedes death, and an openness to the former terms is the only path to a free and rational relationship to the latter.

An ethics thus situated between panic and cynicism, drawing on the energy of both, grounds itself in its own weakness, powerlessness, and mortality, a ground that refers always to the vulnerabilities of the body. As the site of domination and corruption, the body is and must be the source of transformation as much as a site of humility. Just as domination must be continually reproduced and is thus as much a project as a fact, the body's potential for resistance is a question which necessarily remains open. Domination must constantly prove itself anew, and is, for this reason, never a constant. The panicked/cynical appreciation of the penetration of power into every aspect of existence and the appreciation of the fact that, in advanced capitalist society, domination is universally constitutive of subjectivity, renders universal the revolutionary subject.

Every(body), then, and perhaps especially the damaged body, is inherently resistance to the hegemonic, disembodying workings of a transcendent instrumental reason. Every birth is necessarily a forgetting, and thus a time when culture can be undone and recast. Every generation represents the chance for a radical negation of the present, even the negation of de-politicizing generational cliches that insistently contain youthful potentials. Every quixotic act of refusal, faced with its own futility, keeps the need for resistance evident. Every political struggle, overcome in advance by its own convictions, measures the extent to which successful single issue campaigns signal an ultimate defeat. Even the dying gasps of a failed philosophical and theoretical tradition might breathe enough life into the intellect to reveal a utopian content underneath the fading memories of enlightenment.

This brings us, then, to what might be called our singular perspective and aim in this book. Originating in our commitment to exploring the problem of ethical life from within "the context of delusion," to use Adorno's oft-quoted phrase, we write as participant-observers of our own lives. With Maurice R. Stein, we recognize that "we are participating victims as well as participant observers of the forces we study" (1963, p. 181). With Stjepan G. Mestrovic, we recognize that "things have gotten worse than George Orwell imagined" (1997, p. 162). It is in this sense that this book involves a series of studies of *our* world, which is hopefully conceptualized as intersecting with the reader's world as well. It is in this sense also that we write with heightened emotion, if for no other reason than in mindful struggle against the real reality of Mestrovic's "postemotional society" (1997). [6] If we use our bodies and our lives as objects of inquiry, it is out of the conviction that the very nature of post-modern society demands that a critical theory of our society must turn its attention away from the linguistic and toward the body and this earth, toward natural history and that which is contained within it, and the linguistic over-determination of the lot. In this way, we hope to contribute some flesh, our flesh, to the theoretical bones of critical theory.

The ultimate intention of a struggle for an ethical life in the postmodern moment has nothing to do with making things right, for that can never be the case, but refers instead to what Herbert Marcuse (1969) called the "pacification of existence," which entails the end of surplus and unnecessary everything, as though from mass birth to mass death. Nobody can help but live a wrong life, true. But that does not mean that we are not still in need of shared understanding and perhaps, too, some points of navigation now that the ship is most certainly going down. This is the task of critical theory today, at least the sort of critical theory that eschews the search for a timeless ground for rationality in favor of an internalization of Walter Benjamin's (1968) close attention to the "time of the now."

NOTES

1. Although critical theory has always been "empirical theory," this book is self-consciously situated within its recent "applied turn," to use John Forester's phrase, which is also sometimes called the move toward a "critical theory of public life." See Agger (1991), Dandaneau (1994, 1996, 1998), and Forester (1985).

Since this book turns on the meaning of such terms as postmodern, critical theory, emancipation, enlightenment, and the like, we will forego premature attempts at definition in favor of an immanent approach to their elucidation via confrontation with the empirical data that is our lifeworld.

2. If anything, Adorno's stature as one of this century's great sociological and philosophical minds has only grown in the years since his death in 1969. Fredric Jameson, a long-time critic of Adorno's, now suggests that "there is some chance he may turn out to have been the analyst of our own period, which he did not live to see, and in which late capitalism has all but succeeded in eliminating the final loopholes of nature and the Unconscious, of subversion and the aesthetic, of individual and collective praxis alike, and, with a final fillip, in eliminating any memory trace of what thereby no longer existed in the henceforth postmodern landscape. It now seems to me possible, then, that Adorno's Marxism, which was no great help in the previous periods, may turn out to be just what we need today" (1990, p. 5).

3. Following Jameson, it could be observed that Adorno addressed himself to the "traditional philosophical triad of the good, the true and the beautiful," including "the modulation of ethics into sociology ..." (1990, p. 8). Adorno's *Negative Dialectics* and the incomplete and posthumously published *Aesthetic Theory* address the value-spheres of epistemology and art, respectively, as did Kant's *Critique of Pure Reason* and *Critique of Judgement*. Adorno died, however, before he could turn his full attention to the realm of sociology-as-ethics that would parallel Kant's *Critique of Practical Reason*. Of course, Adorno addressed the problem of ethical life in numerous works, including especially in his *Minima Moralia*. Indeed, one could observe that ethical life bleeds from every pore of Adorno's *oeuvre*, which is not only consistent with his reflexive dialectical sensibility and practice, but which is also consistent with his unswerving engagement with his own "damaged life." On this point, see Jameson (1990, p. 74).

4. See Max Pensky's *The Actuality of Adorno: Critical Essays on Adorno and the Postmodern* (1997, p. 11), where he notes that, for Adorno, "The constellation—the dialectic—is a construction out of losses, a lading list of all that is too late to save; critical subjectivity is one generated from loss, and learning from it."

5. See Richard J. Bernstein's *The New Constellation: The Ethical-Political Horizons of Modernity/Postmodernity* (1991) as an example of the best of such "more philosophy."

6. With regard to Mestrovic's *Postemotional Society* (1997), we would be remiss if we did not note the uncanny coincidence of sources and subject matter between his and our work. Among many other topics, Mestrovic analyzes the death of John F. Kennedy and the Dayton Peace Accords, and he draws heavily on the work of Baudrillard, Marcuse, and Orwell for his own novel theoretical contributions. Perhaps the single most significant distinguishing factor, however, is methodological: whereas Mestrovic intends to "sketch the parameters of postemotional society," and does so from a primarily observer point of view, we intend to document our own critical *participation* within this society (1997, p. xvi).

Acknowledgments

We would like to thank Ben Agger, the series editor, for the opportunity he has afforded us to write a book such as this. By allowing us free reign to write the book that we felt the need to write, regardless of its many trespasses against academic norms, we believe it was Professor Agger's intention to use his editorial power to resist the suffocating Foucaultdian discipline characteristic of so much mainstream academic work in the social sciences and humanities. We only hope that we have in some measure lived up to the trust that he has so generously bestowed upon us and in so doing contributed in a meaningful way to the quiet revolution against domination inside and, more importantly, outside of academia.

We have benefited from the presentation of aspects of this work in a number of venues, including the Institute for the Analysis of Contemporary Society, the Society for the Study of Social Problems, the Department of Sociology at Brandeis University, the Department of Philosophy at Michigan State University, and the Department of Sociology, Anthropology, and Social Work at the University of Dayton. Thanks are also due to the University of Dayton Research Institute for several summer research grants and grants in-aid that facilitated the research and writing of this book. Additional financial support to assist in the preparation of this manuscript for publication was received from Fred P. Pestello, Associate Dean of the University of Dayton College of Arts and Sciences, and from Patrick G. Donnelly, Chair of the Department of Sociology, Anthropology, and Social Work at the University of Dayton. The staff at JAI Press has also been exceedingly understanding and caring in their production of the book. We would especially thank Susan Oppenheim, Executive Editor and Gayle Jerman, Vice President for Book Production.

While this book is primarily the product of an unusual domestic collaboration, the authors have benefited greatly from the comments, suggestions, and materials provided by a number of generous friends and colleagues. These include Joe Acquisto, Ben Agger, Justin Biddle, Will Brooke-debock, Tim Bushnell, Marcus Dandaneau Angie Dillman, Pat Donnelly, Erin Dougherty, Stephen Esquith, Dan Finseth, Betsy Hayes, Karen Jonke, Beth McClimens, Michelle McDermott, Tonya McKee, Rachel Meeks-Johnson, D'Arcy John Oaks, Dick Peterson, Maury Stein, Mark Sullivan, Steve Thorpe, Greg Wilpert, and Rick Yuille. In this regard, we wish to underscore the extraordinary assistance and support provided by Erin M. Dougherty, who not only labored arduously to edit the entire manuscript, but who also shared intimately in nearly every phase of its production, from first draft, to photographic assistance, to final publication. The book is much-improved as a result of her sustaining and unfaltering interest and attention.

Finally, this book is dedicated to our respective graduate school mentors, Maurice R. Stein, Professor of Sociology at the Brandeis University, and Richard T. Peterson, Professor of Philosophy at Michigan State University. Maury's long-standing course in the Sociology of Birth and Death is an essential background to the lifespan- and lifeworld-oriented set of studies here presented. This book is thus for Dandaneau a kind of *Habilitation* thesis, which, though he was under no obligation to do so, Maury has generously accepted. Dick's influence is equally expansive, from his formidable instruction in critical theories of society to his specific and caring mentoring of Falcone's Master of Arts thesis in philosophy, which is here presented in revised form as Chapter 6. To Maury and Dick, then, we dedicate this book, and through them we remember all our respective teachers who have helped us develop the concepts that we need to live a wrong life as it must be led.

Needless to say, especially for a book grounded in its author's own particular lifeworld experience, mistakes of fact and judgment, of composition and interpretation, of politics and ethics, are entirely are own.

Chapter 1

Introduction: Lifeworld-Grounded Critical Theory

No reader of The Philosophical Discourse of Modernity *can fail to be struck by the marginalization of the political in both Habermas and his adversaries. This marginalization, this absence of the political is the philosophical discourse of modernity, not, as it were, willfully or by avoidance, but fatefully.*
—J.M. Bernstein, *Recovering Ethical Life* (1995, p. 196, emphasis in original)

The noontide panic fear in which men suddenly became aware of nature as totality has found its like in the panic which nowadays is ready to break out at every moment: men expect that the world, which is without any issue, will be set on fire by a totality which they themselves are and over which they have no control.
—Max Horkheimer and Theodor W. Adorno, *Dialectic of Enlightenment* (1947, p. 29)

The question about poetry after Auschwitz has been replaced with that of whether you could bear to read Adorno and Horkheimer next to the pool.
—Fredric Jameson, *Late Marxism* (1990, p. 248)

[T]he task of providing men and women with that 'sociological imagination' for which C. W. Mills ... appealed years ago, has never been so important as it is now, under conditions of postmodernity.
—Zygmunt Bauman, "Is There a Postmodern Sociology?" (1988, p. 234)

Fredric Jameson has described the central problem of living life in the postmodern era as "the loss of our ability to position ourselves within this space and to cognitively map it" (in Stephanson 1989, p. 48; see also

1

Jameson 1984). This absence is, for us, a visceral experience, *felt* on our shoulders as though it were the weight of the world, on our face as though it were a boot stomping, in our throat as the rising nausea of one facing hopelessly imminent execution, in our tense muscles as spasms of guilt and shame, and in the contradiction of our not unoccassional blank numbness and despair. Our public response as cultural workers (as readers/writers) to this disorientation is the development of a distinctly sociological cognitive map appropriate for those, like ourselves, condemned to living life in the postmodern era. In particular, we are interested in exploring the relationship between such a map and the moral conduct of life. Can sociology function as a stand-in for eclipsed modernist ethical systems? Must it?

The basic idea for our own proposed conceptual map lies in the co-ordinate points left to us from another era, namely, C. Wright Mills' (1959) formulation of the sociological imagination. The sociological imagination was Mills' distillation of the metatheory of the "classic tradition" of modern social theory. Mills describes the sociological imagination as a "form of ... self-consciousness" and as a "quality of mind" that is firmly rooted in "an absorbed realization of social relativity and of the transformative power of history." Once realized, it is experienced as the "transvaluation of values," which is to say, as a type of thoroughly secular epiphany, "a terrible lesson" but, writes Mills, "in many ways a magnificent one" (pp. 5, 7-8, 5). For Mills, this type of "mind" is built around the metatheoretical "co-ordinate points" of "biography, history, and society" (p. 143), each term defining the other in dialectical tension to the rest. Individuals are thereby rendered "minute points of the intersections of biography and history within society" (p. 7). "By means of it," writes Mills, "orientation to the present as history is sought"; the "classic focus" is the human totality at the "historical level of reality" (pp. 15, 128). Mills further contended that the sociological imagination was the "common denominator" of the "post-modern period;" that it was the "most needed" cognitive map around (pp. 15, 166, 13).

For the purpose of regeneration and reinvigoration if also to facilitate a Jamesonian transcoding of the sociological imagination, we read Mills as having developed a version of dialectical imagination along the lines of an Adorno- and Benjamin-style constellation, with biography, history, and social structure as its stars.[1] We assert that, if taken seriously, such a metatheory can continue to provide exactly the "orientation" that Mills (1960) saw as the essential raison d'être for any so-called sociological imagination. Our main theoretical task, then, is the articulation of this new sociological imagination as a constellation appropriate to the vertigo of postmodern times. Our main practical task is the application of this dialectical consciousness in the analysis of a series of interrelated case studies.[2] Our main concern, finally, is the ethical implications of these studies, and, in dialectical fashion, the implications that these studies harbor for the possibility of postmodern ethics itself.

AN EXCURSUS ON METHODOLOGY

Our particular interest in the status of a postmodern sociological imagination as a type of postmodern "ethics" demands, however, special and immediate attention to our chosen methodology, which is a version of what Ben Agger (1992b) has called "lifeworld-grounded critical theory." As Agger explains:

> A lifeworld-grounded critical theory theorizes nontraditional modes of personal and interpersonal resistance, identifying their pre-political potential.

> A lifeworld-grounded critical theory also theorizes *itself*, attempting to adopt a more public discourse in order to prefigure democratic relations between writers and readers (pp. 12-13).

Lifeworld-grounded critical theory is thus a form of self-knowledge that seeks to understand the objective conditions of its own emergence. Such a theoretical approach develops within actually existing lives that transpire/ expire within a historically specific spatio-temporal horizon. In other words, lifeworld-grounded critical theory is situated within a world, this world, our world. It is a form of self-consciousness that begins and grounds itself in its own experience, and, desiring not to transcend its origins, is content to work within its own limits. Accordingly, in our effort to theorize postmodernity, we take our own experience as our point of departure and the standard against which we evaluate our knowledge. We place our embodied selves at the center of our theories, convinced that our knowledge—no matter how sophisticated or immune to criticism—is worse than useless if it does not serve us in our attempts to negotiate the contradictions of our lived existence. Our models are figures such as Audre Lorde, Jackie Orr, and Theodor Adorno. Through their theoretical writings, these cultural workers have written their lives into their textual representations of society, thereby penetrating the processes through which shared struggles are privatized and thus rendered moot and of no public significance.

In the theoretical project at hand, we take issue with critical theory as it has developed within the confines of academic institutions, specifically its pre-occupation with the positive representation of abstract social systems. We agree therefore with Agger's observation that "the methodological injunction of the original Frankfurt School thinkers *to historicize*—to apply the overall method of negative dialectics to the particular historical formations of capital and culture that bear ideological criticism" has been too often forgotten (1992b, p. 10, emphasis in original; see also Agger 1998). While any social theory worthy of the name must understand the systemic conditions and historically determined limits of individual experience and agency, it cannot long remain content at this level of analysis lest it forget its telos toward emancipation.

Involved in our effort to avoid participation in the development of a critical social theory that attends only to the potential for systems crises and has nothing to contribute to the understanding of how these system crises manifest themselves in the context of individual lives, in lifeworld crises, is our intention to address the imbalance between temporality and spatiality that Edward Soja, in his *Postmodern Geographies* (1989), sees as characteristic of the development of critical theory. Using Mills as a point of departure, Soja writes:

> I draw upon Mills's depiction of what is essentially a historical imagination to illustrate the alluring logic of historicism, the rational reduction of meaning and action to the temporal constitution and experience of social being (pp. 13-14).

> To be sure, ... [Mills'] "life-stories" have a geography too; they have milieux, immediate locales, provocative emplacements which affect thought and action. The historical imagination is never completely spaceless ... [But] an already-made geography sets the stage, while the wilful making of history dictates the action and defines the story line (p. 14).

For Soja, critical theory must rethink its historicist tendencies lest its resulting narratives acquire "the oversimplified character of a fable" (1989, p. 24). Implicit in Soja's concern is the recognition that historicism is a form of abstraction that neglects direct confrontation with the spatial limits of individual agency, and that, moreover, evades the intractable dilemmas of that agency by displacing solutions onto an exclusively temporal plane. Such a displacement falsely reconciles the contradictory demands of agency in our postmodern situation. A critical theory that blithely relies on a future orientation for its emancipatory content slides all too often into self-righteous moralism in the embrace of an empty utopianism.

Consider, for example, Cornel West, who is both an astute reader of critical theory and a leading American public intellectual. Yet, West's (1989) advocacy of a "prophetic pragmatism" suggests his unwillingness to disentangle himself from the sheer weight of two contradictory and conservative traditions of irrationalist thought. More to the point, West's combination of theology and pragmatism reproduces an abstract, space-less utopianism wherein a painful adjustment to the given, always its own mythology, is compensated for by the promise of a future redemption. As a public intellectual who positions himself within a grand narrative of American Democracy, West's potentially explosive Marxian critical theory is easily assimilated into the cultural mainstream. It is thus drained not so much of its "progressive" transformative potential, but of its truth content.

Soja's conclusion that, in postmodern times/spaces, critical theory's "historical narrative must be re-entered at a different plane and scale," that is, below the level of grand moralistic storytelling, is crucial to any effort that would aspire to avoid the self-deception and political containment of West's critical theory (1989, p. 24). As we see it, postmodern critical theory must be lifeworld-grounded, where "lifeworld" entails a profoundly spatial as well as temporal dimension, in recognition of the fact that the "background" of social life is about place and space as much as it is about past and future.

The logic of this type of investigation therefore requires that we take our own perspectives as the primary means by which we ground our knowledge in our own participation in hospitalized child birth, our efforts to parent a young boy with various moderate and severe disabilities, our experiences as the subjects of Generation X, our residency in the place called the City of Dayton, and our citizenship in a societally integrated if also mystifying world community of humanity. These experiences, both fragmented and contradictory, come together to constitute our lives, and it is with these experiences in mind and borne in our bodies that we theorize postmodernity.

Equally to the point, we use fieldwork and documentary methods in our analysis of concrete, socio-historical societal relations in addition to our study of everyday life via discourse analysis and other forms cultural studies methods (see Agger 1991, 1992a). In this way, the taken-for-granted, always-already embeddedness of social action and moral choice comes to the fore in a series of situated, immanent, reflexive, critical studies with the institutional and otherwise translocal societal structure of the postmodern, globalizing world forming an essential if (in textual terms) metaphorical background (see Marcus and Fischer 1986; Van Maanen 1988). In short, we are at the center of this work. The "data" on which it is based is either our own experience or the varied materials of social life that have fallen stuck in our web.

In order to present this methodology in a light consistent with our (more shadowy) theoretical approach, we furthermore stage the theoretical applications as types of "force fields" (*Kraftfeld*), the term Adorno (and Benjamin) used to denote, in Martin Jay's concise explication, "a relational interplay of attractions and aversions that constituted the dynamic, transmutational structure of a complex phenomenon" (1984a, p. 14). For Jameson, the entire condition of postmodernity is conceived as a "cultural dominant," as a "force field in which very different kinds of cultural impulses...must make their way" (1984, p. 57). Parallel to Jameson's well-known analyses of such venues as the lobby of the Los Angeles Westin Bonaventure, Frank Gehry's architecture, or Alfred Hitchcock's *North By Northwest*, the main content of this book is a series of specific case studies, whose relation to the fluid postmodern totality is perspectival, if not occasionally utterly fragmentary, but nonetheless—and this is our strongest claim—true. Again, in Jay's unencumbered locution:

> The micrological method that he [Adorno] inherited from Kracauer and Benjamin, which was never fully reconciled with the holistic emphasis he absorbed from Lukacs, was ... not merely a temporary expedient appropriate only to this current fallen world of fragmentation. Like Ernst Bloch, Adorno saw such fragments as prefigurations or traces (*Spuren*) of a possible utopia (1984a, p. 87).

Of course, we do not expect the study of fragments to set anyone, including ourselves, free, much less do we expect these studies to unleash utopian potentials. Mere possession of a cognitive map called the postmodern sociological imagination feeds no one, stops no bullets, prevents not a single act of violence against women, children, or anyone else. In other words, stories of mere mindfulness do nothing, change nothing, except perhaps a single mind, a single reader, which, however, might be something since a "minute intersection of biography and history within society" is the only possible locus of moral decision. In negative dialectics, truth-content, no matter how disturbing, and utopia, no matter how unrealizable under given objective conditions, are inexorably intermingled.

The remainder of this introduction is dedicated to the explication of our póstmodern version of the sociological imagination, including a series of thumbnail sketches of the application of this constellation vis-à-vis the force fields that our lives have foisted upon us for detailed study, and that constitute the main body of this text.

TOWARD A POSTMODERN
SOCIOLOGICAL IMAGINATION

It is our conjecture that fidelity to the exacting demands of the sociological imagination is, sadly, rare among sociologists today, even those putatively sympathetic to Millsian sociology. Parallel to the patterns of bad faith that Jean-Paul Sartre saw as the vexing albeit routine response to the anguish inherent in the ontological freedom that is human existence, we see in the works of most contemporary critical theorists moves that reduce or often fully collapse the tension caused by the "absorbed realization of social relativity and of the transformative power of history," the tension that requires a dialectical embrace of history, biography, and society. The resultant theoretical bailouts may appear to save the sociologist as cultural workman his or her values from transvaluation, and thereby protect some version of a life-lived-rightly, but in reality all that is spared is sociological truth and intellectual consistency.

These patterns of bad faith typical of sociology include: (a) clinging to the sheer weight of a particular and inherently irrational tradition (e.g., in adherence to any particular religious dogma, nationalism, ethnocentrism, humanism, or race-conscious, patriarchal, or heterosexist ideology); (b) hypostatizing and perhaps even sanctifying the essence of sociological self-consciousness itself (e.g., Emile Durkheim, Peter Berger's *Invitation to Sociology*, Mills' own nostalgia for the classic tradition); (c) attempting to spurn the lessons of reflexive sociology in favor of a cool, rational detachment and separation from society (e.g., Max Weber, Anthony Giddens, Jürgen Habermas); or, lastly, (d) the converse, succumbing as though in a sophisticated manner to a self-consciousness built on the myth of societal determination of the self (e.g., Erving Goffman, rational choice theory, behaviorism).[3] In these and other similar examples, the dialectical tension between history, biography and social structure is distorted or erased altogether.

The theoretical minimalism of Norman K. Denzin provides a particularly useful illustration of one form sociological bad faith can take, given that like us, he seeks a postmodern sociological imagination attuned to the intricacies of daily life. Denzin, a former Mills admirer, has developed his minimalist sociology as an alternative to the theoretical practice which Mills habitually referred to as "taking it big." Indeed, Denzin believes that he has unearthed "the lived history Mills sought, but never found" (1990, p. 11). As Denzin writes:

> Mills spoke to an earlier generation [i.e., Denzin's]. His text affected socio-logical lives and set in motion versions of the sociological imagination that are now turning back on him. The mark of a good sociological narrative is its ability to raise questions and to create challenges. Mills did this, but today we must go beyond him (1990, p. 13).

Denzin aims to go beyond Mills' modernist metatheory with an

> ethically responsive, feminist, theoretically minimalist, postmodern sociol-ogy and anthropology of existential experience that is responsive to the death of the 'social' in sociology while it opens itself to the sounds and voices of contemporary American life (1990, p. 2).

What is entailed in this metatheoretical transformation is a type of adaptive response to the collapse of the social, which, following various postmodern social theorists (especially Jean Baudrillard), refers to Denzin's jettisoning of any hope of representing a socio-historical totality in the postmodern age. (The one possible exception to this totality-representation prohibition is, perhaps, Denzin's own positing of this prohibition, which is rooted in his acceptance of, and advocacy for, numerous works of grand postmodern [anti-]theory.)

Denzin wants sociology to eschew big ideas and theory of all kinds in favor of close attention to the fragmented, damaged subject, particularly when the subject is experiencing "epiphanic moments," that is, "when the subject is in-between interpretative frameworks" (1990, pp. 12-13). Denzin has in mind "the ever elusive subject ..., the man, women, and child who cries out and sometimes goes to others for help, [who has] an occasional grasp on who she is and where she is going" (1990, pp. 13, 14). He seeks "the stories of personal trouble that ordinary people tell one another," and not the stories of "self- or society-appointed experts" like Millsian sociologists. He seeks "thick interactional descriptions," not "thick theory" a là Mills; he seeks, in the end, critique and intervention when sociological texts "come up against cultural writings which reproduce repressive ideologies that go against the grain of experience uncovered in the stories we have secured" (1990, pp. 15, 7, 5, 15). Although his is a complex formulation, this is the essence of Denzin's postmodern sociological imagination.

Part of what makes Denzin's effort so useful for present purposes is the apparent affinity between our interest in lifeworld-grounded critical theory and his critically minded minimalist sociology. As is so often the case, however, intellectual work which is apparently similar may in fact be the furthest apart. In this case, it is impossible to underestimate the significance of Denzin's abandonment of a notion of totality (or the social), a move that creates an unbridgeable gulf between Denzin's and this work.

The implication of Denzin's move may be understood as partaking in the pattern of bad faith described above wherein the sociological imagination is captured by what Sartre called the "spirit of seriousness," or the tendency to posit as objective and constraining a social world in which there is no choice but to adapt and conform. Ironically, Denzin does just this in his positivist acquiescence before the condition of postmodernity, which he argues requires that we learn to get along without theory, certainly without dialectical theory.[4] As Denzin at one point asserts:

> ... today our social texts no longer, if they ever did, refer to a fixed reality. Our theoretical signifiers have lost their referents. They now refer only to other texts, which in turn refer to yet others. There is no longer a world out there that can be objectively mapped by a theory or a method (1990, p. 13).

Everything in this formulation turns on the notion of "objectively mapped," with respect to which, unlike Denzin, we mean to give dialectical interpretation and rendering.

We note, for example, that Denzin's minimalism would seem to deny theoretical insight to those whose stories he would prefer to simply listen to. Equally troubling is Denzin's presumption that average folks want nothing more than having their stories heard, as if being listened to by a sociologist (of all people) was an end-in-itself. In any case, it would seem necessary from the standpoint of professional ethics to reflect upon his right to snoop around "epiphanic moments" given that such moments are, by definition, times of vulnerability, precisely when linguistic, interpretive defenses are weakened. To place the textual representations of epiphany on the sociology shelf at the nearest bookstore would seem to involve an

·unsavory alliance between Denzin's minimalism and the crass consumerism of trash TV. Supremely savvy, Denzin is not unaware of the risks that he takes. But having given too much to participation and not enough to observation, his minimalism is lost in space.

We repeat, at issue in the difference between Denzin's minimalism and our perspective is our willingness to represent totality. We insist that an ethically responsive and even feminist postmodern critical theory has a responsibility to retain Mills' otherwise modernist and, yes, masculinist, "taking it big" bravado. Critical theory must obstinately and theoretically engage totality, the complex interactions of social institutions as they operate together to form something analogous to a system. To limit knowledge to small stories out of a concern to avoid the numerous epistemological dilemmas inherent in attempts to theorize totality relieves social institutions, and thus social power, of accountability. This move also reproduces the positivist willingness to sacrifice insight in the interests of certainty.

It is true, however, that the totality is never given, and especially not to the senses or immediate experience. The totality is not a material thing but the combined operation of forces and processes that congeal in the experience of concrete embodied individuals. Lifeworld-grounded critical theory, in its attempt to understand the totality of social processes, thus knows it has no direct access to its object. It seeks to understand the concrete determinants of particular experience through that experience and thereby seeks to understand totality but only as a refracted image out of the corner of its eye. It is true that this project involves the risk of metaphysics, but failing to conceptualize the historical-geographical social totality involves its own risk, namely, as David Harvey has noted (1989, p. 359), the risk of sliding "into parochialism, myopia and self-referentiality," a danger that lies in every attempt to programmatically eschew grand narratives.

What, then, would constitute an adequate formulation of a postmodern sociological imagination? How, indeed, can anyone in this world maintain the mindful tension required in negative dialectics? Some, we think, have accomplished this feat. We would note the extraordinary work of Jackie Orr (1990), who takes her own body/history as the site for critical studies of social structure. In this book, likewise, we offer detailed discussion of each "star" in the Millsian constellation only in direct dialogue with empirical materials, concrete settings, and our own embodied experience. Besides the textual economy therein gained, this style of theoretical formulation and textual representation is, it would seem, at least true to the nature of a conceptual apparatus that purports to be lifeworld-grounded. By way of introduction to the substantive chapters, then, we conclude this introduction with an orienting discussion of each star in our postmodern sociological constellation.

SOCIAL STRUCTURE

We, the authors, live in a place, namely, Dayton, Ohio. Dayton is a city of 180,000 situated in a county of over 500,000 inhabitants. The major employers are Wright-Patterson Air Force Base, General Motors Corporation, and NCR Corporation. The city itself is spatially divided by class segregation. For example, 26.5 percent of Dayton's inhabitants live in what the U.S. Federal Government defines as poverty, and mostly in neighborhoods characterized by high concentration of poverty and which are located near abandoned or dilapidated industrial plants. The median income of city residents is far less than that enjoyed by Dayton suburbanites, the richest of whom live in elegant enclaves along golf courses and secluded, hilly, tree-shaded lanes. Dayton's downtown features the closed department store characteristic of Midwestern, rust-belt towns, whereas its suburban ring is dotted with several popular shopping malls and sprawling strip mall conglomerations. Dayton is also divided racially, where "west side" means African-Americans and "east side" working-class whites (many of whom identify with appalachian culture). What's left of the urban middle class, both black and white, live somewhere in-between. The suburbs and surrounding rural counties are predominately white, including a small countercultural outpost, Yellow Springs—home of Antioch College—which is distant and marginal in both space and time. If Dayton has a reputation or fame that extends beyond its borders, it is most likely as the home of the inventive Wright Brothers or, more recently, as the home of the Dayton Peace Accords. We live in a city that has been dubbed by *Time Magazine* (September 14, 1992, p. 39) an "American microcosm."

Even though we have already given attention to the spatial arrangements of the city, our story so far has clear fablistic tendencies. Indeed, it is a middle-range description that overshoots or undercuts just about everything that might be of more than pedestrian sociological interest. For example, how, given this type of narrative structure, could we relate the idea of Max Weber's "iron cage" of rationality to contemporary Dayton society, much less Adorno's "administered" or Foucault's "carceral" or Baudrillard's "hyperreal" society? Depictions of social structure that do not distinguish themselves from commonsense social theory—the taken for granted consciousness of "race" or "class," or "urban" and "suburban," "microcosm"—seem destined to reproduce rather than challenge and transform everyday consciousness. The centering discourse of social problems analysis, for example, with its ready acceptance of the myth of society and the scourges of conflict and inequality, hardly seems adequate to even the simple everyday reality of an ordinary place like Dayton, let alone to the unprecedented world-historical advent of global warming, species extinction, ozone depletion, the AIDS pandemic, and nuclear winter exterminism, which are part of Dayton, too.

And are there no women in Dayton, no children, no elderly, no clerical, sales, and service workers, rivers or mineral deposits, no plants and animals, no brushes with evil, no strangers from distant lands and climes, no individuals harming themselves daily, no fantasies, wishes, dreams, expectations, aspirations, fears, no sickness and death, no shamanism, totemism, scientism, paranoia, violence, no sense of standing on shaky ground, of staring into a world-historical abyss, no tears, no forgiveness, no forgetting, no remembering, no promise of future times? Is Dayton a postmodern city? Do African-Americans and appalachian whites experience the condition of postmodernity, or is this experience the exclusive preserve of the Eurocentric intelligentsia? Is there even an intelligentsia in Dayton, or is this class primarily a bicoastal phenomena?

We do not mean to appeal to the reified mentality of those who think of such questions as best dealt with via the disaggregation of data sets, nor to those who favor maniacal attention to ever-more closely examined details of situations. Rather, we wish to assert that below the middle-range narrative of place and situation and all manner of concomitant statistical representations lies the real particulars of existence, always already more complex than our theories and methods can explain, much less than they can fully or even adequately (re)present. Projections of social structure are always, thus, in part, matters of choice.

In critical theory, these choices are further constrained by the apprehension of need and a sense of urgency: What do we need to know, and what do we need to know right now? The analysis of social structure is thus something analogous to studying architecture and pyrotechnics while standing in a house that is burning down. People are being immolated all around us (for example, in *this* world, an estimated 10,000 children perish daily from starvation and inadequate medical attention). The house is on fire. The planet is imperiled. Every death is a condemnation of critical theory, and the *sin qua non* of its "structural analyses." Not coincidentally, this is what Mills was talking about when he discussed the compelling nature of "issues" and "troubles"; this is why Mills felt sociology to be the "common denominator" of the postmodern epoch.

In our six studies, we read mass birth and hospitals, disabilities and schools, generations and popular culture, built-environments and neighborhoods, scholarly and public discourse, and the prevailing state of mass death all as "social structure" in need of our theoretical attention. In the course of our lives we have encountered in each of these institutional spaces the disorienting and oppressive effects of postmodern society. We aim past (or through) middle range theoretical discourse to address the extremities of the phenomena at hand. For example, we treat the conditions of our experienced hospital birth as the locus of the overdetermination of rationality at the expense of agency, a specific intersection of biography, history, and society familiar to both Weber and Foucault. But more is needed than simply mandarin criticism of mass birth in mass society, even if accompanied by a Nietzschean fillip that counsels the deployment of artistry before the regime of bio-power. Theory, we assert, must resist the original discipline of an administered birth. We must take it big, holding in mind the truth of mass birth as well as the "new sensibilities" that we are compelled to develop as a means of coping with actually-existing social structure (Marcuse 1969). For us, therein lies the ethical implications of sociological conceptualization, for these new sensibilities, in Agger's words, "prefigure a good society by our treating ourselves, each other, and nature well in the here and now" (1992b, p. 13).

We similarly analyze our experience with the social structuring of disability in terms of Adorno's classic study, "The Stars Down to Earth," for our efforts to parent our disabled 4-year-old son have helped us appreciate the grip pseudo-rational thought has on our culture. Even so, our participation in the various institutions and discursive regimes structuring disability has taught us to appreciate the utopian substratum characteristic of situated human interaction. We also describe the contours of a hyperreal GEN X as a new wave passing through the culture industry and measure it against our experience as post-baby boomers. We discuss the significance of neighborhood "defensible space" plans in Dayton in terms of postmodern spatialization of power, and we turn our attention to the degradation of the public sphere and the role of the public intellectual. Finally, via consideration of the such concrete phenomena as the Dayton Peace Accords and the persistence of the American obsession with capital punishment, we examine the social structuring of death as a mass phenomenon. In each case, we move from within our experience to mediate the most extreme lifeworld experiences (e.g., from Dayton to Bosnia to Ghent; from the birth of our Patrick to the domination of nature at the level of natural history; from the Balkans to the balkanization of neighborhoods and minds and whole generations). And whether it is Habermas' system/lifeworld perspective and his analysis of the public sphere, the classic Frankfurt School studies of prejudice, literature, the culture industry, science, and the family, or whether it is Foucault's analysis of power or Baudrillard's sense for the American "desert," critical theory, especially Adorno's particular version, serves as our benchmark.

BIOGRAPHY

For Mills, biography refers to "the inner life and external career of a variety of individuals" (1959, p. 5). Indeed, Mills suggested that the "signal features" of postmodern times could be registered as the "uneasiness and indifference" experienced by the ever-more powerless members of mass society, which, in the extreme, was tending toward "apathy" and a "deadly unspecified malaise," and, finally, toward the specter of the "cheerful robot" (1959, pp. 11-12, 171-176). In contrast, the felt, inner experience of the "total threat of panic," induced by recognition of a total "crisis," is, for Mills, the first sign of possible liberation, the basis for a politics that points beyond the return of the ever-same (1959, p. 11). Well before Marcuse's "Essay on Liberation" (1969), Mills addressed the "tasks of liberation" in terms of "sensibility," which "includes a sort of therapy in the ancient sense of clarifying one's knowledge of self," and which promises a "society" of the "self-cultivating man and women; in short, the free and rational individual" (1959, pp. 186-187). If it is so that the process of enlightenment and emancipation proceeds from panic to sociological knowledge and back again in the form of sublimated "knowledge of self," then it would seem that the experience of panic (that is, in contrast to uneasiness, indifference, malaise, and apathy), is the essential prerequisite for liberation.

On this basis we might take comfort in Arthur Kroker, Marilouise Kroker, and David Cook's assertion that "panic is the key psychological mood of postmodern culture" (1989, p. 13). However, an "essential prerequisite for liberation" is not itself liberation. Indeed, quite the opposite is true: panic-in-itself is precisely not-liberation, the negation of liberation, the maximal recognition of an absent yet urgent need for healing via revolution. Kroker, Kroker, and Cook describe this:

[In postmodern times,] panic has the reverse meaning of its classic sense. In antiquity, the appearance of the god *Pan* meant a moment of arrest, a sudden calm, a rupture-point between frenzy and reflection. Not though in the postmodern condition. Just like the reversal of classical kynicism (philosophy from below) into postmodern cynicism (for the ruling elites) before it, the classical meaning of panic has now disappeared into its opposite sense.

In the postmodern scene, panic signifies a twofold free-fall: the disappearance of *external* standards of public conduct when the social itself becomes the transparent field of a cynical power; and the dissolution of the *internal* foundations of identity (the disappearing ego as the victory sign of postmodernism) when the self is transformed into an empty screen of an exhausted, but hyper-technical, culture (1989, p. 16, emphases in original).

But might not our anguished panic also help us to discover our own need for a "moment of arrest, a sudden calm, a rupture-point," something to slow the disorienting processes of what Agger (1989a) calls "fast capitalism" and Kroker et al. call the "frenzied scene of post-facts"? (1989, p. 15). Mills defined modern social science as "man become aware of mankind," which he immediately followed with: "It is on the level of human awareness that virtually all solutions to the great problems must now lie" (1959, p. 193). If we come to understand the structural processes that underlie the "disappearance of external standards of public conduct" (ethics) and the "dissolution of the internal foundations of identity" (psychological panic), then is this not the basis for a calming postmodern panic-ethics that could perhaps lead to the formulation of solutions to our great problems?

From this point of view, we can readily agree with Zygmunt Bauman's thesis that "postmodernity is the moral person's bane and chance at the same time" (1995, p. 8), for the vexing, paralyzing, panic-inducing transparency of postmodern times also represents an opening. If postmodernity is as Bauman defines it, "modernity without illusions," then in panic lies the seeds of healing and peace (1993, p. 32).

But as Kroker et al. hurry to remind us, "cynicism" vies with panic for recognition as *the* signal feature of the postmodern period. In his exemplary *Critique of Cynical Reason* (1983), Peter Sloterdijk parallels Kroker et al. in defining cynicism as a type of ruling ideology at the same time that he considers it a "diffuse" phenomena.[5] For Sloterdijk, "cynicism" is an "enlightened false consciousness" that is "reflexively buffered" (1983, p. 5). That is, postmodern cynicism is self-aware or transparent false consciousness. As Sloterdijk writes:

It is that modernized, unhappy consciousness, on which enlightenment has labored both successfully and in vain. It has learned its lessons in enlightenment, but it has not, and probably was not able to, put them into practice. Well-off and miserable at the same time, this consciousness no longer feels affected by any critique of ideology; its falseness is already reflexively buffered (p. 5).

Cynical consciousness is impervious to immanent ideology critique because critique is an essential feature of its make-up and therein always already assimilated and contained. For Sloterdijk, the preponderance of cynical reason renders the postmodern cynic a "borderline melancholic," which even, and perhaps especially, Adorno's "melancholy science" cannot reach. Thus, in sympathy although not in unison with Adorno's "... pioneering work on the pain of the times (*Zeitschmerz*) and [his] ... exemplary healing," Sloterdijk writes:

It is not my ambition to enlarge this honorable infirmary of critical theories. It is time for a new critique of temperaments. Where enlightenment appears as a 'melancholy science', it unintentionally furthers melancholic stagnation. Thus, the critique of cynical reason hopes to achieve more from a work that cheers us up, whereby it is understood from the beginning that it is not so much a matter of work but rather of relaxation (1983, p. xxxvii).

Sloterdijk's appeal to a kynical subjectivity is a call for a new participatory consciousness manifest not simply as a mind or *cognitive* map but, in Andreas Huyssen's words, as a "self-assertive *body*" (1983, p. xvi, emphasis added). Huyssen continues:

The mythic model for the kind of somatic anarchism [Sloterdijk] advocates is the Greek kynic Diogenes, the plebeian outsider inside the walls of the city who challenged state and community through loud satirical laughter and who lived an animalist philosophy of survival and happy refusal (1983, p. xvii).

But we are not convinced that such a "happy refusal" can do the job vis-à-vis cynicism. Nor are we certain that a remembrance of Diogenes' ruckus body-politics from below can turn the tide against the utter preponderance of cynicism. Can Sloterdijk's exploration of the soma-scape for the twitches of a liberatory awakening really overturn the cynicism that is a "... hard-boiled, shadowy cleverness that has split courage off from itself,

[that] holds anything positive to be a fraud, and is intent only on somehow getting through life" (1983, p. 546)? We doubt it.

Sloterdijk speaks of bodily resistance as a philosophy of "flesh and blood (and teeth)" (1983, p. xxxi). Toward the end of *Critique of Cynical Reason*, he writes:

> As in the days of Diogenes, the bearers of the system have lost their self-confidence to the apparently crazy ones. They now can only choose between the false self-experience in collective suicide and the suicide of false subjectivity in real self-experience (1983, p. 546).

In this book, our lifeworld-grounded critical theory aims in between melancholy science and classical kynicism; while we cannot avoid panic ("think globally, act ... globally"!) in a suicidal world ruled by the "apparently crazy," neither can we expect liberation simply by following Diogenes' lead.

It would do us little good, for example, to piss on our son's doctors, vomit on the school administrator's shoes, wave the Mayor out of the way of our sunlight, or walk the streets of Dayton, in broad daylight and holding a lantern, in search of an honest man. Of course, we do not for a moment deny our dire need for new practices of the self (Foucault). We know that we cannot forever go on ingesting Xanax and Prosac, practicing anorexia and bulimia, pumping iron and running long, repairing our broken bodies with screws and rods and new organs, developing our buns-of-steel and airbrushing our images. Or not, and overeating and growing obese instead, lolling about watching television while our hearts beat on involuntarily. We cannot deny, in other words, our embodiment, our intrinsic frailty and mortality, our soft, blemished, fleshy, always already contingent, living/dying, growing/deteriorating selves. Rather, our goal is to give recognition to the everyday reality of seemingly routine social interaction within institutional settings and to stage our (self-) analysis of this level of reality over the course of a hypothetical life span. Diogenes did not confront a phalanx of health and welfare professionals and all manner of street-level bureaucrats. Diogenes did not live in a world so structurally mediated (he did not, for example, confront the paralysis of "acting globally"); nor did he lead a life so long as to be divided into numerous stages and substages. But we must do so.

Yet, our intention is also to explore the spaces/organs of resistance that are available at this albeit necessary level of experience and in these unavoidable spaces/bodies. Bauman, for example, contends that we are, in a "primal" sense, "ineluctably—*existentially*—moral beings" (1995, p. 1, emphasis in original). Our analysis of birth and disability leads us to consideration of utopian implications of new life and wrong life and, in particular, the new/wrong life that is our own being/project-in-the-world. Bauman also furnishes us with a "catalogue of postmodern fears," including the "body under siege," which he notes "ever more frequently...condenses into brief yet violent explosions of body-panic" (1995, pp. 120-121). We aim to explore this and other fears at the level of our taken-for-granted experience, including, for example, the postmodern fear of "the stranger *ante portas*" (1995, 135). In this regard, Bauman writes:

> It is the dream of "defensible space," a place with secure and effectively guarded borders, a territory semantically transparent and semiotically legible, a site cleansed of risk, and particularly of the incalculable risks—which transforms merely "unfamiliar people" (those, under normal circumstances of the city stroll, obscure objects of desire) into downright enemies (1995, p. 135).

We address the issue of defensible space with reference to what is perhaps its most elaborate neighborhood-level manifestation, Dayton's Oscar Newman-designed "Five Oaks Defensible Space Plan." This significant reordering of the Dayton city-scape is an effort to fight crime and reduce fear, but also, perhaps, an effort to live-rightly. Our attention to biography also includes assessment of the outer career of the public intellectual in postmodern times. Indeed, we view death in terms of an expansive transparent field of cynical power that brings the analysis of impoverished critical theoretic public discourse into a text-mediated dialogue with the panicked-of-the-earth.

In all, we address the nature of panic and cynicism as the signal features of the postmodern age (the Panicked Robot?, the Cynical Robot?). We do so from within our own experience and with an eye to discerning the new sensibilities (the new postmodern panic-ethics?) needed to live in a societal whole that is far more untrue today than when Adorno so pronounced it nearly half-a-century ago. This social totality is no cyclops, though, and will not be blinded by a single lantern, a single cognitive map, even if it is sprung in broad daylight or unfolded with great care. Rather, it must be stressed that the "endemic ambivalence" that defines postmodern experience is, as Bauman describes it, "excruciatingly painful to live with" (1995, p. 3). More than simply disorienting, then, the borderland between melancholy and gay science is fraught with such disaster and taut with such tension that only the kindest, softest, most self-forgiving bodies are likely to survive, for only they can, not so much withstand, but incorporate (sublimate) the jolting shocks of postmodernity's force-field electrocution. Of course, as George Orwell understood as well as anyone, every body has its unique limits. Everyone has their own Room 101.

HISTORY

In *The Sociological Imagination*, Mills follows Max Weber in stressing the importance of "historical specificity," that is, the need to pay strict attention to the actual and particular (idiographic, promethean) ways that people have made, or do in the present make, history. This type of historical realism is inherently opposed to grand metanarratives of history, what Soja calls "historicism." These can take the form, for example, of teleological, evolutionary, or other transcendental stories of humanity's immanent self-becoming. Furthermore, in a dialectical move, Mills notes that "the *relevance* of history…is itself subject to the principle of historical specificity" (1959, p. 156). In pre-modern times, the rate of social change was relatively slow in comparison to recent experience and self-conscious "history-making" was of little relevance. Using Orwell's *Nineteen Eighty-Four* as his reference, Mills also points to the possibility of an overdeveloped society in which history is continuously rewritten so as to eliminate entirely its friction with the present, erasing any politically destablizing relevance that history may hold (1959, p. 145). Addressing the status of history in his own epoch, Mills doffs his cap to the prometheanism of Marx, the tragedy of Orwell's *Animal Farm* ([1945]1990), and the thesis of *The Power Elite* (1956), all in one fell swoop: "Men are free to make history, but some men are much freer than others" (1959, p. 181). Of course, none of this matters much today; we live at the very end of history, with the control of the history-making apparatuses, even by a power elite, very much in doubt.

It is a bit like Walter Benjamin's famous depiction of the "angel of history," which he composed shortly before his suicide. Benjamin wrote:

> This is how one pictures the angel of history. His face is turned toward the past. Where we perceive a chain of events, he sees one single catastrophe which keeps piling wreckage and hurls it in front of his feet. The angel would like to stay, awaken the dead, and make whole what has been smashed. But a storm is blowing from Paradise, it has got caught in his wings with such violence that the angel can no longer close them. This

storm irresistibly propels him into the future to which his back is turned, while the pile of debris before him grows skyward. This storm is what we call progress (1968, pp. 257-258).

Bauman thus comments on this passage:

The dead will not be awakened, the smashed will not be made whole. The pile of debris will go on growing. Those who suffered, did. Those who got killed, will stay dead. It is the escaping from (or, rather, being blown away by) the horror of the irreversible and the irredeemable that seems to us—us who have been repelled—to be a "chain of events" (1993, p. 224).

The great modernist moral failing lies in this chain-of-events consciousness, which steps so blithely over the immense and complex wreckage of modernity because of its faith in the redeeming power of societal and cultural progress. Indeed, there is in modernity so little moral energy that it is even difficult to muster the imaginative powers of the "what if" of Benjamin's angelic projection. Who has the time and energy much less the courage to turn around and a face what we have done, and what we do everyday?

Speaking of the masses of postmodernity, Mills understood that the sheer quantity of historical information "dominates their attention and overwhelms their capacities to assimilate it," while their "struggles to acquire (the skills of reason) ... often exhaust their limited moral energy" (1959, p. 5). Having theorized a society dominated by the terror of over-information joined with the problem of moral indifference, Mills imagined that it was as likely that "history-making may well go by default" as made by a "narrow elite." For Mills, while it is only reasonable to "embrace rather pessimistic estimates of the chances" of our making history in "accordance with the ideals of human freedom and reason," the abdication of "social scientists of the rich societies" before this haunting "historical level of reality" is nevertheless "surely the greatest human default being committed by privileged men in our times" (1959, pp. 176, 193, 176). From the many in need of the sociological imagination to the few who could provide it but who were distracted or indifferent, Mills painted a sociological picture of the crisis of "reason and freedom" in an age, the dawn of postmodernity, desperately in need of both.

But our late postmodern space seems to demand even more from the intellectual than sustaining the nearly impossible perspective of Benjamin's angel of history, which sees the human totality and tries, always already too late and without success, as Bauman stresses, to "awaken the dead" and to "make whole what has been smashed." What we need at the end of *human* history is, we believe, a renewed appreciation for *natural* history, which Fredric Jameson, in particular, finds at the heart of Adorno's *oeurve*. As Jameson explains:

> For there is a nightmare of natural history that is even grislier than that of the human one; and it is this that the postmodern mind has been able to repress fairly successfully (save for biological death itself) for reasons that are scarcely mysterious: what better way to avoid being reminded of the nightmare of nature than to abolish nature altogether?

> Yet a glimpse into the interstices that not merely open to view the pecking order of all living species, a hideous eternity of domination and hierarchy designed at least to leave its subjects alive, but also and finally the violence of nature itself, organisms obliged to eat their whole waking life long, and to eat each other (in Adorno's most frequent characterization of it)—this dizzying perspective brings with it a nausea more fundamental than the sight of malice with which humans attempt to culturalize their own internecine slaughter (1990, pp. 95-97).

Lifeworld-grounded critical theory must entail, in the first as well as the last instance, a conceptualization of human history and individual human existence as earth- and body-bound. Adorno and his fellow Frankfurt philosophers understood the suppression of natural history as both idealism and as crushing ideology, even while they were profoundly wary of all manner of posited primordial existentialisms or philosophies of Being, what Adorno ([1964]1973) derided as the "jargon of authenticity." [6] In our time, one need not subscribe to "Earth First's" or the "Unibomber's" one-sided negation of humanism to recognize the continuation of species-centric fable-telling as perhaps the greatest default of the late postmodern intellectual.

Finally, let us not forget that the Angel of History is a projection; there is no privileged or transcendent perspective outside of the course of history, free from embeddedness in some society, somewhere. This is true even for the gifted intellectual, who might just as easily end up dead somewhere in Spain, having her face eaten by rats or, for example, tenured and suffocated or untenured and fearful at some reputable if marginal college or university. The intellectual, like everyone else, wanders in the midst of the train-wreck debris that keeps crashing at history's feet. Everywhere one looks, the victims lie dead or moaning or in a state of shock, or, perhaps, they are semi-conscious, struggling against bouts of panic and cynicism, as in: "My god, what have we done? Everything. My god, what can we do? Nothing." In such a place, history and the future collide; *from* such a place, the past is made and re-made and the future forestalled and perverted.

At our particular intersection of history, biography, and social structure, it would seem that the pile of debris grows skyward, with whole species and whole human populations regularly dismissed as surplus. This magnificent pile looks to soon reach the earth's upper atmosphere, where, like a postmodern cherry on a modern ice cream sundae, we shall plop the future itself on top just for good measure. Perhaps—the natural scientists cannot be sure—we have already done so.

In this book, we must necessarily tromp around in the wreckage of history as postmodern fieldworkers, regardless of the futility of our roamings or the limits of our intellect. Nor in the course of our sojourn can we ignore our own kind, the species *res intelligentsia publica*, especially those who stand in the debris and survey it at long stretches, only to then recommend, as the leading contemporary American philosopher, Richard Rorty (1992), does, a "more banal politics," by which he means greater attention to this and that social problem here and there, and less, or none at all, to the totality, the same totality that the angel of history cannot escape much less redeem. If in the course of these pages the reader does not feel the blowing the winds of progress nor the inviting refuge of provincial small-mindedness that Mills called American "liberal practicality," it is because we are huddled down in our world, hoping that from within here we can somehow slow or even stop we-humanity from realizing our crowning ur-achievement: the return of the always already preponderant natural history to its uncontested position as the *only* history there is.

THE QUESTION OF POSTMODERN ETHICS

We have never been very impressed by the criticisms of Adorno that dismiss him as the philosopher who *merely* circled the ineffable, or who inadvertently or ironically brought critical theory to a standstill or into a dead end (see Buck-Morss 1977, pp. 189-190; Jay 1984a, p. 161). Instead, our assessment runs more along the lines of Jameson's:

> [Adorno's] introspective or reflexive dialectic befits a situation in which—
> on account of the dimensions and unevenness of the new global world

order—the relationship between the individual and the system seems ill-defined, if not fluid, or even dissolved.

The over-emphasis in Adorno on what he called theory—defined as the detection of the absent presence of totality within the aporias of consciousness or of its products—is not a bad lesson for intellectuals today, when the older notion of critical theory as permanent negativity and implacable social critique seems better to characterize the practice of a Sartre than the ideals of postmodern thinkers.

The "current situation" to be sure has any number of urgent demands besides dialectical theory; still, "not only theory, but also its absence, becomes a material force when it seizes the masses" (1990, pp. 251-252).

Yet, if dialectical theory is pitched at too rarified a level of abstraction or, which is the same thing, if it overshoots the very disorienting spatial experience that undergirds the vertigo of postmodern lives, then the hope of making theory practical vanishes in the postmodern fog and the work of intellectuals becomes indicative, not of our task and promise, but only of our alienation.

The many specifics of our present effort at lifeworld-grounded critical theory, like Bauman's, "draw life-juices from, or dry up and wilt in, the daily life of postmodern men and women" (1995, p. 8). The reader who chooses to drink with us from these juices must know that, in certain respects, we (writers/readers) are like vultures haunting the remains of some carnage. In other words, it is not a clean business to write or to read a book about postmodern ethics; that we regularly suck our own blood does not improve matters. We still must accept what Bauman calls "responsibility for the responsibility" of making moral choices, like writing dialectical theory versus doing something else (1995, p. 5). Like drinking down a nose-bleed, then, this exercise leaves us with a raw throat and a sense of cannibalism, and a thesis that we can only direct toward fellow readers/writers: *the trace-fragments of postmodern ethics lie in the negativizing tension of dialectical theory, the adoption of which requires the moral energy to give up believing in believing and adopt responsibility for responsibility, or what is the same thing, developing a postmodern sociological imagination that once set in motion and carried to those most in need, could provide enough orientation to the postmodern situation so as to, perhaps (who can say with certainty?), arrest the otherwise probable eclipse of humanity, and thus constitutes the one essential content of post-*

modern intellectual life and therefore the closest thing we have to a post-modern moral imperative.

NOTES

1. In his *The New Constellation: The Ethical-Political Horizons of Modernity/ Postmodernity* (1991), Richard J. Bernstein has initiated a similar project. Like ourselves, Bernstein deploys the methods of negative dialectics in his Deweyian assault on philosophy's re-occurrent false antinomies. Like ourselves, Bernstein's philosophical labor is oriented to matters of an "ethical-political" nature in this hyphenated space of the modern/postmodern. We even share Bernstein's recognition of Richard Rorty as a philosopher of paramount importance and sophistication, as do we share Bernstein's profound ambivalence before Rorty's original contribution. But this present work departs fundamentally from Bernstein in the most obvious, methodological sense that ours' is a work in lifeworld-grounded critical *sociology*, whereas Bernstein's series of "exercises," as he calls them, remain, despite their self-conscious pragmatic orientation, *philosophical* treatises.

2. Mills himself spoke of how the sociological imagination was coming to be perceived as the "common denominator" of the modern/post-modern age because, first and foremost, it was "coming to be felt as a need" (1959, p. 21). How many sociologists "need" sociological theory as a "cognitive map"? How many understand their "theory" as Audre Lorde understood her "poetry," as the answer to the questions: "What are the words you do not yet have? What do you need to say? What are the tyrannies you swallow day by day and attempt to make your own, until you will sicken and die of them, still in silence?" (1984, p. 41).

3. In her study of Sartre's relevance for sociology, Gila J. Hayim terms these four patterns of bad faith "the traditional solution," "the ontological solution," "the stoical solution," and the "positivist solution," respectively (1980, pp. 23-26).

Some readers will undoubtedly be scandalized by our assertion that so many of sociology's great theorists, even Mills himself, might fail the "dialectical" test. While it is perhaps obvious how adherence to religious dogmas or their secular equivalents contradicts Mills' insistence on the "absorbed realization of social relativity and of the transformative power of history," it is less clear, on the face of it, why and how, say, Berger's *Invitation to Sociology* (1963) reifies the role of the sociologist as a type of seer possessed of special and sacred qualities (what Berger calls, for example, "reverence" for the "world of men," where the sociologist is "possessed" as by a "demon," conceived as engaged in "a very special kind of passion," etc.), or why and how Giddens' (1982) Kantian fact/value separation (his "two house conceptualization, the factual house and moral/practical house, that you move between") is falsely rationalist, or especially why and how Goffman, the theorist of actors, could be seen as having assumed a particular stage in history as *the* stage (but see Gouldner [1970, pp. 378-390] for starters).

4.   On the relationship between positivism and postmodernism, see Jameson's intriguing comment that "positivism becomes postmodernism when it has, like philosophy on the older paradigm, fulfilled and thereby abolished itself. Adorno insists on the one side of its mission, thereby giving us one useful description: it wants to abolish the subjective, as that takes the form of thoughts, interpretations and opinions (perhaps it also wants to abolish the language that corresponds to those things: poetic, emotive, rhetorical). This to say that it is a nominalism, and as such wants to reduce us to the empirical present (or to use the empirical present as the sole pattern for imagining other situations and other temporal moments)" (1990, pp. 248-249). Of course, positivism is used here in the usual broad sense that is common practice in critical theory, referring in this case to Denzin's hypostatization of "the postmodern," which is an assumption shared with those who would see law-like regularity in the world, and who would attempt to "objectively" map it (that is, without recourse to an always-already theoretical, subjective background). The only difference is that Denzin's postmodern formulation, ironically, leads him to an attempt, we would argue, to "reduce [sociology] to the empirical present."

5.   Note Huyssen's (1983, p. xii) attention to the special usefulness of Sloterdijk's insight for the analysis of the "mind-set" of today's elites.

6.   Jameson is correct, we believe, to credit the Frankfurt School as "among the philosophical ancestors of the ecology movement" as well as, in a related connection, as one of the most important sources for "proto-feminism," their having suggested that "gender also and preeminently marks the spot where human and natural histories bewilderingly intersect, reminding us of the high stakes in their disentanglement" (1990, p. 96).

CHAPTER 2

Mass Birth: The Lifeworld Begins
in the System

One factor about a spinal anesthetic which I think is important to mention is that you do feel manipulation, but you do not *feel pain.... Watching the birth of your baby is entirely up to you; no one will make you watch, nor will anyone say that you may not. After all, who's having the baby? The way we manage to do this is by a system of mirrors. These are connected with the lights used to illuminate the delivery field. The anesthetist uses the same mirrors to watch what the doctor is doing....*
—Dr. Laura E. Weber, *Between Us Women* (1962, p. 110, emphasis in original)

The memory of water, along with the indivisibility of particles and the black hole hypothesis (there being a secret correspondence between all these things), is the greatest gift science has made to the imagination in recent times. Even if this function remains eternally improbable, it is true, from now on, as a metaphor for the mind.
—Jean Baudrillard, *Cool Memories II* (1996, p. 5)

The mystery of every phenomena is solved in its history.
—Ernst Block, *Natural Law and Human Dignity* (1986, p. 268)

We are also without memory. We have reached the point of searching the water for signs of a memory that has left no traces, hoping against hope that something might remain even when the water's molecular memory has faded away.
—Jean Baudrillard, *The Transparency of Evil* (1993a, p. 96)

In many ways, Horkheimer and Adorno's *Dialectic of Enlightenment* (1947) is a flawed work. It presents its thesis at such a general level, it is easy to forget that the internal relation between enlightenment, mythology, and domination is real. Since Horkheimer and Adorno enter the history of enlightenment by way of myth, literature, mass culture, and racist ideology, none of which claim for contemporary consciousness to be true, save perhaps as metaphors or parables, this almost guarantees that the work will be understood as a moralistic tale or fable. "Science" is implicated, but only abstractly, as an ideology or as a form of discourse. As a material practice, science is left alone, untheorized and unaccountable. This failure to take on science as a form of practice, as real power, encourages the pragmatist defense of science. This defense points out that, regardless of whether or not science can justify itself, it "works"; regardless of whether or not scientific claims about itself and the world are true, science as a practice enhances the human ability to control our environment. Who can argue with this?

In spite of this basic flaw, the honesty of *Dialectic of Enlightenment* does much to absolve its authors from blame. Horkheimer and Adorno's willingness to question the part played in the persistence of domination by enlightenment and the elite intellectuals who claim it as their own is an act of treason against their own kind, a betrayal of the lie that Reason will set anyone free. This, without forgetting the promise of enlightenment, its utopian content, and its truth. This failure to forget, in its Blochian insistence on remembering the past promise of future times, underwrites the tragic sense of *Dialectic of Enlightenment*. Here, we read the implicit though the unjustifiable claim that it could have gone—should have gone—otherwise. That history should have gone otherwise is a claim that protests against time itself, that places the past on the same ethical plane as the now, and that grants unfulfilled hope the same metaphysical status as what currently exists. It is a perspective that cannot help being melancholy if not melodramatic.

In refusing to privilege that which currently exists merely because it exists, Horkheimer and Adorno insist with Benjamin that history does not march endlessly forward through empty time and, here, they intimate the "spatialization" of history. Even as *Dialectic of Enlightenment* enters history at the most abstract philosophical level possible, its thesis suggests, points to, even demands the concrete, the specific, the determinate. In other words, *Dialectic of Enlightenment* seeks to negotiate the distance between the concept of enlightenment and its actuality; it attempts to penetrate and thus violate the process through which enlightenment becomes mythology and domination, especially in its realization.

Science *is* power and must be analyzed as such. Only then can the prag-matist line be countered on its own ground: Yes, science *does* work and this is the reason for our concern. Science, in general, is a historically spe-cific form of domination appropriate to our time. Its appropriateness can be read directly from its efficacy; it is thus far able to control for the contin-gencies of late capitalist society. These contingencies are, above all, human contingencies, even when they appear in an estranged, alien form. The purest expression of this lies in medicine, the direct application of sci-ence to the human body. The overwhelming success of medicine cannot be denied, and any critique of science must squarely confront this fact, resist-ing the urge to explain it away or otherwise devalue its efficacy. If critique is to prove itself worthy of even the slimmest hope, it must test itself against power's strongest claims.

Medicine, as knowledge, is first and foremost self-knowledge. Medicine refers directly to our collective, institutionalized understanding of what it is to be human. It is thus the form wisdom takes in postmodern society. Doctors, not mystics, priests or our community elders, see us into the world, and doctors see us out. Medicine, more than any other authority, rat-ifies our existence. It tells us when we are sick, and increasingly decides if we are well. It sets the minimal standard for participation in the human community. The practice of medicine is our primary defense against inter-nal dissolution, both socially and individually. It negotiates the line between life and death, and only with its signature can we attain an honor-able discharge from the struggle for existence.

As *Dialectic of Enlightenment* was being written, its thesis was being enacted on the stage of history. With respect to political history and even public culture, this much is obvious. Fascism in Europe and the emergence of a conformist consumer culture in America both bear witness to this enactment. Less obvious, the *Dialectic of Enlightenment* found a particu-larly pure form of expression in the guise of medical science as it came to increasingly control the experience of women giving birth. Thus, in 1900, 95 percent of all American births took place in the home (Wertz and Wertz 1977, p. 133). By 1955, the year Adrienne Rich, author of the classic work, *Of Woman Born* ([1976]1986), gave birth to her first child, only 5 percent did so (Leavitt 1986, p. 269). Hidden within this sea change in the place of birth lies a radical reorganization of the practice of procreation, a transfor-mation in the relations of power surrounding the birth process, and a thorough reconceptualization of the activity of birth. All this without notice, despite the grave consequences for women giving birth, who until this century were necessarily considered both essential and at the center of human procreation even as they suffered cultural devaluation and material deprivation for their typically unavoidable bodily commitment to childbearing.

In this chapter, we aim to further the analysis of enlightenment as myth, of science as domination, by bringing the interrelated theses of *Dialectic of Enlightenment* into a dialogue with the conceptual and, importantly, material and concretely experienced transformations evident in the last 50-odd years of birthing in America. In Part One, we offer a phenomenology of our own experience of mass birth, one which falls somewhere between the happy, gratifying birth experiences of popular mythology and the horror stories of obstetrical abuse that form the undercurrent of such mythology. In this phenomenology, we necessarily accent the participatory perspective implied in any self-conscious methodological distinction between system and lifeworld (see Habermas [1981]1987b). Here, we mean to reveal and document one instance of the spatialized microprocesses of domination that undergirds the overarching discourse of domination proffered in Horkheimer and Adorno and, by extension, raise doubts concerning the liberatory significance of Habermas' disembodied, rationalistic, methodological dualism. In Part Two, we regroup and address the issue of a postmodern sociological imagination that draws into its constellation of history, biography, and social structure the fact of the always already overdetermined domination of biography, the fact of new life as a function of mass birth. The essence of our position is that the all too common theoretical repression of the daily annihilation of "birth" renders any effort to ponder the recovery of ethical life as an always already evaporating countermyth, insufficiently rooted in the historically specific facticity of systemic domination. We therefore begin at the beginning, which is also our endpoint.

PART ONE. NAVEL GAZING

As we near the end of this bloody century, it can be said that birth, long a symbol of renewal and transformation, the ultimate mystery, the most human of experiences, no longer happens. Divested of its power and long-banalized, childbirth, the bringing into being of new life, has become nothing more than a human-interest story, for example, a hook to increase the viewership of a sitcom a few seasons past its prime. Women still get pregnant and come out of it with babies, to be sure, but women no longer give birth, and birth, strictly speaking, no longer happens. Nor is anybody born anymore, a situation even more astounding.

We repeat: babies are made, but childbirth no longer happens. Consider, in this regard, the birth of our own child, who came into this world six weeks prematurely and accompanied by the best medical science had to offer. There is no simple way of relating the unfolding of events which led to the emergence of our child for there is no plot line or narrative; there is no logic of unfolding which could capture what *really* happened. Certainly the physiological story of parturition is well known: conception, rapid cell division, hormonal changes, and so forth, but no one, not mother, father, or baby, had any experience of these events which can be recollected and retold. The physiological logic—the only true logic—is irrelevant to the birth of our child; the social/historical logic is itself impossible to recover. Equally to the point, our personal memories of the pregnancy and birth are fragmented and often contradictory. Many of these have been lost or distorted out of recognition.

As it turned out, we had very little say in the birth of our son and equally little say in our respective roles as parents. Early in the pregnancy we sought the expertise of a nurse-midwife with the intention of protecting ourselves from the variety of abuses obstetrics offers women. However, at thirty-two weeks gestation, labor threatened a premature beginning, and we found ourselves on the wrong side of the line between normal and pathological birth. Our Certified Nurse Midwife referred us to a Medical Doctor, who referred us to another Medical Doctor. After being admitting to the Miami Valley Hospital Berry's Women's Center, and after several days of confusion, we found that we were under the care of The Clinic. Compelled to play a new game with different roles, we were no longer involved only in a struggle with our species-inheritance and the biological challenges of procreation, in themselves great enough, but were now obliged to contend with real, live, institutionalized social power. And this is where our stories separate: our "we" fragments into different "I's" as each of us found ourself in a specific relation to social power.

I, our son's mother, would spend the next ten days on my back, object of the medical gaze/glance and a variety of its manipulations. And, I, our son's father, could only observe and defend, test my power against that of the doctor's and the hospital's in the hopes of ameliorating the situation of one who was, as a matter of social fact, my wife. Our success in playing this new game depended on our willingness and ability to settle into our respective parts of husband and wife and to take advantage of the cultural norms surrounding those roles. It was a game we played but not because we chose to; the time was not ripe for the feminist revolution at Miami Valley Hospital in Dayton, Ohio.

So, for ten days we exploited our genders, sometimes panicked, sometimes cynical, but never because we believed in our respective femininity and masculinity. Of course, we weren't required to actually believe in our roles, but only to act as if we did. About a week into my hospital stay, a doctor, herself a woman of sorts, informed me—the mother—that it had been decided that amniocentesis would be performed to determine fetal lung maturity, with the outcome of said test determining if labor would be artificially induced. I, our son's mother, protested that I was only 34 weeks along and had been told by another doctor upon admission that an effort would be made to prevent labor until 36 weeks, or what is, I was led to believe, technically a situation know as "full term." I wanted to know the reasoning behind the change of plans; I wanted to know what options were available. She informed me that she would have no answers until the next day, after "the committee" met. My birth, she assured me, was being actively, regularly, and conscientiously managed, and there were 70 other GYN patients waiting to see her "in clinic" and she didn't have time for conversation. I responded that I would have to confer with my husband, meeting her evasion with an evasion of my own. Thus, two women, both unwilling to act on our own accord, together agreed to displace our agency on absent masculine authorities, however malignant or benign.

Indeed, that our birth was the responsibility of a committee was news to us and shed a new light on our situation. Since admission, it was like a made-for-TV movie scripted by Kafka: "K Gives Birth." We could not get any but the most basic information about our situation, decipher the structure of medical authority within the hospital, nor even discern who, in particular, was responsible for the birth. Still under the spell of childbirth education classes in the first few days after "admission," we requested to speak with the doctor who would attend the delivery so that we could go over our "birth plan." We were told, however, that there was no way of knowing which physician would attend until it happened. Other questions and requests faced a similar demise: the expression of my—the mother's—desire not to have an episiotomy or use anesthesia was met with the vague comment that "each birth is unpredictable" and that "women trained in natural childbirth often have difficult births because they are unwilling to give up control." When it became apparent ("became apparent" being the only apt description), that the committee, which we never laid eyes on, intended to induce labor, we asked the roving hospital childbirth educator about the dangers of induction. She responded with a soliloquy on the evils of the Canadian system and of socialized medicine in general. It wasn't an answer to our question, but we listened in silence nonetheless.

On the tenth night of my hospital stay, an electronic fetal monitor determined that my uterus was contracting, again. I, the thing to which the fetal monitor was attached, felt nothing, but I secretly willed my body on for I was tired of the whole affair. I was tired of being in a bed soaked with fetal urine, the inner spaces of my body open to the world; tired of being a woman; tired of the intrusions of the nurses, educators, religious counselors and other well-meaning, though no less irritating, visitors and caretakers. I had no thoughts for the underdeveloped being inside me; *that* had surely ceased to be my responsibility ten days ago, if it ever was.

They moved me to a labor room, which sported wood floors, comfortable chairs, and homey decorations. I called my husband to come in spite of the nurse's insistence that it wasn't necessary, that nothing would happen until morning. I presumed she meant that nothing would happen until after the committee met the next morning, when physicians congregate to exercise their greatest powers. At any rate, my husband arrived, and we spent the night, more or less together, somewhere between sleep and watchful wakefulness.

The next day a doctor informed us that they (the committee?) thought it best to induce labor, or so we understood it, primarily to see if the fetus could withstand the stress. It was an awkward conversation carried out in simplistic terms, given the doctor's attempt to translate his technical expertise into something meaningful to a layperson, which wasn't necessary since I, our son's mother, had a working understanding of obstetrical techno-jargon. Both of us were playing dumb, respecting the demands of our respective roles. In any case, according to the Electronic Fetal Monitor, the fetus was not doing well. It was uncertain at that point whether or not the fetus could withstand a vaginal birth. It was apparently necessary to jumpstart my uterus in order to see if the fetus could stand it: oxytocin challenge; trial by labor. I, our son's mother, consciously avoided reflecting on the tautology involved in this plan of action and, instead, asked only about the side effects of induction. The doctor denied that there were any side effects of consequence and I thought a minute, searching for some basis for consent. Finally, I remembered that I, once a fetus, had been induced—I think that my mother's obstetrician was going on vacation—

and this made the well-known evils of oxytocin seem bearable. After all, I had been through an induced-labor once before and could thus do it again.

And so we were "pitted," the professional slang for administering oxytocin. I had already been attached to an external monitor, the machine that goes beep, the night before, and to this were added the IV carrying oxytocin and a glucose solution which would provide nourishment through the impending ordeal. I was also fitted to an automatic blood pressure cuff which would, on its own accord and much to my consternation, inflate itself at regular intervals. The external fetal monitor (EFM) left me immobile: the slightest movement would disrupt its ability to read the fetal heart rate, which was not responding well to labor. The first hours of labor were mostly a tedious wait, interrupted only by the nurse who would come to adjust the rate at which the oxytocin was delivered. According to the EFM, the contractions were irregularly spaced with the double peaks characteristic of induced labors. At one point, after a shift change, a different nurse came in to offer the brand name analgesic, Tylenol. I responded with a very polite "No thank you, I feel okay," and my husband assured her I was fine and added that I was not planning on using any anesthesia. I, the mother-to-be, wasn't feeling any pain, just the tedium of idle waiting, and they had no drugs for that, at least not legal drugs, the kind a doctor would prescribe.

At one point the doctor arrived to explain what the fetal monitor had produced. The news was still not good: the fetal heart rate was sharply decelerating with each contraction and taking too long to return to normal rhythm. This suggested the need for a cesarian delivery. Knowing we were more or less out of control of the situation, I stated that I wished to deliver vaginally, but if a "C-section" was, in fact, necessary, I hoped it would be done under local anesthesia. Whatever.... The doctor also wanted to employ an *internal* fetal monitor, he said, which involved attaching a wire to the fetal head. I ritualistically asked about side effects and he ritualistically denied any of consequence.

I consented. There was no real choice but to do so. In so doing, however, we found ourself in a new game, a different interactional ritual of managing the contradictory demands of a shifting set of BIOpower relations. Until that point, I had negotiated these particular contradictions by seeking the care of female practitioners and was, because of a combination of luck and planning, able to avoid directly and personally confronting the sexual politics of gynecology (Daly 1978). My luck, as I knew it, ended; my labors began in earnest.

I lie on my back, knees bent, legs apart. Three male doctors gather around my vagina, tending to their project. I focus my energies on maintaining the usual careful indifference to their attention while simultaneously riding out the rise and fall of labor-induced pain. Occasionally, I let my knees fall together in a futile attempt at modesty and because whatever it was they were doing *hurt* really, really bad. I breathe through the pain, unaware at the moment of the irony suggested by the fact that the only time I relied on "natural" childbirth "techniques" was when the doctors were doing something—what, I was never sure for more than the few seconds it took them to explain it—to me. As my legs close, the doctors request that I spread them again. I dutifully comply, knowing well that my resistance is symbolic, merely suggestive of an other world, a different world where women control access to their bodies. With each spoken request, I am assured that their right of access is not simply given, but must be established through language. I take some satisfaction in this but do not carry this game too far, uncertain of the consequences of testing the doctors' patience. I do not want to know what it feels like to be a noncompliant woman and have no desire to find out what women went through thirty years ago when their legs were restrained, strapped down, and forced open as a matter of routine. To be honest, I don't even know if stirrups and leather are ever used on birthing women anymore, no matter how non-compliant they become.

This odd game of modesty, where I feign indifference to the manipulations of the doctors even as I allow my body to resist those same manipulations, is interrupted with comments and questions intended to establish my presence in the moment. I joke about alien abductions and continue my ritualistic inquiry into the side effects of this or that procedure the doctors deem it necessary to perform. Predictably, no one laughs at my jokes or admit to any side effects. Yet, I persist, feeling a little feeble and naggy. I am compelled by a sense that it is better to be irritating than mute, lest they—the makers of my reality, the controllers of my body—forget that I was even there. Their interest is pragmatic, focused on my vagina as an object of medical perception/procedure. The rest of me is of interest only to the extent that I am an obstacle to the completion of their tasks.

At one point, as the doctors are doing something especially painful—I think they were inserting a catheter into my uterus to bathe the fetus as it was being born, but I can't be certain—I announce the arrival of a contraction, expecting the doctors to pause in their labors so I could focus on my own. My announcement is, of course, redundant given that the EFM is recording every uterine pulse and twinge. The doctors have no intention of delaying their business and, instead, merely seek my patience, informing me that they are almost done. Soon after, I tell the doctors I am getting dizzy from lying on my back for so long. Again, a doctor informs me that it won't be much longer. He is dismissive in his reassurance.

When we are alone, the father-to-be and me, I work hard to be in my body and feel the fullness of its pain. As each contraction peaks, I concentrate on *not* resisting the pain. I allow it to overwhelm me and annihilate me. I actively seek to disappear into the envelope of my body's effort. As I get used to the rhythm of my womb's ritual of expulsion, I come to welcome its challenge. The pain satiates me, embracing me in its totality, offering respite in its intensity. In a funny reversal, this pain allows me to bear, to "manage" the other pain, distracting my attention from that sophisticated mental pain, taking the form of anxiety and bordering on panic, of having been penetrated and overcome by medical science. With each contraction I feel myself getting stronger even as I lose myself to my embodiment.

As I labor, the fetal heart rate, graphically represented on the screen of the fetal monitor, appears stronger. The massage of my body must be a source of strength, of life. The thought suddenly occurs to me that we have somehow avoided a surgical delivery. I share this by exclaiming, for the first time in my pregnancy, "We're having a baby," a cliché, perhaps, but so is every real-live experience. We feel triumphant in our newly found purpose.

I am startled out of my labor with a pain as sharp as it is urgent. I announce that I am pushing with the excited conviction of body-knowledge, of discovery and recognition. I am told to go ahead and push and I do as I must. The urgency subsides and the nurse checks me. I am fully dilated and a doctor is called. He is a doctor we haven't met before, young, probably our own age. We still remember his name, like all the doctors before him. We prepare to depart for the delivery room and this young doctor explains what to expect when we arrive. He smashes his hand between the mobile bed and the door jam as we hurry out of the labor room. He is young. He tells me, the father of our son, that I must change into scrubs and can use the doctor's locker room for this transformation. He tells me that I need not hurry, for the main event will not happen for a long time. I, the mother of our son, interrupt the situation from my mobile bed, partially panicked at the thought of my husband's absence, partially resentful at the bond between the doctor and my husband, and partially offended at the doctor's arrogant assumption that he knew the intentions of my womb. Most of all, I am ready to be done with this business of birthing, so much so that I reject the very thought of a long delivery and insist that my husband does, indeed, hurry becuase the baby is coming fast. He assures me that he hears what I am saying and promises to hurry.

As we make our way to the delivery room, I overhear a casual conversation carried on between the doctor and my husband over my prostrated body. Apparently, the doctor's wife had recently had her first child. My husband asked if he had delivered it, to which the doctor replied, in effect, "No, I didn't want to be a hero. My place was at my wife's side." What a guy. I am put off by the doctor's assumption that as a doctor he is a hero *in potentia*: arrogance springs eternal.

As we enter the delivery room, I feel the certainty of a contraction, one for which I am not ready, one for which the confusion of our journey has prevented me from preparing. I feel panicked as the pain tears at my body, depriving me of breath and presence. I cast about for an anchor. My husband has gone to change. I grab a hand close to me, any hand, and press it to my mouth to stifle the scream building in my body. As the pain recedes, I look into the eyes of the person whose hand I have kissed. It is the hand of a nurse who was just passing through, on her way to someplace else. She jokes with the doctor about my having broke her sterile field. I feel ashamed at our intimacy. She decides she may as well stay for the duration.

They are not ready for me in the delivery room; they have not received the message that we were on our way. Despite the hours of constant monitoring, the unrelenting regulation of every detail of my labor in the interests of control and predictability, chaos ensues, or what seems like chaos in so sterile an environment, and I am left alone as medical personnel rush to prepare the instruments of hospital-approved childbirth. It seems in this moment that my body is the only instrument ready for the delivery. I feel redundant.

Another contraction rips through my body, clawing at me with its unexpected surge of power. As if ambushed, I scream so long and so deep that it seems to issue from some underground well of resistance formally unbeknownst to me. I am carried by its force, riding it through the contraction. In its aftermath, I feel clearheaded and, in fact, awestruck at my own body's power. I am amazed by the volume of my voice as it betrays me. Cool. I scream through the next contraction, this time even louder and stronger. As my voice ebbs, I find that my husband has already returned from the locker room, decked out in pale green scrubs, a shower cap on his head, balloons of sterile cloth covering his shoes. He looks goofy. Proud of this power within me, one which remained a secret to me until that moment, I ask if he heard my yell. He did, he was there, and is also excited. We are both happy. The nurse interrupts us to scold me. She condescends, telling me that I produced a very nice yell but that the energy was, unfortunately, misdirected. Feeling frivolous and again shamed by this nurse-just-passing-through, I attempt to get back to the task before me.

Waiting for the next contraction, the nurse explains the technique of pushing. As each contraction builds, I am to take two deep cleansing breaths, and push (not scream, I presume she meant) on the third. It is noisy, and I can't focus. My pushes are not effective, my breathing uncoordinated. As the contractions peak, the doctor and nurse both loudly and in unison urge me to push. Pushhhh.

I am fortunate, profoundly fortunate, that my midwife responded to my call to assist me in what was going down. She had been waiting outside through my labor, and I asked for her so that she could give what support she could. I am told, however, that only one lay person is allowed in the delivery room. That one lay person would be my husband.

Then, another contraction, again to a loud chorus urging me to push and breathe. I am not in my body and the pushing hurts, offering neither the satisfaction nor relief previously experienced. There is too much confusion, too many instructions on breathing and pushing. Certainly, my body knows how to birth after aeons of evolution. Certainly, it can manage to breathe without the help of expert advice.

As the urge to push subsides, the doctor begins, from his station between my legs, a sermon on the technique of giving birth. My raised knees serve as his pulpit. Irritated with his intrusion, I cut him off. As if speaking in tongues, I begin talking back to the doctor, throwing in medical jargon here and there as I explain how I intend to birth as I need to and according to the demands of my body. Convinced that there is no turning back, I tell the doctor how I will push and when I need to, that I will breathe as I see fit. I accuse him of withholding food and drink from me and of keeping me up all night. I tell him that I am tired and inform him that unless I am left alone to birth as I need to I will be driven into exhaustion and a forceps delivery will be necessary. I know I overstate my case: this poor kid-doctor just happened to be there when I had had enough; he only just came on rotation and probably had little authority over the details of my situation, especially given the committee's central role in decision making. In any case, they, the attending physician and his cronies, back off. I inform them that a contraction is approaching, that I am getting ready to push. They are now quiet through my efforts.

My midwife is there. Apparently my words had a greater impact than I knew. She takes one look at me and starts talking about the birth of her first child and how she pushed so hard, pushed so hard *with her face*, that she broke a good many of the blood vessels that called her face home. I was doing the same thing. That little bit of advice meant a lot. It allowed me to redirect my energies toward pushing out the child and not popping out my eyeballs.

At the urging of my husband, I sat up-right to see our child born. I don't think I really cared, absorbed as I was in actually *giving* birth, but I complied with the vague thought that that was what a good mother did; I thought, I ought to act like a good mother given the (omni-)present regime of observation. Our first sight of Patrick as he was born was of him with his fist to his cheek, the cool blue of the umbilical cord that was wrapped around his neck contrasting sharply with his red and pink skin. With another push, maybe two, our child was fully born and the second sight I had of him was of his penis and scrotum. Since our prenatal ultrasound had indicated that the would-be Patrick was a girl (Katherine "Kate" Frances Falcone, we anticipated), I was surprised and exclaimed "It's a boy!," repeating a ritual which must occur thousands of times every day in every corner of the globe. The cord was unceremoniously cut and our child, six weeks premature, was placed on a table for the first test of his independent life: an Apgar. He did well. After some confusion about which baby was which (another had shown up at about the same time, and they all look alike), the as yet named "Patrick" was whisked off to the neighboring neonatal intensive care unit (NICU).

And so our child was born. But there are many gaps in the story thus far, things which are not amenable to retelling. Such as the fact that whenever the doctors busied themselves with my pelvic region, I experienced them as being very far away, as if the distance between my chin and my pubic bone was at least fifteen feet and no less. Clearly unable to resist their attention yet unwilling to reconcile myself to it, I had created a psychic distance to replace the real distance of which I was deprived. Even so, the fact remains that my experience of my body literally changed, its felt dimensions expanding to meet my need for space. I cannot integrate this fact into my sense of how things are.

And then there is my mother who was present throughout my labor, at the edges of my awareness. While she was there throughout my labor, we did not once talk nor, in my recollection, did I acknowledge her existence. I was angry and resentful at her presence, her status as a witness. But she meant well and I could not bear to ask her to leave. I suspect she did not want to be there any more than I wanted her there. So we endured the labor, if not quite together, then side by side as if caught in each other's orbits, neither one of us having enough speed to escape the gravitational pull of the other. Postmodern mother and daughter, a relationship which depends on silence for its maintenance.

There is more. We, mother and father, became parents at the same moment but experienced fundamentally different initiations. This is the case even though we parted just once and for but a few minutes. A mother becomes a mother according to the logic of the panopticon, simultaneously with her reduction to an object, that is, on her back, legs open to the medical gaze, a masculine gaze. The penetration is total, extending to the child inside with a monitor clipped to its skull and the regulation of labor via the oxytocin drip. As I, our son's mother, experienced it, the pain of birth was the pain of penetration, and my becoming a mother was a public spectacle: an object lesson for medical students, a curiosity for those who had never seen an unanesthetized woman give birth, and a perplexing, perhaps traumatizing, vision for those close to me watching the events unfold according to their alien logic.

When a father becomes a father, a different code is in play. Just prior to the birth, I, our son's father, was offered the protection of the doctor's locker room where I could change into scrubs, the doctor's uniform. It was a modesty and privilege not afforded to mothers, and premised on my very alienation from the birthing process itself. Dressed in scrubs, like the doctors and nurses, and able (trained all my life, in fact) to make small talk, body talk, face-to-face talk, to communicate with authorities, the likes of which include medical personnel, I was able to make use of a kind of magical power that a well-honed and self-conscious masculinity sometimes affords. I ordered the doctor not to perform an episiotomy, for example, and *he listened* and, for whatever reason, obeyed. Later, when I would see him trailing along among a gaggle of student-physicians doing their rounds in the NICU, I could cause him to acknowledge me, sheepishly, as I stood beside Patrick's "isolette" home, simply by setting upon him with the fixed gaze of a potentially menacing zoo animal, intent on saying something from behind the bars of his cage.

PART TWO. THE DEATH OF BIRTH

As it stands today, a woman is seriously limited in making birth her own, shaping its progress according to her life experience, fully integrated in the rhythm of its unwinding. Birth stands apart from and against the biographical life-history of the individual woman who births. This estrangement is the culmination of many social historical processes that, over a stretch of time/space, combined to create mass society, a historically unprecedented form of social organization, which was firmly established in the United States of America by the middle of this, the American Century. Never immune or separate from the whole of social organization, childbirth was no less implicated in this transformation. Recall once again that by 1955, 95 percent of American women bore their children in hospitals under the guidance of modern medicine. Birth had become mass birth, a term which refers not so much to the quantity of birth but to the qualitative treatment of childbirth as a mass phenomena, wherein individual agency is thoroughly subordinated to institutional logics that exist and are perpetuated as if independent of anyone's control.

The very presence of medicine in the birth chamber is a direct manifestation of the structuring of procreation by social forces. The power of medicine is thus a social power and an institutional power. More than this, medicine is a material practice, and, as such, it is more than a passive description of birth or a form of ideology abstracted from the activity of birthing. Medicine is, in fact, constitutive of the experience of birth. The dominance of medicine vis-à-vis the structuring of birth expresses a previously asserted/established material control over procreation. Knowledge is power: To know something is to control it.

In the hospital, birth is freed from the constraints of the particular conditions of each woman's experience of birth,[1] signifying birth in the abstract, birth-in-itself. This primary structural feature of contemporary childbirth is conditioned on the decreasing material significance of a "natural division of labor" (Marx [1846]1977, p. 51), relevant to procreation in favor of its social division. In other words, birth as a social fact is quickly overtaking birth as a natural given, and this situation calls into question the continuing utility of positing a natural division of labor as an analytic category relevant to the production of new humans. The relative contributions of males and females given by biology is of increasingly minor influence in shaping how birth occurs in contemporary America.[2]

This is especially true of the biological participation of males who are not universally necessary to the bringing forth of new life. Not all cultures have posited a relationship between sexual intercourse, pregnancy, and fatherhood, which typically requires a social definition for its establishment. Even in the West, where such "ignorance" of the biological origins of paternity is thought to have been left behind, a definite ambivalence concerning the details of male participation can still be found. The legend of Christ's birth within the Christian mythological tradition is suggestive of the nagging persistence of this ambivalence even in our own, ever so advanced, times.

In late twentieth-century America, where the necessity of male participation in procreation is generally accepted as an incontrovertible fact, the participation of particular males is not so certain. Biologically, males are more or less interchangeable. This interchangeability is only intensified by such technological developments as artificial insemination and *in vitro* fertilization. Such practices mean that a given male does not even have to be present at conception: just sperm, any sperm. While the specific biological relation of *this* male to *this* neonate is always open to question, this question has been pried open even further by science. DNA testing, now commonplace, only offers further evidence that paternity must be socially established if it is to be established at all.

Until recently, there could have been no concept of a maternal ambivalence corresponding to the problem of paternal ambivalence, primarily because of the biological relation between particular females and particular neonates. A female could not help but give birth to the same fetus which gestated in *her* womb as a result of *her* ova and a spermatozoa. However, the emergence of the so called "new" reproductive technologies has radically undermined this certainty. Through such technologies, particular females are becoming more and more tangential to any given newborn. With the emergence of embryo-transfer technology and *in vitro* fertilization, it is now possible (even mundane) to speak of more than one biological mother, of one woman giving birth to another woman's genetic offspring.

While it is true that the relation between particular females and particular neonates is not quite as contingent as that which obtains between particular males and particular neonates, it is also clear that the differences that remain are becoming increasingly less important and meaningful. At the moment and for the moment, some bodily involvement on the part of *a* female is necessary, given that it is not yet possible to sustain the development of fetal life from conception to "birth" entirely outside the uterus of a female. However, neonates *have* been born of brain-dead females, a fact which suggests that the necessary uterus does not have to be attached to a *fully living* female. This apparent dependency of a fetus on the uterus attached to the body of a more or less living female, who may or may not be the origins of the fetus's genetic material, is hardly fixed in stone. Intrauterine gestation is no longer necessarily nine months but may be as short as twenty-one weeks. Conception no longer must occur in a female body but can and does take place in a petri dish. These facts are well known.

At issue, here, is the decreasing contribution of particular biological beings to the continuation of our species. The historically necessary participation of entire bodies organized according to biological sex can no longer be taken for granted as "natural" as opposed to "social." Furthermore, the bodily commitment of females is less subject to the dictates of "nature" than ever before. The presence of a female body is still necessary but her conscious involvement, the commitment of her entire being, is not. More and more, her biological participation is becoming analogous to that of males. It is a contingent involvement, one which is increasingly uncertain and permeated with ambivalence.

In general, the significance of the natural division of labor is steadily decreasing while that of the social division of labor is increasing. So long as childbirth is taken for granted as a natural phenomena, its social structuring will remain implicit, and not subject to control. In the current context, the labor of childbirth is socially divided, the unitary experience fractured. Divided labor is no longer subject to the dictates of nature. The body in birth is obedient to a different dictator, that of science as an expertise embodied in the form of the doctor. Divided labor demands organization: it is managed labor. In other words, the social division of labor relevant to the bodily contribution to the bringing forth of life requires a further division, namely that of mental and manual labor. This division renders minds and bodies separate from each other and occurs in fact and not just in philosophy.

This brings us to the social epistemology of mass birth; to the world of Michel Foucault and his concern to map the intersections of knowledge and power. By social epistemology, the genealogy of knowledge/power, we refer to the social structuring of authority over birth and birth's representation (Adams 1994). Knowledge and authority demand each other, a fact implied in the meaning of the term "representation" itself, a term which has connotations for both politics and knowledge. To represent means to both describe an object as in a picture and to speak for someone as in Congress. In both cases, a given representation is a stand-in or replacement for that which is represented, if anything at all. In short, representations are constitutive of social relations.

As with the shift in the place of birth from home to hospital and the increasing division of labor characteristic of the birth process, transformations in how birth is represented exerts a determinate influence on childbirth. It is this productive dimension that most interests us, for it is the power of representation to create realities, and, in this case, further the centrifugal processes that form the problem of mass birth and its concomitant erasure of birth itself. The problem of "how birth is represented" consists of two analytically distinguishable dimensions: the vehicles or means of representation and the significations of the representations themselves.

Regarding the means of representation, prior to the medical-technological advances of this century, the unborn child could be known only through the woman in whose womb it resided. Interested observers had no access to the fetus independent of the body and the voice of the woman who carried it. Equally important, there was no possibility of influencing fetal development independent of the mother. The advance of medicine has made possible a different kind of knowledge about the fetus with different practical implications. Maternal blood tests, amniocentesis, chorionic villi sampling, and urinalysis are examples of prenatal tests that provide information about the fetus without involving the woman's subjectivity for its availability. The information takes an esoteric form recognizable only to the medical literati and not to the birthing mother, or anyone else, for that matter. Ultrasound and electronic fetal monitoring take this process of surveillance one step further by providing an immediately available visual representation of certain elements of the fetus and the uterine environment. Neither of these require the physical penetration of the mother's body nor the retention of its matter (blood, urine, tissue).

These "windows on the womb," as they are called, allow direct access to the developing fetus on the part of the trained specialist. The effect has been to displace the authority of women to represent birth in favor medicine's representations. Additionally, the alienation of the fetus from the mother creates for the fetus the possibility of an independent social status (Katz-Rothman 1989; Raymond 1993). The fetus is viewed and even medically treated as an autonomous human being long before birth, the rights of which are debated, advocated for, and often legally protected, against the articulated concerns of the woman in whose womb the fetus resides (Katz-Rothman 1989; Raymond 1993). The woman-with-child is reduced to merely a maternal environment, a reduction which devalues her bodily contribution to the birth process as a whole. Her involvement in the bringing forth of life has evolved to the point where she is but one element in the process of reproduction, and not a particularly significant one at that.

Having gained independent access to the fetus *in utero*, medicine claims for itself the legitimate authority to represent not just birth but the substantive interests of the fetus. Such a claim to authority can only be made at the expense of the authority of the woman in whose body the fetus resides. This is because the expert knowledge of medicine and the knowledge grounded in a woman's experience of the life forming within her body are qualitatively different kinds of knowledge, with different foundations and different vehicles of representation.

A woman's experience of birth is primarily sensual: she cannot hear or see the contractions of her body in labor nor can she see the developing fetus within her without the aid of advanced technologies. In contrast, the doctor perched beside his EFM or ultrasound can *only* see graphic representations of the body of the fetus, the function of its organs and uterine activity, from which he is required to *infer* knowledge of the thing itself. The advantages of the latter cognitivist approach are many, including that the doctor does not even have to be in the same room as the birthing mother, as he can watch the goings-on of her body on a monitor across the hall or across the world.

Moreover, a woman's experiential knowledge of life forming within her and her body birthing can be made intersubjectively available only through the very intimate forms of voice and bodily expression. The moan, the sigh, the grimace, and the clenched fist punctuate the words a woman speaks to convey what she is feeling, lending bodily substance to abstract verbal expression. The doctor relies on a different kind of communication, one which takes the form of the increasingly inhuman language of technology: numbers, graphs, figures and computer-generated images reinforce the inevitable alienation of the attendant to the birth from the actuality of birth. Indeed, the somatic languages of childbirth are meaningless and have no objective status within medicine, except possibly as indications of impending risk, cooperation, or in any number of ways, as the symbol of something else tangible and real.

Two realities are thus created in the conflict between the understanding of the birthing woman: the women's own understanding which is saturated in her experience of giving birth, and that of the doctor which is premised on "his" inevitable alienation from the same experience. These realities are, by virtue of their origins, incommensurable. Saturation and alienation exclude each other, and, while alienation can be partially compensated for, saturation can only be accepted or denied. Like any bodily experience, the experience of birth, if it is to be made available to an outside observer, is always dependant on mutual recognition and intersubjective understanding. Its objectivity can only manifest itself intersubjectively, and this depends on the willingness of the one who is Other, Other-to-the-birth, to open themselves to the intimacy of the moment and allow themselves to be touched by the woman's voice in its various and always particular forms. It is an act of surrender involving a thorough acceptance of the fact that a woman births as if there were no other, and no possibility of another birth. It is only by respecting this void of intersubjectivity that the unending is-ness of the body birthing might be transcended and alienation partially compensated for. Put differently, it is only by recognizing *the limits* of intersubjectivity that an intersubjective understanding of a woman giving birth might be broached.

Needless to say, medicine doesn't do this, or even attempt to do this. Insisting on its own image of a physiological birth abstracted from a given woman's experience, medicine approaches the birthing woman with its own language and its own vision. From the alien perspective of medicine, birth is incommensurable with its experience. The medical claim to authoritatively represent the activity of giving birth and the fetal product is a form of epistemological privilege grounded not in the "truth" of birth, but solely in a particular form of institutionalized social power. Through this epistemological privilege, medicine organizes the reality of birth, creating a metaphysics of birth that involves the temporal and spatial conceptualization of the project of birth.

In *Reproducing the Womb* (1994, p. 171), Alice E. Adams describes her pregnancy as having occurred in what she calls "real time":

> I felt the constant tumult as the baby hiccoughed, flexed her body, and tested with elbows, knees, and feet the limits of my inner space. She was a bulky, impertinent, spirited presence in my body, simultaneously an integral part of me and an independent entity. In the months before her birth, our relationship was mediated through touch not vision.

Pregnancy is sensual and spatial, occurring in and through time but not of time. Its form, medium, and essence is that of bodies and their movements.

For the most part, and especially from the perspective of the woman, birth constitutes a unity of time and space; the unformed child develops within the spaces of a woman's body, making a place for itself where previously there was none. The woman's belly grows to accommodate the child, perhaps resenting, perhaps forgiving it its trespass as it stretches her skin, stretches her body, and transforms the shape of her very being in space. When the time comes, her body gradually opens to allow the child passage. The woman works cyclically to move the child through the newly created innerspaces of her being. As the head of the child passes out of the body of the woman, she again stretches to accommodate it. In and through time and space, the woman and child share in the intimate project of birth.

From the medical perspective, pregnancy and childbirth is conceptualized in such a way that time and space are considered separate from and often in opposition to each other. The focus here is on discrete units: gestational age is a matter of weeks while pregnancy is divided into trimesters; labor is divided into stages, each with its maximum duration; the dilation of the cervix is measured in centimeters and the child's movement into and through the birth canal is again described in terms of stages. Not to be outdone, the human scientists have insisted on their own rationalized conceptualizations that parcel out the proper psychological, affective and social responses and adaptations, taking the physiological template as the basis for their more airy forms of normalization.

In essence, the basic principles of Frederick Winslow Taylor's scientific management are applied to the management of labor, where the continuum of fetal development and birth is divided into a series of units, each allotted a certain amount of time to unfold before intervention is considered necessary (Adams 1994). Accordingly, a woman in a typical American hospital does not birth in and through time but against time. The body space of the woman and the abstract time of medicine are pitted against each other. Her—or rather her cervix's and the fetus's—*rate* of progress is considered a primary indicator of her uterus's efficiency. The woman who wishes to avoid the array of interventions medicine has developed is placed in a continual state of emergency, for she does not confront the challenges of birth directly but only as they are temporally mediated. She knows it is only a matter of time before a normal labor turns pathological and intervention is necessary to contain its deviance. She must either beat the clock or reconcile herself to accepting whatever assistance medicine may deem necessary and appropriate.

Not only does the medical management of labor involve what Herbert Marcuse (1964) called a process of "one-dimensionalization" of the experience of childbirth, wherein women's bodies are effectively redesigned according to a narrow objective instrumental standard (see also Adams 1994, p. 53), but in this process of flattening the lived experience of birth, the very nature of time is changed. The medical representation of birth involves a reconfiguration of time itself in which time is no longer anchored in space, and, in particular, body space. Instead, time is emptied of content so that its neutrality and universality are assured. Time can be considered a common denominator applicable equally to all because it no longer applies to anyone. It has become the abstract, "empty time" pointed to by Walter Benjamin (1969) as the chief characteristic of modernist consciousness.

As time is reconfigured, so is space. The logic and practice of medicine transforms the infinitely dimensioned micrological material spaces of a woman's body into a two-dimensional field that privileges vision. The body is, for medicine, a plane, as transparent as it is flat. Birth has been reduced to the problem of how to get the perinate from point A to point B in a timely fashion. Through this reduction, the body becomes pure space, nothing more than that which lies between two points. The resistant materiality of the woman is here reconceptualized as that which produces friction, inhibits progress, and threatens inertia. More than this, the body of the woman herself denies visual access to the fetus. Carrying the unformed and unborn child like a secret protected by the obstinate material of her skin, her tissues, her blood, and her bones, the woman comes between medicine and its object; she interferes with knowledge of the fetus. In her very being, she produces ignorance and mystery. She casts a shadow. She *is* a shadow, nothing in her own right but still darkening the light so necessary to vision.

Together, the medical reconfiguration of time and space re-creates reality on its own terms. It is a virtual reality where relations between humans are replaced not so much by relations between things, as in Marx's ([1867]1977) notion of commodity fetishism, but by relations between signs and images, as in Baudrillard's vision of a postmodern order. In the old order, nausea, dizziness, a missed period, or quickening often established the subjective reality of the life forming inside a woman. Today, it is the result of a pregnancy test, hearing the heart beat, and seeing the fetal image on the screen of the ultrasound device. The representation now precedes the reality, establishing and grounding the subjective experience of that reality.

This reversal demands a second: the various windows on the womb which allow medical access not just to the unborn child but to the unformed child, means that the social birth of the child precedes its physiological birth. Social categories, including gender and disability, are with increasing frequency assigned prenatally. In cases where the pregnancy is terminated on the basis of these categories, social death also precedes, or, more accurately, interrupts the real birth of the child. The child thus lives and dies without being born: virtual child.

As Baudrillard (1991) has shown, virtual reality demands virtual catastrophe. While, in general, birth is considered a normal physiological function, each birth is increasingly a potential disaster. Indeed, the very normalcy of birth creates the pathology such that, no matter how predictable and regular birth may be, each birth is treated as an emergency. The rationalization of childbirth, its standardization and detailed management, has not led to a pacification of the birth process. Quite the opposite has occurred: the perceived danger has multiplied as if to mock its attempted evasion. This is the case despite the fact that women and full-term babies rarely die in childbirth.

The logic is one where intervention does not reduce risk but both encourages risk-taking and redefines previously acceptable labors and fetuses as "at risk." At the same time, however, as a state of emergency is created, medicine never quite fulfills its own self-induced expectations. Instead, the emergency is contained within and by the logic of intervention which redefines every potential problem as a field of action before it asserts itself. Every birth is potentially pathological, but the pathology is anticipated and overcome before it ever emerges. Prophylaxis.

Consider the following: A prenatal test results in a positive diagnosis for downs syndrome and a pregnancy is, on this basis, aborted. It is a virtual death, the mourning of which can only refer to the loss of a normal child who never was and never could have been. The abortion of the genetically anomalous fetus is a nonevent coupled with a virtual one; the life of the real child is terminated but it is the loss of a different, nonexistent child which is mourned. The real child—the one with the diagnosis—can be nothing more than a contingency dealt with, a disaster avoided, the negative of the image of a perfect child. Yet it is the latter child, the one who never existed, who is missed. The "could have been" replaces "what has been" as the privileged reality. The catastrophe applies to the child who never was. It is virtual.

The metaphysics of birth, more than anything else, points to processes of world-maintenance through which social boundaries are constructed and maintained such that birth is integrated into social organization. Birth becomes an organized reality; the more threatening the birth the more intervention is considered necessary. Early in this century, before medicine had consolidated its monopoly on childbirth, all birth was considered pathological (Arms 1975; Wertz and Wertz 1977). Controlled by old women, superstition, unregulated general practitioners, and "nature," it represented the limits of science and logic. It was disorderly because order had not yet been imposed. This is no more the case: birth has been normalized and subjected to science's regulation. Birth was not so much discovered to be normal but was made normal and forced to submit. How could it be any other way?

Until the last century, childbirth was a women-centered affair, and, in childbirth, women reproduced not just individual humans, but a distinct women's culture. As Judith Walzer Leavitt, in her *Brought to Bed*, observes:

> Childbirth, through its often repeated reminders of how important women were to one another, was a very significant part of a woman's world. Childbirth customs and rituals formed a cornerstone of women's group identity .... The support network that women gathered around them at the time of their confinements provided the necessary base for women's ability to resist some medical practices and to keep considerable control in their own hands (1986, p. 210).

Attending each other's confinements, women offered each other support, both practical and emotional. Even when a physician was invited to attend a birth, "his" power and status as an expert was limited by the real and continuing presence of a woman's friends and family at her bedside. His influence was thus subject to the constraints of those who had much to offer a woman in labor. The shared experience of giving birth created a material foundation for solidarity among women through which a distinct woman's world was created and maintained.

This culture was not a universal culture, but was subject to class and other divisions. While women depended on other women for support in childbirth or felt their absence when they were unable to find such support (Leavitt 1986, p. 95), the specific form of this support differed according to her particular situation. This is perhaps the most significant fact about birth in the last century relative to our own. A hundred years ago, the only certainty about birth was that the way a woman labored was dependant on her life situation. It would be impossible to infer how a woman birthed from the fact that she gave birth. Any further understanding would require an understanding of her general situation: her class, racial and ethnic identity, marital status, religious convictions, where she lived, where her mother lived, and so forth. All these details directly influenced the how of each woman's birth. This is so because before our time there was no such thing as Birth, independent of the women who gave birth and the particulars of how they did so. Only recently is it possible to infer many of the details of a given birth from the fact that it occurred.

Today, one can know with relative certainty almost as soon as a woman is pregnant that she will receive prenatal care beginning in her second or third month, attend childbirth education classes in her seventh month, visit the hospital in her eighth month, stop smoking or feel guilty if she can't, cut down on coffee, drink six to eight glasses of water a day, and take vitamins throughout her pregnancy. When she goes into labor, she will call her doctor, leave for the hospital when her contractions are five minutes apart and a minute in duration, breathe through early labor, receive an anesthetic in active labor, take two cleansing breaths before bearing down with the third, have a small cut made in her perineal tissues, and watch herself give birth, husband or his surrogate at her side. And through the entire process she will try to think positive, pleasant thoughts, reminding herself that nightmares and other worries are natural; a woman generally has the right equipment, and if primitive women can squat in the woods, bear their young and get back to work without a second thought, then certainly she can do it with the best modern medical science has to offer. After all, birth is perfectly normal, Normal, NORMAL.

There are variations, to be sure, but the point is that they are variations on a consistent set of widely regulated practices that do little more than measure a woman's deviation from what is nearly always reproduced as normal. Even if no woman births according to the norm—and it is difficult to imagine that any actually do— it would just mean that all women are deviants, and in that fact the nagging suspicion that women giving birth border on the pathological would be confirmed. That birth is normal, in other words, doesn't mean that women are, or even can be, without the assistance of medicine. In the typical situation, the obstetrician can

intervene to restore the integrity of the bell curve by bringing a noncon-
forming labor into line.

More importantly, many variations, particularly those which have potentially dangerous consequences for the mother and child, are strongly associated with life lived on the wrong side of line between rich and poor and
are exacerbated by institutional discrimination against ethnic and racial
minorities. It is well known, for example, that mal- and under-nourish-
ment, little or no quality prenatal care, high stress levels, and many similar
social factors related to social stratification and the degradation therein
produced, increase the potential for complications in the birth process.
This knowledge, however, is transmuted in the classic tradition of the medicalization of social problems, in which the dire effects of systemic social
domination are rendered and treated as technical problems requiring for
their solution specialized medical interventions and treatments. Social
problems are treated in the emergency room, on the delivery table, and in
the neonatal intensive care unit, and later, in early intervention programs
serving children at risk for or with established developmental delays. The
result is that the lethal and damaging consequences of advanced capitalist
society's inability to assure an adequate and general standard of living are
treated as myriad unrelated individual problems, caused by either personal
or subcultural shortcomings, bad luck, or a defective physiological constitution.

There is a bitter logic and a vicious circle involved here. The abstraction
of birth from the experience of particular women has harmed all women
birthing but has been especially disastrous for those who are furthest from
the American white middle-class norm of risk-reduction through early prenatal care, childbirth preparation, and six to eight glasses of water a day.
Such women carry the double burden of birthing according to some
abstract norm in an alien institution, in addition to facing the everyday
challenges of making ends meet in a society that could not care less about
their survival. On top of this, they are then blamed for failing to take measures to reduce risks to their health and that of their children, blamed for
our country's high infant mortality rate, and blamed for reducing our country's standing on United Nations quality of life indices, all as if persistent
poverty were a alternative lifestyle choice.

Women who are prevented from achieving a white middle-class standard of living suffer more in childbirth: African-American maternal mortality rates are twice as high as those for white women; black infants die
in their first year at four times the rate of white infants. [3] The persistence

of institutionalized white supremacy is neither limited to marginal right wing extremist organizations nor does it leave childbirth practices unaffected. Behind the statistics lies hidden a way of life, a way of birth, and a way of death.

Through the medicalization of human procreation, mass society literally reproduces itself in the birth of each of its members. Mass birth is a birth which is consistent with mass society, where life means little more than not-dead. It is a painless birth, neither challenging the order of things and people nor the order of the woman's self. In an event that hardly happens, nothing is felt, no agency is risked, and the human project of bringing life into the world occurs without any experience of transformation. A woman does not create *new* life but just *more* life.

A woman does not and cannot birth as an individual who brings to the birthing room a particular life history. It is precisely this, the experience of a lifetime residing in the tissues of the body, which is explicitly and emphatically denied in the culturally hegemonic and institutionally dominant conception of human procreation. Accordingly, women birth not as humans, not as women, nor even as a Woman, but as a function of her reproductive system. Biography is irrelevant; agency not devoted to conformity is impossible. Birthing women can be nothing more than their social-medical construction.

The emergence of birth in the abstract where "Birth" is conceptualized independently of its experience, as an event which does not require the involvement of the entire woman, assumes that women are somehow separate from their birthing bodies and are not directly implicated in the activity of their uteruses. An exploration of pain relief in childbirth helps to draw out the significance of treating birth as a physiological event abstracted from a woman's life in its constitutive influence on the experience of birth.

At the extreme, as was routine and considered progressive in the middle of this century, women were rendered unconscious as they gave birth. This does not mean that they were necessarily relieved of pain, for women did not spend their entire labors in a state of unconsciousness. The relief of pain involves a compromise between the health and safety of the mother, that of the fetus, and the continuing efficiency of the uterus. It has never been easy to strike a balance between these three interests and at the same time provide a reasonable amount of pain relief for a woman in labor. Thus, various drugs were used to partially dull the pain throughout labor; often it was not until the woman was actually about to give birth that she was fully "put under." As Dr. Laura E. Weber informed her readers in *Between Us Women*, after the work of pushing is complete:

> When they put you on a stretcher or roll your crib bed into the delivery room, you are now finished with your work. This is where the doctor, anesthetist and nurses take over, while you go to sleep. When you wake up, you will probably be in your own room and your baby will be in the nursery. It is to arrive at this point that you have conceived, carried, worried and labored (1962, p. 105).

In this scenario, the birthing woman is brought right to the point of actually birthing before she is put to sleep. This means that she most likely felt much of her labor pains *and* is deprived of the experience of birth.

The use of the drug scopolamine, supplemented with morphine and chloroform, takes this paradoxical situation to its extreme. In general, "Twilight Sleep," as this practice was known, "dulled the awareness of pain and, perhaps more important, removed the memory of it" (Wertz and Wertz 1977, p. 150). Leavitt described the specific form of "relief" provided by this procedure:

> Women's bodies experienced their labors, even if their minds could not remember them. Observers witnessed women screaming in pain during contractions, thrashing about, and giving all the external signs of "acute suffering" .... But few women described such suffering after they emerged from a twilight delivery, the amnesiac properties of scopolamine eliminated their memory of any discomfort (1986, p. 129).

Twilight Sleep did not so much relieve women of their bodily pain as it destroyed their power to remember and voice their experience of it. Thus, not only was their experience of birth lost to the unconscious, so was their pain. In other words, women were radically alienated from both the fact of having given birth and their own suffering.

At mid-century, the alienation of women from their own activity of birthing took the extreme form of the medically sanctioned disabling of her consciousness of having given birth. The agency of the birthing mother, her mind drugged out of existence, is replaced by that of the expert and his or her staff, who, working as a team of professionals, are responsible for overseeing the birth of the neonate.

In the contemporary context, such scenarios are rare since they eventually caused more problems than institutionalized medicine was prepared to accept. In the late fifties, both medical professionals and the lay public began to question the various practices of anesthesia which were danger-ous to both the health and long-term well-being of mother and child (Wertz and Wertz 1977). Now, after several decades of institutional change, spurred in part by the Feminist Women's Health Movement but also, par-adoxically, the anti-feminist cult of heterosexist motherhood or the Femi-nine Mystique (Freidan 1963) current at mid-century and facilitated by a growing critical awareness even among health care professionals regard-ing the value of so-called "natural childbirth," women generally expect, and they are likewise expected, to remain conscious throughout the birth.

Instead of unconsciousness, women are today offered the relief of anes-thetics that numb only their bodies, or parts of their bodies, to the sensa-tions of labor; anesthetics can mean, in other words, anything from total paralysis of the woman from the waist down to the localized numbing of only the uterus and the cervix. In any case, women remain conscious but do not *feel* themselves giving birth. They are placed in a position with respect to their own activity of birthing analogous to that of the doctor: educated as to the physiology of reproduction in childbirth preparation classes and expected to take an active part in the birth, women are aware that they birth; they can see it and hear it and know that it is happening, but they cannot feel themselves birth; they do not experience it as an actuality.

The inevitable alienation of the physician from the particular births they attend and that of male physicians from birth in general is effectively rep-licated in the experience of birthing women as a matter of obstetrical rou-tine. Thus, a woman giving birth must typically be told when to push, how to push, and how to breathe when pushing, necessary instructions which indicate that a women might not finish her task without some form of external motivation in addition to whatever practical aid routinely offered to complete the delivery. A prepared woman, "well-trained," as the self-help manuals keep referring to her, can birth this way with only minor complications (of her own or the newborn's condition). At issue is not only safety but also the extension of the division of labor into the birth canal itself and the resulting fragmentation therein implied.

This fracturing of the experience of birth leads to a situation where it is possible to speak of two women birthing: the mind-woman who manages the work of the typically literally senseless body-woman according to the direction of medical expertise. The social division of labor in childbirth, particularly that between the labor of minds and the labor of bodies, involves a division of the woman herself; she is subject and object, mind and matter, producer, consumer, low-level manager and worker. She is man, she is woman, she is a gender-neutral physiological event. Most of all, she has no more power or authority than any other lay person in the face of any other expert. She knows better than anybody what she is going through, but the very status of her knowledge is diminished by its foundation in her saturation in the process of giving birth. That is to say, her authority over her own body is institutionally devalued because that knowledge is contaminated by the particularities of her own experience.

The assumption that women are not full participants in the births they give underlies both pharmaceutical and psychoprophylactic pain relief techniques commonly employed in mainstream hospitals. In seeking to relieve a woman's pain, the goal is for the mother to achieve a state of perfect relaxation in order to enhance the efficiency of her uterus. Again, in Dr. Weber's (1962) words:

> Patients who are very apprehensive and tense are frequently given some mild sedative or other medication to relax them and this in turn will help their labor progress more satisfactorily. A very tense patient actually seems to hold herself back to some extent (p. 98).

And, further:

> The medicine we give you helps dull your pain and also relaxes you so that your labor will progress more rapidly and satisfactorily (p. 100).

Underlying the medically encouraged use of pain management techniques is the assumption of a "fear-tension-pain cycle." The idea is that a woman's fear of childbirth produce muscular tension which both increases pain and interferes with the functioning of the uterus. The use of various techniques of physical and emotional relaxation, either pharmaceutical or neuromuscular and psychic dissociation, are encouraged to interrupt the fear-tension-pain cycle and thereby ease a woman's labor.

The guiding assumption behind "pain management" is that women are closed systems and the source of the perceived danger is internal to that system. The cornerstone of childbirth preparation is the reforming of a woman's taken-for-granted understanding of childbirth, which is said to be informed by superstition, myth, and old wives tales. In addition, childbirth preparation aims to recondition her "automatic" inclination to resist the pain of childbirth simply because it hurts. Women are taught the physiological facts of birth in the hope that this knowledge will allow them to contextualize their pain, and, in the end, to see their pains as something positive to work with and not as a negative to work against.

The assumption that women are closed systems that respond only to previous learning implies that the source of danger and bodily tension is within her; she is the problem. The alien and threatening hospital environment and medical regime being practiced *on* her body are in this way rendered innocuous and invisible. As natural childbirth pioneer, Dr. Robert A. Bradley, informs the readers of his *Husband-Coached Childbirth*, childbirth "training displaces ignorance, superstition, fear, anxiety, and the resultant bodily tensions which are such obstacles" to childbirth (1965, pp. 10-11). Moreover, through the practice of natural childbirth, Bradley suggests that: "Women can enjoy the process of birth and add to their dignity by being educated to follow the example set by instinctive animals" (p. 12). Evidently, a woman's very humanness presents an obstacle to the birth process: while birth may be natural, women are not. A woman's task is to dissociate herself from what is happening to her body so as not to interfere with its operation.

As a rule, a woman is taught to dissociate from herself and identify with her medical construction as a physiological process identical in all women. There is no recognition of woman birthing in her own way, as she is for herself. Such an approach to the activity of birthing could only interfere with the predictable progress of her labor. Rather than birthing as she has come to be as a body and as a self and coming to an understanding of her body's powers to not only create life but to withstand the onslaught of its emergence from within her, a woman is simply deprived of self-experience through pain relief.

As discussed earlier, in the middle of this century a woman would have likely been unconscious at the moment of giving birth and therefore unable to take part in her body's ability to resolve the challenge—contradictory in its essence—of birth. Today, she is typically numbed and feels neither pain nor pleasure but rather a sensationless manipulation of her body parts. Feeling nothing, a woman has no experience of her birthing body as anything other than a thing disconnected from herself and controlled from the outside.

In general, offering to relieve women of their pains, medicine promises to deliver women from the legacy of their bodies. In so doing, medicine takes on eshatological dimensions (Raymond 1993), even if this is only an appropriation of the body's own capacity to deliver itself. By definition, the actual birth will alleviate the pain of giving birth, a fact which signifies that pain is but one aspect of a complex experience, and a limited one at that.

Pain relief is our culture's only accommodation of women as they give birth. Birth, like death, is an end game pointing directly to the limits of experience. Unlike death and by definition, one can and often does live through it. If all women died in childbirth, it would soon cease to be an issue. As obvious as this is, its significance should not be overlooked. The social accommodations, the means cultures have developed to integrate the overwhelming facticity of birth into the communal experience, are as many and various as human culture itself. However, in all cases, rituals have direct implications for the women who birth. This stands in contrast to the rituals surrounding death, which are necessarily indifferent to the person who has died, at least after the point which they have, in fact, died.

Promising only to relieve physiological pain, our culture receives a woman into motherhood with indifference. The institution of medicine, in treating birth as a physiological event, steadfastly denies the continuity of birth with a woman's experience, denies that birth is not an event isolated in significance, but a passage for *both* woman and child. Receiving no public recognition for her entry into motherhood, save for the Hallmark Card type of pseudo-recognition perhaps best exemplified by the giant storks increasingly appearing in new mother's front yards, a woman births as if alone.

This fact strikes at the heart of the paradox of mass society and is perhaps its purest and most immediate expression. Perceptible only from within the lifeworld, this paradox refers to the combination of high levels of social integration with the extremes of isolation which have long been considered a prevailing feature of 20th century American life. The American practice of birthing is no exception to this rule, in spite of the fact that it has not, to our knowledge, been analyzed in these terms.

Thus, childbirth in our society is a public affair. Any variety of strangers can claim authority over and access to a woman's body throughout the "perinatal period." The visibility of pregnancy constitutes an open invitation to invade the culturally established personal spaces of a woman's body and violate the boundaries of her being. A woman birthing in the (ever-same) hospital births on a ground not her own and is subject to rules and rituals to which she is incidental but which manifest for her real power over her life. Hospital business is conducted, if not in a foreign language, then in the alien, technical language of medicine, which can only be partially translated to the lay person at the will of the doctor and various other attending specialist professionals. Having no guaranteed private space or time, a variety of strangers, including doctors, nurses, technicians, religious counselors, and childbirth educators, have access to a woman's bedside throughout the day and night.

In and through this publicity, this overwhelming press of the social, a woman births alone, in a psychic wilderness miles from nowhere. Up until the mid-seventies, women in hospitals typically spent their first stages of labor warehoused, sharing space with several other women. However, the shared space was not and could not have been a social space. It was, instead, serial space, more like waiting in line at a grocery store. Surrounded by strangers, a woman was never alone and at the same time she was never specifically with or for anyone. And, no one was with or for her.

Even now, when it is common for women to labor and deliver in private rooms, perhaps surrounded by close friends and family, there is no common culture specific to birthing which acknowledges the communal reality of childbirth. The trend toward "family centered maternity care" only reinforces and glorifies the isolation of the heterosexist nuclear family. Separated from each other in private rooms and supported by their dutiful husbands, each woman labors in much the same way and according to identical institutional demands; there is no opportunity for creating a woman-centered culture surrounding childbirth (Cosslett 1994).

The isolation of women birthing, while rooted in their embodiment, is primarily a social isolation. A woman birthing has no name, just a description. A woman birthing has no life story, just a medical record. A woman birthing has no vocation, just a reproductive function. She has no friends and family, just labor coaches and supporters who "support" her. There can be no public recognition of a woman's initiation into motherhood, no way of easing her transition, no communal understanding and accommodation of her passage, for she is just passing through.

Yet, it is precisely this which makes for the continuity between mass birth and mass society; in this moment, the lifeworld begins in the system and is thoroughly permeated by its logic. The very distinction between system and lifeworld is an analytical distinction and, even as such, it is difficult to sustain. Almost as soon as it is posited, the life-world takes on mythological dimensions, tinged with a nostalgia for a home no one can today make a claim to. In a mass society, there are only systems and subsystems, and no amount of conceptual make-believe can change this. We birth and are born according to an alien logic which structures agency in a direction that conforms to the requirements of institutionalized social power.

The overdetermination of biography by social structure, such that there is little opportunity for women to exercise their agency in any but a conformist direction, has direct implications for the continuing possibility of history. The institutionalization of childbirth specifically implies that the social organization of childbirth is self-perpetuating. Human reproduction refers to both the reproduction of bodies and the reproduction of the conditions under which those bodies are reproduced. A basic consistency exists between the preservation of the species and the preservation of society. In the last century, there was a real distinction between the reproduction of humans and the reproduction of society, such that reproduction and production were organized according to different logics. Indeed, the nineteenth century was a time of massive sociocultural as well as economic transformation, where the means of social reproduction and history-making (relations of social production) were changing as rapidly as the means of industrial production. Living and making a living came into direct opposition. This, however, is no longer the case. We have created and cemented a new order of things.

The social structuring of procreation by medicine is a consolidation of power to create and regulate life itself (Foucault [1976]1978). Having displaced the birthing woman from the center of procreation and having taken all the necessary precautions against the unanticipated emergence of individual agency, obstetrics has managed to neutralize the tension between biography and social structure. In doing so, history is stopped in its tracks. It is unimaginable that any qualitatively different experience, any unanticipated or unforeseen development, might occur that could threaten the social structuring of the relations surrounding childbirth.

The development of (the science of) obstetrics and its institutionalized practice has severely limited a woman's ability to determine the specifics of how she gives birth, thus depriving her of any power to make accommodations for her own needs. Unfortunately, real, existing women arrive at the doctor's office or the hospital admissions desk, the materiality of their bodies intact, and insist on the particularity of their flesh and bones, but this particularity is neither acknowledged nor allowed to exert itself. A woman's capacity to mindfully integrate and effectively respond to a variety of complex stimuli, both environmental and internal, is systematically, and as a matter of course, disabled. Simply stated, she is without agency.

Without agency, no qualitative change and certainly no intelligent trans-formation of social institutions can take place. There can only be implo-sions and explosions, entropy, atrophy and hypertrophy; in a word, catastrophe. In spite of it all—all the science, all the enlightenment, all the marching forward of reason—the future appears to be in the hands of nature. But how much more can it can bear? Agency evaded is history deflected; a short-term victory for institutional interests is but a recipe for long-term self-annihilation.

Human history, stopped in its tracks, grants the upper hand to nature, and the struggle for survival intensifies. At the same time, reduced by science to its essence, nature shows itself as a projection of social relations, which is what it always has been for modern consciousness anyway. Science is a form of power intent on overcoming the resistance of nature. But nature is a construct: nothing more than human nature on its knees. Nowhere is this contradiction more apparent than in the sphere of human procreation.

In the late 1590s, Peter Chamberlen the Elder is said to have invented the forceps, the first practical intervention into childbirth introduced by physi-cians. While their design was kept secret for almost a hundred years by the entrepreneurial Chamberlen family, who were intent on preserving their competitive edge, the invention of the forceps established for the first time the possibility of acting on what was then considered the "course of nature," initiating the practice of "meddlesome midwifery," as it was called by its opponents. Forceps were not used in America until the middle of the eighteenth century when physicians began to attend women in child-birth. By the middle of the nineteenth century, the episiotomy had been developed, the first ovariotomy performed, and the stethoscope invented, making it possible to hear the fetal heartbeat. In the same period, the anes-thetic properties of ether and chloroform were discovered and applied to birthing women, and a program of "demonstrative midwifery" was initi-ated at the Buffalo Medical College, initiating the practice of parturition. In this span of a hundred years, physician-assisted childbirth became firmly established in America and radically altered "nature's" design. Within another one hundred years, obstetrics gained full control over par-turition, having successfully supplanted midwives and home-birth in a move to the hospital which not so much altered nature but eliminated it.

What is this nature which medicine has so successfully competed with? In the case of the successful attempt by physicians to establish a hegemony over childbirth, it is clear that "the natural" referred simply to the aeons-old control of birth by women (Merchant 1980). Physicians thus opposed themselves to the taken-for-granted assumptions and layered experience of generations surrounding childbirth. More than this, they opposed the traditional relations of power in the birth chamber that allowed women to take an active part in shaping the immediate social conditions of giving birth. The medicalization of childbirth transformed that activity from one grounded in and saturated by the cumulative experience of women birthing to an activity dominated by an expert science whose primary practitioners would never and could never give birth.

The struggle against nature is the struggle against other humans. It is also a struggle against human nature. The medicalization of childbirth, through which procreation is reconfigured according to a logic external to its movement, literally involves a re-design of the means of reproduction, namely women's bodies. This suggests the immediate identity of nature and human nature and the domination of nature through the domination of human nature. The penetration of the mystery of birth as a natural phenomena is a penetration of women birthing. The overcoming of the resistance of nature is the overcoming of the resistance of women. The use of anesthesia is just one way of overcoming resistance, and the fact that the domination of nature is made more bearable by its use only increases domination's efficacy. According to the same logic, the use of pain relief allows the doctor to bear what would have otherwise been a most difficult duty. It thus does not liberate women from the pain of childbirth, but institutionalizes insensitivity to that pain.

More than this, anesthetics, in interrupting the biological body's so called fear-tension-pain cycle, eliminates any stimulus for action. The bodily tension resulting from fear and/or pain is a preparation for action, and when action is impeded, fear and/or pain continues or intensifies. The action which does not ensue would have been oriented toward avoiding an anticipated disaster. In rendering women insensitive to pain, anesthetics disrupt the relation between the human body and both its own experience and its environment; it thus deprives women of any grounds for resisting inhuman childbirth practices.

The significance of this extends far beyond a woman's individual interests; being unable to defend and protect her own body, she is unable to protect and defend the perinate. Humans, like all mammals, have evolved such that the youngest and most vulnerable of the species are assured security and protection by virtue of the fact that they develop within the body of another of their kind, one fully grown and capable of acting in self-defense according to her interests. The self-interest of the mother and that of the perinate are identical: treating herself well and seeing to it that she is treated well is the best protection she can offer the life forming within her. The selfish pursuit of her own needs for nutrition, bodily comfort, peaceful living conditions, and a pacified existence generally, immediately benefits the still unformed child.

The life forming within the body of a woman depends on the ability of its mother to protect her own body; when she is rendered insensitive to threats, she can no longer provide this minimal assurance. A woman coerced into dependency, forced to trust the will of others, and numb to the pain of her own situation, is reduced to a passive container, unable to act on her own behalf. A vacuum is thus created into which the social power of medicine flows. The most vulnerable and dependant members of our species are thus placed in a direct confrontation with social power, unmediated by the fleshy comfort and support of the human body. The consequences of this can be seen in any neonatal intensive care unit, the NICU, with its rows of plastic boxes containing little beings with feeding tubes up their noses, wired to heart monitors, and dependant on respirators for their survival.

Depriving women of their ability to feel pain deprives women of their ability to feel when something is wrong and thus take measures or make adjustments to accommodate their bodies. It destroys the necessary interchange between intelligence and feeling, reflection and experience, an interchange essential to learning and survival. Bodily pain, itself a form of knowledge, conveys the powerful and unmistakable message that something must be done now or disaster will ensue. With anesthetics, the urgency of this message is evaded and its content goes unheeded. The anesthetized woman feels no pain, can't do anything anyway, and the potential for disaster remains unchecked. The ability to respond, in a word, *responsibility*, is either mediated by the insight of the doctor or displaced onto nature and how much insult it can absorb. In other words, expert science and its practitioners, having assumed responsibility for directing the process of birth, interrupts the bodily interchange between sensation, reflection, and action. This eliminates the potential of birthing women to take actions which might alleviate their pains and at the same time establish an equilibrium which might preserve the well being of the newborn and her self.

Science, in its systematic, empirical orientation towards the abstract and the general, must wait for problems in the technique of birth to manifest themselves statistically, that is to affect a large number of women and/or newborns, before it can take action. High rates of maternal and infant mortality relative to other countries have, in the past, been the impulse for much scientific hustle and bustle, but only after it was already too late for those who died. Given science's systematic focus, the individual case, as such, cannot be of significance. Only epidemics, pandemics, and endemics receive attention, suggesting that it is only when problems threaten the social order in mass society that they become real.

In evading the subjectivity and responsibility of women who give birth, scientific cognition and its institutional accoutrements have established a relationship with nature such that it only recognizes death, nature's loudest protest. Rather than caring for individual women and responding to their verbal or bodily protest, however hesitant or disorganized, science only sees the threat of nature, writ large, a threat which directly challenges science's own limits and legitimacy. Interested only in eliminating chaos, it steps in only when things have already gotten out of control. In this movement, human history is replaced by natural history.

A line has been drawn between the acceptable and the pathological, the high-risk and the low-risk birth, a line even the midwife and the natural childbirth enthusiast will not touch. The pathological birth belongs in the hospital because only the hospital can contain its threat. The pathological birth is potentially debilitating, even fatal for both mother and child. More importantly, however, the distinction between normal and pathological birth suggests that one of the primary functions of medical metaphysics is to maintain the illusion that birth and death do not demand each other. The American attitude toward birth is primarily an attitude toward death, and the domestication of birth is, more than anything else, an attempted domestication of death.

CONCLUSION

Prior to the hospitalization of women birthing, obstetrical science had no universally recognized access to its chosen objects. As was the case in so many other spheres of social life, the nineteenth century was a time of transition in which the terms of birth and the relations of power surrounding this most human of activities were renegotiated. Only in the twentieth century was the result of these negotiations consolidated and it became possible to speak of institutionalized childbirth, that is, of mass birth. Only in the twentieth century did obstetrics gain unquestioned access to women's bodies in the modern hospital, allowing obstetrics to develop an independent science of birth in general, a phenomena abstracted from the experience of particular women. No longer attending to women in their homes, physicians were freed from the compulsion to negotiate the complexity of power relationships permeating the social atmosphere of a woman's bedside. In a woman's home, the physician remained an invited guest, whose power was limited. In the hospital, however, a woman is alone among strangers who are above all dedicated to support the doctor. Even now, with the admission of fathers to the bedside of the birthing woman, the alien nature of the hospital environment persists. The birthing women has no power to bring the birth chamber under her direction and definition. She remains at the mercy of institutionalized medicine, masculinity's clearest expression.

This shift from home to hospital as the place of birth points directly to a shift in the normative context of birth. So long as birth remained in the home, it occurred within a space saturated with moral ties which could potentially ameliorate asymmetrical power relationships of gender and generation that may have existed between herself and her attendants. This is especially significant at the time of birth, given the inherent vulnerability of a woman in labor. In the hospital, women cannot depend on such protection, for, in contrast to the home, the hospital environment is one permeated with instrumental reason. Doctors, nurses, and the variety of technicians necessarily approach the woman as a task to be completed, a problem to be solved, and an object of professional concern. Each laboring woman is just one of many to be tended to in any given shift, and the needs of each woman are in direct competition with the needs of other women. Moreover, the relation between a woman and her attendants is devoted to a specific task of achieving the live birth of a healthy child and doing so without losing the life of the mother. This primary task-orientation limits the relationship to a one-sided, instrumental type, which privileges obstetrical technique at the expense of larger issues. Conflicts, to the extent that they arise, are articulated and resolved in technical terms. Questions of what is best for the narrowly defined health of the fetus and mother are the only questions that arise. Honor, dignity, integrity, spirituality, and autonomy are values which are best left at the admission desk. That it might be better to die in childbirth or that it might be better to sacrifice the life of the child inside rather than submit to the degradation of a particular obstetrical technique, such thoughts can hardly be thought, much less articulated or acted upon.

The general result of this normative shift, a shift which signifies a change in power relations surrounding childbirth, is essentially paradoxical and immediately captures the nature of authority in our time. Science, in general, is oriented toward the control of nature and medicine towards the control of human nature under the professed goal of easing the torment of human existence. Science and medicine have promised to eliminate what religion could only accommodate. Thus, science's promise to ward off illness, disability, and even death, and its demonstrated ability to do so, if only temporarily, almost guarantees its hegemony as a form of authority. Its authority over our internal processes, our very being, is based on the fact that medicine can, much of the time, make us better.

But "better" is a relative term and the power of medicine is not. As the influence of medicine steadily increases, its power expanding into ever-more areas of life, the fulfillment of its promise of pacifying human existence continues to remain out of reach. Indeed, the hope for such fulfillment seems to grow ever dimmer. Medicine, a formal discipline, is indifferent to the substance of life and promises only to keep death at bay and nothing more. Like the Christian religion which it has effectively replaced, it will help us in our vulnerability but only on its terms and according to its logic. And this, only if we accept its definition of health as meaning nothing more than not-dead and not-quite-dying. Providing only a longer life, medicine is indifferent as to whether it is a life worth living.

Still, it is true: women today no longer expect to die in childbirth. In this sense, medicine has had some success in controlling for the contingencies of procreation. Medicine has won its fight against nature. But at what cost and at whose expense? It is this question which haunts the postmodern consciousness, a consciousness forced to reckon with the consequences of utopia realized (Baudrillard 1988a). It is a consciousness unhappy with its own victory (Hegel [1807] 1977, p. 127), a borderline melancholic suffering from a disease which appears to affect primarily the engineers and technicians of our existence (Sloterdjik 1983). It is *they* who have assumed responsibility for curing what ails us, and it is they who suffer the burden of callousness inherent in treatment.

This callousness threatens even the attempt to understand the development of obstetrics, given that such understanding hinges upon the ability to integrate and thus neutralize the power and significance of human suffering. Even here, it is success which poses the greatest threat: the actuality is so potent that it replicates itself in the very attempt to overcome it. Any understanding nullifies its own originating impulse in empathy with those who have been overrun by the march of progress. It involves the attempt to make sense of a history which can no longer be made sense of, whose only sense has already been made, has already been felt by the bodies of women in pain. The first forceps delivery, the first C-sections, the first ovariotomy, the development of a treatment for vesico-vaginal fistula, all occurred without anesthetics. That obstetrics developed at all, now *this* is the mind-numbing issue which tests the limits of human empathy. The pain felt by the women on whose bodies these techniques were practiced could only be matched by the callousness of the physicians attending them. Only one as hard as rock to human suffering could have been able to respond to a woman's cries with iron hands and metal knives, could have been able to respond to a woman's suffering with the infliction of more suffering.

Given this situation, it is unlikely that many of the invasive treatments obstetrics has developed would have been accepted in any but the most dire of circumstances without some method of relieving the attendant pain. It is unlikely that even most doctors would have engaged in such painful practices if they had to bear the burden of women's unavoidable bodily resistance. While modern consciousness is indeed a callous consciousness, it only rarely strays into such extremes. Some way of evading the body's struggle would certainly have been necessary for the routine use of invasive procedures to become established.

Pain relief thus occupies a central position in the history of modern childbirth, but this recognition does not so much provide us with an insight as it points, instead, directly to the vanishing point of history. The simple statistical fact—a fact this chapter is premised upon—that in 1955, 95 percent of all American births took place in hospitals, suggests that the vast majority of women undertook their births unconsciously. Later such "pain relief" would be replaced by the numbing of women's bodies as they give birth. Either without mind or without feeling, women, since mid-century, have ceased to birth fully with their entire being. Of equal importance, women have no experiential knowledge of the births they have given. All they have is, at best, abstract hyperreal representations such as might be captured for your viewing convenience on a video tape.

History, as an experience, thus disappears, not so much vanishing into a void, but *itself* becoming a void. An image comes to mind, that of a black hole. A black hole is a star whose mass was so great that it could not support its death. It therefore collapses under its own weight, ultimately taking a less burdensome and thus more efficient form. A black hole is a star that has died but continues to exist. A black hole is a star that no longer needs to prove itself in good works but can rest confident in the tautology of its own existence. A black hole is infinitely more stable, so powerful that even light cannot escape. But do we know what happens to a black hole after *it* exhausts itself?

This point on the horizon where history becomes a void has been anticipated by George Orwell, who, in his best-known novel, *Nineteen Eighty-Four* ([1949]1990), invented in his imaginary Oceania the reality of "the memory hole." For his part, Studs Terkel, the author of the Pulitzer Prize-winning study, *The Good War* (1984), sees his effort to preserve the experienced memories of World War II in terms of such an effort's futility: Terkel understands the insistent forgetfulness of youth who cannot remember events which were unbearable for those who lived them. Finally, in his masterwork, *Slaughterhouse 5* ([1966]1988), Kurt Vonnegut repeatedly and steadfastly refuses to represent the firebombing of Dresden. In this, Vonnegut refuses to privilege *that* reality, privileging instead the reality of Billy Pilgrim, the frail being lost between worlds but firmly grounded in his silver boots and draped in an azure toga. Ultimately, though, Billy Pilgrim could not sustain the gravity of his own situation, and so he collapsed, taking refuge in a more efficient form, overwhelmed, as he was, by the sheer weight of facticity.

I am—the mother of our son—thinking of these things as I drive along, taking our 4-year-old son to his physical and occupational therapy appointment at Dayton's Children's Medical Center. My son is disabled. He cannot talk, walk, stand, sit, or even roll over from his back to his belly. As explained to me by the rehabilitative therapists, my son's primary struggle is one against persistent primitive reflexes and, of course, gravity, the simple gravity of physics. He cannot, it seems, escape the prehistory of the species nor the pull of the earth's center. But my son is better equipped for the struggle against metaphysics. For he understands, even relishes, the myth of the given. He takes joy in his own lack of balance. He plays with gravity itself, laughing when he falls, not so much at the sheer facticity of his fallenness—although at this too—but, rather, at our futile attempts to catch him, to protect him, to support him, to prop him, to in every way plot against him by plotting him against a set of fixed coordinates. Unless he gets hurt. Then, he cries.

At any rate, I am—the mother of our son—now spinning my wheels at a stoplight in Dayton, Ohio, and I see a woman, belly big with child, waiting to catch a bus. I realize that she is very young, a girl of no more than 14 or 15 years old. I look away, and I hope she did not see me looking at her because I know she must get a lot of looks, odd looks, curious looks, vindictive looks, resentful looks, in any case, a lot of looks. Her's cannot be an easy way. I see another, an older woman who looks like the first, and who must be the girl's mother. It dawns on me that maybe this is the secret of teenage pregnancy, that these teenage mothers about which there is so much hand-wringing, have, in fact, cracked the code of the big bang and offered a unified field theory all in one stroke. It is simple: they have figured out that it is best to become a mother while one is still a daughter. That is, they live the truth that a chain is only as strong as its weakest link, and that a broken chain is just that: broken. They are thus the masters of the universe, and a better role model than Stephen Hawking for our son.

NOTES

1. Historians such as Judith Waltzer Leavitt in *Brought to Bed* (1986) and Richard and Dorothy Wertz in *Lying In* (1977), as well as others such as Suzanne Arms in *Immaculate Deception (1975)* and Jessica Mitford in *The American Way of Birth* (1993), all focus on the shift from woman-centered birth practices to hospital-centered birth practices as *the* defining element of contemporary practices of giving birth. For an excellent overview of this and other issues surrounding the transformation of birth in modern society and culture, also see Robbie Pfeufer-Kahn's *Bearing Meaning* (1995).

2. For discussions of the poltical and cultural significance of reproductinve technology, see especially Barbara Katz-Rothman's *Recreating Motherhood* (1989), Janice Raymond's *Women as Wombs* (1993), and Gena Corea's *The Mother Machine* (1985).

3. U.S. Bureau of the Census (1996, p. 92, Table 124).

CHAPTER 3

Dried Beans and Beethoven:
The Art of Parenting the Ineffable

"Lived experience" is only a moment of a comprehensive notion of experi-
ence, a moment that is both fallible and suggestible. Works like the Ninth
Symphony exert a mesmerizing influence; the power they have by virtue of
their structure is translated into power over people. After Beethoven, art's
power of suggestion, originally borrowed from society, has rebounded on to
society and become propagandistic and ideological.
    —Theodor W. Adorno, *Aesthetic Theory* ([1970]1984, p. 347).

A culture is not completely wrong just because it failed, so affirmation in art
is not completely wrong either.
    —Theodor W. Adorno, *Aesthetic Theory* ([1970]1984, p. 357).

In Beethoven's Piano Sonata op. 31, no. 2 in D minor, the second theme of
the Adagio is...one of the most overwhelming ones Beethoven ever com-
posed, because in it the spirit of Beethoven's music reveals itself most com-
pletely. This spirit is hope.
    —Theodor W. Adorno, *Aesthetic Theory* ([1970]1984,p. 398).

Art is not alone in holding the dignity of humanity in its hands.
    —Ernst Bloch, *Natural Law and Human Dignity* ([1961]1986, p. 280).

If reification is forgetting, then every birth is, *in potentia*, a forgetting of
forgetting. Birth is difference personified. New human flesh is the stuff of
freedom. Babies are nonidentical, even identical twins.

This thesis is especially true in the case of wrong children, like Patrick,
who embody an extreme, recalcitrant form of nonidentity. Patrick cannot
help but resist integration, premature reconciliation, normality, and in this

way, his very existence makes him a type of existential hero. It is not so much that he brings freedom into the world via his Sartrian nothingness as, unexpectedly, via his Sartrian being, his mere facticity. Patrick reverses the poles in the traditional Western philosophical story of humanity's self-becoming. Patrick prereflectively lives Audre Lorde's counterintuitive demand that "I feel, therefore I can be free" (1984, 38).

Of course, like Audre Lorde, Patrick doesn't get off the hook quite that easily. Earnest attempts are made to forget him, to reify him, to conceal his body/freedom from the world and from himself. As an uncommitted, not-much-participating, artful threat to the order of things, Patrick is met in the field of battle with the full force of a jealous science, a science which, we know, barely tolerates the lightening genius of Beethoven and Bobby Fischer, and not at all the crippled and dim-witted genius of wrong children. While Patrick-in-himself may be hope, his life in the world *is* the dialectic of enlightenment.

In this chapter, we engage our lived experience of coming to know our son Patrick, our "third thing" that makes us a family, for what it might teach us about what Adorno called the "third thing," which is neither science nor art, but critical reason, or what might also be called the sociological imagination. We do this because, as parents, we remain intellectually oriented people who wish to recover and, perhaps, redeem, the utopian yearning implicit in enlightenment. This, if anything, involves anticipating a life liberated from the overdetermination of instrumental reason and, as we have come to think, from communicative reason as well. We do this so that we can understand the life-chances of our son, the world he projects, and to prepare ourselves for our unique role of being his guardians and protectors. How odd this must seem and how strange, how curious *we* must seem to take ourselves so seriously. How many standard deviations from the mean this urge to position ourselves in such a world-historical context places us, we do not know.

We assess social structure and its significance for everyday life through the consideration of our son's body as a site of domination, as a template which charts the form domination takes in the administered society. At the same time, as parents and critical theorists, we are responsible for resisting domination so that Patrick might become himself and live for himself. We thus show how Patrick, in his very being, calls out power's human essence and in so doing extracts the utopian element preserved in domination. More than this, Patrick's biography demands remembrance and allows for no simple affirmation. His presence in the world cannot help but remind us of the untold and unacknowledged stories of children like himself who have been put away in attics and institutions, subjected to abuse and medical experiments, and generally left to languish in the closets of their otherness. His biography is thus tinged always with regret for a history of utopias neglected and hopes unredeemed. In conclusion, we return to the question of aesthetics and politics and to the implications this study has for ethics, where the experience of parenting the ineffable is rendered a window on the truth of nonidentity.

But first, we turn our attention to Patrick's life in the world. Since Patrick does not speak for himself as normal four-year-old children do, parental phenomenology is all that we have to go on.

PART ONE. THE TORN HALVES OF FREEDOM DO NOT ADD UP

There are two things that our son, Patrick, enjoys as much as anything else. The first is running his hands through a bowl of dried beans, picking them up and letting them fall. And, when finally bored with this activity, he enjoys listening to Beethoven's Ninth Symphony, especially the choral tribute to Schiller's "Ode to Joy," which he desires endlessly repeated.

Our Patrick is not a genius. He is more dried beans than Beethoven. Born on April 30, 1993, this 4 pound, 11 and one-half ounce premature child spent two weeks housed in an isolette in the Neonatal Intensive Care Unit (NICU) at our local Level 3 hospital. Patrick required postpartum assistance with respiration and treatment for elevated bilirubin, lest he die of asphyxiation or develop a disabling case of jaundice. It was also necessary to closely monitor Patrick's intake of nutrition. Breast milk was forwarded from home, where a mother was locked in pitched battle with an electric-powered breast pump (though it was almost one week before Patrick was allowed to drink of this offering). We were told that Patrick would live; the intensive medical intervention visited upon Patrick was sufficient cause for our neonatologist, in a face-to-face conversation, to all but guarantee his survival.

By the time of Patrick's release from hospital custody, we were informed *both* that Patrick would likely be delayed in achieving early developmental milestones, which is typical of premature infants, *and* that he was healthy and normal and there was therefore nothing to worry about. With this in mind, we gathered up the assortment of corporate freebies nicely packaged in an attractive and useful diaper bag, a gift from Ross Pharmaceuticals, makers of infant formula and other nutritional supplements, and made our way for the door. The birth of Patrick had been an ordeal, but now it was time to retake control of our lives.

The months passed, and Patrick's development was, in fact, delayed, although we did not experience it as such. As Patrick is our first and only child, we had no sense for typical development. We could only compare him to the general, abstract standards stated in popular guides to parenting and child development, and, like many parents, we used these guides as a substitute for our nearly nonexistent practical knowledge. With the nearest family several hundred miles away, we were more or less on our own. We worked very hard to construct Patrick as normal, albeit delayed, naively interpreting any and everything he did as "progress." Thus, at four months, when Patrick flipped from his stomach to his back, we concluded that he could rollover. We did not know at the time that the *way* he did so was atypical in the extreme. Patrick wasn't really rolling over at all. He had so little control of his body that when he pushed himself up onto he arms, he immediately lost his balance and was carried by momentum onto his back. His body was, in effect, rolling *him*, whether he liked it or not.

Patrick was six months old when his pediatrician gently suggested that he be "assessed." She did not indicate that there was any reason to worry. Rather, our primary care physician justified her suggestion in terms of a "better safe than sorry" logic. We took her at her word and, without worrying much, returned with Patrick to the hospital where he was born, to the NICU where he spent his first two weeks of life for an assessment conducted by the staff occupational therapist, a specialist in Neuro-Developmental technique. Based on her expertise, she recommended weekly therapy sessions, primarily in order to determine whether or not Patrick's delays were the result of an underlying neurological problem. This was early November.

In January, when we returned from a holiday visit with Patrick's grandparents back east, we found a message on our answering machine from the doctor that requested that we come in for a visit. And so, when Patrick was eight months old, a "diagnostic work-up" was begun, involving first blood work and a CT scan, the results of which were normal, and then an EEG, the results of which was not. Patrick had epilepsy. This fact established, we were then referred to a pediatric specialist in neurology who ordered an MRI (magnetic resonance imaging) of Patrick's brain, the results of which were also abnormal. Patrick had epilepsy, and he also had brain damage. More blood work followed, the results of which suggested the possibility of a metabolic disorder. Roughly one-third of the approximately 250 types of metabolic disorders are treatable, which, it bears to keep in mind, does not mean that they are curable. Without treatment, such congenital metabolic disorders result in varying degrees of mental retardation and physical disability and finally death, with a potential life span of three to thirty years, varying with the specific condition. We learn these facts when Patrick was eleven months old.

When Patrick's pediatrician suggested the need for a diagnostic workup some months earlier, we asked her for an educated guess as to the potential nature of the problem. She indicated that "cerebral palsy" was a likely explanation for Patrick's delays. Thinking this to be a worst case scenario, but familiar with the hard edge of reality, we launched a preemptive strike at the United Cerebral Palsy Center (UCP), which is located next to Dayton's Children's Medical Center. This was a difficult initial foray into the marginal but sizable world of the severely disabled. Indeed, the U.S. Bureau of the Census (1996) reports that, in 1991-92, 12.1 percent of the U.S. population over 15 years old is severely disabled, with another 11.5 percent reporting less than severe disabilities. In absolute numbers, there are 23,588,000 severely disabled Americans, and an additional 22,435,000 who are in one fashion or another otherwise disabled. Even so, the fact that nearly one in every four adult Americans shared with our son some form of disability provided little emotional comfort inside the UCP building. Our family's future was laid out before us; we were more than mildly disturbed by the sheer number of people in need, who as often as not were milling about, staring hitherto, framed by their numerous and various mechanical devices, and/or pondering the presence of so nimble a couple trying desperately to manage their impression so as not to mirror in their faces the anxiety and shock in their stomachs.

As it turned out, though, by the time Patrick was eleven months old, cerebral palsy had become the best case scenario. This occurred during the thankfully brief period in the search for a diagnosis for Patrick when his neurologist was very much worried that Patrick did in fact suffer from an incurable metabolic disorder. As parents, we spent several months imagining that Patrick might not live to his fourth year, or that, regardless, he might have a severely foreshorten life expectancy. Forced to think concretely about our son's death, our efforts to meet the challenges of his care were entwined with conflict and sadness as we each struggled to assimilate what appeared to be an already determined, though for the most part unknown, fate.

I—the father of our son—felt in my gut that cerebral palsy would be a great and good eventuality, for the alternative promised only the unbearable heaviness of Patrick's not-being. But I—the mother of our son—was not so certain. Having assumed primary responsibility for the details of Patrick's care, and thus familiar with a different kind of heaviness, namely, the tangible, exhausting heaviness of Patrick's being, I could not avoid feeling that death would at least relieve me of that burden. Such thoughts somehow helped me through very long days, one after an other, spent with an infant who required constant attention his every waking moment and even then would sometimes scream or whine or fuss no matter what you did and you spent all day alone with him and hated to be alone with him and would count the minutes until his dad got home and would slide into a panic if he was late because something had to give and then you would fight because nobody was sleeping because the baby wasn't eating and would scream every time you fed him and you hated breastfeeding because it would only make your baby scream and it was nothing like the books said; the doctor said it was colic and would go away but that was months ago and it didn't go away and wasn't going away and wouldn't go away for a year or so or more.

So you would spend hours in the car, the baby screaming in the back seat, sitting in the car seat, so you put it in the front seat so you could hold the pacifier in his mouth because he couldn't do it by himself even though he was nine months old. And you'd wander through the shopping mall, your baby in a pouch sucking on your finger because he was hungry but you didn't want to feed him and you would think security was following you because you knew you fit a profile of a housewife with no direction who was playing with the edge and might see something to catch her fancy and put it in her pocket because it was shiny and it was pretty and caught the light which was bouncing all around her in all directions.

You would have to leave the shopping mall and feed your baby in the parking lot or go back home to an empty house and try to get your baby to take a nap for twenty minutes or maybe thirty but never more so you could do the dishes or make some food for dinner all the while worried that you may not be able to take it and you might hurt your baby or you might hurt yourself and you knew that either way it was the same thing because you had somehow bonded even though you can't remember when and you can't remember how but his big brown eyes were open wide with softness and his smile was a wonder and he'd look at you with a question on his mind even though he couldn't ask it and he thought you were the center of the universe and you knew you had to be there for him if only for a little while. And sometimes you had fun together even though he couldn't do anything and he liked to hear you sing and he liked to watch you dance and would laugh when you were silly and sometimes he would scream and you'd start crying with him and he'd quiet down a bit so he could listen, to hear what you were saying with your tears. Then you'd be together, crying for a while and he would start to change his voice to mirror yours and then you'd be conversing in a funny kind of conversation, mostly crying. And the doctor thought that maybe he was dying and that somehow made it better even though it made you sad 'cause it wouldn't last forever and you couldn't stand the word forever and you didn't like to think about it because you knew that it was bad.

And, I, Patrick's father, was once a child and once had biological parents myself. My father was a small man, not more than 5 feet and 2 inches tall. But he was exceedingly strong and masculine. To hear tell of it, he was a Marine Corps boxing champion in his lower-end weight class and, despite his stature, a notorious bully throughout his abbreviated adult life. When, in the midst of a domestic dispute, my mother shot him in the throat with his own handgun, he did not die. Somehow he survived the night, severely wounded on the living room floor. In the next room, my mother aimed better the same gun at herself, and did not survive. At any rate, having averted death, my dad lay for nearly a month in the hospital, breathing and talking through a tracheotomy, aware that he was permanently paralyzed from the waist down, but living nonetheless and likely to stay that way.

I never saw him myself because, at the age of six, I was deemed too young to withstand the trauma of the hospital if not also the more pressing facts of my father's condition. He would be released soon enough, anyway. But stories related to me about this time included that my Dad, although he had considerable difficulty speaking through the hole in his neck and was as a result nearly impossible to comprehend, did in fact manage to talk with great energy and purpose; he had, so the story goes, a tremendous will to live, and at least one nephew who could understand him. My Uncle John would tell me that his younger brother, my Dad, would point to his head with his index finger when Joe, the nephew, had made sense of my Dad's unusual locution, as if to say with a wink and a nod, "he's smart," and even, "he's smarter than you dunces."

Unfortunately, the nursing staff's attention lapsed one night, and my father choked to death due to a clog in his breathing tube. There was mourning, of course, animated by a deep sense of tragedy. My family was also generous with the nursing staff, who they saw as sufficiently apologetic and remorseful as to cause them never mention the words "law suit." But as far as I know—and this is my main point—it was not unusual for my Dad's family to adopt the attitude that his death was for the best. For Lenny was a small but altogether virile man. How could Lenny live as a paraplegic, confined to a wheelchair? How could this macho man in a rough and tumble General Motors town raise three young sons in such a crippled condition, with their mother's suicide a front-page story, the results of which all three of children had personally witnessed the morning they woke up to find that they lived in a new world? Lenny's death was tragic, but perhaps, in the great scheme of things, not so much of a loss.

This reminds me of the initial response to Patrick's condition expressed to me by my closest and dearest Uncle, who, with my Aunt Helen, would raise me from the time of my parents' deaths. He would say things like, "maybe it would be best if Patrick did not survive," as well as share stories of other children he knew over a lifetime who also were born with defects, and whose families made the decision to institutionalize them and as much as possible forget them. Difficult, tragic, but perhaps for the best. This also reminds me of my Uncle's parents, my grandparents, who sent a mentally retarded son, my Uncle Franklin, to live in a group home located some distance from Flint. I would see Uncle Frankie only at Christmas family get-togethers, and then only rarely. Last I heard, he is still alive.

I, Patrick's mother, have my own child memories, most of which come to me second hand. In the stories told mostly by my mother, I was a passive baby, slow to walk, slow to talk, hard to reach, in a world apart. The Doctors assured my parents that I was fine, would grow out of it, was the sister of a very active, hyperactive brother, and who therefore only seemed slow by comparison, but was really, in the larger scheme of things, on the easygoing side of normal. My mother knew that I wasn't hearing, not all the time but only some times and she told the doctors so. In response, she was informed that a child cannot be deaf part time and that a child hears what a child wants to hear. My problem was a behavior problem. Eventually, I went to kindergarten and within a week or two my teacher informed my mother that I wasn't hearing, not all the time but only sometimes and should be checked out by a doctor.

As it turned out, or at least as I understand it now, I was having some type of allergic reaction that affected my middle ear. This resulted in a deafness which would come and go as it pleased. I have very few memories of this time. I went to speech class until the fourth grade. In fifth grade, I attended adaptive physical education because I was "uncoordinated," a term that meant something like "retarded" (whatever *that* meant, although I knew it was something I didn't want to be). I was a poor student through elementary school, though nobody was certain if I was in fact mentally retarded or simply an underachiever. I do know that I didn't like school. I was always in some kind of trouble, usually for not doing my work or not paying attention. I was an easy target for the other kids. And nobody expected much of me anyway because I was passive and slow and hard to reach and in a world apart. Or so the story goes.

So neither of us came to Patrick unencumbered by memories of disability and its significance. And neither of us can pretend to a less than ambivalent relationship to Patrick. Our love for Patrick and our ability to parent him are both conditioned on our having been confronted by his death as a real potential and our ability to confront the physical and emotional challenges of his care. This challenge includes working through our own memories and, in effect, bringing our identities up to date. This challenge also includes withstanding the knowledge that many people (at times, even ourselves) cannot imagine that our child will ever have a life worth living. Patrick's existence is both temporary and unjustified. Of course, he is not alone in this.

We never received a firm diagnosis for our son. Rather, we were informed that the results of Patrick's second MRI were consistent with "hypoxia," meaning that at some point during the pregnancy or perinatal period Patrick had been deprived of oxygen to the point where his brain was damaged. I—Patrick's mother—responded by pointing out that hypoxia meant a diagnosis of cerebral palsy. The specialist that we were with at the time did not directly respond to this lay diagnosis, but instead asked if any other medical personnel had uttered those words in our presence. Our response was as ambiguous and as guarded as the question: We shrugged our shoulders. During another visit with the same specialist, it was suggested that Patrick attend a specialty clinic at Children's Medical Center designed to efficiently care for the large numbers of children lumped into the cerebral palsy pot. We would come to know this service as, simply, the "CP clinic." Naturally, we inquired if this recommendation meant that was Patrick's diagnosis was finally determined. In response to our question, the specialist physician indicated that by attending the CP clinic, Patrick would have access to the range of services that he required. At about the same time, another doctor, a geneticist, told us that cerebral palsy was a "garbage can diagnosis." For her part, our early intervention specialist (we began early intervention programming when Patrick was sixteen months old), informed us that cerebral palsy did not really mean anything in particular, given the wide range of prognoses it implied. Thus it was that Patrick was eighteen months old when we began thinking that he really did "have" cerebral palsy. At age two, we took him to the CP clinic.

The story we have just presented tells of a progression of events organized chronologically, but it barely skims the surface of what was happening: there are many other stories constitutive of the two-year process through which we became parents of Patrick. These stories refer to Patrick's own coming into being as a person, whose primary wish is that we take him as he is, as much as to our own ongoing effort to negotiate a compromise between the contradictory demands of Patrick's specific being as a body in-the-world. This latter effort, in particular, requires that we resist reconciling our knowledge of Patrick as a damaged body with our understanding that he insists on his body as fully intact, simultaneously deconstructing and reconstructing in his being the meaning of integrity, of wholeness.

To be honest, we spent a good year or two completely baffled by the advent of Patrick. We spent a good year or two (we cannot be more precise) almost completely at the mercy of medical and educational authority. As with the birth experience, we were again Mr. and Mrs. K, the parents of infant K, floating with a sense of foreboding from one examination and test to another, without knowledge of what they meant or how they were connected or where we and Patrick would, in the end, end up. All the highfalutin theory in the world could not save us from the slow but steady integration into a loosely coupled set of institutional arrangements that never really talk to one another and thus never cohere. Anecdotes might help to convey this sense of loss.

Consider a moment from a visit to the Cerebral Palsy, or rather, the CP Clinic. A young doctor-in-training is assisting Patrick's orthopedic specialist. At issue is whether Patrick requires braces, which might deter his toes from contracting under his feet. We sit in the usual sort of examining room, one of many families visited in a serial manner by the clinic's team of specialists (e.g., the dietician, the social worker, the orthopedic team, etc.). The young doctor is inquiring about Patrick's medical history while he thumbs through Patrick's now rather substantial chart, which has already by this time overflowed into a second folder. Finally, perhaps to impress his mentor, Doogie Howser openly deduces the ultimate cause of

Patrick's condition. Looking not at us but directly to the attending orthopedic specialist, the young doctor reasons: elevated bilirubin postpartum
caused hypoxia, which, as it often does, resulted in Patrick's brain damage.
Though his logic was impressive, on this account, Patrick was fine at birth.
His brain damage was the result of the NICU's failure to sufficiently
address his need for treatment. We fully and immediately understood the
implications of this student-doctor's theory: If correct, our son's condition
would be the sole result of negligence. We sit in silence. Later, after a brief,
private discussion, we decide not to go down *that* road and forget about our
doctor-student's moment of professional indiscretion. In retrospect, it
seems unlikely that there is much truth to this theory. Patrick has spastic
cerebral palsy, which we understand is generally not the result of jaundice.

Patrick's case is also followed by a neurologist, a good man, whose spir-
its seem uplifted since moving into a newly constructed neurology suite at
Children's Medical Center. Early on, as we have indicated, the big question that Patrick's neurologist needed to answer was whether or not
Patrick's condition was static or progressive. If it was static, then the damage was done, period. If it was progressive, then an ongoing process was
at work, and Patrick would perhaps get worse and worse before dying. A
series of initial tests in search of microbiological clues to his condition and
an answer to the basic static/progressive question were all, in the end, negative. Patrick's neurologist is now reduced to occasionally inquiring if we
observe in Patrick any form of regression, anything that might suggest that
Patrick is losing the ability to do something that formally he could do. Our
neurologist is looking to us for everyday signs of a progressive malady that
he could not otherwise, with the best of science at his disposal, find.
Thankfully his and our search so far has turned up nothing. Every six
months or so, we troop down to his new office and we report no observable
regression in Patrick's condition, and every six months or so, Patrick's
neurologist sends us home.

At one point, we were so confused as to Patrick's situation that we
requested a special meeting with the neurologist. We met him in his closet-
size office (or so were his digs before the new suite), he behind his desk,
we in front of it. Before we knew what happened, we were immersed in so
serious a discussion of mitochondria that we wished we had better recollection of our now-distant educations in elementary biology. At some
point, it was also halfheartedly suggested that we might consider taking
Patrick to the local pediatric geneticist and, if we planned a second child,
undertake genetic screening for ourselves. It was also reported to us that in

about 50 percent of similar cases, no diagnosis is ever made, no cause is ever determined. And as long as Patrick's condition is not, in fact, progressive (this remains a possibility), knowledge of the origins of his disabilities is not essential to his care. It may have been at this point that we finally realized our own complicity with enlightenment-as-myth, for we honestly expected more from science than acknowledgment of the fact that all the kings horseman and all the kings men couldn't put Humpty Dumpty back together again. We thought, erroneously, that they might at least find the wall from which he fell.

By the time Patrick was nearing his fourth birthday, we had inadvertently stumbled across what we have come to consider the secret logic regulating the exchange of information between pediatric specialists and the guardians of their patients. It began innocently enough with a simple question concerning whether or not the specialist could offer any insight concerning when Patrick would be able to understand his cerebral palsy. Already Patrick recognizes the term, although naively. He beams in his proud way when we use it in the same way he beams when asked if he is four years old or if he is Patrick. In response to our question, the doctor suggested that we take Patrick's cues and wait for Patrick's questions, which, he assured, would come as his communication skills improved. In other words, his advice was: don't answer questions which haven't been asked. And don't respond to those unnamed, inarticulate fears parents typically have about their children. For example, how is Patrick going to learn how to talk and think about his condition—his birth defect and his damaged brain, his muscles that freeze up at the slightest effort—unless we first talk about it? How is he to proceed unless he has the tools to think about himself as both defective and fully human, damaged and perfectly well, that right and wrong demand each other? And if his parents do not do this, how can he bear the burden of having been born into a society so ill at ease with the fragility of bodies? How will he cope with the stigma of disability? Surely we cannot wait for Patrick to articulate the questions that penetrate his very being, for he lives that being now, and he needs those answers today.

This tautology is the same tautology as that behind the theory of supply and demand, a tautology that will encircle you in the frustration of *silent need*, just like economic theory vanquishes all needs in its preference for *effective demand*. In medicine, the supply of information should not exceed the express demand for information, lest the client be terrorized by overinformation and the expert held accountable to a responsible public.

And so we leave the good doctor's office, our quest for insight into our son's inner world truncated by a vicious and effective circle.

We hear Patrick's questions, although Patrick does not actually ask them; perhaps he does not even know they exist. But we hear them in the same manner that parents impose meaning on the undifferentiated wail of the newborn and the inexplicable tantrums of the two-year-old. When Patrick sees other children, he becomes mesmerized with interest in their activities, as if he's studying the kinesthetic principles underlying their movements, cataloging the finely tuned twitches of their muscles, and storing knowledge of the competency with which they go about their business. Who could help but wonder at the intensity of his interest and the motivation behind his study?

In educational environments, which Patrick entered at 16 months of age, the situation was more disturbing. Here, we were closer to our own intellectual turf; we were relatively more familiar with the theories of child development and child psychology that informed the practices of what is called "early intervention." These included, most predominantly, the standardized measurement of Patrick's physical, cognitive and psychosocial developmental progress as well as the social engineering of small group relations. While the various theoretical schools in play were obvious enough to us, they were, on our reading, more or less opaque to those charged with their enactment. Needless to say, the shock of witnessing bad theory practiced poorly did not soon wear off.

For example, it is difficult to describe fully the vertigo that results from being asked to participate, as parents are expected to do, in the application of the Hawaii Early Learning Profile (or HELP-strand) to our own son's development, requiring of us a rationalized, compartmentalized, empirical study of his many facets and particulars, knowing all along where this type of analysis would end up, and worse, where it came from. In addition to working with our son in the classroom at the Early Intervention center, we were also expected to attend the parent education sessions held in the "family room" across the hall. Sometimes, these so-called educators would simply photocopy articles from mass market, glossy covered magazines, such as *Parents* or *Child*, without even attempting to interpret their significance for parenting special needs children. Other presentations were devoted to explaining the food pyramid (as if it were not self-explanatory), teaching very rudimentary sign language, toilet training, and childproofing techniques for the home. We learned how to make playdough from Kool-Aid and flour, one hundred phrases of praise for our child, and the difference between discipline and punishment. In other words, rarely did the parent education component of our son's program squarely confront the fact that the majority of the children involved in the program were there because they had disabling medical conditions. Playdough and praise are nice, but they hardly address the challenge of raising a disabled child, just as learning how to toilet train the typically developing child sheds little light on the task of teaching *our son* to toilet independently, if at all. Ultimately, we became less trusting of professional authority the more we encountered semiprofessional practitioners, with their forms to be completed and their pet theories and their half-educated appreciation of their place in the order of things. We were thus reminded that we live in a mass society, that professions in practice diverge from professions in theory, and that theory itself is no match for the carceral workings of institutions.

At about this time, while sitting in the parent's lounge at Southview School, our county's Early Intervention Center, we chanced to pick up an issue of *Exceptional Parent* that was lying on a table. While Patrick was receiving his socialization into the world of "education," we read an obituary for Irving Kenneth Zola, who was professor of Sociology and Public Policy at Brandeis University, expert in the sociological, cultural, and policy-oriented analysis of disabilities, founder and editor of *Disability Studies Quarterly*, and, last but not least, a board member of *Exceptional Parent*. Irv, who was himself disabled (he used crutches to walk), had passed away unexpectedly. We already knew this. We did not know Irv well, but he was an admirable and inspiring presence even at a distance, someone who added tremendously to the educational milieu of Brandeis University, where I—Patrick's father—studied sociology. The extent of the loss that his death brought into the world struck us fully, however, only in *this* particular milieu, a setting that Irv helped to create in his years of advocacy for the disabled, but a social world, we were sure, he would have never have simply affirmed. His obituary was, for us, received as a message in a bottle, confirming not only the untimeliness of our parental and theoretical task, but also its marginality. In this centrifugal time/space compression, we felt thrown away from the center of a wheel spinning out of control. Out of control.

Patrick now attends the Dayton Public Schools Non-Categorical Preschool program. He rides in a yellow school bus, has a book bag, and wears a blue-pants/white-shirt uniform, the latest trend for discipline-conscious urban schools anxious to acquire the magic formula of parochial school success stories. Patrick's favorite activity is "circle time," where the children sit around the teacher, singing songs and learning such basics as the days of the week and how to recognize their written names. Patrick sits in his wheelchair; the others sit in little blue chairs reserved expressly for the circle time activity. In the circle, Patrick is a full participant. He is limited only by his four-year-old attention span, which, in such a group, is not unique to himself. When the teacher asks for "a quiet hand," Patrick, as often as not, volunteers one of his own, stretching out at a 45-degree angle to silently salute the request. He is in the game, and he is an eager player.

From Patrick's perspective, circle time is an equalizer. Here, his physical differences are minimized as his enforced passivity works to his advantage. When bored, Patrick is able to enter into the silent conspiracy of children as they create a world apart from the tedium of numbers and colors. He plays with their hair and they are content to let him do so. They busy themselves with the parts of his wheelchair, pleased to have such a convenient, and, in its way, magnificent diversion. He drops his name card so that one of his schoolmates can pick it up. His disability becomes a guise for what may well be a shared strategy. At any rate, we picture him in league with others.

We have in our minds another picture, too, one far less endearing, one that depicts a little girl who never was and who will never be. Her name is Kate, and though we cannot see what she looks like from the picture itself, we save it as a reminder of the our own virtual reality. The picture is tangible, however. It is stored away in a box where we keep mementos of our child's first weeks of life (e.g., the hospital ID bracelets, the impossibly small knit hat Patrick wore when straying from his isolette, the ruled tape the NICU nurses used to measure the circumference of his head, the pink card that the nurses used to keep a daily tally of Patrick's weight gains and losses, etc.). The picture is a printout from an ultrasound session at five month's gestational age. The obstetrician reading this image led us to believe that it indicated the presence of a labia: a medicalized beaver-shot produced through the knowledge/power of our very own Dr. Larry Flynt. And so we expected the birth of a baby girl, our own American version of a Chinese small happiness. But disgruntled that our "daughter's" first baby picture was wrongly focused, I, her mother, refused to bring it into our house and instead stored in the glove box of our car, which is where it stayed, for how long, we cannot remember. I do not even remember if I showed it to "her" father, nor do I remember if I was the one who finally carried it over the threshold. I do know, however, that it sat on our bedroom

dresser for months before I finally put it with the other things that had out-
lived their usefulness, but were kept, without reason, nonetheless.

Kate never was and, though we fully expected her, we did not miss her
when she failed to emerge. We were both, instead, glad to see this boy who
had managed to outwit the panopticon. We took this as a good omen. Even
though we knew that, statistically, preemie girls do better than preemie
boys, this did not matter.

This non-Kate newly born interloper went without a name for three days
during which he was known officially as "boy Falcone." We, as parents, had
decided that, given our different last names, our first child would be given
his mother's surname and his father would choose the first and middle name.
If, we thought, a second child was ever in the cards, this GEN X, make-it-
up-as-you-go formula would be reversed. So, I, our child's father, was in
charge of finding a replacement for "Kate," and this would take some time.
It is an age-old custom of many cultures to delay the naming of a newborn
until its chances for survival are high. My reason was for delay, however,
was a combination of surprise, ill-preparedness, and distance from any cultural customs that would provide firm guidance. Finally, after much consideration, and after much battle with anomie, I chose my own middle name
for my son's first. The tag on his isolette was duly updated, and boy Falcone
was in this moment christened Patrick Falcone, for life.

The NICU is where it all seemed to begin, for us, where we became a
family. The regime of observation that continues to this day is totalizing
but it is not total. In one minute everything is fine, and in the next, a stern
looking doctor is telling you that your son has a 90 percent chance of survival, even though no one had prepped you on the fact that his survival was
in question in the first place. Then, it departs as suddenly as it appears, like
a disaster that leaves in its wake the wreckage of an event past. As parents,
our status is analogous to the Red Cross: having no role in what actually
happens, we stand ready, in a constant subjective state of emergency, but
at the sidelines, where we wait for the objective emergency to abate long
enough for us to rush in. Our job is to clean up and rebuild, even if we can
never make things right again.

Writing this, we suspect we are fudging, presenting ourselves as more
knowing, our own lives as more intact, and our own theoretical consciousness more set, than they really are. To be sure, our story reads like a proto-
myth, a revisionist account that represents our particular disorientation in
the face of these emergent, amorphous phenomena as a despatialized
heroic struggle to parent our little boy. Even worse, the attempt to undercut

this myth intensifies it, leaving the myth itself intact. This is the lie of reflection: it depends on and even creates the illusion of distance that allows for the reconfiguration into a narrative form what was originally inchoate and nauseating. In this sense, reflection is a defense against an unspeakably real reality, which we experienced as an ongoing disaster. Of course, it is precisely as a defense that theory demonstrates its use value: for better or for worse, it allows us to escape the overwhelming press of our particular fate so that we might simply be parents to our child. It is thus a form of resistance, but one which is of only limited significance.

PART TWO. REFLECTIONS ON ASTROLOGY

What is needed is a "cognitive map," and "all of us have them." These are the words of the expert coordinating Montgomery County's September 1997 "NICU Training Project" workshop for medical, educational, and therapeutic specialists, as well as a few chosen parents. As an example, this expert distributed to the assembled workshop participants a critical comparison of the standard Mercator two-dimensional projection of the world, which he dubbed a "white, European map," and, in contrast, the politically correct Peters projection, which, among other things, depicts more accurately the relative sizes of Europe and Africa. The former dates from the sixteenth century while the latter was first published in Germany in 1974. According to the handout, the Peters projection "is an excellent tool ... to help students see the importance of the 75 percent of the world's population who inhabit the Third World." While a two-dimensional projection of a three-dimensional sphere cannot help but be a distortion, the Peters map is offered as a more apt representation of what really exists. The lesson seems to be: we need cognitive maps that are less false. Sir Karl Popper, we imagine, would have been pleased.

This is the way of systematically distorted communication. Reform and progress make their way within institutionalized falsity, where the politically less false emerges from within the politically more false. Every positivist projection, even of the whole wide world, reconfirms the failure of the subject who would apprehend the totality as a flat plane. It is not the *will* to understand the whole that is false; rather, it is the whole itself that is false, its only truth lying in what cannot be positively projected without violence to itself. The NICU Training Project coordinator was surely right: we need better cognitive maps than the ones that we already possess. But the only means to acquire such a map is through negation, by turning full force against the given astrology.

Our own experience of the given objective structures constituting the disabled world of cerebral palsy leads us to a reconceptualization of Adorno's analysis of specifically modern irrationalism, which is contained most vividly, perhaps, in his study titled "Stars Down to Earth" ([1952-53]1994, pp. 34-127). This, because the institutional culture of disability shares many of the features pointed to by Adorno as being characteristic of astrological thought. The similarity is troubling because the complex of factors that would lead one to engage astrological expertise are very different from those which might lead one to engage professionals expert in the care and education of disabled children.

In Adorno's telling, one seeks the advice of the astrologer for largely psychological reasons, as a way of coping with generalized anxiety and the climate of uncertainty in which people are said to operate. The astrologer thus potentially provides a form of comfort. It is true, as Adorno emphasized, that the need for astrology was and probably still is expressive of objective social needs that are sublimated in the psychological disposition of the reader, but these objective needs are, in Adorno, given secondary status relative to the psychological needs. In contrast, the advice of the expert in the care of disabled children is sought because there is an objective need to "access" the esoteric professional knowledge purportedly at the exclusive disposal of the professionally trained. In this situation, one is faced with the concrete daily challenges of care that, within the confines of the isolated nuclear family, are burdensome and baffling in the extreme. While such a situation certainly has psychological ramifications, these are secondary to the objective motivation for seeking expert advice. This all important difference renders the similarities between the astrological forecasts and the advice dispensed by professionals working in the field of early childhood intervention suggestive of the general and compelling tendency in our culture to actively pursue and acquire forms of pseudo-rational irrationality. We *need* something, and what is offered seems less false than what we already have.

At issue here is the division of labor characteristic of the production of knowledge and its subsequent refraction in the lived experience of mass society. In Adorno's accounting of astrology, this division of labor results in a fetishization of facts without meeting the need for synthetic knowledge. There is no resulting coherent and meaningful whole; the opaqueness of the social system is in no way lessened by the tremendous increase in the amount of information available. This creates an absence at precisely the point where individuals must decide on courses of action and ways of being, decisions that, if nothing else, require a solid understanding both of one's place in the system and of the nature of the system itself. All manner of hucksters understand this dilemma and stand ready and willing to fill this gap with their various formulas for living rightly.

Adorno's critical intervention is directed at understanding the social-psychological nature of the need that astrology and its intellectual cousins fulfill. He assumes, perhaps rightly, that the basic needs of human existence are generally met by the productive infrastructure of society, that, in other words, the readers of the daily horoscope are relatively secure in their material survival. Astrology is thus directed at the quasi-spiritual needs for meaning and guidance, needs which are created in the production of knowledge itself. A science which avoids interpretive insight as metaphysical only partially fulfills its obligation to those who must depend on it to guide their practical judgements. In our experience, this situation certainly obtains, but is intensified by the fact that, in the absence of a traditional approach to the raising of a severely disabled child, we are dependent on institutions to assist us with the practical challenges of care. The actuality of our dependency is real and immediate; that it is met with predigested formulas so closely reminiscent of astrological forecasts is, needless to say, profoundly disturbing.

More than this, the modern division of labor results in overspecialization and a fragmentation of knowledge domains, and this has further direct implications for its usefulness as a guide. From this angle, the not-quite-thirty-pound being in our care is splintered into functionally differentiated spheres of action and corresponding regimes of discourse that, as often as not, come into conflict with even each other. Thus, there is Patrick the object of medicine and medical discourse, with his truncal hypotonia, dynamic spasticity, persistent primitive reflexes, his abnormal EEG with continuous slow spike waves, his MRI showing a loss of cerebral white matter throughout the hemispheres, and so forth. There is also Patrick the object of education and its discourse of Individual Educational Plans, Multi-Factored Evaluations, Least Restrictive Environments, its Developmental Domains and Developmentally Appropriate Curriculums, and the like. There is also Patrick the object of rehabilitation and its peculiar discourse of gross and fine motor development and speech/language pathology, and so on and so forth. (We are fortunate that we have not yet had to consult with behavioral and psychological experts and thus do not know what vocabulary they use.) Each of these general fields are further broken down into an endless variety of sub-specialties. Here, the fragmentation of knowledge results in a fragmentation of Patrick himself: some practitioners tend to his bones and joints, some tend to his lungs, others to his brain, still more take his fingers as their focus. What may be appropriate for one part or within one institution may not be appropriate for or in another. Even more to the point, any given recommendation or bit of advice may radically depart from Patrick's own intentions. Patrick is the object of fragmenting administrative procedures and rationalities that threaten his integrity and erase his subject-centered reason. He is a disability requiring intervention, an object to be manipulated or, just as often, a subject in need of an array of augmentative communication devices, lest he fail as a participant in the great linguistic community of humanity.

As parents and theorists, our task is to negotiate with and to resist and manage these discourses so that we do not become complicitous in institutional logics that seek nothing but to intervene in Patrick's development in order to integrate, rehabilitate, and contain the cost of his continuing care. Even so, we are necessarily compelled to participate in these processes; we ourselves take Patrick to his doctors, therapy sessions, and early intervention programs, in full knowledge of the fact that we have the right to refuse such participation, and knowing well the full significance of the fact that each and every attempt to help our son and other damaged children is historically and structurally a form of domination. We deliver Patrick to the agents of domination with a smile on our face and, from Patrick, a big hello. Why do we do this?

In addition to the real material benefits of participation (e.g., free diapers, a small amount of financial assistance for such things as respite care, adaptive equipment and recreation, stipends for meetings and practical parenting advice, etc.), there are other less obvious and perhaps more important factors encouraging our participation. Of primary significance is the isolation of the nuclear family, an isolation that is a long-recognized structural feature of mass society and a fact of our everyday existence. Without institutional support, we would have nearly no support at all. That disability is a stigmatized condition in our culture, and that those who care for the disabled are stigmatized by association, only intensifies our isolation by making general (i.e., nonspecialized) social interaction difficult and emotionally exhausting (e.g., see Cahill and Eggleston 1995). At the same time, because this stigma spills over to include professionals working with children like our son, particularly those working in educational environments, we have often felt a certain alliance with those who have made it their vocation to spend their days caring for and teaching children who have been designated as uneducable or, in today's politically correct anti-language of euphemism and evasion, developmentally challenged.

For example, in a recent conversation, a special education teacher, who in years past worked in a segregated facility, described the discrimination against children who were severely disabled and used wheelchairs to get around. Fully aware of the bitter irony, she emphasized that "even in a segregated building, they did not want us," referring to the fact that her class was excluded from assemblies and other building-wide activities. She continued by pointing out that even now, in the age of mainstreaming, the location of classrooms in regular schools is rarely a function of what is best for the students, but, instead, is a matter of "who has room for them." The controlling factor is simply whether or not the principal will accept a special needs class. As we listen to her story, the image that comes to mind is of refugees begging for asylum and a place to simply be. It was clear that this professional felt personally implicated in the fate of her students, and that the stigma of disability attached to her work and thus to herself was more than a matter of simple courtesy (Goffman 1963).

Adding to this stigma is the fact that much of what the professional does will not add up to anything of consequence; it will neither contribute to the productivity of the nation nor reduce the taxpayers' burden of caring for the disabled. Indeed, it is likely that a good number of the children in their care will not even develop the intellectual or affective skills to appreciate their teacher's efforts. It is this saturation in the is-ness of what they do that forms a basis for a bond between ourselves as parents and the professionals who provide for Patrick "direct service."

We find in this situation more than the echo of the concentration camp; we find also the trace of utopia. This comes not from above but from below, in the situated interaction between Patrick and those devoted to his care. Here, the face-to-face give-and-take conflicts with the pre-given faceless script. Patrick is a full participant in these interactions, inserting himself into the closed systems of instrumental domains. He thus overshoots his incarceration within the fragmented enclosures. If there is a banality of evil in the documents and directives of his institutional existence, there is also a banality of utopia in his naive, dim-witted desire to establish his human presence, to make his wishes and feelings known, and to make friends despite his not living up to the functional social standards of his society. Patrick does this on his own, exercising his autonomy, despite our own theoretical misgivings and ambivalence, to make the world safe for himself. He is therefore able to wave away the fetishism of facts as if by magic wand and establish in their place the plain fact of domination as a human affair, which is not eagerly engaged in by even the most hardened techno-fascist.

It is thus true that we are sometimes horrified by our son's treatment as a disabled person, and more frequently, simply overwhelmed by the straightforward irrationality of institutional logics. It is also true, however, that when we are able to penetrate the endless layers of bureaucratic regulations, institutional justifications, and all the competing discourses describing our son, when we are able to understand the professionals' own self-understandings and set aside our doubts and our panic, when we are thus able to finally look at what actually happens in Patrick's medical treatment and in his education, we cannot help but notice that he does in fact benefit from the institutions serving him. More importantly, he enjoys himself. Patrick enjoys going to the doctor, he enjoys the give-and-take of "assessment," he enjoys the attention lavished upon him by his therapists and teachers as much as he glows in response to the pitying smiles of passers by. Even when he's subjected to a gross indignity, such as the regular blood lettings at Children's Medical Center, he gets over it quickly enough to more or less grudgingly accept the sticker given to him for his pain. By the time we get to the car to go home, Patrick is pleased to show off the sticker stuck to his hand.

And so it is that we continue our participation in organized domination, knowing that the varying and competing discourses overdetermining Patrick are only one aspect of the complex phenomena of damaged life, and knowing that they are only loosely related to the way such lives are lived. It may well be that these discourses so refract the reality they intend to represent that they have already lost all contact with it. It may well be that it is we who are guilty of the sin of positivism by assuming that the regimes of discourse that so occupy our attention refer to something other than their own internal necessities.

Patrick, at least, seems unscathed. Still in the period of grace called early childhood, he looks power in the eye and with a grin calls its bluff, betraying institutionalized social power's human essence. And power—in the form of doctors, therapists, and educators—smiles back. Patrick, who is too dumb to know any better, manages to engage power in a moral relationship, if only for an instant, merely by insisting on his pleasure in communing with other people. He willfully imposes on them his understanding of the good life and in this way extracts the utopian element preserved in domination. We imagine that Foucault would have approved, that he would give Patrick's body/pleasure form of resistance two thumbs up, if for no other reason than to distinguish Patrick's resistance from his parents' merely average accomplishments.

It is precisely the institutionalization of domination, with the consequence that individuals can displace their responsibility for the way things are onto abstract bureaucratically regulated systems of action, that allows for this moment—but only a moment—of freedom. In buffering the potential impact of individual decisions and actions on the collective, institutions allow a limited space where people might do right, in spite of it all. Institutionalized social power can afford to be lenient with transgressors against its own logic because its stability is all but guaranteed. The long march through the institutions is filled with well-meaning deviants who affect the totality of domination not at all. Of course, this is no justification for domination. Though institutions preserve the possibility of utopia, they also prevent its realization in any but the most accidental and fragmented fashion. It is as much a mistake to privilege the utopian moments still allowed as to privilege the institutional social power itself.

So we have come to rest, for the time being taking up residence in the Grand Hotel Ambivalence. Our theoretical efforts are devoted to maintaining the tension between thinking of the administered society as an "open-air prison" versus a postmodern utopia that finds in body/pleasure at least the momentary means of escape. It is from this borderland that we view the works of other theorists, even those who, like ourselves, have turned their intellectual powers toward understanding their own children.

Michael Berube, author of the recent memoir *Life as We Know It: A Father, A Family and an Exceptional Child* (1995), is one such thinker. Berube has explicitly considered the tension between his intimate experiential knowledge of, and relation to, his son Jamie, who was born with Down's Syndrome, and the twisted social construction of "Jamie," which requires of the elder Berube, for Jamie's sake, an act of deconstruction, not only of the phenomena of "disability," but of the received understanding of humanity in general. Needless to say, Berube's reported experiences and his mindful theoretical sentiments are much like our own. Nevertheless, Berube's diagnosis of the problem is strangely at odds with ours, and it is thus perhaps worth a moment's reflection to juxtapose them in the artificial light of the written word.

The sticking point seems to replicate in some respects the long-standing tension between the classical tradition of German critical theory, which we hold in high esteem, and the growing lines of mutual admiration between American pragmatism a la Dewey and Mead and French social theory a la Lyotard and Derrida, which Berube seems bent on furthering. For his part, Berube concludes his journey through the human condition decidedly less skeptical than he once was of grand "appeals to our 'common humanity,'" because, for him, he has found in his son a concrete reason to reevaluate the universal human "desire to communicate, to understand, to put ourselves in some mutual, reciprocal form of contact with one another" (Berube 1994, p. 51). Berube is not naive. He writes:

> I thought such appeals were well intentioned but basically inconsequential. Clearly, Muslim and Christian do not bond over their common ancestor in *Australopithecus*. Rwandan Hutu and Rwandan Tutsi do not toast to the distinctive size of their cerebral cortices. The rape of Bosnia, and Bosnian women, does not stop once Serbian soldiers realize that they too will pass from the earth (1994, p. 51).

Still, Berube maintains—he hopes?—that the universal human capacity and desire for reciprocal communication and the mutual realization therein attained "stands a better chance" than anything else he can think of as a means to achieving a pacified, peaceful, inclusive human existence. In a doff of the cap to semiotics, one imagines, Berube concludes with a catchphrase meant to suggest a postmodern ethics: "Sign unto others as you'd have them sign unto you. Pass it on" (1994, p. 51).

Of course, there is at least one German critical theorist who might sympathize with Berube's analysis. Throughout his storied intellectual career, Jurgen Habermas has appealed to the healing, albeit counterfactual, solidarity that lies in the potential of an undistorted human communication that seeks nothing other than simple understanding. For Habermas, the dialectic of enlightenment is most certainly not a story that must, inherently and ultimately, veer toward a form of total domination. Rather, for Habermas, the dialectic of enlightenment is "unfinished." In Habermas' telling, instrumental reason is opposed by communicative reason, by the liberatory rationality of Reason's arguments with itself (see Habermas [1981]1984, [1981]1987). What is required, in Habermas' divining, is a decentered analysis of this differentiation of reason, one that upholds the as-yet determined contest between instrumental and communicative reason by exploring, even in the abstract, the human potentials of the latter against an overzealous, overdetermining real-time documentation of the former. For Habermas, this move from a subject-centered reason a la Horkheimer and Adorno to a consideration of intersubjective reason as communicative action is *the* urgent theoretical task. For Habermas, we need more enlightenment, not less. What we need is no less than a more enlightened enlightenment, lest the "dark" critique of enlightenment sunder all hope for the realization of a rational modernity, rest in an indefensible performative contradiction, and provide fodder for the very reactionary, anti-enlightenment forces that, if successful, ironically portend the actuality of total domination.

Like Berube, then, Habermas turns his attention toward the transcendent, the universal, the potential; he likes Mead, too. In this way, he leaves behind the immanent, the particular, the irretrievably past; he distrusts Nietzsche. For example, while Habermas remarks that Horkheimer and Adorno's *Dialectic of Enlightenment* (1947) was "inspired by Benjamin's now ironic hope of the hopeless," Habermas does not (perhaps out of simple respect for the dead) take the next step in this direction, which would lead to reflection upon Walter Benjamin's actual corporal death. For his part, Berube wants to draw from his experience with Jamie, and from his considerable knowledge of the long-standing discourses of domination used to squash Jamie's predecessors, a lesson concerning the productive power of discourse to create a world in accordance with our description of it. He bases this project on his wildly divergent, otherwise inexplicable experience with Jamie, for which reference to such terms as "mongoloid idiot" become incomprehensible as anything but virulent reification. Out of his parental concern for Jamie as much as from his wish for an inclusive humanity generally, Berube would have us tear-down such received impediments to human-to-human understanding, and let flourish in their wake a free, unpredictable course of human communication between always already underdetermined, not overdetermined, actors in-the-world. His, then, is a struggle against the prejudice of a normalizing discourse, much like Habermas' is a struggle against the prejudice of a total critique. In Habermas' words, both falsely assert that "there is *no way out*" ([1985]1987, p. 128, emphasis in original).

We also face prejudice. Patrick is the object of a panoply of unwarranted discursive constructions, to be sure. In program after program, from Twos-in-Transition to our days spent at the CP Clinic, we, as parents, are systematically stung by the alien definitions of Patrick as Other writ large, other, that is, than the child we know, our son, *himself*. But his difference is much more and much less than an instance of mere *difference*, we think. He is more than and less than a new and potentially destabilizing element in an open system of communication. His emergence bespeaks more than and less than the potential of an emergent paraology of the postmodern condition. Patrick's significance is simply not determined by, exhausted by, nor contained within his communicative action, even though he does everything Berube and Habermas would wish of him in this regard.

Instead, we believe, Patrick's genius lies more or less in his always already built-in *refusal* to correspond, to form an identity, to forget his difference. Of course, this is true with regard to the blatantly dis-membering workings of medical, educational and all other forms of instrumental discourse, but it is also true with respect to the humanistic, hopeful, performative discourse of communicative action and mutual realization. Patrick is a more or less subtle critic of subtle affirmative social theory like Berbue's and Habermas'. Here's why we think so: Patrick is ultimately ineffable, and *that* is the difference.

Patrick's condition gives new meaning to Foucault's charge against Habermas: that he, Habermas, is engaged in enlightenment blackmail (see Foucault 1984; Miller 1993). What if Patrick never learns more than the 10 or 15 words he presently uses with great distinction? What if he never quite manages to acquire the skills necessary for use of a motorized wheelchair? What if the various and sundry press-the-picture, augmentative communication boxes never allow him anything but minimal forms of communicative action? What if he never works a day in his life nor competes in the all-too-Special Olympics? What if, his usual happiness notwithstanding, he is socialized just enough to feel the painful gaze of the pitying specific Other toward himself, but not socialized enough to sublimate this pain, to talk it out with a Humanistic Generalized Other? Indeed, what if his life had been cut short by a genetic abnormality?

Patrick is happy and we are happy to be with him. He is amazingly well-adjusted and enjoys immensely his public school preschool classmates as well as playing with the kids at United Cerebral Palsy day care. But these facts of life do not vitiate his corporal difference nor do they mute his biological resistance. Below the level of the discursive construction of the self and of humanity lies the nondiscursive, *natural* realm of politics. There is no solace in this radical alterity. What's done is done. Damaged life cannot be made right anymore than forever damaged bodies can be fixed.

Even so, it is just as wrong to refuse to recognize that, even within the open air prison of the administered society, people are able to build for themselves lives that insist that the concentration camp remain a metaphor for most people most of the time. Such refusal denigrates the memory of those who have perished in real prisons and furthers the logic of identity which is the logic of domination. The administered society is not a concentration camp and astrology is not fascism. As Agger has written:

> Adorno's negativizing formulation of critical theory ... makes it impossible to ignore deception disguised in the banalities of the quotidian as well as in the outright falsehoods of philosophy and social theory .... At the same time ..., theses of the decline of the individual and eclipse of reason leave a good deal to be desired in the way of practical intervention. Although friendly fascism, disguised as liberalism, abounds today, the metaphor of society as a concentration camp is overly undifferentiated (1992, pp.12-13).

Returning then to Adorno's discussion of Carol Righter's early 1950's *Los Angeles Times* astrology column, we are forced to question Adorno's own complicity with totalizing systems logic. In that essay, Adorno looks down upon the world of the astrological adept and finds in this phantom subject a childlike psychological dependency founded upon narcissism and ego-weakness. More than this, Adorno projects a system that flirts with the grand paranoia of irrationalism if only to explain the virtual fascism of American consumer-oriented capitalism. In short, Adorno's essay on astrology shares a strong affinity with the pseudo-rationalism of his object of analysis.

Thus, Adorno attempts to relate the half-serious triviality of the daily horoscope to the ominous threat of fascism by reference to the insights of the depth psychology of psychoanalysis. In so doing, Adorno posits such explanatory vehicles as a desire for "sex without threat" and a "repression of the sense of smelling" to account for some of the details of the astrology columns (1994, pp. 43, 84). To be plausible, such explanations would seem to require empirical contact with the reader of the columns. Of course, Adorno did not have such contact (1994, pp. 38-40).

Even if Adorno's astrology essay is read as a research program, it still replicates many of the "pseudo-rational" qualities pointed to by Adorno as characteristic of astrology.

Just as Adorno's fascist propagandist regularly makes oblique references to a multitude of impending threats as well as to the propagandist's own frailty before these threats, the reader of Adorno on irrationalism cannot ignore the panoply of his own allusions to a faceless menace lurking, such as those quoted above, or to Adorno's own reflexive gestures of impotence, such is implied by his own erudition vis-à-vis Carol Righter and Righter's daily musings on the stars. Just as the purveyors of irrationalism never argue the merits of the opposing views on their own terms, so, too, does Adorno eschew treating astrology on its own terms. Indeed, in our time—a time when Adorno's essays on irrationalism comes to us nicely packaged in a smooth covered softcover book whose face is graced with a cover photo in black and white of a women blissfully gazing upward to the stars—"Adorno" himself comes to correspond to the late capitalism he so utterly detested, always already as luminous thought-commodity requiring the rare sensibility of the fully erudite who would open the mystical cover in search of esoteric enlightenment.

To read Adorno against his own grain is to reorient discussion of irrationalism from itself toward its objective context of delusion, from "Adorno" to late capitalist society, from the universal to *our* particular, here and now. In our reading of the overarching reification of Patrick, we therefore seek a corrective to the critical theory industry. In our confrontation with disability astrology—from HELP-Strands and Multi-Factored Evaluations to the mindless formulas about human brains disseminated at professional workshops—we mean to advance a lifeworld-grounded version of negative dialectics, where the tendency of critical theory to dissolve into myth is weighed against the necessarily ongoing press of a life lived wrongly.

In this sense, the division of labor that specializes in and fragments a new life and that renders parents as the go-betweens among institutional agents that refuse to speak to each other (much less to the object of their concern) is the structure that also makes the ethereal machinations of medical and educational astrology the only viable guide to life within the protection racket. The counterculture has only produced alternatives, from alternative radio programming to alternative medicine to alternative education, and even these only for the marginal elites with the intellectual and financial means to gain access to these safety valves for the system. In Dayton, which is no Boston or Berkeley, the system of systematically distorted communication is hegemonic, and we, as parents of a disabled boy, cannot avoid taking the role of affective specialist first-class among a team of caregivers and careproviders upon whom we are effectively dependent for services and insight. Our one common territory is the ubiquitous professional workshop, land of the half-serious lecture meant as much to create the illusion of meaningful activity as to purvey real knowledge about real people and actual situations. The structure of our situation demands what

Adorno called a "bi-phasic" life activity recommended in Righter's astrology: to live then to die, here's mud in your eye.

In this regard, Stephen Crook has observed:

> The question of "paranoid" thinking arises here once more. Contemporary authoritarian propaganda ... might be thought to display two features which Baudrillard identifies in contemporary (post)culture. First, authoritarianism has the air of a panic production: its elements of syncretic pastiche and nostalgia ... are a bid for cognitive reassurance in the face of a "loss of reality." Second, and in consequence, such propaganda simulates a meaningful and shared symbolic order. Baudrillard characterizes "simulation" in terms very close to those used by Adorno in relation to "paranoia": "a short-circuit of reality and its reduplication by signs." Adorno's theme of bi-phasic ambivalence might find a place here, too: individuals might be conceived as moving in and out of simulations (family, work, sport, politics, etc.) that project systems of action and meaning which would be radically incommensurate if translated into a propositional form (1994, p. 28).

Upon our reading, Crook's allusion to the metamorphoses of "Adorno" into "Baudrillard" is both true and false. Crook's theoretical sensibility is not in doubt; the similarities between these signs are arguably sound, for things are undoubtedly much worse since Carol Righter walked the earth. Yet, Crook is, like us in one part of our live, seduced by the magic of theory, which must always concede primacy to the object lest it devolve into the very thing it means to oppose. In the other part of our life divided against itself, there is the unavoidable fact of our participation in (post)culture and its consequences for practice as well as for theory. The cognitive map that we seek must therefore take into account the cognitive maps for sale at the nearest workshop, both in the sense of their necessity as well as in the sense of their horrible projection of a world that affirms their necessity. The critique of a bent logic is only possible through that logic, for we have nothing else to go on.

This is the truth of theoretical exaggeration, which lies in thought's own unavoidable complicity with the reality whose limits it would test. If Adorno's seminal analysis of astrology is itself, at base, astrological, then our lived experience of imposed dependency upon astrology is itself, at base, true to Adorno's own self-negation.

In Adorno's reading, one of the purveyors of irrationalism's chief techniques is to ominously draw connections among apparently discrete and unrelated phenomena, such as between the movement of the stars and one's life chances, in general, and more absurdly, one's chances on this very day. Here, Adorno charges irrationality with the error of positivism. What does not exist is given existence (astrology's efficacy, divine intervention, luck), and thus what really does not exist (*Geist*, negation, the not-yet) is forgotten. For Adorno, the psychic appeal of this half-serious, clownish irrationalism meets the half-adults' need for a normalization of a contradictory and threatening existence over which they have no effective control. This, for Adorno (1994), is but a "symptom of the regression in consciousness ... that has lost the power to think the unconditional and to endure the conditional" (p. 128); it represents thought's capitulation to the demands of "late capitalist forms" (p. 129), for, as Adorno forcefully states, "the horoscope corresponds to the official directives of the nations, and number-mysticism is preparation for administrative statistics and cartel prices" (p. 129). One thinks, for example, of the Million Man March and of the Promise Keeper's Washington, DC mass assemblies.

At issue here is the evasion of history and history's overdetermination by social structure. Forces, both natural and supernatural, are invoked to account for and guide individual conduct, thereby displacing the responsibility of institutionally empowered social actors onto abstract systems outside human control. As the above allusion suggests, this is the traditionally masculine escape route to the abstract and to the patriarchal. In *our* world, however, it is neither the stars nor a distant masculine deity that is responsible for regulating human behavior. Rather, the all-too-human, frail and feminine application of systems of legal and scientific discourse to the bodies of the masses forms for us a complex of everyday domination. So it is that we turn our (feminist) attention to the law and neuroscience which cut short the process of reflecting on one's place in the system.

In the beginning was "the law," specifically Public Law 94-142. PL 94-142 was passed in 1975 and is now popularly known as The Individuals With Disabilities in Education Act (IDEA). This law has since undergone a series of successive mutations, the latest a 1997 reauthorization, or PL 105-17. The most significant mutation for our purposes, however, occurred in 1986 and was known as PL 99-457. PL 99-457 included Part B and Part H. The latter is now known as Part C. These legal limbs extend the mandated provision of intervention and educational services to children with disabilities between birth and age five. In general, the federal IDEA law provides financial incentives to encourage individual states to provide educational services to individuals with disabilities. The law sets forth the minimal criteria for compliance necessary to receive federal funds. For the most part, states are charged with developing and implementing these programs. This devolvement of administrative responsibility to the states has resulted in a proliferation of lesser executive orders, committees, initiatives, projects, et cetera, ad infinitum, ad nauseam.

It is, in other words, a long road from the federal mandates encouraging the provision of a Free and Appropriate Education (FAPE) to children like our son, to Patrick's getting on the school bus. If one maintains an awareness of the decades of medical, psychological, and educational research that has in the past and continues today to motivate policy makers and legislatures at the national level, this road appears more like a deer path through an ideological thicket. Indeed, the law itself serves a hygienic function in cutting-short the overwhelming effort to understand both the system at the local, state, and national levels and one's place within this system. In biblical fashion, IDEA is treated as the sacred origins of educational programming for the handicapped, making it unnecessary to reflect further on its genesis. One's place in the system is thus clearly determined by a faraway legislative maneuver that occurred some twenty-odd years ago.

Moreover, the various legislative acts that frame the world of disability as a real, actionable reality also allow for the floating of moral and otherwise philosophical responsibility. This further allows institutionally empowered actors to dispense with the need to either explain or legitimate what they do. Time and time again, when confused or disturbed by an aspect of our son's programming, we are put off by the simple declaration that "this is the way the law says it has to be." For example, at our first Individual Family Service Plan (IFSP) meeting, we were asked to name and empower a "service coordinator." After receiving clarification concerning what a service coordinator was, I—Patrick's mother—indicated that I would be coordinating his services. We were then informed that "the law" specified that the service coordinator had to be someone other than a parent and that the child's teacher usually performs that function. Somewhat put off, I asked about this law, which we had never before heard of, and how it was applicable to our family. The IFSP facilitator indicated that she did not have a copy of the law, but offered to make me a co-coordinator of Patrick's care. Not wanting to be difficult, I consented. Two women thus worked it out, but the law remained the distant, largely absent, final authority.

Service Coordination (a.k.a., case work), is the legally mandated "process of helping families and children receive all the early intervention services they choose for the child," ensuring "that parents and providers know who is responsible for each phase of the child's IFSP."[1] In our case, it was in fact us, Patrick's parents, who provided such "coordination." In this example, invocation of the law is used by professionals to avoid arguing for and justifying their positions in the face of questions from the laity. More than this, the law has no clear relation to reality. While it may well be illegal in the State of Ohio for parents to coordinate services for their child, it is our experience that it is precisely parents who organize the variety of medical, educational, and rehabilitative interventions; it is parents who investigate programs that offer financial assistance, schedule appointments, and see to it that their children get to those appointments. It is also parents who bear the burden of guilt and responsibility when things are not going right. It is difficult to imagine how things could work any other way.

An analogous process occurs with the reliance on "science" to justify the expansion of publicly funded programs along the lines of Early Intervention. The science itself may be sound, but the policy recommendations and guides for individual conduct that are drawn from its conclusions are as questionable as the conclusions astrology draws from the stars. At the moment, neurological development in the first three years of life is receiving considerable national media attention (e.g., *Time* 1997; *Newsweek* 1997). Environmental conditions such as sensory deprivation, inadequate nutrition, and early childhood trauma have all been found to directly affect neurological development, proof of which can be had through newly developed sophisticated imaging techniques such as PET-scanning. Commonsense is thus reproduced as insight, dressed up in the garb of sophisticated biomedical science, a reproduction which evades the very political issues of the social structural causes of inequality and poverty in favor of reforms that promise only to add to the burden of parents, who are expected to raise children with middle class brains whether or not they have access to the means of middle-class life.

At issue here is the definition of the "normal brain." As soon as it is recognized that the brain itself is subject to immediate environmental influence, the definition of normalcy becomes a directly political issue. If impoverished brains receive lower scores on scholastic achievement indexes, it is also true that privileged brains have proven unable to do little more than blame the brain of the victim for the endless variety of structural conditions contributing to the impoverishment of brains. Indeed, the ability to treat the brain as a thing-in-itself, abstracted from bodies and lives, is a disorder that appears unique to the unevenly developed brains of middle class professionals.

Consider, in this regard, another tale from the ubiquitous workshop. In August 1997, a lecture titled "Workshop on New Findings on Brain Development" was presented to an audience of teachers, therapists, and others working in Montgomery County's Early Intervention programs. Once again, a few parents were in attendance. Attendees received a packet of information summarizing the lecture. [2] The first page is titled "The Learning Machine" and contains a two-paragraph summary of the last fifteen years of brain research. The paragraph begins: "Neuroscience, with the use of powerful and sophisticated research tools has recently reached 'one peak moment of discovery and opportunity' and that is new knowledge about how the brain develops." This is followed by a brief discussion of neurons, axons, and dendrites before concluding: "Environmental conditions and early experience dramatically and specifically influence not only the number of brain cells and number of connections but how the intricate circuitry of the brain is wired." In other words, and as the lecturer informed us, "sensory experience is the architect of the brain"; by age three, "the brain is hard-wired." If this crucial early childhood sensory experience is poor as a result of inadequate or harmful environmental conditions, then early childhood deprivation can mean a damaged brain.

A few pages later, a 1994 report by the Carnegie Task Force on Meeting the Needs of Our Youngest Children, titled "Starting Points," is summarized. The conclusion of the task force is that "a staggering number" of the 12 million children under the age of three in the United States are "affected by one or more risk factors that make a healthy development more difficult." Such risk factors include low birth weight, inadequate health insurance, child abuse and neglect, and the abandoning of newborns to hospitals.

Following these two summaries are two pages of practical recommendations. The first, which is titled "The Day-to-Day Care of Young Children's Brains," includes such basic parenting tips as "limit television," "encourage safe exploration and play," and "recognize that each child is unique." The second, also titled "The Learning Machine," lists a variety of public policy recommendations, including expanding parent education, expanding access to prenatal care, and improving day care. While these recommendations are in themselves innocuous, even praiseworthy, they are also without substance. They avoid controversial structural issues such as the fact that poverty and class polarization are built into our economic system and exasperated by the decades-long American "retreat from public policy" that has been identified, for one, by sociologist and antipoverty public policy expert William Julius Wilson (1996).

It goes without saying that, since the above commonsense practical advice is derived from neurological research, we have before us an instance of the medicalization of social problems. In a world where medical research and medical authority appear increasingly dominant, policy recommendations, like Wilson's, that derive their bearing from the social and historical analysis of institutions and empirically ascertainable social inequalities, appear increasingly to be loosing their once-strong credibility and public purchase. In this process, political matters are transformed into technical discussions of brain development and neurons. Even more disturbing, children themselves are instrumentalized and reduced to the function of their brains, as if the point of human existence were neurological development, that is, as if the greatest number of synapses for the greatest number of people was an appropriate social goal; as if the accumulation of synapses were a viable national purpose. One can imagine a new quality of life indicator being developed, Per Capita Synapses, which would be derived through dividing the Gross National Product of Synapses by the total population. Where would the United States rank among the world's leading industrial powers?

The unwillingness and unpreparedness of medical experts to confront directly the structural causes of poverty and the consequences of asymmetrical power relationships slides into an insensitivity to the situation of those living on the wrong side of the line between high and low risk everything. Child abuse, malnourishment, emotional and sensory deprivation, are not "risk-factors"; they are painful and damaging human experiences. To contain the potentially transformative horror and revulsion that might come from attending to the burdens that abused and neglected children must bear on their small shoulders by reformulating these subjects into discussions of healthy neurological development is a form of systematically distorted human awareness and empathy that silences the pain of the most vulnerable of beings. It is an extreme form of the banality of evil that would pile insult after insult on top of injuries to the most fragile of bodies, which are really babies hardly out of the womb. Equally insidious is the stated long range goal of this latest brand of phrenology, described by the above discussed lecturer on brains as helping to "guarantee 100% normal babies."

It is interesting, in this regard, that Lennard J. Davis should begin his "Constructing Normalcy" (1997), a historical review of the place of disability in the birth of a modern understanding of normality, with an epigram drawn from Adorno's *Minima Moralia* which reads:

> If such a thing as a psycho-analysis [sic] of today's prototypical culture were possible ... such an investigation would need show the sickness proper to the time to consist precisely in normality (1997, p. 9).

Here, disability studies and critical theory cross swords against a common enemy. Davis reaches back to antiquity to contrast the meaning of the "ideal" body, which referred to an unattainable because divine form, to the early modern meaning of "normal," which meant "perpendicular" (and which derived from the carpenter's square, called a "norm"), to our present concept, which came into existence only after 1840 and which means "constituting, conforming to, not deviating or different from, the common type or standard, regular, usual" (1997, p. 10). Davis then proceeds (without reference, by the way, to Foucault, much less to *Dialectic of Enlightenment*) to trace the genealogy of normalcy through the development of statistics, the writings of Quetelet, Freud, and Marx, to Marx's object of great admiration, Charles Darwin, and most importantly, from there to Darwin's cousin, Sir Frances Galton, who, among other things, invented the procedure of fingerprinting, ironically, "out of a desire to show that certain physical characteristics could be inherited" (1997, p. 15). It was Galton who also coined the henceforth loaded term, "eugenics" (1997, p. 15).

The ubiquity of eugenics as a most pressing form of identity thinking is doubly underscored by Davis. Not only did the eugenics movement seek the practical elimination of all manner of deviance, from the criminal type to the twisted body, it was also so attractive to the modern mind as to bring together such unlikely adherents as Emma Goldman, George Bernard Shaw, Sidney and Beatrice Webb, Harold Laski, and Theodore Roosevelt on the one hand, and, of course, Adolph Hitler, on the other. According to Davis, "We have largely forgotten that what Hitler did in developing his a hideous policy of eugenics was just to implement the theories of the British and American eugenicists" (1997, p. 19).

In 1933, for example, "the prestigious scientific magazine *Nature* approved the Nazis' proposal of a bill [a legislate act, that is] for 'the avoidance of inherited diseases in posterity' by sterilizing the disabled" (p. 19). Davis continues: "The magazine editorial said 'the Bill, as it reads, will command the appreciative attention of all who are interested in the controlled and deliberate improvement of the human stock'" (p. 19). Even though Alexander Graham Bell, among others, was also drawn into this thicket of racist/eugenics ideology (based on comments Bell gave in a 1883 speech titled "Memoir upon the Formation of a Deaf Variety of the Human Race"), Davis shows great restraint in relegating the publication and initial reception of Murray and Hernstein's modern day classic, *The Bell Curve* (1994) to a footnote. In following this lead, it is with attention to another seemingly innocuous footnote in "Creating Normality" that we conclude our discussion of this text.

Davis, a professor of literature, writes in Footnote 10:

> The genealogical family line is both hereditary and financial in the bourgeois novel. The role of family is defined by Jurgen Habermas thus: 'as a genealogical link it (the family) guaranteed a continuity of personnel that consisted materially in the accumulation of capital and was anchored in the absence of legal restrictions concerning inheritance of property.' The fact that the biological connectedness and the financial connectedness are conflated in the novel [*Oliver Twist*] only furthers the point that normality is an enforced condition that upholds the totality of the bourgeois system (1997, p. 27).

If it is so, as Davis and, by reference, Habermas argue, that the modern bourgeois family was a mechanism for the entwined reproduction of both capitalism and the larger domination of normality, then what of the contemporary family whose spawn fits neither the plot of *Oliver Twist* nor the workings of these larger systems? Is it here, in the birth of the ineffable, with his primitive reflexes which remember the radical alterity of natural history, that nature really wins out over nurture? And not, as in Davis' retelling of Dickens, where Oliver's workhouse experience is no match for his bourgeois heredity, which in the novel overcomes poor Oliver's wrong environment, but, rather, in Patrick's irreconcilability with the workhouse itself?

The question of normalcy is a profoundly historical and spatial matter. It was not long ago or far away that bodies like our son's were a violation of extreme manifestations of the will to normalcy, the pathology of the "100% Normal," and thus destined for the incinerators of Europe and the asylums of America, each complicitous in the dream of a racially pure, eugenically engineered utopia. In our particular universe of time and space, however, Patrick is considered a threat to no one and is himself threatened only by the sympathetic pity of those who half-accept his existence. But *we* know sympathy cannot be trusted, for sympathy feels nothing beyond its own discomfort with twisting writhing bodies. Sympathy may seek, at a moment's notice, to cut them down, thereby cutting forever the thread of hope which is wrapped like a noose around our neck, a tether which keeps us here, right now.

According to Martin Jay, Adorno once remarked that Marx "wanted to turn the whole world into a giant workhouse" (1973, p. 57). Adorno apparently intended to distance himself from Marx's flirtation with economic determinism, and, moreover, his positivist faith in a productivist utopia won through modern man's mastery over nature. Marx is too much a mirror of what he criticizes (a point also made by Baudrillard). Marx's Hegelian dialectic is viewed as not nearly extreme enough, for Marx's inverted Hegel still manages to walk, whereas today, the project of enlightenment and emancipation needs a dialectics with primitive reflexes that can barely manage to crawl. Ours, then, would be a new postmodern novel: *Oliver Twisted*. Our cognitive map is grotesque, for it has an ugly hole in it, a memory hole stuffed with public laws and the latest brain research, through which we cannot remember anything in proportion to anything else, for each fragment is a trace always already damaged and lacking in coherence. We do know, however, that the intersection of a damaged biography with a normalizing society is a historically dangerous affair, but the final outcome not even a postmodern sociological imagination can imagine. At its limit-experience, negative dialectics cannot avoid the shadow cast by astrological predictions and workhouses any more than we, our family, can avoid medical non-diagnoses and the long-arm of the educational workshop. There is no reconciliation in our world, no coming to rest, no prefigurement of a life worth living that is not a disfigurement of damaged life already lived.

CONCLUSION

There is no liberation in a one-sided celebration of damaged and hurt people as the truth, as more free than the normal, as more beautiful than Beethoven, for there is no primordial organic balance that brings deviance and disorder into harmony with normality and the reproduction of the ever-same, nor is there a sociolinguistic equivalent whose carefully chosen words would substitute for such an order. The world is not right, nor can we make it so by simply adjusting our description of it. Our bodies are not right, and the expropriation of the expropriators will not change that. Nothing waits in the wings to save us; nothing normal or basic awaiting its self-realization. Thus, revolution today must be a pitiless revolution for the dumb, the dim-witted, the sick, lame, and lazy, for the non-identical, the ineffable, for those who will never know the difference and will never know enough to show gratitude. Something like hope lies in their modest refusal to integrate. They can't help themselves.

Recently, a friend loaned us a bevy of Beethoven CDs, mostly piano concertos. At the same time, Patrick, now four and a half years old, finally eclipsed twenty seven pounds in weight. Both Beethoven and Patrick grow heavy and what remains of their subaltern utopian content may fast be growing too burdensome. If there is hope in this situation we doubt if even Oprah could bring it out.

But Adorno remarks somewhere that the struggle for life and for art requires today a struggle *against* Beethoven's Ninth Symphony, a work of art issued to the world by a man who at the time could hear only himself think. There is no doubt that this proscription against premature reconciliation is still very much needed. Still, Adorno never meant by this to foreclose the memory of redemption that, in reflections from damaged life, is rendered as the gesture of a clenched hand pawing through a meaningless pile of dried beans. Herein lies the genius of Adorno, and, we think, of Patrick as well.

At times, we picture Patrick with his dried beans, some left by chance in the bowl, most strewn on the floor. We hear the music that he makes, the pop, pop, pop as they first obey his desire, then gravity, and finally entropy, before coming to rest, apparently exhausted of energy. When Patrick himself is exhausted, he slumps over, all the supports of his meticulously adjusted wheelchair no match for the weight of his body. We think how vulnerable he is, how his imperfections are probably indefensible. At times like these, we think also of the Euro-Elites enjoying their Ninth Symphony over the din of screams and moans from the Balkans. We imagine that they are moved to tears by the fourth movement, for it is so beautiful, so hopeful. We read in the newspaper that the Dayton Philharmonic is to perform this symphony, which is popular, and which lots of folks will pay good money to hear performed for their amusement. At times like these, we say to ourselves: "Wouldn't it be nice for Patrick if he could go to such a performance?" But, no, he would disturb the norms of such gala as much as he would any performance, and we, no, we couldn't bear to hear this.

NOTES

1.   Early Intervention Document 1: "Service Coordination for Infants and Toddlers with Developmental Delays or Special Needs and their Families." Service Coordination Committee of the Ohio Interagency Early Intervention Council.

2.   Early Intervention Document 2: "Workshop on New Findings on Brain Development." August 21, 1997.

CHAPTER 4

Generation X:
An Essay on Liberation

Marcuse and the New Left were defeated, *not* refuted.
—John Bokina, "Marcuse Revisited" (1994, 22, emphasis in original)

The contrast between the presentational form of The Aesthetic Dimension *and that of Adorno's work on aesthetics, to which Marcuse links his, is compelling. (...) [Marcuse] was attempting...to take the imagination and its utopian potential, as explicated in* Eros and Civilization, *and to lodge it within the aesthetic dimension in the narrower sense of the aesthetic experience of works of art and culture. So lodged, it would be safe to some degree from the ideological battles of a troubled Left and from one-dimensionalization. And he placed it explicitly—and, by virtue of the contrast in presentational form, emphatically—under the aegis of Adorno's aesthetic work ....*
—Shierry Weber Nicholsen, "The Persistence of Passionate Subjectivity"
(1994, pp. 152-153)

It's a strange world. Some people get rich and others eat shit and die. A fat man will feel his heart burst and call it beautiful. Who knows? If there is, in fact, a Heaven and a Hell, all we know for sure is that Hell will be a viciously overcrowded version of Phoenix ....
—Hunter S. Thompson, *Generation of Swine* (1988, p. 11)

Who would have thought the kids would start taking over so soon? Or that they would even want to? They were supposed to be slackers, cynics, drifters. But don't be fooled by their famous pose of repose. Lately, more and more of them are prowling tirelessly for the better deal, hunting down opportunities that will free them from the career imprisonment that confined their parents. They are flocking to technology start-ups, founding small businesses and even taking up causes—all their own way. They are making

111

> *movies in and out of Hollywood, making money, spending money. Slapped with the label Generation X, they've turned the tag into a badge of honor. They are X-citing, X-igent, X-pansive. They're the next big thing. Boomers beware! It's payback time.*
>
> —Margot Hornblower, "Great Xpectations" (1997, p. 58)

Generation X, strictly speaking, does not exist. It is a sign without a signified. There is no empirically observable referent, no age-bound cohort sharing in a common and defining set of experiences, no collective identity, no historical self-consciousness, no authentic, organic project in-the-world, that unites or compels those born since the post-World War II baby boom or serves as an independent check against perpetual redescription by the Hornblowers of the mass media. There is no need to quibble about defining boundary dates, nor is there a need for conceptual subcategories, such as to divide "Atari" busters from "Nitendo" busters, further inserting in between these what our local newspaper recently dubbed "Gappers" (i.e., those born between 1963 and 1969, which includes ourselves) (*Dayton Daily News*, 1997, p. C2). Even if we could summon the moral energy and could overcome our attention-deficit disorder long enough to weigh through the details of the popular psycho- and socio-babble and shameless marketing rhetoric that discursively *constitutes* "Generation X" at the same time that it violently repels serious discussion, the point would be moot: Generation X does not really exist "as an actuality," to use Karl Mannheim's phrase from his classic, "The Problem of Generations" (1952, pp. 302ff). Also, in this sense, Generation X does not really exist as a phenomena worthy of humane, gentle, critical theoretic analysis. Generation X exists, at best, only as a simulacrum where all simulacra must, in hyperreality (see Hultkrans 1994). Unfortunately, analysis at this level is, by definition, nauseating for both author and reader.

This is not to say that actually existing young bodies do not occupy a very real temporal/spatial position within the postmodern order, or that these bodies fail somehow to register the domination characteristic of the postmodern period, or that our lives, such as they are, do not transpire and tend, as they always do, toward biographical expiration. We still eat shit and we die, to be sure. As such, and in spite of its failure to exist, Generation X is a potentially pregnant term, in the sense that it is a triple negative, a negation of the negation negated. On the surface, the appellation refers to nothing, to "X." Some of its adherents delight in this fact, as though enthralled in a libertarian epiphany, where "X" stands for something like "You can be anything you want to be." For our part, however, let this "X" refer to something absent, namely, the palpable absence of a life worth living, which is the ultimate desideratum of critical theory, especially as expressed in the many theoretical works of Herbert Marcuse. Finally, and here we move past Marcuse, the something that we have identified as nothing must be digested if only because it nauseates us to do so. The resulting waste product, which is the truth of this ideology, may be picked through for clues of a new sensibility. It is only through this sort of cannibalistic dialectic—and not some cheap, unserious, one-sided, one-dimensional anti-label, or even the old theoretical art of a quickly retreating high modernity—that immanent critique must today work its way.

Thus, Generation X is not only not for-itself, it is not in-itself either. Generation X *is*, we are suggesting, detritus, and we are the "generation of swine" feeding on the shit that we are drowning in. Switching metaphors, this is what immanent critique has devolved to in an era as often described as post-postmodern as straightforwardly postmodern: chewing off the leg trapped in hyperreality, which means overthrowing the order of things at the cost of our limbs, and, given the predictable loss of blood, perhaps at the expense of our lives as well. We must risk everything in confrontation with that which negates us (one thinks of Hegel) but without any genuine hope of a resulting pacification of our existence (one forgets Hegel). In contrast, and by way of example only, Habermas' mandarin Kantian tendencies, his "thin" version of the lifeworld, his distance from Baudrillard's American "desert," fuse together and diminish his liberatory value for the young much more than his sheer verbosity ever could. In this sense, Marcuse is still the critical theorist for the American young, for he never abandoned his tendency to exaggerate and to live his theoretical contradictions. What's more, once he was defeated, and the revolution postponed indefinitely, he had the good sense to hide his utopian discourse from the overexposure it would receive in the blinding light of a twilight world.

Born in the United States in 1964 and 1966, respectively, we do not take solace in, much less gain inspiration from, such American-born texts as Marcuse's *One-Dimensional Man* (1964) or the "Political Preface 1966," which stands before his re-issued *Eros and Civilization* (1955), for that would entail our growing up absurd(er). Rather, if our analysis is grounded in such texts —and, importantly, their defeat and subsequent retreat to the "aesthetic" as though under the aegis of Adorno's oeuvre— it is precisely because they provide no solace and represent only reflections of that which does not exist because that which might have existed was extinguished before it could be born. We therefore cannot tolerate such texts, for that would surely be repressive. We cannot take pleasure in them, for that seduction would dissipate yet again their already dissipated compassion and love. We cannot *be* the next Marcuse, the "next Left," the new iconoclasts, the voice of hope for those who have no hope. We have no hope. (What is "hope"?) Marcuse is dead. We have only a corpse to nurture us, and the barest chance of surviving our own survival. This is not meant as more melodrama or self-pity, the very sort of pseudo-interiority mass marketed *as* Generation X. Far from it. We mean only to speak truth to nothing and to no one.

Anticipating credulity toward this metanarrative, Part I of this chapter addresses the hyperreality of Generation X in order to introduce into our discussion the particulars that make for the free-floating quality of our existence, sans lifeworld. Here, we occasionally and more or less haphazardly invoke our familiarity with the popular films, novels, and Gen X lexicon that delineate the cultural field of our "object" of analysis, and that, subtextually, establishes our (admittedly pathetic, halfhearted) generational authority. In Part II, we aim to articulate and elucidate an impossible if nonetheless necessary cognitive map that works against the melodramatic and *sidereal* tendency of Gen Xness in order to concretize the truth of its/our nonexistence. As though having found Marcuse's and Adorno's messages in a bottle, somehow entwined, perhaps fused together as though in subterranean firestorm radiating from a belowground, 1950's Nevada nuclear test, we hope to sketch on the reverse side the outlines of a new message, a new sensibility with (post-)ethical ramifications.

PART I. GROWING UP ABSURDER

In the final scene of Richard Linklater's 1990 Gen X film classic, "Slacker," which is set in Austin, Texas, a group of young men and women gleefully are enjoying each other's company on a bright, sunny day while riding and filming one another in a convertible automobile. Accompanied by a light and peppy tune reminiscent of Frankie and Annette beach party music, this final scene climaxes when the party arrives at a precipice on the outskirts of town. Here, one of the filmmakers hurls a handheld camera off one of Austin's famous cliffs so that it ultimately comes to its shattering demise some hundred-odd feet below. Just prior to this joyous act of self-annihilation, the camera is quickly aimed toward the ground, where two books lie, front-cover up. Only one of the book's titles is readable to the ordinary viewer (that is, us). It is *Growing Up Absurd* (1956), Paul Goodman's famous social criticism on behalf of the new generation of American youth forced to face the new postwar social order, or what Goodman calls simply "the organized system." In this way, *Slacker* figuratively and reflexively "grounds" itself in the history of literate, intellectually inspired, social critique by and/or for the young, the "youth," or what Goodman also terms, the "problematic."

That *Slacker* is, however, a far cry from *Growing Up Absurd* is evident more than in their obviously divergent forms. *Slacker*'s screenplay is as pure a phenomenology as one is to find in cinema: a brilliant depiction of what Alfred Schutz famously dubbed the "multiple realities" of social life. Moving, often seemlessly, from one situation and one person's reality to another situation and another set of realities, Linklater makes good on his own "theory," as told by a hyperactive Linklater to an uninterested, deadpan cabby on their way from the bus terminal to some unknown Austin destination in the first scene in the movie. Linklater relates that he just had "the weirdest dream back on the bus." This dream was unusual in that there was "nothing goin' on at all, man; it was like the *Omega Man* ...." Linklater then remembers that he dreamed a book, the premise of which was that "every thought you have creates its own reality," resulting in a world of many and various interconnected although ultimately "separate realities." Fantasizing about some of the interesting realities that might have befallen him had he not chosen the taxi ride into town, such as his meeting a "beautiful girl" and eventually "moving in with her," Linklater bemoans his sobering and already determined fate: "man, shit, I should have stayed at the bus station." From this follows countless eavesdropping scenes where dozens of shadowy and mostly youthful characters appear and intersect and disappear and disconnect to reveal the fragmentation and alienation of social life in one corner of a presumably larger, similarly structured, and similarly experienced world.

Parallel to Linklater's blend of phenomenology and narcissism, the substantive nature of the characters' various worlds are weird and untethered as well as shot through with pain, delusion, utter apathy and even moments of insight. For example, in the first scene following Linklater's opening, a young man, perhaps in his early twenties, murders his mother by running her down with the family station wagon. The accident scene is elaborated on through the appearance of a series of individuals, each of whom approach the dead body from their own self-absorbed perspective. Thus, a woman stumbles across the hit-and-run crime where Linklater is hovering over the body. The woman is jogging and veers toward Linklater, telling him, "Don't touch her," "Call the police," "Get her ID," "Don't touch her." A man drives up apparently agitated by the delay caused by his path having been blocked by the splayed body of the elderly women, her groceries strewn about her. The jogger informs him that everything is under control, to which he quickly replies, as if seeking leave, "Then you don't need me." Before returning to his car, though, the man notices the jogger as a women. He gives her his business card and asks that she call him, presumably for a date. Another bystander approaches and wonders "Whose body is this?" and asks the jogger if the groceries are her's. The jogger gives this second man the first man's business card and tells him to call the first man as she heads off to continue her workout, leaving the corpse under the authority of the guy who wants the dead lady's groceries. Soon thereafter, it is implied that Linklater calls the police as well as the women's son, who has returned to his home. The son is perched in a window in an apartment just above the scene of the crime. After taking the phone call concerning his mother—he is interested in only whether anyone caught the license plate of the hit and run vehicle—he ritually burns some picture cut from a photography album and prepares to dictate from a book into a tape recorder. Just as the police arrive at his door to place him under arrest, he plays a reel-to-reel film that repeats what appears to be old home-movie footage of him and his mother. She is first pushing, and then jabbing with her foot, the back of her young son's go-cart, effectively propelling him forward with a kick in the back.

Another scene involves a student-type who lives in a room filled with dozens of working television monitors, including one strapped to his back. He tells a friend about a murder he once witnessed but found unsatisfying, in part because he missed some good scenes (especially the knife being plunged into the body), couldn't replay the whole scene in slow-motion, and could not adjust the hue of the blood, which he felt was simply not right. He plays a video of a graduate student who, just prior to taking his committee hostage, films himself bemoaning the human condition. Throughout the entire scene, video footage from "The Atomic Cafe" (1982) and the Space Shuttle Challenger disaster play on various monitors, and is presented in much the same manner as the FOX network's ghoulish marketing of death and mayhem as though under the banner of "World's Funniest Tragedies Caught on Film, II." Here, hyperreality is presented as mundane and preferable to reality, although also insane and thoroughly antisocial.

Another scene depicts an older gentleman and his young adult daughter, who together interrupt a young trespasser in the home that they share. The elderly gentleman, who claims that he is an anarchist and pines for the day that he will blow-up the State of Texas legislature, takes the young man under his wings, offers him whatever he wants, and regales him with apparently apocryphal stories of his stint fighting fascism with Orwell and the Lincoln Brigade and of his near-miss with death beneath the University of Texas tower once infamously occupied by Charles Whitman, the unexpected mass murderer. The anarchist blames his deceased wife for his bad luck at having missed the excitement that day.

Additional memorable characters include a young JFK conspiracy theorist, socially awkward but compassionate toward the obscure works of the long-suffering "buffs"; a right-wing Nietzschean, counselling scorn and indifference toward the poor and homeless, for whom charity does more harm than good; and a young women hawking on the street what she insists is Madonna's pap smear in a bottle. One of this women's potential customer's has recently been released from a mental hospital in Dallas, having been placed there by her parents. And so forth.

Occasionally, theory rears its ugly head, only to be resubmerged into the morass of a fragmented normalcy. For example, a found, if not well understood and hence quickly discarded, text is a set of postcards that read like a postmodern suicide note. These postcards are authored by "Paul" under the pseudo-name, Juan Apagotos (or so his name sounds). They are discovered and read by Paul's former house mates, who enter his empty room and pause for a moment to consider his evident theoretical imagination and despair. Their reading and commentary is as follows:

> Juan Apagotos spends a lot of time walking around town. He tried college for awhile, but that consumed too much time, so now he's looking for a job that doesn't involve much work. He rents a room in a large house and rarely sees the people he lives with. He thinks one is called Frank-something, and he thinks there are some more, but he can't be sure.
>
> Housemate: I guess that means us.
>
> He comes from a *light* blue-collar family. He doesn't see his parents much anymore. He quit going to visit when they quit sending him money. One of his grandparents died last month, but he can't remember which.
>
> Housemate (looking at the front of the postcard): It's Uncle Fester.

Last summer he thought about sticking his index finger in a fan. Someone told him his fingerprints are unique, and he believes there's too much direct evidence against uniqueness. He thinks the differences are minor compared to the similarities.

Housemate (looks at the picture of a military parade on the card's front; says nothing).

All his days are about the same. He wakes up at 11:00 or 12:00, eats cereal or toast, reads the newspaper, looks out the front door, takes a walk, goes to a movie matinee, listens to the radio, watches sitcom reruns 'till 1:00, and usually falls asleep about 2:00. He likes to sleep. Sometimes he has good dreams.

Housemate: This is the finale.

Watch for the next episode. Juan joins up with an emerging European terrorist organization, and soon returns to the United States with a supply of homemade nuclear weapons.

Housemate: Huh, interesting.

While it may be reading too much into the film to label it a work of post-modern critical phenomenology, the usual interpretation—that the film is "in form and content" the depiction of "the meandering, painful, but always ironic and amusing slacker lifestyle" (Rushkoff 1994, p. 40)— seems to miss the mark. *Slacker* is not about overeducated young people who lack 9-to-5 ambitions; it is not a depiction of a "lifestyle," much less an indictment of the intrinsic failings of the last born.

A more charitable and, we think, more intelligent, reading would explore the connection to *Growing Up Absurd*, the central thesis of which Goodman often repeats and underscores.

It is the argument of this book that *the accumulation of the missed and compromised revolutions of modern times, with their consequent ambiguities and social imbalances, has fallen, and must fall, most heavily on the young, making it hard to grow up* (1956, p. 217, emphasis in original).

In Goodman's perspective, and likewise, we suggest, in *Slacker*, the "burden of proof, as to who is 'wrong,' does not rest with the young but always with the system of society" (1956, p. 238). In his case, writing in the midst of what C. Wright Mills called the "American Celebration," Goodman was moved to detail the oppressive nature of advanced capitalist society and all the many forms of irrationality that the classic sociological analysis of modernity's rationality had by this time produced. Framed as a set of ambivalent social and cultural developments with dubious and pernicious consequences for the young, the unfinished project of modernity is, in Goodman's reading, called to account for itself. He does not blame the most innocent and least responsible victims, who would otherwise be easy targets. For Goodman, the organized system, among other things, was making growing up quite a chore. And Marlon Brando, we imagine, didn't make things any easier.

Goodman does not, however, deny the young their agency by treating them as passive victims of an omnivorous social system. Rather, he explicitly supports their independent efforts to "vomit up the poisonous mores" (1956, p. 239). As Goodman continues:

> They won't eat them—they are sick because they have eaten too many of them. And they are "in the right" because they are obviously in the right, everybody knows it (1956, p. 239).

Indeed, the social critic Goodman wishes to form an alliance with the bare facticity of nausea among the "crazy young." For in their very newness, their freshness, what he calls their "spirit" and their "existential reality," he finds a source of resistance to the organized system's own defining "role playing, its competitiveness, its canned culture, its public relations, and its avoidance of risk and self-exposure ...." "That system and its mores," writes Goodman, "are death to the spirit, and any rebellious group will naturally raise a contrasting banner" (1956, pp. 240, 241).

In *Slacker*, if there is a "contrasting theoretical banner," it is certainly not rendered banner-like. Today's resistance, such as it is, cannot be directed against so clear a target as the "organized system," nor can the form of a generational manifesto—such as in *Growing Up Absurd* or later, in the call-to-arms known as "The Port Huron Statement"—stand as sufficient to the current situation. Instead, today's resistance is more likely to take the form of an ironic third-person autoanalysis composed on postcards, or a cryptic message of critique that points, like Goodman, to the objective societal causes of disgust over-against the merely subjective attitude of apathy. Nonetheless, today's resistance remains a secret, esoteric message passed from hand to mouth rather than a billboard best seller that predicts the emergence of a new generational collective consciousness/conscience.

Slacker articulates a new politics for the postmodern condition where perhaps the greatest struggle is for a connection to reality itself.

This new politics is not, however, less theoretical because of its form. Indeed, in a age when "the personal is political" is an urgent everyday reality much more than it is a thin slogan barely worth mouthing, such new political forms are an appropriate vehicle for resistance to the dominant micro-dominations characteristic of the current malaise. Who, now, for example, could so unself-consciously repeat Goodman's masculinist opening line to his chapter on "Jobs," "It's hard to grow up when there isn't enough *man's work*" (p. 17, emphasis added)? Man's work, indeed, is still in short supply, for who, today, is a "man" (see Butler, 1990)? And who, today, could have such a merely ambivalent attitude toward modernity, in this, an age of extreme emotions, of panic/cynicism? Imagine what it is like to "grow up" when children are always already mature, when the meaning of "man"/"women" are no longer fixed, when, indeed, nothing is fixed but so much is in disrepair, when even our "generation" does not exist, and certainly not as an authentic and independent emergence of a counterculture, counteraesthetic, or counterhegemonic activity, that is, as a political class-in-and-for-itself, such as that posited, in the now-dated, wholly modernist social imaginary of *Growing Up Absurd*? In other words, the throwing-up-as-growing-up, Brandoesque, macho process advocated by Goodman so many years ago has taken its toll at the level of aesthetic and critical forms themselves, such that a new generational "essay on liberation" must fundamentally recast itself lest it become nostalgic, masculinist Left propaganda, or, in myriad otherwise ways, bad art. Today, Brando is old and fat, but hyperreality may still get around to recycling him, as has been the happy fate of Sinatra and the Rat Pack, Tony Bennett, and even Tom Jones.

Slacker, the postmodern film, thus sets itself apart from the linear bookish tradition of modernist social critique, in that its tracking-shot-laden exploration of a local setting, Austin, Texas, addresses the vertigo of postmodern time/space at the same time that it offers, however tentatively and incompletely, a theoretical map for comprehending the everyday pastiche of contemporary social intercourse. The film is also more reflexive and subsequently more self-critical and less burdened by its own illusions than works such as Goodman's, which appeared prior to the death of authorship and similar facets of the cultural sea change called postmodernism.

Slacker, as phenomenology and as art, attends primarily to the subject in his and her superficial, immediate and local milieu at the expense of the transcendent objective context and its substratum of depth psychology, its history, and its translocal integration into system and meta-system. More than this, it also captures the refraction of that context as it passes through the prismatic lifeworld which bends and fragments reality into its constitutive parts. This is the truth of *Slacker*, a truth incorporated in its self-conscious and self-destructive conclusion which openly acknowledges its radical particularity and world-historical insignificance. Indeed, its own acknowledged powerlessness thus directs our attention to the absence of a vital, potentially transformative culture; it directs our attention to the absence of a generation.

If a film such as *Slacker* describes the bending logic of the lifeworld from within that lifeworld, other Gen X classics take a more straightforward theoretical stance vis-à-vis the same object. Take, for example, Gus Van Sant's 1989 *Drugstore Cowboy*, which thematizes the problem of gender and generation and thus of social reproduction, specifically, the reproduction of the lifeworld. As such, *Drugstore Cowboy* not only describes the fact of multiple realities but explicates their emergence and shows their structuring. This film is set in Portland, Oregon, in the year 1971, and opens with "Bob" (played by Matt Dillon) lying on a stretcher in an ambulance on his way to the hospital. Only his face and shoulders can be seen, the rest of his body covered by a sheet. His face is slightly distorted, so that half of it resembles the made-up face of a corpse displayed at a wake. From this position, Bob narrates the story of his life, how he came to be riding in an ambulance via his life robbing drugstores of their mind-bending wares. The question raised by the film—"Why do drugs?"—is a simple enough one, but the answer offered eschews the typical explanations, such as peer pressure, escape, excitement or psychological dependency, all of which are brainless in equal measure. Avoiding both glorification and didactics, then, but not without humor and a compelling sense of tragedy, the film explores the consequences of failed social reproduction for the isolated individual in a mass society.

While *Drugstore Cowboy* places itself squarely within the classic tradition of outlaw movies such as *Bonnie and Clyde* and *Sugarland Express*, it avoids the sentimental romanticism characteristic of this genre. As a rule, the mythos of the outlaw genre concerns the chances for individual survival in which energetic youth exploit openings or breakdowns in the system, bypassing normal channels and established procedure in order to make their way in a society of closure. In traditional takes on the outlaw, the individual lives on the margins, unsystematically working the system in order to survive. By accepting their marginal status, outlaws are able to establish their independence by creating a private world composed exclusively of social relations resembling an ideal typical family.

Equally important, the outlaw is knowledgeable about both his/her own self and the nature of the objective system on the margins of which he/she operates. Knowing one's place and keeping one's cool are conditions for survival to the extent that cynical self-consciousness is the foundation for action. Objective reality, from the perspective of the acting outlaw-agent, constitutes a transparent unity that is easily penetrated. In a typical formula, the young outlaw opposes the middle-aged cop made soft and slow by the leisurely life of the small town or the rigidity of the city administrative apparatus. In either case, the freshness and vigor of youth are enough to provide an edge over the status quo.

In *Drugstore Cowboy*, however, this mythos is no longer intact. While Bob's self-conception is that of the outlaw, traditionally conceived, his social, cultural, and generational marginality undermine his attempts to evade the logic of the closed society. Additionally, the social system itself, while thoroughly corrupt, appears as a totality which cannot be avoided through the sheer force of will. The overwhelming sense is of the dissolution of the confident and self-conscious agent sitting at the center of a reality easily understood and thus easily conquered. Or, as Bob informs the viewer in the introductory voice-over, "we were playing an game we couldn't win."

Thus, Bob and his spouse, Diane, are working with another couple, Rick and Nadine, younger than themselves and untrained in the ways and means of petty crime. Through the voice-over, Bob establishes his relationship to the others: "I carried the whole goddamn crew on my back like it was my own newborn son." Feeling himself to be a father of sorts, Bob accepts responsibility for raising 'em right, even as he is convinced that his charges are unprepared to follow in his footsteps, having been, as he speculates, spoiled by television. Like a classic bourgeois father, Bob's paternalistic concern for those for whom he feels responsible is limited by his interest in their ability to help him maintain his habit. This essentially instrumental attitude towards those who, within the logic of the film, constitute his family, is brought into the open in an exchange with another young junkie in which Bob, only half-jokingly, offers to sell Nadine, the youngest, least experienced, and most vulnerable member of the crew. Later, after Nadine dies of an self-induced, apparently suicidal overdose, Bob chastises Rick for feeling bad for the death of a woman who beat him out of his cut of the illicit booty.

Bob's personal relations are an unstable tension between a paternalistic concern and self-interest, suggesting that his inner-world is a twisted reproduction of broader contradictory social relations. This permeability of Bob's inner-world is further manifested in the increasing vulnerability of the private sphere of his crew, both with respect to the unpredictable intrusions of the system writ large, as well as to internal conflicts rooted in gendered values that embody the tension between production and reproduction. For example, after the first drugstore heist presented in the film, Bob shoots up in the car, irritating Diane. She asks him why he can't wait until they get home, like everybody else. At issue is the confusion of means and ends, such that the pursuit of appropriate means towards achieving the good life endangers the possibility of living that life. This low-voltage tension is further elaborated in an argument between Bob and Diane over "sex." She wants to and he doesn't. Instead, Bob desires only another drugstore heist, and this despite the fact that the crew is already well supplied with contraband. Bob's devotion to his work of stealing drugs, drugs which earlier in the film had been referred to as a "shortcut to success," and everything that entails, has become for Bob a clearly irrational obsession that consumes all other potential values. As if to underscore the vulnerability of Bob's private world, Bob and Diane are interrupted in the middle of their argument by the explosive entry of Officer Gentry and *his* crew of fellow cops, who are intent on busting Bob for his latest heist.

Here, for Bob, the overwhelming and stressful press of the social takes the form of the more powerful fathers of the criminal justice system, and, in particular, Gentry, who has taken a paternal interest in first bringing Bob before the law and later protecting him from that same law. After forcing their way into Bob's and Diane's house, Gentry's partners proceed to tear apart their home piece-by-piece, as Gentry and Bob spar with each other in a twisted male bonding ritual in which golf handicaps and insults are exchanged with equal significance. The basis of this complex of interactions is that Bob and Gentry are playing some kind of man-game. Diane, Nadine, and even Rick, having no interest in Gentry as a father figure, observe from the side-lines, if not passively, then at least within entirely different logics that are immune to the bourgeois dominance rituals being enacted before them. Thus, Gentry also interrogates Diane and Nadine in an attempt to appeal to their apparent gendered weaknesses, but is unable to establish a bond amenable to negotiations of mutual interest. Unwilling to play along, Diane receives Gentry with a straightforward, fuck-you hostility. Nadine, apparently unable to play at all, simply and honestly answers Gentry's questions, and *that* gets him nowhere.

In spite of their general immunity to the symbolic paternalistic power of Gentry, it is clear that his actual power, which is backed up by the full force of the law, is real. In other words, the familial bonds of the crew are in fact threatened by Gentry and his partners. Not only is their home left in utter disarray, but the mantle piece over the fireplace, long considered the symbolic center of the bourgeois family, is struck in half by an ax wielded by one of Gentry's partners, a move that clearly establishes what is at stake in the confrontation. As a consequence of the search, Bob moves his "family" from their freestanding, if rented, house, first to an apartment complex, and, later, into a roadside motel. But even there, in this most temporary of residences, they are again forced to move on due to the prior reservations associated with a local sheriff's convention.

In and through this basic storyline, wherein the material determinants of Bob's actions are laid out, another story unfolds, revolving around Bob's reliance on an untethered fatalist system of superstition to guide his actions. In other words, the power of the social and of other men is twisted by Bob into a body of pseudo-rational beliefs about a fate that can be known in advance only if one can read "the signs." Thus, after an altercation in which Gentry unmistakably establishes his dominance and orders Bob out of town, Bob takes his crew "crossroading" in search of security. Through a self-protective logic, he rationalizes his having been overpowered by another man by blaming it on Nadine. According to Bob's thinking, Nadine had placed a "hex" on the crew by virtue of her having asked Bob if she could get a dog, "a little something to hold and to pet" during those times that the more experienced members of the crew were away on business. Apparently, in Bob's astrological worldview, which Diane seemed to share, the simple mention of a dog guaranteed that "luck flew out the window for the next thirty days." Later, Nadine rebelliously places a hat on a bed, which, for Bob and Diane, is the illest of omens, perhaps suggestive of a mixing of the sacred and profane as well as the collapse of a bi-phasic worldview where contradictory activities are kept in strict conceptual separation. The hat on the bed foreshadows Nadine's suicide by drug overdose.

Nadine's death compels Bob to seek treatment at a methadone clinic, not so much because he feels guilt over the death of a young woman, but because he desires to make good on his debt to "the hat." Given that it was

Nadine herself who placed the hat on the bed, Bob is able to evade his own responsibility for her demise, and, indeed, blames Nadine for both her own death as well as for her having placed the crew in danger by saddling them with a very inconvenient corpse. Additionally, Nadine's rebellion against Bob's arbitrarily invented taboos was a one-sided negation that, in the end, proved to be more of a threat than Bob's own idiosyncracies. If Nadine tacitly understood the irrational logic of Bob's fatalism and dismissed his leadership and authority on that basis, she also dismissed the truth content of Bob's system, which included the recognition that narcotics are poison and, if abused or used carelessly, potentially fatal.

In any case, Bob's bargain with fate means he must leave his crew, which includes his wife, and stop using drugs. His immediate self-interest is to avoid being charged with murder. Explaining himself to Diane, Bob says:

> I said God, son, devil, whoever you are, please have pity on me. Please let me get this poor girl's body ... into the ground so I don't have to spend the rest of my life in prison. And God, if you do that for me, I'll show you my appreciation by going home, getting on the methadone program, getting a job, and living a virtuous life.

In the last scene of the film, Bob is once again stretched out in the ambulance, on his way to the hospital. By now the viewer knows that Bob has been shot, and that his having taken a bullet has freed him from his debt to fortune. It is left an open question whether this new found freedom means that he is about to die or simply return to his drug using ways. In any case, Bob is pleased to have gotten himself a "police escort to the biggest pharmacy in town."

Earlier, when Bob is seeking entry into the treatment clinic, the intake counselor, a kindly middle-aged woman who is apparently impressed by Bob's take on his life, asks him if he has ever considered becoming a counselor himself. Frustrated, Bob responds in the negative, explaining that:

> To begin with, nobody, and I mean nobody, can talk a junkie out of using. You can talk to them for years but sooner or later they're gonna get a hold of something. Maybe it's not drugs. Maybe it's booze. Maybe it's glue. Maybe it's gasoline. Maybe it's a gunshot to the head. But something, something to relieve the pressures of everyday life, like having to tie your shoes.

In Bob's own estimation, addiction and death are synonymous, both means to the same end of evading the dissolution of the lifeworld and the crisis of social reproduction. A perpetual outsider, perpetually persecuted by the powers that be, Bob is compelled to eke out a life in an era of rationally organized systems that portend world where there is a place for everything and everything is in its place.

Everything, that is, but 'me,' Bob must think to himself, for this "everything is in its place but me" is the primary problem of the individual in a mass society. Mass society is thoroughly collectivized by the systematic and impersonal operation of organized capital and the administrative state. Every individual must solve the problem of finding their place in a timely manner so that they can have a life complete with spouse, kids, house, and dog. From this participating perspective, the world is a seemingly impenetrable set of "structures" regulating all facets of behavior and ultimately determining one's life chances. It is as though the individual were Mr. Sperm in his top hat and bow tie (and we all secretly identify with Mr. Sperm), as he races the teeming millions who are just like himself to the monolithic Ms. Egg. In mass society, there are so few pathways to success and so many fighting for the same prizes that the individual, as such, has little realistic hope for success. But despite the disheartening results of rational probability analysis, each individual must nonetheless try and try again. The odds are against any single one of us, but, barring suicide, we have no choice but to push on.

Given the alternatives provided by the system, neither death nor the pseudo-existence provided by drugs seem so bad. To be sure, from the perspective of a life in which tying one's shoes presents itself as a challenge, blowing one's brains out might well be a rational choice. For example, at one point in the film, Bob and the crew plan to rob a pharmacy, which is located next to the unemployment office. In *Drugstore Cowboy*, these are the most readily available options. Indeed, the "virtuous life" Bob promised to lead turned out to be the dreary existence of a drill press operator who spends all day in a dingy and dirty and loud factory "drilling holes that bolts fit into." Justifying his new life to an incredulous Diane, who visits Bob in hope of enticing him back to the life of crime, Bob insists that his existence is altogether tolerable: "Sometimes, I wake up and feel like something good is going to happen," he tells her. Needless to say, she is not convinced and rejects his invitation to stay the night and find out for herself.

As in *Slacker*, no alternative is presented within *Drugstore Cowboy*, nor does one follow from its logic. Given that it is the *system* itself that is diagnosed as wanting, and given that the *system* controls the available options, this pessimism is neither surprising nor cause for concern. Unlike *Slacker*, however, because *Drugstore Cowboy* thematizes the crisis of social reproduction as a historically specific phenomena, it exhibits a more sociological significant tension than *Slacker*. In addition to the value conflicts rooted first in gender and second in the structural conflict between the organization of societal production and reproduction, there is also a generational tension suggestive of a historical awareness absent in *Slacker*.

This historical awareness first presents itself in the fact that the story told by *Drugstore Cowboy* takes place in 1971, and is clearly an historically sensitive commentary on the *origins* of our current situation. There are at least four generational perspectives presented in the film, each of which represents a valid take on reality. There is Gentry and the intake counselor at the treatment program, both of whom are middle-aged and provide different angles on the systemic accommodation of deviance via the criminal justice and the social welfare systems. As such, they represent the interests of institutional social power, and they are thus impotent to actively deal with real systems crisis much less to understand that crisis, immersed as they are in the pervasiveness of systematically distorted communication.

This systematic distortion of understanding is wedded to the impotence of agents charged with compensating for breakdowns in social reproduction, an impotence which remains even when they take their responsibilities to heart, and is portrayed through a discussion between Gentry and Bob late in the film. Bob had been beaten and shot by a younger junkie who was convinced that Bob's going straight was a scheme worked out to beat the system. Of course, it *was* such a scheme, but not in the way the younger junkie assumed. Finally convinced that Bob has no drugs to offer them, the junkie shoots Bob, apparently for kicks, but also perhaps as retribution for his past treatment by Bob, which was flippant and condescending. Gentry, suspicious that Bob was shot by a fellow cop with a grudge and a publically stated vendetta, questions a quickly fading Bob before he is slipped into the waiting ambulance, apparently in a sincere attempt to find out who done it. Bob first tells Gentry that it was the "TV babies" that got him (a reference to the young junkie), then, as if regaining his composure, he tells Gentry that it was "the hat." Unable to get within Bob's peculiar logic, where signs fast absorb their signified and leave no trace of their referent, Gentry mistakenly assumes "TV Baby" and "Hat" are street aliases when in fact they refer only to Bob's idiosyncratic system of meaning. Needless to say, the information is useless.

On either side of the conflict between Bob and the immediate representatives of the system are the very old and the very young, each of whom embody truths which are unavailable to those directly implicated in social conflict. For example, Father Tom Murphy (played by the Beat Generation author, William S. Burroughs) is an elderly ex-priest who had been put to pasture due to indiscretions related to his own addictions. From his marginal position, Father Murphy can and does speak truth to social power. The voice of wisdom rooted in memory and experience, Father Murphy informs Bob of the global systematic implications of the demonization of narcotics:

> The idea that anyone can use drugs and escape a horrible fate is anathema to these idiots. I predict in the near future, right wingers will use drug hysteria as a pretext to set up an international police apparatus. I'm an old man, and I may not live to see a final solution of the drug problem.

Remembering a time when drugs were not considered the root of all evil and knowing from his own experience that the "horrible fate" faced by junkies has as much to with the social construction of deviance and scapegoating as the drugs themselves, Father Murphy's insight reflect the systematic pathologies resulting in both widespread drug use and its persecution.

Father Murphy's historical and systemic perspective on the drug problem is, in part, presented and received as a type of redemption through which Bob is forgiven his sins. Father Murphy shows Bob that he is a victim of a world-historical process in the face of which Bob has no effective power. But this perspective does not stand alone, for it must be considered in dialectical tension with the perspective of Nadine. Nadine, as innocent and naive as any child, embodies the refraction of system's crises into pathologies of the lifeworld. As such, she has access to a different truth, passively reflecting from within Bob's own complicity with the same social power he resisted. She is the silent witness to the irrationality of the adult world; seeing the game but ignorant of what is at stake, she pays for her naivete with her life. Nadine's willingness to run headlong into the furor of the system is established early in the film, in the scene, discussed above, where Bob is making a deal with another junkie, the same one who later shoots him. Easily the smarter of the two, Bob intentionally gets the math wrong in an attempt to bilk his client out of his fair share of speed.

Nadine, apparently aware of Bob's unethical intentions, openly corrects him, and thereby undermines the scam. Immediately after this exchange, the young junkie requests from Bob an asking price for time spent with Nadine. Bob is at first offended—he's no pimp, he says—but then jokes with the junkie-turned-john. For the sake of argument, he asks how much the young junkie would be willing to pay for Nadine, doing so in front of Nadine's boyfriend, Rick, who Bob describes as "his muscle." Bob means to convey to Nadine, and to everyone present, their respective statuses in the family. Paybacks.

Later, Nadine looks on as Bob is beat up by Gentry and his partners. Having witnessed this, Nadine alone among the crew members understands why Bob takes the crew crossroading; she knows the truth behind Bob's rationalization that they need to outrun "the hex."

Together, Father Murphy and Nadine reflect the multiple truths of Bob's situation. Taking the transcendent perspective of the priest, Bob is blameless, a victim of broader social processes that are as opaque to him as to most everyone. Taking the immanent perspective of the child, Bob is shown to be complicitous with that system, reproducing the broken logic of the system in the next generation. This next generation, however, is unable to manage the system's irrational tendencies. There is thus no youthful utopia on the horizon. The telos of the system is either its own infinite replication or death, which are the same thing.

But we have promised a phenomenological account of Generation X, and instead we have delivered an analysis of two movies which are already highly self-conscious representations and thus hyper-mediations of the phenomena in question. This is because Generation X is exhausted in its media representation, having no existence independent of its image. Our method thus lives up to its name, if only because a phenomenolgical account of a simulicrum has no business seeking something real beyond the appearance because that something is not there.

We might at this point reveal what the young themselves, the real, actually alive members of Generation X, think about their lot in life. We might consult Douglas Coupland's works of fiction or peruse Sarah Dunn's especially lively and emblematic *The Official Slacker Handbook* (1994) and thereafter make reference to the tidal wave of "Gen X" newsmagazine and newspaper stories and popular films that pursue and/or deride "Gen X" themes. Or we might consult the results of survey research, which the above sources often do, or simply go on our own gut feeling and experience and what we've picked up from our friends and acquaintances over the years, which doesn't seem too firm a ground for much of anything. Or we might just as well throw up on the laptop before us, not having the stomach for so much pointless image-management and mass society dross, for Gen X does not really exist, and someone, somewhere, must reject out-of-hand what Foucault called the "immense verbosity" and "giant mill of speech" that is characteristic of any institutional discourse of domination (see Breines 1994, p. 52). No amount of newly released documents can save us, much less ease our nausea or quell our bipolar panic/cynicism.[1]

Of course, reading too much Baudrillard is bad for the soul, like too much Foucault, too much French wine, and so forth. If we are to make use of their theoretical insights in our work within and against the power of a specific simulacrum, "Gen X," we cannot—we dare not—take them too seriously. Baudrillard teaches us not to make a fetish of reality. Foucault insists that, when it comes to practices of the self, there is a lot more than meets the eye, namely social and historical determination. Together, they provide a theoretical antidote to reification, but only if we resist the urge to reify them as well.

And so, even if we insist that Generation X is a sign without significance, both in the sense that it has no actual referent and that, as a sign, it has lost the ability to evoke any potential beyond the given, then it is also true that, as such, Generation X refers to an absence. Referring to nothing—not even itself—it still signals away, and we suspect that this is more than just media magic.

For example, Baudrillard, in his *America* (1988a), notes that the "energy" from the assassination of President Kennedy, a "murder ... neither avenged nor elucidated," "radiates out over present-day America" (1988a, p. 88). This describes one such potential (absent) referent. Baudrillard's point may be given concrete expression vis-a-vis the brain-matter strewn over the back of a powder blue Lincoln and splattered onto a few shell-shocked motorcycle policemen. It is even tempting to suppose that this event was filmed precisely to assist its transportation into the political safety of hyperreality. For his part, the elder of the authors vividly recalls first seeing Zapruder's famous footage in seventh grade history class; this was in 1977, after Gelraldo Rivera's intervention that made the footage for the first time widely available, and before the emergence of "Gelraldo." With a big screen held up by a rickety frame and an old projector clicking away under the cover of dimmed, technologically backward lights, and with the teacher and his Boomer colleagues transfixed on the events unfolding, the students sat passively in their rows and columns as the

President's head exploded, his body violently thrust back and to his left before disappearing altogether, with secret service agent Clint Hill now securely attached to the limo, and the film flickering to black. This reminds us of a question: Given what Nixon *didn't* erase, what must he have said during those precious minutes of silence? We have other unanswerable questions, too, such as: Wasn't "deep throat" a rather strange, not-very-politically-correct, name to assign a coup-plotter?

And then there's *JFK*, the bright and colorful movie, and Oliver Stone again, who would later give us *Nixon* (we suspect it is only a matter of time before he delivers *Mills*). It is quite a distance between seventh grade history class—and a wonderful teacher would dress in his Revolutionary War getup and fire his musket for his appreciative students—and the hyperreal glorification of John F. Kennedy's promiscuous paternity of the Generation of the 60's, which might be considered his all-time greatest, mind-blowing fuck. In this film, which labors to reclaim history because there is no history—notwithstanding Jerry Ford's, J. Edgar Hoover's, and Arlan Spector's best efforts—we find the most radiant example of our contemporary one-dimensionality, so astral that perhaps only Baudrillard can really get the full effect of the joke. In *JFK*, as elsewhere, the universe of political discourse, like this case, is closed, and the mind quickly wanders to the precociously young Bill Clinton being filmed in the rose garden with his hand in JFK's cookie jar.

One is reminded of Marcuse's *Counter-Revolution and Revolt* (1972), where Marcuse blithely notes on the first page that "the murder of the Kennedys' shows that even Liberals are not safe if they appear too liberal ...," implying, of course, a theory of these assassinations that eschews the official "lone-nut" explanations in favor an albeit oblique treatment of them as straightforwardly political events. (We are reminded of yet another free-floating question: Who, now, remembers that Walter Reuther, recently revived as a 1950's monster movie in Nelson Lichtenstein's *The Most Dangerous Man in Detroit* [1995], was also perhaps "too liberal"?) Like Baudrillard, Marcuse does not, of course, analyze the crime-scene specifics of this or that political assassination, although he does eventually include Fred Hampton and George Jackson, among others, in the field of analysis. Instead, it is as though Marcuse is treating these all-too-high-crimes-and-misdemeanors as the background assumptions of the theoretically and political sophisticated. It is as if Marcuse anticipates Baudrillard's contention that we live in a *posthistorical* era. Baudrillard writes:

> We tend to forget that our reality, including the tragic events of the past, has been swallowed up by the media. That means that it is too late to verify events and understand them historically, for what characterizes our era and our *fin de siecle* is precisely the disappearance of the instruments of this intelligibility. It was necessary to understand history when there was still history (1993c, p. 160, empahsis in original).

Perhaps drawing from his own considerable experience working for America's intelligence agencies ("Intel Inside"), Marcuse also assumes that documentation cannot be had, but that the dialectical imagination dictates that the worst must be assumed. It is worth pausing for a moment, then, to draw a connection between Dallas and Dayton, between Marcuse's pre-astral and Baudrillard's fully fictitious America, for the death of that President is still with us (and here we refer to ourselves, "us"), and is perhaps the last marker of the beginning of the end.

The mainstream white American suburban Baby Boomers tend to define themselves culturally as coming of age in the wake of that fateful day in Dallas ("the city of hate"). In retrospect, it could be observed that they did not handle very well the straightforwardly brutal assassination of their father-figure, the youngish, apparently virile (viral?), Jack Kennedy, or "The Prez," as he once suggested his friend Ben Bradley call him, or "Chicky Baby," the term of cynical endearment that Frank Sinatra for his part, and all on his own, coined, or "my husband," as Jackie would say whilst in earshot of media types (and who knows what Ms. Billy Jean or Jimmy Hoffa or Fidel or the rest of his significant others called him). We might think that the Boomers simply accepted it without comment were it not that large segments of this sizable generation absolutely, and in short order, freaked-out, mainly in a gush of tears and hands clenched around the sod trammeled on by the lads from Liverpool (Elvis, of course, had prepared the ground), and later, in their manic delight with the delivering of the head of Richard Nixon as though in ritual sacrifice. That is, the Generation of the 60's settled, predictably, for TV Generation circuses (many, perhaps most, of them never having been in need of bread), and political farce, as though in exchange for letting the real dead dogs lie. Therein, and this is our theory, they participated in the destruction of historical reality because they were unable to redeem the vanquished angel of history.

In contrast to black Americans—who were too often then and still are today in need of bread, and who torched their own neighborhoods in a sort of pyrotechnic handwringing in the wake of Martin Luther King's pitiless slaying (a bullet racing down from the mountain top), evidence of which remains a pressing reality in Dayton and nearly every other major American city with a significant African-American population and a significant burned-out section of town, or passed silently through Fred Hampton's bullet-riddled apartment (Chicago winters kill), or shook the walls of Attica post-George Jackson (but the Harlem Globetrotters made amends, right?)—the best that the newly educated although, in retrospect, semi-erudite, American white middle class youth could do was a much more mediated, often strangely misdirected ("baby killers"?) rebellion against the Vietnam War, which eventually devolved into watching the whole world watching themselves change the whole world, and later still, Billy Joel's "We Didn't Start the Fire." And finally, let us not soon forget, there came the esteemed *Forest Gump.* Unlike Correta Scott King, the white queen Jacqueline Kennedy went to her grave in silence, as extremely affluent people with children to protect often do. Unlike the firestorm in the streets of Newark and Watts and the panic in Detroit, the defining, controlling mass element of the New Left settled, ultimately, for *JFK*, the movie, and William Jefferson Clinton, one of their own, playing the part of the first baby boomer President interchangeably with his other presidential roles, and doing so even better—that is, even more effectively—than Ronald Reagan played the part of John Wayne.

Think now of Foucault, of whom it has been reported (in full high-brow intellectual reverence for the appeal of "Inside Edition") that he long scoffed at the emergence of what he sometimes derided as a strangely and obviously homophobic, all-too-American, fear of a "gay cancer" (see Miller 1995). While Baudrillard simply cannot get enough of AIDS-as-metaphor—his *America*, for example, is full of its usage in this way—Foucault, for his part, could not stomach it as a lethal reality. Since it is not uncommon for the emergence of the AIDS pandemic to be viewed as the marker of Generation X, an indication of the onset of a new reality, where "Silence = Death"—and where just about everything else, too, fits this equation, backwards and forwards—we might dwell for a moment in comparative analysis of two kinds of death, world-historical political assassination, on the one hand, and the death of millions of ordinary people, on the other, many of whom, we should immediately recall, were once just trying to get laid or, in lesser numbers, get high, and even more obscurely, get blood or, in still more minuscule numbers, get even, by raping or killing someone or both.

In his *History of Sexuality* (1980 [1976]), Foucault might as well have named Marcuse as his chief target, for who but the Freudian critical theorist of "polymorphous perversity" was, at that time, better qualified to serve as the whipping boy of the critique of "the repressive hypothesis" (see Breines 1994)? Of course, even Goodman had taken pride in the youth of his era for having achieved, as he put it, "a simpler fraternity, animality, and sexuality than we have had, at least in America, in a long, long time" (1956, p. 240). But it was Marcuse who perhaps most of all put sexual liberation on the map of political liberation, and it was the generation that barely understood a single thing that he had to say—could Oliver Stone have read *One-Dimensional Man*, much less his large, enthusiastic audience that flocks to *JFK* in equal delight as to *Forest Gump*?—that understood sexual liberation to mean, effectively, the more fucking the merrier—get laid for the revolution!—without thinking about who was fucking whom, why, and with what consequences? This, we take it, was Foucault's point about power and about sexuality, that even The Revolution was dammed. In retrospect, so, too, of course, was the libertine critic who would seek out too many "limit experiences." Indeed, it is as though Foucault became exactly what Marcuse imagined as the epitome of polymorphous sexuality: "the determinate negation of Nietzsche's superman" (1966, p. xiv).

But where does this leave us, today? Marcuse once wrote that, "'by nature,' the young are in the forefront of those who live and fight for Eros against Death, and against a civilization which strives to shorten the 'detour to death' while controlling the means for lengthening the detour" (1966, p. xxv). Of the young today, it might be said that they are slackers whose slacking is a blow against the "performance principle." They are posthistorical experimental subjects, whose irony and whose cynicism are as necessary as popcorn and Good-'N-Plenty for enjoyment of a necessarily affirmative Hollywood docudrama. They are consumers of historical simulacra, not the makers of new sensibilities, not those who would, in a resublimation of a new reality principle after the repressive desublimation of the old, realize our real utopian possibilities. They are instead "fractal," and they are nothing, the stuff of the ever same, determinately negated before they got started. And so it is probably today more true to say that AIDS is a better "biological ground for socialism" than sexual liberation ever was, that physical harm and every sort of systematic detour to death, in other words, always outweighs pleasure as a source of revolution.

We live, after all, in the shadow not only of world-historical political assassination not even recognized as such, but also of the Panama Deception and the Gulf Non-War. We live in an age when the State Attorney

General from Mississippi can wonder aloud on "60 Minutes" about the health and safety of his whistle-blowing star witness against the Tobacco Industry, and President William Jefferson Clinton could ride if he wished through the streets of Dallas (home to "America's Team") without so much as a bubble top. There will be no Dallas for this President, who is more likely to end up hosting the first post-Presidential TV show, perhaps, "Live from Little Rock with Bill and Hillary," sponsored by a born-again American Tobacco Industry grown fat on worldwide sales stretching from the newly rehabilitated Vietnam in Southeast Asia to the newly capitalist Russia, which needs American cigarettes, in part, to smooth its transition from competitive-mafia capitalism to organized-crime-syndicate capitalism. We can take no pleasure in this recurrent dream.

If not the first self-conscious generation in American history, surely the Generation of the 60's was the loudest and most self-righteous, the most imbued with a sense of entitlement, as though voted most likely in their high school yearbooks to use their power to transform the Whole Wide World and remake it in accordance with their new sensibilities. But this is the same lot who missed their chance to grapple with history, in part, *because* of their "generational" hubris, which cut them off from a historical consciousness. This is the same generation who today market the very idea of "generations" in order to corner their children and their children's children in ever more discrete and manageable market niches, and who thereby cannibalize themselves as much as their offspring in a grand effort to prop up a consumer capitalism that feeds on narcissistic personalities. Gen X is the product of a defeated Boomer culture that is in search of new raw material for its voracious media. Once a generation that carried *One-Dimensional Man* in its back pocket (perhaps Angela Davis would have made more sense?), today they have embraced the "comfortable, smooth, reasonable, democratic unfreedom" which was that book's dystopia. And the commercials today selling 50-something health care products are covered by snippets of the Rolling Stone's "Time is on My Mind," and the amount of their own shit they will gladly devour unto their deaths knows no end in a permanently recycled "culture" of feces.

But perhaps there is more to it than this, given especially that our knife maintains a masculinist, Eurocentric edge that distorts the reality it refuses to represent. After all, there was a lot more to the youthful rebellions of the sixties and seventies than draft dodging and fucking, wasn't there? There was feminism, gay rights, an emerging ecological consciousness, a tentative war on poverty, and obstinate struggles against the racism that so grips our nation. Yes, it is true we have heard rumors about these alternatives, but it is also true that there has been little follow through on their utopian promises. There has been some real social change to be sure, but not at ground zero, which is where most people live and where it is needed most. Bodily violence against women and children continues to increase, and a redistribution of wealth necessary to the elimination of poverty has not occurred. Class polarization appears to be intensifying; in spite of the current economic boom, the poorest twenty percent of our population has not benefitted. Incomes may be rising, but not for everyone. Racism persists; white flight has created a de facto segregation of schools and housing seemingly immune to legislative fixes. Even those middle class whites who remain in ethnically and economically diverse urban centers often send their children to private schools in the interests of doing right by their kids, which, however, in practice results in schools segregated along race and class lines.

Not that groups concerned to fight poverty, racism, sexism, homophobia, and other forms of bodily violence are to blame. They have simply proved inadequate in their struggle against the forces working *against them*; they have been simply overpowered. There is no shame in this, unless, of course one still clings to a masculinity of mighty street battles and visions of resistance, in which case we have nothing to offer. This game is a crying game.

What are we and what is our world, then? Ask the Nike Corporation, whose access to hard social science research rivals if not surpasses any department of sociology: "I am Tiger Woods," an advertising trick which must have been made an infinitely easier to deploy given that Spike Lee had already pirated the line from the memorial to Fred Hampton for his sickening "I am Malcolm X" epilogue to *Malcolm X*, the movie. Who killed JFK? Forget the CIA, the Cubans, the Mob, all the false leads, and all the messages from a rebellious French Intelligence. It might as well be Tiger Woods (i.e., us), although, admittedly, he lacks the lone-nut assassin's penchant for the standard use of his middle name, which underscores for the public the assassin's low self-esteem and/or inferior cultural heritage as an explanation for his lone-nut mental state in the first place. (In fact, "Tiger" is at the other end of the name-as-prestige continuum from "Lee Harvey," "James Earl," "Sirhan Sirhan," etc. He is more likely to own something someday, like the "Golden Bear" has done.) And don't we all want to "be like Mike," pal around with him as well as covet our front-row tickets for Kicks games, especially when Mike is in town. We're all

Tiger Woods and we're all Michael Jordan and Spike Lee, hyperreal Others, whose chief real talents are outweighed by their tremendous Gen X talent for cynical media self-promotion. We are Madonna, too, and we are Bart Simpson (both white and black); we are fans at the title fight between George Bush and Orientalism's favorite son, Sadamm Hussien. We are the condemned living in a hypperreal prison. And, as the main characters of Stone's ironic critique of the hyperreal, *Natural Born Killers*, derisively insist, "there's no escaping here."

A slacker phenomenology, then: never really begun, with heavy reference to surface images, and necessarily dissipated and unfinished.

PART II. TOWARD A GENERATIONAL POST-ETHICS

History does not conform to theory. This is true even of critical theories, which, Habermasians excepted, are resolutely historical. Or this would be true, except that our current time/space warrants, for historically specific reasons, a posthistorical self-consciousness. The critique of historicism that empties into its own historical specificity derives from the firm rejection of various and sundry Kantian, Hegelian, and Heideggarian certainties in favor of Nietzschean and, perhaps, plainly sociological ambiguities. As Mills-the-plain-Marxist once explained (and, in this regard, echoing his Weberian tendencies), even the "relevance of history ... is subject to the principle of historical specificity" (1959, p. 156). That is to say, whether or not history matters is itself an historical matter. That history does not conform to theory does not mean that it should, or that, vice versa, theory should actively conform itself to history. When we speak of a cognitive map as a dialectical sociological imagination, we do not mean a flat concrete apron upon which to set up positivist glass-bead games.

That is why it so difficult to straightforwardly address ourselves to the phenomena of "Generation X." Generation X, not existing in the usual historical sense of "existing," is itself a powerful blow against historical consciousness. On the surface, it is part of a larger conceptual movement to supplant sociologically warranted historical narratives with the pseudohistorical specificity of generational intervals. It reduces social history to the fact that people are born and die, and that, at some more or less demographically discernable times and places, a bunch of people are born, and, life expectancies being what they are, a bunch of people die within some variance from a mean. What is otherwise a great blur of contemporaries daily changing in composition is, in crass, positivist generational theory carved into discrete subpopulations. Indeed, with the help of a hodgepodge of ancillary conceptual markers whose job it is to rationalize this blur into an orderly progression that regularly gives birth to "the next generation" (or, as the Pepsico prefers these days, "Generation Next"), the larger forces that shape modern history fall prey to reduction and loose their salience. Parallel to Mills' criticism of the increasingly untenable, because ahistorical, Marxian theoretical attention to the "proletariat" in terms of a Marxist "labor metaphysic," we propose the immanent critique of today's "generation metaphysic." The crux of the matter has to do with choosing concepts. The ethics of the matter has to do with choosing the concepts that we need, and that are productive of enlightenment and emancipation.

Let us be clear: we do not need generational categories. They appeal primarily to a narcissistic tendency in contemporary American culture. The fear of a slippery, contradictory, managed, postmodern identity feeds cultural discourses that transforms a fuzzy cohort into a meaningful collective historic actor, grounded in a time and a place, and perhaps, too, with a sense of purpose and a future to be realized. In the Generation X metaphysic, as in its Baby Boomer predecessor, the affirmative qualities of popular culture provide the primary source for the images that play the part of hypperreal stand-ins for a genuine, transformative social solidarity. In its sway, a generation comes very quickly to refer to the people who, by themselves or together with their families, watched many of the same television programs, or heard from their parents and sometimes found out on their own accord about something a bit unusual in the world had happened, as in the explosion of the Challenger and the attempted assassination of President Ronald Wilson Reagan. As though via the magic of their somehow always have been playing the same Trivial Pursuit game, such a cohort then becomes a pseudo "generation as actuality," that is, for Mannheim, a generation that is self-consciously and collectively engaged in a concrete "common destiny" (Mannheim [1928]1952, p. 303). This was perhaps less true of the Boomers at those scattered times and places when they really existed as a generation, but is no less true of them today, as they sit before Nick-at-Night's lineup of TV Heritage.

This much is perhaps relatively straightforward. But what historical concepts *do* we need? How do we acquire a liberatory orientation toward history or an understanding of "the present as history" (Sweezy as quoted in Mills 1959, p. 146), when the means of genuine history-making have migrated so far from our daily life?

Bear in mind, too, that the resulting absence of world-historical agency characteristic of postmodernity is filled with free-floating representations of history and history-making, issued at a mind-warping pace from the world of Oliver Stone, Spike Lee, and many lesser skilled Hollywood myth-makers, and whose chief quality is their power to overwhelm the real, to be more real than real. In this context, it is not possible to simply ignore the hypperreal, and instead set down to a good library of historical monographs and scholarly research papers, as though that would produce a firm ground for historical consciousness rather than an empiricist fetish-ization for firm grounds of all kinds, historical and otherwise. Nor is it pos-sible to peruse the slow-moving oral histories of Studs Terkel, or talk with Grandma, as though direct, unmediated contact with the past were really possible via such tonics, however pleasing, therapeutic, or educational such attentive listening might be.

We share with Baudrillard, then, the thesis that we have lost contact with the past, which is now irretrievable by ordinary means of historiography. Or, more truthfully, we share with Baudrillard the intuition that it makes sense to exaggerate this point, indeed, insist upon it, even if it is not really true. This is what an obstinate theoretical approach to history requires of us, and in this way, its internalization becomes a matter of ethics for what would have been an organic intellectual, in an age without anything organic, including especially intellectuals.

At this point, we might suggest the need for an alternative historical con-sciousness so extreme as to violate the very tradition that has made such a consciousness possible. We seek to recover once again, like a dog sniffing its own feces, natural history, which is set in geological time, embedded in rock, and intimate with the expanding and confounding universe of planets and stars. We mean to articulate a postmodern sociological imagination that transcends the usual multiple realities, real though they may be, and envisions the utter uselessness of Austin and Phoenix and every similar no-place, in all its pseudo-complexity. In this view, the grand world-historical human tragicomedy loses its appeal, and the modern subject is humbled before spatially specific mountains and oceans and all manner of an evolv-ing nature, which cares not at all, exists not at all, for its emboldened and self-absorbed human inhabitants. The postmodern subject is thus the last man, though not as a critical conceptual fulcrum, but instead, as a real real-ity, that is, an historically specific reality.

Freed, if only in the mind, from the cacophony of the manic American culture and set in relief against the dark churning of the north Pacific and the fog settling over the Alaskan mountains that jut from the sea, Gen X discourse attains its peak absurdity. To sit on that part of Earth, to sense one's position and place on the planet, is to begin the work of immanent critique against the age of *posthistorie*. We hesitate to write in this way, lest we be misunderstood as purveyors of a romantic-historical naturalism, members of such an undialectical troop as *Earth First*, or conjure in the reader's mind the opening scene from David Lynch's pathetic *Blue Velvet*, for we recognize that the sea and fog are deadly, the natural world our fate, more so now than ever before, and that it is impossible to re-present a non-alienated, mimetic, human relationship to the nonhuman natural order of things, which doesn't care if it's first or not. Mannheim must be credited with having discerned as equally false as an Anglo-American positivist generational theory its Germanic romantic-historical alter ego ([1928]1952).

But, still, to be a fleshy body exposed to a cold patch of rock is, nonetheless, productive of a new enlightenment that eschews the arrogance of the old. The problem is that one needs concepts in order to do this, including especially, following Mannheim, sociological concepts. There is simply no way to disentangle one's self from our sociocultural second nature and thereby directly approach a posited primordial substratum without recourse to conceptual/sociological mediation. We thus share Norman Denzin's concern that most American sociologists are unwilling "to develop a sociological imagination relevant to the times" (1991, p. 21), but differ with him in the sense that we mean to suggest a sociological imagination that refuses to be completely submerged within "the social." In other words and as Max Horkheimer noted in the conclusion to his own reflections on "The Revolt of Nature," "The sole way of assisting nature is to unshackle its seeming opposite, independent thought" (1947, p. 127).

Perhaps this is a potentially unique generation, upon whom it is incumbent to make the effort to acquire a meaningful orientation to natural history and its object, the Earth and its celestial environs, for never before has so much depended on the achievement of a world-historical realism. This requires, first of all, a jagged break with Humanism, especially its popular manifestations in everything from *Star Trek* (regardless of which generation) to the Jet Propulsion Laboratory scientists' slick marketing of their vested interest in publicly-funded research via infantile Mars rock names. This is, after all, (potentially) the last generation, and it must face its real nonexistence squarely by negation of its hyperreal non-existence, which is anthropomorphism par excellence. This would of course require the ability to deconstruct the weighty disinformation that characterizes debates over ecological calamity (e.g., see Gelbspan 1995). At the level of cultural studies, for example, one would have to address texts like *Focus on the Family*, an evangelical magazine that, in a recent issue, counselled parents of Generation Xers to provide what "school programs, textbooks and popular culture" do not, namely, a "balanced view of environmental problems" that would correct the (mis)impression that "the current generation" has "brought the Earth to the edge of doom" (Sanera and Shaw 1997, p. 10). But aside from such critical intellectual interventions, what could be more easy than to accept that biology (not anatomy) is our destiny, and that only the revolt of nature can serve the ends of a humble human liberation? What could be more easy, more basic, than finding ourselves grounded on this Earth, always already *of* this planet? What could be more ethical in a non-Humanistic sense than experiencing the guts that constitute our species being *sans* illusions?

But where shall the guts, the new sensibilities, to think "independently" come from? Here, we might fruitfully turn our attention to the level of the panicking body that is and is not Nature, and is strung out between life and death. In this regard, consider the productive theoretical labors of Jackie Orr, a young sociologist, who writes as a "postmodern woman-body somewhat panicked" (1990, p. 474). She is, indeed, pissed. Orr lives in a postmodern world dominated by the machinations of liquid, or by a different name, hyperreal capitalism. She is hypermediated and she is sick to the core of her being, having had her fill of this society and its socialization and medicalization and all manner of invasive BIO-power processes. But, she still has enough guts left to "perform" an indirect assault against that which is so menacing to her and to us, and to issue a "collage" that is rooted in the flesh and blood of Jackie Orr, but which is less an act of self-sacrifice than an act of visceral revolution. Orr, as she writes herself into her work, possesses the new sensibilities that we need (even though we, and we suspect, she, wouldn't wish them on anyone); her example is, at minimum, instructive for any post-ethical GEN X existence.

In what is perhaps her masterwork, "Theory on the Market: Panic, Incorporating" (1990), Orr gives her readers what she calls a "gift," or, rather, an "ambivalent gift" (1990, 480). In essence, the gift is her continuing performance, her ongoing being-in-the-world, which, though necessarily an act of self-expression, is less art than politics; indeed, it is the only politics left. Orr's texts are thus meant more as actions toward than expressions of. Their value is more in their staging of a struggle than in their sheer status as exemplary if otherwise politically inert text products. Stated somewhat differently, the ambivalent truth and the transformative power of her work lie not so much in their content as in their incomplete form, in their self-conscious refusal of flow-chart logic and in their tacit recognition of a future world yet to be wholly determined. While it is therefore inappropriate to celebrate her evident theoretical virtuosity—for that would be missing the point entirely by furthering reifying tendencies of a reading and scholarly audience rarely able to fairly weigh what an author says in relationship to what she is talking about—we might still venture to note her consistent application of the sociological imagination in the postmodern epoch, this, at any rate, before turning our full attention to the structure of this epoch and its significance for an ethics for its younger members.

The casual reader of Orr might only see in her penchant for slash marks and parenthetical neologisms an indication of her postmodern theoretical sympathies, overlooking that Orr is firm both in her analysis of postmodern social structure and in her conceiving of postmodern social structure in its objective primacy. As she writes, her interest is in "postmodernism *not* as a theoretical style or intellectual position, but as a profound and powerful social configuration in which I find myself inescapably implicated" (1990, p. 480, emphasis in original). Orr, for example, queries:

> How might panic be read, from the vantage point of sociology, as an emergent social text complexly connected to the crises in cultural meaning, social collectivity, and capitalist (re)production articulated as "symptoms" of the postmodern [Harvey 1989]? In what ways might the panicked body be researched as a gendered inscription of an urgent, disruptive language of individual dis-ease and social crisis (1990, p. 481)?

Her's, then, is an engaged self-reflection on sociocultural panic that treats her body as one site, one particular instance, of domination, among a constellation of historical and structural forces that systematically produce domination in myriad locations. It is not that her "trouble" is to be subsumed under the concept of a larger "issue," she but an instance of something general and thus truly important. Instead, the reverse is more to the point: in her own survival lies the prerequisite for her resistance to the false and consuming whole of late capitalism, and, by political/theoretical analogy, to any such resistance, such as a generational resistance. It is simply that survival depends upon the transformation of a society that eats it young.

Orr's theory/practice is, furthermore, articulated through a reflexive
sociological discourse that invents itself in its critical friction with the
always already implicated, suspect disciplinary knowledge/power that is
sociology-in-itself (also see Agger 1989) but that also simultaneously
deconstructs itself as an always already impotent act of merely textual
refusal (sociology-against-itself). Orr writes:

> [I]n pursuing the recognizably sociological project of weaving autobiogra-
> phy and history, of investigating the complex cultural text(ure)s of individ-
> ual consciousness and social structures, I am also trying to do something
> more. Or less. In contrast to most sociological techniques of storytelling, I
> am interested in finding a practice of writing that evokes the political imper-
> ative, but also the *impossibility* of writing our social bodies in relation to
> their multiple levels of determination (1990, 482, emphasis in original).

A dialectical imagination, in other words, even one that is fully embraced
as a negativizing self-consciousness and rendered as a self-critical, if venerable, textual practice, nonetheless remains a quality of mind and a text.
It is not and cannot be an action in-the-world that by itself reconfigures
social structure or refashions cultural patterns. Like late capitalist society
as a whole, sociology lives on, mostly ignorant of Orr and her colleagues
performing a radically new sociology in the basement of its annual meetings. The last lines of Orr's "Theory on the Market" are telling in this
regard: "Is it possible to resist to any effect? And will efforts to do so be
recognized as sociological" (1990, p. 483)?

While a sober positivist sociology is fated to predict a negative answer
to these questions, a dialectical sociology maintains its allegiance to those
engaged in the futile struggle for something different, which is precisely
not a senseless struggle, for real lives are a stake, here and now. This helps
to explain why Orr sees her feminist theoretical and practical work as both
"a convulsive *and* considered disruption that does not seek membership in
any recognized body of existing social knowledge" (1990, p. 482, emphasis added). While resistance depends in the first instance on the convulsive
refusal to go with the flow (panic-in-itself), the organization of this disruption into the purposeful and considered act of political will requires a
degree of alienation from the immediacy of panic-onto-death (panic-for-
itself). The location of the dying self is consciously rendered as the mediation of alien tendencies both subjective and objective while the fight for
self/society is therein engaged from this no-man's land of a particular feminist critical self-consciousness. It is therefore no surprise that Orr calls her

"Theory on the Market" an "essay," for she is both the author and the subject of her topic, the fragment whose voice rises in argument against final integration into the predictable text of her own dismissal and demise (see Adorno's "The Essay as Form" [1958]1984).

Thus, although it rubs against the grain of her own sociological practice, her own attention to the primacy of the object, we here (re)present Orr's sociological theory for the lessons she teaches us about the intersection of history and social structure which is biography. She advances the work of theory borne of "damaged life" in her historically specific attempt to do all that she can do, which is offer herself and us a "gift." Her gift is that she pursues the truth of her own dis-ease. This requires her to face herself as a sick women, and to convulse at this sickness; she must work from within her panic to shake the very foundations of the suppressed and typically diverted panic of others. Orr tells her reader: "I would give you my dis-ease. For free" (1990, p. 480). The ethics of this exchange require that we accept her gift as ambivalently and as freely as she offers it, which means that we, too, must pursue the truth of our own damaged lives; that we, too, must reflexively engage the false whole from within the (con)text of our specific site of domination; that we, too, must survive mere surviving, if only for the sake of those who have succumbed before us, and who cannot organize their resistance through and against *theory* because, for them, the jig is up. Orr's sociological imagination therefore pushes us to ground our critical theory in the anthropological limits of human existence.

For those who live on to fight another day, as whole swaths of any given generation must do despite their own reasonable suicidal longings, the eery target that emerges is the (non)condition of post-postmodernity. Habermas, for example, provides a well known way of analyzing our situation: Gen X is the butt of a joke called the crisis tendencies of late capitalism, as the raw material for new social movements that would protect the "gammer of forms of life" (i.e., the very integrity of a life worth living), or as the subjects constrained by the need to finish the project of modernity, laboring under the constraints of the highest stage of moral development, that is, postconventional morality, and guided by communicative ethics, ultimately, toward the counterfactual of systematically free dialogue oriented toward reaching a utopian "understanding" (see Kelly 1990). Indeed, sociology can easily—all too easily—document the unprecedented empirically discernable structure of our twilight epoch, a modernity without illusions. But such a classical sociological tableau, rich though it undeniably is, does not provide a useful way to approach anything like a meaningful shared set of lived, biographical experiences, for *our* lifeworld, as opposed to Habermas', is not so much structurally differentiated, advanced, rational, albeit besieged by the steering media of instrumental rationality *cum* money and power, as it is, simply, overwhelmed and tending in the extreme toward sheer obliteration. In an epoch defined by its tendency toward cultural fragmentation, and by the non-existence of its subjects—an epoch that is the product of mass society, come full circle in that it has reproduced itself from within itself—only frank examination of the nullity that we've become (announced by Weber and fleshed-out by Horkheimer and Adorno and today's best feminist theorists) can offer any hope of avoiding our annihilation by the systemic forces that would subsume us and cancel our potentialities. Postmodern critical theory is, we are suggesting, much-*needed*; it is as *necessary* as new forms of art.

The issue of our generation as an actuality vis-à-vis the postmodern is, we think, profoundly connected to the question posed in Max Pensky's 1997 edited volume, *The Actuality of Adorno: Critical Essays on Adorno and the Postmodern*. That is, the liberatory transformation of our generation from a phenomena of mere generational location (i.e., the sheer fact of our existence in relation to contemporaries born in competing eras), to self-conscious phenomena of generational actuality, requires much more than the emergence of a distinct, humble (if still) maybe unavoidably Leninist intelligentsia (what in Mannheim's formal sociology would be a free-floating "generational unit" [1952, pp. 302ff]). Such an intelligentsia would find its historical ground in natural history because history itself is foreclosed to it. Such an intelligentsia would work out its social criticism and resistance to social crisis from within its various experienced dis-eases, its damaged life, because these are the sites of domination that otherwise thwart an active being-in-the-world, and that, moreover, reveal the telltale workings of capillary postmodern capitalist BIOpower. What is needed is resistance to the hyper-real stratification of old and young in the interests of building a solidarity of all bodies; a solidarity of those fated to have been born, live, and die on this earth. This puny, busted generation facing the extinction of a life worth living needs an alliance through, across, and beyond generation, indeed, the very annihilation of generation itself.

This is where Adorno's legacy diverges from Mannheim's, for had Adorno written his own essay on "The Problem of Generations," he would have certainly eschewed the straightjacket of formal sociology and the flattening anti-utopian tendency and sheer delusion of a scientific sociology of knowledge in favor of a fully (non)participating, Beckett-like, theory of the end game. A parallel may be drawn between Adorno's all-too-famous prohibition on lyric poetry after Auschwitz and what we here announce as a postethical prohibition on generational theory and generational self-consciousness. The actuality of our positive existence, such as it is, lies in our present-day accounting for the fact of our "spiritual" nonexistence. We are a generation too late, not one that is on the make. We are the fiction, not the authors of our own world. We require the mind of a loser (as in Beck: "I'm a loser baby, so why don't you kill me"), which is the truth of our chosen predecessor's actuality. As Pensky remarks of Adorno's theory of the postmodern "constellation, the centerpiece of Adorno's historiography,"

> The constellation—the dialectic—is a construction out of losses, a lading list of all that is too late to save; critical subjectivity is one generated from loss, and learning from it (1997, 11).

What we must learn, of course, is not so much a positive, traditionally ethical lesson—a set of rules to follow, a code—but rather the truth of our own abandonment before the unprecedented monster of an evermore unitary, one-dimensional, comfortable, smooth, rational, democratic, unfree, postmodern nonexistence. This is the sociological *gestalt* that beckons us.

Yet, within this lies the postethics of the damaged life and the negative lesson of the Generation of the 60's, whose narcissism is as objective for their children as Vietnam was for their parents. The Generation of AIDS—not of Kennedy, but of the "Dead Kennedys"—must refuse easy assimilation into the quick fix culture of reckless self-destruction, lest they repeat the unrepressed failings of their naive oppressors. In this sense, then, the work implied in a good course or two in the sociological nature and historical development of mass society in the postmodern epoch is as necessary to surviving our surviving as is meditating on the pharmo-capitalism that pulses through our veins and the fictitious reality that is more real than the real, and that appears in the form of a TV viewer's guide in everybody's Sunday morning newspaper. The middle-aged doyens of postmodern theory sometimes forget that their own modernist educations are necessary to their postmodern revolts and their own mid-life crises and do an injustice to the young by depriving them of anything against which to revolt, save for their own hyper-self-conscious stories and airy cultural studies of this and that popular film. The need for empirical sociology remains; the young need to deconstruct it *for themselves.* [2]

In this context, it is only apparently incongruous that Orr would care a fig about sociology and whether her panic theory will be considered sociological, for it is necessary to do more than survive alone, the false hope of the cynic. Premised on a disappointment which it cannot admit even to itself, cynicism soon becomes a reactionary defense against anything new, including especially a desire to reestablish a link with a tradition. Deconstruction is not enough; it is necessary to also recover the past hopes of a tradition once moved by the promise of the future. That it turned out all wrong is no excuse for bitterness against this hope, even if it is adequate justification.

CONCLUSION

Essential to the project of "lifeworld-grounded critical theory" is the prefiguring of a qualitative alternative to the existing order of things in the very enactment of the theoretical project itself. This follows most directly from Marcuse's work. Yet, even Marcuse was defeated and resigned to hide his open longings for something different from the burnt earth tendencies dominant and hegemonic in his twilight years. It is strange, for example, to imagine as contemporaries Marcuse's fresh corpse and Margaret Thatcher's rise to power, in the same year as we, the authors, struggled our way through the coming-of-age gateway of middle school, ignorant of this passing and blurring of generations and such contradictory sensibilities. How can we, from this vantage point, prefigure anything when all that we know is loss?

Thankfully, the total society is perpetually destabilized by birth and by death, and by its false relationship to the natural world. This, even we, a nonexistent generation, can count upon, even when the total society's own internal contradictions seem perpetually and forever contained and depoliticized, and even when our most courageous predecessors shrink away and die behind the veil of art. It is the recognition of the falseness of the whole within us, then, that prefigures the immense will needed to recognize our own true needs, and in this primary project we are, despite ourselves, aided by the forgetting that is birth, the remembrance that is death, and the humility that is our earth-boundedness, and that, together, calls us to accept our abandoned state and to thoroughly reject our supposed fate. This said, then, it becomes our task and our promise to eschew the easy way out and to refuse to participate in our much-anticipated X-tinction. If we are the Generation of Swine, then let us come together before we die as the other white meat.

NOTES

1. For those who would wish to consult GEN X sources, or who would be interested in the sources that inform the present work, please consider the following as of special importance: Abrams and Lipsky (1994); Andrew Cohen (1993); Cohen (1994); Cohen and Krugman (1994); Coupland (1991); Giles (1994); Gross and Scott (1990); Howe and Strauss (1992, 1993); Karlen (1994); Kunen (1997); Liu (1994); Martin (1993); Nelson and Cowan (1994); Ratan (1993); Shapiro (1993); Shapiro et al. (1994); Joseph Star (1984); Star (1993); Strong (1994).

We would also acknowledge the students of the 1994 and 1995 University of Dayton Honors Social Science Seminars, whose 160-odd original "Slackers" project interviews were helpful background in the preparation of this chapter. The overriding "message" that was received from this project, however, was the students' own disdain for the "GEN X" genre itself, which we have, of course, taken into direct consideration in these pages.

2. One might profitably begin such a "course" by reading Stanford M. Lyman's *Postmodernism and a Sociology of the Absurd: And Other Essays on the "Nouvelle Vague" in American Social Science* (1997). Authored by a sociologist imminently grounded in the theory of mass society, this collection is an exceedingly erudite and substantive effort to critically mediate the tension between modern and postmodern social theory.

Chapter 5

Defensible Space, Communitarianism, and the Origins of Neighborhood Panopticonism in Dayton, Ohio

It is the dream of "defensible space," a place with secure and effectively guarded borders, a territory semantically transparent and semiotically legible, a site cleansed of risk, and particularly of the incalculable risks— which transforms merely "unfamiliar people" (those, under normal circumstances of the city stroll, obscure objects of desire) into downright enemies.
—Zygmunt Bauman, *Life in Fragments* (1995, 135)

In reflecting on the problem of the increasing social distance between the white middle classes and the Black poor, Oscar Newman, the renown theorist of "defensible space," argues for the federally ordered dispersion of the poor in the suburban residential landscape. He insists, however, that "bringing the poor and the black into the fold [sic] must be conducted 'on tightly controlled quota basis'" that is non-threatening to the middle class and ensures their continuing social dominance.
—Mike Davis, *City of Quartz* (1990, p. 261)

Oscar Newman, who coined the term "defensible space" as the answer to urban crime, may well now be one of the most influential of all thinkers about urban design in the United States.
—David Harvey, *Justice, Nature & the Geography of Difference* (1996, p. 408)

In our society there are few instances of shared beliefs or values among physical neighbors. Although this heterogeneity may be intellectually desir-

149

ble, it has crippled our ability to agree on the action required to maintain
the social framework* necessary to our continued survival.
—Oscar Newman, *Defensible Space* (1972, p. 1, emphasis added)

It wasn't until the very day before we sat down to draft this chapter, in the
spring of 1997, that we realized for the first time that we lived in a defacto
"defensible space" neighborhood. Prior to this realization, we had imagined ourselves only surrounded by defended spaces, that is, only adjacent
to the street closures and sundry artifacts of traffic control, theoretical territoriality, and the creation of enclosed mini-neighborhoods that constitute
one of America's most alluring postmodern planning responses to ubiquitous urban crime and, to believe Oscar Newman, the father of defensible
space architecture, to the disintegration of viable modern urban life *in toto*.
Indeed, the southern border of our northwest Dayton Mount Vernon neighborhood butted up against Five Oaks, America's most touted defensible
space experiment, lauded by Henry G. Cisneros, Clinton's first-term Secretary of Housing and Urban Development, widely discussed in the major
print and television media, and the subject of several scholarly studies,
including studies conducted by friends and colleagues at the University of
Dayton (see Donnelly 1988; Donnelly and Kimble 1997; Donnelly and
Majka 1996, 1998; Majka and Donnelly 1988; also see Cisneros 1995;
Newman 1996). Defensible space plans were also in effect in the neighborhood adjacent to the east and, to the west, residents of a private lane used
their own money to erect a barricade that would seal the end of their street,
making it a dead end to would-be cut-through travelers. In fact, all across
Dayton, from disaster area HUD housing complexes to gentrified historic
districts, not to mention Dayton's expansive and well-heeled suburbs,
defensible space is a significant feature of a city that Jon D. Hull, writing
for *Time* magazine, dubbed an American "microcosm" (1992).

In part, we had experienced the effects of these surrounding closures in
the rush-hour congestion on the nearby major thoroughfares, as commuters
avoided the now maze-like neighborhood streets of Five Oaks to our south
and Santa Clara to our east for the arteries called Main Street and Salem
Avenue. From such experiences, we knew that Dayton's defended spaces
were an unavoidable, difficult, and paradoxical presence that demanded
our critical theoretic attention. But we were nonetheless slow to appreciate
the inexorable movement of this concept and its institutionalization as the
latest thing that any neighborhood with commonsense would do. This
came to us, as we have said, only upon reading our neighborhood association newsletter of May 1997. Apparently, many of the remaining entrances

to our neighborhood were to be altered to slow traffic. Normal square intersections were to be converted to traffic circles for the same purpose. Temporary inconveniences, it assured, would be forthcoming, but, in the end—and this was only implied—our own Mount Vernon neighborhood would be closer to the contemporary ideal: adjusted, fortified, in a word, defensible.

In Part One of this chapter, we further describe the intricacies of Dayton's Five Oaks flagship defensible space experiment in order to provide the lifeworld-grounding that is the distinctive contribution of our reflections upon the ethics of postmodern living. We argue that neither celebration nor straightforward rejection are appropriate responses to this spatial development. Instead, a sober sociological accounting that draws its meta-framework from the venerable sociological imagination points to the thoroughly contradiction-ridden nature of late capitalist society. Any local "solution" that operates within this framework is necessarily caught-up in these contradictions. This is an unavoidable and inexorable problem that does not in itself vitiate the value or immediate rationality of the defensible space movement (and the larger growth industry called "crime prevention through environmental design," or CPTED). But our rendering does, at minimum, complicate any pious reading of the social, political, and cultural significance of America's experimentation with defensible space urban planning.

In Part Two, we turn our attention to the implications that the anticrime administration of the spatial lifeworld has for contemporary ethical life. As residents of a defensible space neighborhood ourselves, as "victims" of more than one breaking-and-entering experience, and as the new owners of black, intentionally uninviting, commercial-lock security doors, we do not offer, we hope, a sanctimonious point of view on the problem of urban crime and the defensible space response to urban crime. On sociological *qua* ethical grounds, however, our position is ultimately opposed to defensible space initiatives, for we never make recourse to the positivist theoretical paradigm of order that undergirds the discourse of "community disorder," but instead choose to historize, as must be the case with dialectical theory and practice. It is not only the unintended and perverse consequences of social action that worry us, although these are not negligible. Our concern is primarily with the totality, another name for the intersection of history and biography within social structure, and the not-too-faint repercussions that defensible space creates there. That the meaning of this perspective takes some explaining is the burden of this chapter.

PART I. DAYTON: A CITY OF NEIGHBORS

We began to hear about defensible space projects shortly before our move to Dayton from Flint, Michigan, Dandaneau's hometown, and, at that time, the focus of his research into the workings of General Motors-led deindustrialization (Dandaneau 1996). The year was 1992. As we would later fully appreciate, researchers at the University of Dayton, particularly the Sociology Department Chairperson and Five Oaks resident, Patrick G. Donnelly, had acted as a leading advocate of the defensible space project, and working together with his university, neighborhood, and city government colleagues, was essential in bringing the Five Oaks defensible space plan to fruition. Indeed, we visited Professor Donnelly's residence several times during our transition to Dayton. As we recall, we were encouraged to discuss our reactions to the mini-world that Five Oaks residents had labored with significant industry and resourcefulness to bring into existence. (With respect to Professor Donnelly's leadership in this effort, we must immediately note that few academics have acted so effectively as public intellectuals, at least in Edward Royce's formulation [1996], and used their knowledge and expertise to so forcefully address a social problem in their own community.) We asked (implicitly): Are the people here concerned about unintended consequences? Racism? Institutional racism? Who paid for this project? Can changing traffic patterns really affect crime rates? What of the structural basis of crime? So, folks here really support this? Does everyone? Do you think it will really work in the long run?

But it was not until 1995, when City of Flint Mayor, Woodrow Stanley, and with him 50-odd Flint residents, made the 250-mile bus trip south on Interstate 75 to view the Five Oaks plan for themselves and to ponder its promise for Flint that, for us, this defensible space chicken really came home to roost. We felt that we knew Flint fairly well, in part because we had ourselves felt the fear of random violence and petty criminality that so pervades that particular city. For example, one night in Flint, while Steve was lolling away the evening watching television in the basement of our rented house and Maude was two floors above writing at the computer, Steve was jolted out of his TV-induced coma by an explosion and the sound of shattering glass. Steve's immediate reaction was to bolt from the basement futon and dart upstairs in a commando body posture shouting for everyone to "get down, get down," for it was obvious to him that the living room window had just been blasted out in a drive-by shooting. What else could it be? This was a city of notorious economic decline and social corruption. We lived in a hardscrabble innercity neighborhood, a working-class, predominately white neighborhood, not far from the factories, strip bars, and drive-through beer stores. Steve's own brother and sister-in-law had been nearly mugged while walking over one night; his elderly parents, and nearly everyone he ever knew over a lifetime who could afford them, had security alarms and steel doors, and even these precautions had not prevented Grandma Pruder's picture window once from catching a beer bottle flung from a passing car. The advice had always been the same: keep your shades drawn at night and watch out for the kids, whose apparent innocence could be deceptive. Was it not true that everyone under 20 years old (as well as many above that age) was packing heat? *Anyone* can buy a gun. This was Flint.

It turned out, much to our embarrassment, that the culprit that night was a small bomb made only of fermenting orange juice in a gallon-size wine bottle, left under the basement stairs and forgotten on some garbage day long past. The home-made bomb was not the creative product of some senseless gang bangers or Michigan Militia types out for some let's-make-the-picture-window-go-away fun, but the unintended consequence of our own apathetic domestic hygiene. In any case, the chilling effect was telling. Our own reactions that evening demonstrated that in the not-to-distance recesses of our minds was an easily activated fear of senseless violent crime. Random violent criminality was thus taken-for-granted and the resulting fear always already present. Flint, and our neighborhood in particular, was experienced not so much as a war zone—war being too organized and predictable for what obtained there—but more as a place where crime operated with the same effect of terrorism, that is, with few discernable patterns and with a constant state of low intensity fear as its chief psychological result.

And so, Flint's Mayor, the popular Woody Stanley, was here in Dayton, wandering about the enclosed streets of Five Oaks, the neighborhood next door, in search of a new world for Flint that would be free of such fear. And he was not the only policy tourist to make the trek to Dayton. Officials from other cities, such as Aurora, Colorado, and Buffalo, New York, have also found their way to Dayton, in part encouraged, no doubt, by the golden imprimatur of the U.S. Department of Housing and Urban Development. Secretary Cisneros, for one, writing in his *Defensible Space: Deterring Crime and Building Community*, states:

The Five Oaks neighborhood of Dayton, Ohio, is probably the most impressive example of the creation of neighborhood defensible space (1995, p. 16).

This sentiment is echoed by Oscar Newman, who writes in *his* latest HUD publication, *Creating Defensible Space*:

The successful reorganization of the existing urban grid of streets to create mini-neighborhoods in the Five Oaks community in Dayton, Ohio, has created a trend that is now sweeping the country (1996, p. 5).

Perhaps it was the extraordinary national media attention lavished upon Five Oaks that made the trip seem worthwhile to Flint officials. From prominent stories in *The New York Times*, *Boston Globe Magazine*, *Newsweek*, *The Los Angeles Times*, *Christian Science Monitor*, *Denver Post*, *USA Today*, *The Economist*, and coverage on CNN, NBC's *Dateline*, and National Public Radio, Five Oaks has over these past several years had its fifteen minutes of fame and then some and, as a result, a secure place in the archives of hyperreality. Newman, who was paid to design the initial Five Oaks plan, helps to clarify the desirable spin:

There is a trend in the US to have gated communities, but the suburban kind, with a guard controlling access, is withdrawal action. In Dayton, the residents took back the local streets for themselves and the community (quoted in *The Christian Science Monitor* 1995).

Whether it is like bugs to a bug-zapper or pilgrims to the wailing wall, Newman designed gates and enclosures for Five Oaks, and the king, he is pleased, and the lords from far-flung dominion, they have come.

Pause for a moment. Barbara Trent, the documentary filmmaker, recently explained that she chooses film projects based in part on watching "what goes by her face" during television news broadcasts. For example, when President Bush announced the 1989 invasion of Panama as the means of choice to arrest the wayward Maximum Leader, Manuel Norriaga, Trent decided not to "let that one go by." The result is her Academy Award-winning *Panama Deception*, which documents both the covered-up tragedy that resulted from the nighttime invasion by 17,000 U.S. troops of an unsuspecting Panamanian nation as well as the venal, *Real Politick*, behind the invasion itself, which was to recover the Panama Canal and dominion over the Canal Zone by exploiting a clause in the Carter-era Treaty that provided a return of the Canal to U.S. control in the event that the Panamanians themselves could not defend and secure it. The destruction of the Panamanian Defense Forces (PDF) was thus *the* strategic objective of the Christmas-time blitzkrieg, and what better cover for a Pearl Harbor-style assault than the story of a long-distance Latin American drug bust?

While intrinsically important, Trents' experience is here retold as a useful prolegomena to any future lifeworld-grounded critical theory that imagines for itself a meaningful public audience, for, contrary to her own assessment, *Panama Deception* has had, in *this* country, no discernable political consequence. The former President and his Administration have not been in the least affected by its documentation of the facts nor by the film's subsequent exaltation as a superior work of investigative journalism. There have been no show trials much less even a hint of post-Presidential stigma-creep. Rather, the life-history of this film documents something even more important than the corrupt workings of American political, military, and media power in the case of the Panama invasion, and that is the prevailing "one-dimensionality" of contemporary late capitalist American society (Marcuse 1964). This society has proven itself capable of containing every form of critique thrown at it, reducing critique to one technical achievement among others, as in this case, to little more than exemplary documentary film. The "universe of political discourse" is as easily foreclosed at this emergent and increasingly preponderant level of hyperreality as it is at the level of the policy machinations of the welfare/warfare state, which was Marcuse's primary concern in 1964.

The eclipse of meaningful public life—which, to reverse the usual formulation, is now *less* real than television reality—means that lifeworld-grounded critical theory must proceed circumspect of media reportage and image-proliferation, paying much closer attention to the capillary workings of power in the trenches of specific locales. Counter-mythmakers— from Bill Moyer's loving portrait of Joseph Campbell to 60's radical Barbara Trent, from the sacrificial Anita Hill to the self-sacrificing Oliver Stone, the *auteur par excellance* of hyperreality—none of them are effective forces of counter-hegemony in a world where even the "gulf war did not take place," as Baudrillard (1995) rightly insists. Working from within the medium of mass deception, without an audience educated in the theoretical deconstruction of this deception, let alone with access to a political force *beyond* image-management, political critics are defeated long before they get started. This, in a postliterate society, is true also—or, should we say, even more true—for book writers. Still, perhaps there is value in one sort of message in the bottle over others, especially when staged without expectation of any public consequence. Perhaps we need not follow Baudrillard so far as to "forget Foucault," but instead realize that no one knows who Foucault is, academic Foucaultdians least of all.

Back to Dayton. Dayton's defended spaces and their mighty justifications are, as we have noted, in-our-face. Anecdotes pile up, one on top of the other. For example, thoroughly unprompted, a City of Dayton fire fighter/paramedic, who at the time was moonlighting as a life insurance company's home visitation nurse, reports to us of his and his comrades' distaste for the Five Oaks gates, which they find difficult to negotiate. This is the case even though precautions for emergency vehicles have been taken: the gates can be unlocked and, when necessary, removed, say, for snow-plowing equipment or in order to further experiment with traffic patterns. Speed bumps, too, make the squad's blaring horns and warning lights unnecessary at five miles per hour, says our volunteer informant. Of course, defensible space in Dayton also has a host of more established critics, including the alternative media, civil rights groups, grassroots opposition, and an odd political leader or two. Most of these, however, have receded before the sheer fact of the gates. The plan proponents once dubbed these critics "the opposition," much like JFK assassination investigators are labeled "buffs." Like people who, in political matters, cite information from "the internet," the opposition are in Dayton stigmatized and of little import in whatever goes for serious policy deliberations (even though we still hear from them occasionally, as during our door-to-door work for a fringe Dayton City Commission candidate, or when we hear the rumblings of JFK conspiracy theory as it works its way into sociology [see Simon and Henderson 1997], which has long been deaf to the workings of the postmodern state and its unsavory agencies and exigencies). The bottom line is: there is no meaningful, potentially transformative opposition to defensible space in Dayton. Opposition is stigmatized, fragmented, silenced, and stymied.

Perhaps the most telling of our personal anecdotes, however, comes from the immediate reactions we witness as myriad visitors to Dayton confront for the first time the Five Oaks gates. Indeed, we have never in six years of welcoming visitors to Dayton *not* had them express palpable disquiet and just as often alarm at the presence of the defensible space gates and associated traffic barriers (that is, speed bumps of various types, mini-traffic circles, cul-de-sacs, one-way traffic restrictions, such as one close-by intersection that divides the perpendicular street into opposite direction one-way streets).

Our studied explanations to our generally educated guests emphasize the plan's positive points: crime is a real problem, the immediacy of which is not to be easily brushed aside; Five Oaks' experience with crime was, to hear the tell of it, intimately tied to *traffic*, that is, car traffic that originated in Dayton's *suburbs* in search of access to the informal economies of prostitution and drugs existing in the Five Oaks area. Thus, the story goes: there was a white, middle-class suburban clientele bent on satisfying the desire for vice by preying anonymously upon the commonplace sins to be found in the dark cityscapes, who dropped easily into and out of the neighborhood via nearby interstate access ramps, and who deserved what they ultimately got. We then switch gears: the majority of the Five Oaks residents *wanted* the gates; they participated in well-attended informational forums held before ever a gate was erected; indeed, Five Oaks residents participated in the implementation process all along the way. Then, the final tact: the short-term results seem encouraging, for crime rates have in fact decreased in the neighborhood, and have not, as might have been expected, simply increased elsewhere. It seems an ironclad case.

But these representations do little to comfort our guests from out-of-town. Heads sway slowly back and forth as we pass side street after side street closed by the brick-anchored gates, as though our explanations were but local justifications for something terribly wrong with the big picture, as in, "so this is what we've come to," where "we" refers to all of us, an inclusive universal humanity. One sociologist colleague, when hearing of the plan over the phone, made a connection with Israeli policy in the Occupied Territories (we thought, too, of Apartheid South Africa, and everyone thinks of the gated suburban enclave and Davis' "City of Quartz," which Newman and every other decent, knowledgeable Five Oaks proponent are at pains to distinguish from that which Dayton has done to itself). But our friend was spared the full effect of her comparative sociology by arriving and leaving Dayton under the cloak of night, the "barricades" safely hidden in the shadows. Given, however, that "crime prevention through environmental design"—a practice as well as a concept that predate Newman but which are intimately associated with defensible space—has become part and parcel of the contemporary planner's and architect's mission and have been realized in constructions the world over, it is simply impossible to avoid or ignore this aspect of the postmodern built environment. Who, now, can avoid trespassing defended spaces?

The sum total of these experiences contribute to our trepidation vis-à-vis defensible space near and far, in communities "known" as well as those so mediated by modernity as to be immediately "unknowable" (see Marcus and Fischer 1986). Knowing Flint, for example, we made the educated guess that defensible space would not appreciably lessen Flint's disastrous crime; even less would it "build community." We naturally compared defensible space policy in Flint ("Buick City") to a policy once not long ago proposed by one of that city's millionaire car dealers, who, as an aspiring mayoral candidate, suggested a special force of crime fighting police in "50 new Buicks," that is, the sort of local initiative that has more to do with fear, ignorance, self-interest, and political expediency than with anything like dialectical reason. For the bottom line in Flint has everything to do with General Motors' roughly $2 billion annual payroll and its long-term and long-standing policy of disinvesting in that city, its hometown. Commonsense suggests that a community cannot build upon a foundation of joblessness and despair, which, just ask anyone, make an excellent foundation for decay, crime, and violence. Was this any less true of Dayton, which, among other things, is itself a General Motors town?

Furthermore, the mostly positive media attention that Five Oaks has received means nothing, except perhaps the exciting, if, on second thought, unwelcome transportation of "Five Oaks" into the netherworld of the infinitely reproducible surface image, from the maudlin tableau of a black child peering through the jail-like gates to the more rosy depictions of black and white children, smiling and bound together, safely at play on reclaimed streets. Even the commanding judgments of Washington, DC policymakers, city officials, and resident scholars must be bracketed and treated with skepticism, for a series of particular interests and local perspectives inexorably guide them, as they guide us.

Even setting such interests aside, the attempts to establish the scientific objectivity of the reduction in crime or an increase in community cohesion postdefensible space cannot, we think, be borne out without, at minimum, (a) a method for controlling for the national trend in declining crime rates that is coincidental with the implementation of the Five Oaks plan; (b) sufficient longitudinal data necessary to distinguish between, on the one hand, the short-term effects of what could be a temporary neighborhood mobilization leading to a short-term "community stabilization," and, on the other hand, the sought after long-term consequences of the closures themselves; and (c) sufficient longitudinal and comparative data necessary to discern the relative importance of defensible space vis-à-vis the crime-producing effects of larger community- and society-wide structural changes, such as with respect to the loss of automobile manufacturing and military-industrial base jobs from Dayton's two primary high-wage employment sectors, or respect to the local and particular qualities of the specific types of crime and the demographic specifics of the Dayton neighborhood in question. We might also want textured qualitative data that speaks to the perspective of the actors themselves, to decide what meaning the phenomena of the enclosures has for those who pass by and live within them.

Much to their credit, Dayton's local defensible space researchers stress not only the tentative nature of their otherwise encouraging short-term empirical findings, but they also cast doubt on the potential applicability of the Five Oaks defensible space strategy for other neighborhoods and communities, underscoring, for example, the many "unique features of this plan and this neighborhood which may not be present in other neighborhoods experiencing crime problems" (Donnelly and Kimble 1997, p. 18), as well as the need for attention to the relevant "broader social forces that are not and cannot easily be addressed by local community groups" (Donnelly and Majka 1996, p. 27). But, in the end, neighborhood property values are up and crime is down, and in the scales of local rationality, the balance is thereby tipped against the would-be critic.

But let us suppose that the Five Oaks defensible space anticrime/community-building initiative were to be shown effective in an instrumental sense by means of social science and that the local meaning of the gates was found innocuous. We argue that there would still be room for critical analysis at a more expansive historical/spatial, political/ethical plane, for here we confront a new set of measures and a new set of imbalances. After all, Bentham's idea for a panopticon worked well enough in practice. One need only visit a state-of-the-art penitentiary or *either* local shopping mall, that is, following GEN X comedian, Chris Rock, the mall that white people go to or the mall that white people *used* to go to. In other words, instrumental reason cannot address Foucault's point about panopticonism, for his larger point hinges upon a "working" panopticon and is a critique of the instrumental reason that produces it. Instrumental reason cannot even get Rock's joke, for it knows only a humorless, abstract world disconnected from multiperspectival, situated critical reflection.

This is the intersection that interests us in this reading, the painful spot at which the needs of the isolated subject, the terrain of place and personal property, and the weight of logic and local rationality collide with what Mills, in the last few, and it seems, mostly unread, chapters of his *The Sociological Imagination*, called the "historical level of reality." At this plane, a series of world-historical questions draw our attention to political economy, race, the space of the unknowable, and, at some distant, far-flung point, the dialectic of enlightenment. We are also, therein, returned to our experience and our immediate reactions, to the level of the gut, and to a reconsideration of what goes for commonsense. Like the potential student of medicine who, in Horkheimer and Adorno's telling, and against all apparent "logic and rationality," would rather be a writer than a credentialed medical practitioner, if for no other reason than "to explain more clearly [to him or herself] ... the terrible state in which everyone lives today," we hold that "contradiction is necessary," and that, when confronting crime and defensible space urban design, *this* is the only way to "remain within the bounds of common sense" (1947, pp. 237-240).

PART II. FIVE OAKS AS STRATEGIC HAMLET

Andreas Huyssen concludes his now classic essay "Mapping the Post-Modern" with a statement reminiscent of C. Wright Mills' general perspective on the contradictory demands plaguing the public spirited intellectual living and dying at the end of modernity. Huyssen writes:

> No matter how troubling it may be, the landscape of the postmodern surrounds us. It simultaneously delimits and opens our horizons. It's our problem and our hope ([1984]1990, p. 271).

Here, Huyssen evokes the sense of being surrounded, even threatened, on all sides by the strangeness of the postmodern and the real abstractions— World Capitalist System, Mass Society, The Culture Industry, The Social—which grip the mind. At the same time, he calls forth hope, pointing to an opening on the horizon. Mills, in his characteristically macho style, expresses a similar sentiment in the closing remarks of his programmatic "Letter to the New Left":

> Let the old men ask sourly, "Out of Apathy—into what?" The Age of Complacency is ending. Let the old women complain wisely about "the end of ideology." We are beginning to move again (1960, p. 347).

If, as we are suggesting, Mills' sense of being both "trapped" and "on the move again" is still salient for intellectuals today, then perhaps Mills' cognitive map, his sociological imagination, can help us to make sense of The Five Oaks Defensible Space Plan. Mills' analytical triad of history, biography, and social structure, once it is inflected through a postmacho culture and driven up against the wall of the apparently mundane developments of everyday life in a midwestern American city, might well prove useful for drawing out the significance of one instance of a populist and not-at-all avant-garde desire to defy death through the conscious institutionalization of what is presented as community but may well in fact instead constitute a field of perpetual surveillance. We thus treat Five Oaks as a force-field where biography intersects with social structure to further the historical trajectory of a carceral society. Specifically, the cynical instrumental logic of public administration and social engineering entwines with the panicked embodied logic of frail individuals faced with real threats and real gun-down-your-throat criminality to render unassailable the conclusion that there must be gates, barricades, spaces protected, and free movements managed. The stranger, *ante portas* as Bauman puts it, must be checked.

One thinks first of Hobbes, then of Weber and Foucault, and finally of Baudrillard, for where else but in a virtual prison will we, the upstanding, right living inhabitants of declining urban centers, find personal security, mitigate our salvation anxiety, and bring to order the institutional systems that we, the self-conscious builders of the iron cage, have brought into existence, and that still, even as it lies in ruins at our feet, escapes our ability to control. But the dialectical imagination that is the sociological imagination demands that more than this be said. As Hauke Brunkhorst has so eloquently stated, Adorno never imagined that the "ethic of damaged life" proscribed "the possibility of right *action* ..." (1996, p. 319, emphasis in original). Instead, Brunkhorst writes, in direct reference to a line from *Minima Moralia* that reads, "there is no true life in a false one":

> [T]he thesis confirms only that there is no *entirely* true life in a false life. But thus it is still a long way from the claim, as Nietzsche suggested, that everything is allowed. Every individual act can still be judged as to its rightness or wrongness. Moreover, the actions and characteristic traits of modern man and the various aspects and all individual moments of his lifeworld are assessable to moral evaluation. *Minima Moralia* is nothing other than a collection of such judgements as, for example, that it is an outrage when one says "I" (p. 319).

"Moreover," continues Brunkhorst:

> Adorno's thesis only confirms that *no true life* would be possible in the case of a completely false life. But this does not mean that a *non-forfeited* life cannot be imagined (p. 319).

And, a moment later:

> *Minima Moralia* are "reflections from damaged life," as the subtitle con-
> firms, and the damaged life is *not yet* the completely false life (p. 319).

With respect to the case of Five Oaks, the apparent fixation of the historically specific panicked body within social structure must be further discussed, or, to use the root meaning of the word discuss, it must be "struck
apart." In other words, reification must be engaged so as to unlock the
yearning for a pacified existence that is submerged and refracted in the
Five Oaks defensible space initiative. Such an engagement can potentially—and only potentially—uncover the moral impulse that both moti-
vates and legitimates such programs but which are distorted out of
recognition by the objective context of their implementation. This hope,
however elusive or esoteric, constitutes the best hope for doing right in a
world that is wrong. Such a theoretical effort can perhaps enable the originating moral impulses that, in the attempt to live rightly, manages to only
further the damage that objectively obtains.

In what follows, we seek to articulate the tension inherent in the Five
Oaks plan in order to show that it is not a simple replication of Davis' *City
of Quartz*, in spite of its intimate relation with Newman's manic, zealous
march to the sea. Our dialectic demands confrontation with contradiction
within the not-yet entirely false totality. We thus begin with an analysis of
the urban middle class as a strategic bulwark for a crisis-prone late capitalism, and its significance for a dialectical understanding of Five Oaks'
defensible space initiative.

To be sure, neither the White House nor the president who lives there are
immune to assault. Like the typical Five Oaks residence, the White House
and its occupants are vulnerable. It thus should not come as a surprise that
the emergence of defensible space neighborhoods in Dayton, Ohio, has
received the full support of the Clinton administration. Indeed, Oscar Newman is the darling of an embattled HUD and manifests more concretely
than Amaiti Etzioni and his amorphous communitarianism the *sin qua non*
of the Clinton-led "New" Democratic Party, for Newman appears as the
logical outcome of the crisis of the liberal welfare state.

In recent years, the real and symbolic residence of the American Head of
State has been sprayed with machine gun fire and assaulted by the Kami-
kaze flight of a single-engine aircraft pilot. The proximity of the front
porch of the White House to Pennsylvania Avenue means also that any suicidal bomber in a Rider rental truck could potentially obliterate that

alabaster structure, leaving it and its inhabitants, including the president's family, devastated. Calls to reopen the Avenue for symbolic reasons—to reflect an open, democratic, fearless society—echo an undercurrent of disquiet in the face of the vastly expanding security apparatus surrounding the President and other political leaders, an apparatus that developed only in the wake of the Kennedy assassinations and other acts of violence against the nation's political elite, and as a more recent response to the enhanced danger that terrorism poses to the life and security of all Americans. But a hard-boiled calculus that weighs symbolism against reality and finds the latter wanting demands a phalanx of secret service protection and, now, the enclosure of Pennsylvania Avenue.

This type of calculated, instrumental realism undergirds most of what goes for national policy in the 1990s. Like the threat of terrorism, the 1980's budget deficits and the resulting Reagan Era national debt, the need of international capital for expanding markets and increasing profit margins, the ongoing reality of a reactionary American racism fueled by the rejection of the essence of the civil rights movement, and so forth, form for the New Democrats the hard barriers within which political choice must operate. Such realism demands that so-called Reagan Democrats be brought back into the electoral fold via, in part, the imprisonment of a sizable chuck of the African-American population and the enactment of punitive welfare reform. NAFTA must be enacted over the vehement opposition of organized labor, and federal, state, and local government spending must be curbed so as to bring the upward flow of income and wealth back into line with the polarizing tendency of liberal capitalism. To win an effective governing constituency for this inegalitarian policy agenda and with it, at least, the appearance of legitimacy for the retreat from the now-dead New Deal compromise, Clintonism embraces the rhetoric of the "New Covenant," the "Vital Center," and the moral goodness of "Americorp" volunteerism, at the same time that it smoothes the way for the balkanization and further stratification of everyday life. As seen from the point of view of America's "truly disadvantaged," Clintonism is California Blue Sky Reaganism with a Southern Baptist face and a heartfelt tear welling up in the eye.

The forced devolution of federal responsibilities for maintaining the so-called safety net to catch those who are ground-up by the vicissitudes of the market, including affordable public housing and public-sponsorship of "urban development," means that new solutions to the old problems of the urban underclass and working poor, and, most urgently, to the problem of urban street crime, must come more and more from the policy goodie bag of the political right-wing. While American progressives like William Julius Wilson (1996) continue to advocate to deaf ears a return to aggressive New Deal-style national policy, including a return to WPA-types of public employment initiatives, the only real game in town appears to be the more or less easy acceptance of a resurrected pre-New Deal "liberal" capitalist agenda, buttressed by racist and class-based ideology. Even former House Speaker and the epitome of old-style Democrat Party politics, Thomas "Tip" O'Neill, lent his considerable weight to the ideological notion that "all politics is local," thereby pointing to the collapse of the modernization and moderating tendencies of organized capitalism that has run through American politics since FDR and through the first-term Nixon administration, but that came to an end with the rise to power in 1981 of Ronald Wilson Reagan. In this new era, even the nation's leading Hispanic politician, former HUD Secretary Cisneros, jumped on the bandwagon, as are a good many other former liberals. We imagine that Cisneros backed "defensible space" initiatives with the zeal of a political leader without options or envisioned alternatives; in other words, he simply signed-off on them. What else could he do?

Of course, this broad context of the structural dimensions of the long-analyzed and long-coming "crisis of the welfare state" are little and rarely acknowledged influences on the coming of defensible space to Dayton, Ohio (see Offe 1984). The understanding of capitalism as a contradictory, exploitative, and life-damaging economic system—which underlies the theoretical analysis of a tenuous, unstable "welfare state compromise"—is antithetical, not only to the prevailing wisdom of nineteeth-century market theory and its related liberal social doctrines of individualism, but also to the ideology of "community," relentlessly propounded as a type of secular salvation strategy.[2] In Dayton, the post-Civil Rights Era (and more to the point, post-urban riot era) accommodations to public participation in policy making have been adroitly used to legitimize the appearance of a democratic, bottom-up decision-making process, something especially easy for policymakers from on-high to embrace and promote. The people, via their ubiquitous neighborhood associations and, in Dayton, via their "priority boards" (funded with federal Community Development Block Grant monies), have "bought into" the idea of their effective democratic participation in local politics, and so participated in their own social engineering. This participation provides all the legitimacy needed for most politicians,

·including the President, Secretary Cisneros, and many lesser representatives of the people.

It is doubtful that the emergence in Dayton's Five Oaks neighborhood of a grassroots response to the perils of today's civil society represents anything like the "solidarity" that Habermas and others point to as the much-needed corrective, regulating force vis-à-vis the integrated, although contradictory, semi-autonomous systems logics of market and state at the twilight of advanced capitalist society (Habermas [1981]1984, [1981]1987). It is doubtful, in other words, that a neighborhood-level upsurge of participation in public policymaking represents a rebirth of democracy that would tame the one-sided rationalization of civil society by market forces and state domination, much less heal the wounds inflicted by this "colonization of the lifeworld," that is, in Habermas' astute if albeit simply classical sociological view, the pathologies of personality disorder, alienation, and anomie, and at a more obtuse level, the clipped project of modernity itself (Habermas [1973]1975; see also Dandaneau 1998). While defensible space initiatives certainly mesh nicely with Clinton's thinly veiled neoconservatism, it would appear that something more corrosive also characterizes them. To his credit, Habermas calls the likes of Clinton "the legitimates," "the real conservatives" of our time (1986, p. 10). But the specifics of their concrete time/space enactment brings to mind the perspective more of Foucault and Habermas' Frankfurt School predecessors than his own support for communicative ethics and the legitimacy of new social movements. The simple participation of a neighborhood association in the making of the carceral society seems enough, at least in the short-run, to vitiate Habermas' otherwise intelligent hypotheses concerning motivation and legitimation crisis. How can this be?

The United States is not the continent of Europe and Dayton, Ohio, is not Paris, France. There is much truth, it would appear, in the thesis of American Exceptionalism, for on this side of the Atlantic, the crisis of the welfare state has not been met with massive national strikes and the election of a Socialist/Communist/Green governing coalition, as it has been, for example, in France, nor, as even a positivist sociology would have to predict, will it. The reasons for this are well-known: despite its recent revival, America lacks a labor movement of consequence (Clinton has shown this); racism is as divisive a force as ever, mitigating industrious and heartfelt attempts to create a class-based "Rainbow Coalition" (Clinton has shown this); the putative party of the people, the Democratic Party, is, as we have noted, bereft of ideas and exhausted by the prospect of a return to populism (Clinton has shown this), while fringe parties, for their part, face ideological barriers at least as daunting as the institutionalized electoral barriers are to popular democracy, which includes, among other things, the overwhelming effective disenfranchisement of the electorate and the related overwhelming control of political power by the American Plutocracy and their paid representatives (the marginalized efforts of the Greens, New Party, Labor Party, and various populist independents, including even Texas billionaire, H. Ross Perot, have shown this). These factors and experiences as well as others are evident to even the most casual observer of American politics, such that it is increasingly tiresome to rehearse the obvious.

Back in Dayton, a bevy of private schools, including two located in Five Oaks, along with proposed "charter" schools, compete with a withering public school system; the possibility of a minor league baseball franchise and a gussied up river front are the latest plans to resurrect the city center and are receiving considerable support, even from the suburbs; a massive "Job Center," the main replacement for the safety net, is now operating out of a refurbished warehouse, open to the job-seeking public and blessed with the support or at least the begrudging participation of nearly everyone in positions of authority and influence, including, in some respects, even ourselves; General Motors is threatening to close two of its eight local factories, the very same plants whose UAW local representation brought GM's North American operations to a two-week standstill in 1996; and the assessment of Five Oaks defensible space plan continues as new areas of the city marked for traffic re-routing receive, when the funds become available, their cement traffic circle barriers, while low shrubs are planted at public housing complexes to enhance the resident's feeling of ownership over spaces they do not, as a matter of fact, own.

It is within this general context that the relationship between the rationalization of public and private spaces, institutional social power, and the advent of the postmodern can be seen to be more than the simple production of artistic, theoretical imaginations. Rather, there has always been a fluid dialectic between postmodern concepts and the condition of postmodernity—between, for example, the perspectival pastiche resulting from Lyotard's (1984) "incredulity toward meta-narratives" and the basic changes on the ground that race ahead of theoretical conceptualizations as often as they recycle as affordable it-sort-of-resembles-the-Pompedieu-Centre simulacrum Kitsch. Theorists of all sorts live in the quotidian world, just like everyone else, and the spatial structure of daily life—the real, material expressions of societal contradictions chiseled into the built environment— have as a flipside the tortured agency of its architectural and planning overseers as well as the bad faith of their would-be free-floating theoretician critics.

In the present analysis, the historical genealogy and structural archeology of Dayton's progress toward the defensible space ideal have a remarkable, coincidental entwining. Architectural theory and practice is typically regarded as the historic origin of postmodernism self-consciously manifest. Indeed, it has been famously observed by Charles Jencks that the public expression of the postmodern epoch can be dated precisely at July 15, 1972, at 3:32 p.m., the moment in St. Louis, Missouri ("The Show Me State") that the Le Corbusier-style Pruitt-Igoe federal housing complex was demolished and renamed as a symbol of the utter failure of modernism as social structure ("the machine for living"). While, for some, mainly those at the top of the aesthetic hierarchy, the implosion of this particular brick-and-mortar monument was tantamount to a liberatory unshackling of the theoretical imagination, for others, particularly the stewards of late capitalism and those otherwise mindful of the unrest whelming-up at the bottom of the brutal, dog-eat-dog social order, the failure of Pruitt-Igoe signaled an era in need of rearguard defensive strategies, including anything that would work, even the melding of premodern and hypermodern, or even some airy new postmodern aesthetic, anything, that is, to stabilize and pacify the agitated, abused urban masses.

With respect to the former, we have in mind the great postmodern architects, planners, and their theoretical exponents, who would transform cityscapes and public life with their use of color, antiutilitarian materials and design, historical quotation, and a heavy dose of sheer *jouissance*. With respect to the latter, we have in mind a young professor at St. Louis' Washington University, whose firsthand observation of the fall of Pruitt-Igoe modernism led him down a decidedly serious, not at all playful, path. We speak here of Oscar Newman, the planner, architect, and defensible space visionary.

In a nutshell, Newman's defensible space architecture aims to resurrect integrated urban community from the disenchanted, rusted cage ruins symbolized by Pruitt-Igoe's one-sided, top-down rationalization of public housing domesticity, but not with postmodern aesthetic flourish or anything resembling postmodern theoretical acumen (one thinks of Frank Gerhy's cynical complexity). And if Weber's world is the problem, Durkheim suggests the solution. Newman's main concern has always been and remains the most pressing, in-your-face result of modernist anti-

gemienschaft: urban street crime. Where there is community, sociology has found since time immemorial, there is a powerful, informal containment of this sort of crime. Where there is crime, there is not only a lack of community (social "disorganization"), there is a profound threat to civilized human life itself (anomie, a concept Newman shies away from, perhaps to remain accessible to various state bureaucrats and neighborhood opinion leaders). While Newman appeals (ironically, as we will suggest) to the intellectual legacy of Jane Jacobs' seminal *The Death and Life of the American City* (1961), it is the death and life of real American victims of urban crime that is his vision's major selling point, politically speaking and otherwise.

Part of Newman's amazing and apparently growing success is in part explained by the fact that his antidote for the pathologies of the lonely crowd blends so seamlessly with Clinton-era communitarianism. Newman addresses the genuine, all-too-human fear of crime via the gaze of the all-seeing urban planner *cum* savior from on high: someone who can be hired as a consultant, a fixer, in other words, but one who promises much more than downturns in crime statistics, for Newman also promises a return to community. Here, in offering an alternative, Newman departs from the Weberian tradition, and most of what makes social theory, in its own way, a dismal science. As a telling refraction of Bentham's zeal for utopian public policy, Newman's is a prophetic vision of a self-imposed and democratically-selected panopoticon solution to the most pressing sort of social problem, a solution which, furthermore, does not entail alteration of the basic institutional order or macro-level societal power relationships. For in Newman's inspired divining, community is the coordination of self-interest: mutual surveillance and neighborhood *cosa nostra* are viewed as an everyday protection racket. The domicile—HUD apartment or freestanding house—is a turret in a postmodern neighborhood castle; mini-neighborhoods and other erected alignments of class interest are *capo regimes* in a larger family of neighborhoods and sectors of integrated interests; "territoriality," Newman's ingenious operationalization of community, is a theoretical and emotive touchstone with personal security the basis for any hierarchy of human needs as well as the basic *raison d'être* of the legitimation-seeking state. Newman promises a new totality, a new order, "a means for restructuring the residential environments of our cities so they can again become liveable and controlled, controlled not by police but by a community of people sharing a common terrain" (1972, p. 2).

The appeal of Newman's work is that it evokes a sense of crisis both within the lifeworld and at the more abstract level of the social order. Newman emphasizes that a prevailing sense of personal insecurity undermines the state's legitimacy. That is to say, street-level criminality undermines the world of the upstanding, law-abiding, non-drug using, non-body selling/buying, property- and space-respecting, struggling middle-class average Joe and Jane American urban resident, who, it would seem, just want what they feel entitled to under the 90's communitarian social contract: simple middle class peace of mind, a space to call their own, and stable property values. Any threat to this class is a threat to the prevailing order of things because it destabilizes the buffering, legitimizing fact of the upwardly mobile middle class. Such as threat to middle class existence therefore requires fine-tuning the system, not so much for *their* particular strategic benefit, of course, as for the benefit of order itself. Given the perpetual need for the reproduction of systemic state domination and class hierarchy, Newman's message is loud and clear. Viewed this way, the apparent immediacy of the Five Oaks problem is sociologically mediated and thereby politically and ethically complicated.

For his own part, Newman presents in a decidedly pragmatic spirit this intersection, on the one hand, of the immediate interests of the urban middle class in creating a secure inner-sanctum within the general state of urban decay, and, on the other, the interests of the state in preserving the loyalty of the same middle class essential to its legitimacy. Not only does Newman explicitly distinguish his positions from his 1920's laizze-faire predecessors, he also avoids the bleeding heart sentimentality and flabby idealism typical of arguments favoring increased government involvement in the details of urban existence. This is evident, for example, in Newman's 1972 discussion of "Image and Milieu," which focuses on the capacity of spatial design to manipulate individual perceptions as well as the very fabric of social relations.

Newman first waxes apparently compassionate and egalitarian in his self-conception as middle class intellectual benefactor of the poor and needy:

> While we have come a long way from our laissez-faire attitudes of the 1920's in developing a more enlightened approach toward less able members of our society, we are still apparently incapable of providing housing for them which looks better than the worst we provide for ourselves (1972, p. 105).

But Newman then returns us to Pruitt-Igoe, his base-camp, where a representative sample of "the less capable members of our society" once resided, and there, to Lee Rainwater's 1966 analysis of Pruitt-Igoe's failed surface appearance, where Rainwater is quoted in his observation that:

> ... the consequences for conceptions of the moral order of one's self and of others, are very great. Although lower class people may not adhere in action to many middle class values about neatness, cleanliness, order and proper decorum, it is apparent that they are often aware of their deviance, wishing that their world could be a nicer place, physically and socially. The presence of non-human threats conveys in devastating terms a sense that they live in an immoral and uncontrolled world. The physical evidence of trash, poor plumbing and the stink that goes with it, rats and other vermin, deepens their feelings of being moral outcasts. Their physical world is telling them that they are inferior and bad just as effectively perhaps as do their human interactions (quoted in Newman 1972, p. 108).

Newman is, however, quick to eradicate even the hint of liberal idealism suggested by Rainwater's barely concealed contempt (for "the stink" of the "immoral and uncontrolled world") and his guilty anguish ("their ... world is telling them that they are inferior and bad"). Speaking for himself, Newman immediately reassures his readers (who, it would seem, he assumed to be his sought-after and, it turned out, soon ingratiating state-sponsors), that:

> *We* are not advocating aesthetic treatment of halls and apartments for the sake of beautification alone .... In our discussion, aesthetic considerations assume importance for the ways in which they can contribute to the definition and subdivision of the environment as well, [sic] as to the psychological state of the inhabitants (1972, p. 108, emphasis added).

For Newman, the aesthetic dimension of his plans are plainly secondary to the main goal: control through manipulation of "the environment" and the "psychological state of the inhabitants," as though what were at issue were a better maze for the poor rats, who have been in the past given very poorly designed mazes indeed, causing them to eat themselves in quantities unacceptable, indeed, pathological, to the smooth functioning of the totality.

Let us for a moment dwell on the meaning of "Strategic Hamlet" as applied to Five Oaks. Newman's evolving theoretical baggage is not, it turns out, limited to welfare state social engineering. The crisis that he sees afflicting our system is instead sunk deeper than merely in his fear of an unenlightened late capitalist society; an America still stuck in the ideology of nineteenth-century Social Darwinism, laissez-faire nonintervention, and brutal racism; a system proscribed from engineering itself, with the help of regression analysis and statistical assessments, for rational outcomes. This still-deeper level of analysis is suggested by our use of the term "hamlet" but is viewed most directly in Newman's specific theories of "Animal Territory," "Human Territoriality: The Social Contract," and "Collective Security" (1973, pp. 13-17).

Consider Newman's take on the connection between modernity and the encompassing natural order of things:

> In modern society, group identity has been detached from its moorings in shared, community-oriented space. With this transformation of the group, the concept of "strangers" and "familiars," so long an active shaping force in animal evolution, has been given over to social utopian conceptions of man: that to define someone as a stranger dehumanizes the opponent and is the source of racism, social strife and war. This humanistic philosophy would have it that all strangers be treated amiably as members of the "family of man" (1973, pp. 13-14).

Contrary to the modernist cosmopolitan attitude—of the *flaneur*, perhaps—Newman advocates a return to the ways of animals. For even though we are "resigned, perhaps doomed, to live a deterritorialized existence in contemporary cities," we need not treat all others "amiably" or as "familiars" (1973, p. 14). Instead, like individual animals protecting their territories amid innumerable, closely cohabituating, sometimes competing, and even threatening predator species, we might learn from animals how to "share habitats," despite the fact that *what* we learn "may be blind to reason" (1973, p. 15).

What compels our retreat to the animal world is nothing other than the frailty of our perhaps-too-optimistic "social contract," where "The State gives to the individual or group a wide range of options and means of recourse if his person, his property or even his ideas are violated" (1973, p. 15). But, Newman further explains, "as we are beginning to recognize, it is harder and harder to feel secure about the effectiveness of these non-biological, legal supports" (1973, 15). Newman concludes from this that the state cannot effectively or at least sufficiently secure the lifeworld of mass society; it cannot, in other words, make good on its promise of (a) civil society. He writes:

172 / *A Wrong Life*

This breakdown of confidence in law unearths a latent danger for society, especially provoked by crimes of violence committed by strangers. These crimes come perilously close to reevoking a biological instinct to survive. They threaten the ability of the individual victim to sustain his faith in an abstract system of justice; they tend to precipitate a widespread loss of faith in the capacity of the system to provide people with a sense of justice in their day to day lives (1973, pp. 15-16).

The breakdown in civil society, as measured by the real and perceived inability of the state to secure individual rights, brings us "perilously close" to the suppressed state of nature, which, if fully "re-evoked," would entail an unmediated, animal-like, struggle for "survival."

Newman then explains that "the last frontier on this urban battlefield may be the apartment door." Newman warns, ominously, at least from the point of view of the state:

Should this barrier become subject to ready violation, there may be, as a result, less willingness to surrender the individual power of self-defense to the corporate wisdom of society, to the police and the courts (1973, 1p. 6).

From this imagery, Newman concludes:

The human social contract is, then, gravely threatened by the inability of cities to insure basic freedom from anxiety and insecurity for its citizens (1973, p. 16).

Lest modernity (i.e., urban life) fall prey to the evil of naive cosmopolitanism in a mass society, Newman proposes the reordering of undifferentiated spaces so to enhance "collective security" by means of well-defined "spheres of influence," or home territories modelled on the "penumbra of safety" characteristic of animal dwellings. This zone, in Newman's rendering, is defined by an instinctual prohibition against hunting, which Newman presumes as an evolutionary "mechanism for preventing animals from instinctively attacking their own young in the midst of a hunting foray" (1973, p. 16). For while "we have come to believe that man is free of his biological heritage," it is "time to recognize the positive function of [our instinctual, animal] legacy as a means of reducing conflict and enhancing identity and security" (1973, p. 16). "Perhaps," Newman wonders aloud, "these and other lessons of animal societies state a biologically defined minimum relationship to habitat which has to be understood, addressed, compensated for, or overcome by planners of modern cities" (1973, pp. 16-17).

At issue in Newman's analysis is a posited intersection of a biologically rooted human nature and the interest of the state. This intersection legitimates for Newman the manipulation of the immediate built environment of the urban resident as well as a further extension of state power in the interests of containing the "other" within. It is precisely because biologically determined human nature sets a limit on how much cosmopolitan modernism humans can stand that, in Newman's vision, the state is compelled out of a concern for its own stability to recognize the practical efficacy of creating mini-communities of "familiars."

The implementation of Newman's theory of defensible space directly signifies the collapse of modernity as the enlightened attempt to live perilously among strangers, without dependable security or any guarantees and barriers to protect us. Newman's theory is thus truly post-*modern*, seeking to evade the all-too-human demands of negotiating the unavoidable tensions of urban life and taking refuge in a posited primordial survival instinct that is, by definition, immune to Reason. As such, the theoretical alternative proposed by Newman, and in part enacted in our lifeworld, just a few blocks down the way from where we live, is at least as threatening to *our* vision of the good life as is the street-level criminal, who, more often than not and when all is said and done, only wants our property. In contrast, defensible space signifies in institutionalized and mundane form the emergence of the repressed undercurrent of modernity which would have its extreme manifestation—were civil society actually to collapse, were the moral capacity of the trapped and threatened individual totally overcome—in fascism. Five Oaks is not fascism, but neither is it freedom. It is, then, strategic hamlet: Five Oaks as a local bulwark against a fear that carries us, because we cannot help ourselves, closer to the most frightful of world-historical eventualities.

But is it not a stretch to draw a connection—to make a fantastic allusion, really—between the fear of a lurking, jungle-entrenched, "gook," Communist Vietnam, fortified in the infamous sweep-and-clear anti-language of that police action, by well-placed "strategic hamlets," and a simple neighborhood "stabilization plan" in Dayton, Ohio, whose Other is merely the usual assortment of gun-totting drug dealers, cut-through traffic, low(er)-class renters, and prostitutes with their circling caravan of johns? We suppose Vietnam would be a fantastic allusion were it not that Davis has already, years ago, proposed it (see Davis 1990, pp. 267-271, subtitled

"Vietnam Here") and was generally well received in doing so (see also Davis [1992, 1994] for his even more alarming discussion of a post-Chicago School "ecology of fear").

Several years before the collapse of modernism in the implosion of Pruitt-Igoe, Irving Howe addressed the issue of the emergence of a postmodern literature grounded in the mass consumer society, which he perceived as taking hold in the postwar years. For Howe, mass society resulted in the fact that:

> our society no longer lent itself to assured definition, one could no longer assume as quickly as in the recent past [e.g., the 1930s] that a spiritual or moral difficulty could find a precise embodiment in a social conflict (1970, 198).

Illustrating this problem, Howe invites the reader to imagine an improvement on Dostoevski's *Crime and Punishment*. In Howe's improved version, just as Raskolnikov is resolving to murder the pawnbroker, "a miserly hunchback whose disappearance from the earth would cause no one any grief" (1970, p. 190), Raskolnikov receives a letter notifying him that he has won a Guggenheim fellowship "for the study of color imagery in Pushkin's poetry and its relation to the myths of the ancient Muscovites" (p. 190). In this way saved from the bitterness of his situation:

> Raskolnikov sinks to his knees and bows his head in gratitude. The terrible deed he had contemplated can now be forgotten; he need no longer put his theories to the test; the way ahead, he tells himself, is clear (p. 191).

At issue in Howe's reading are differences in the objective context that directly affect the necessity of an ethical consciousness. For the postmodern subject, an ethical consciousness is irrelevant, almost comical. Howe, then, understands the condition of postmodernity in terms of a redundancy of individual attempts to justify their actions, given that such actions occur in a context that make it simply unnecessary to do much wrong. The challenges of ethics as an individual problem, itself, would appear to have been overcome, or at least displaced.

And yet, while it is true that individuals, as such, are rarely given the opportunity to act with consequence and thus have no need for a well-developed conscience, it is also true that a distinguishing element of our culture is its vulnerability to "moral panic" (Goode and Ben-Yehuda 1994), those great spasms of moral indignation that appear as if out of nowhere and recede almost without a trace. Media driven crusades against this or that social problem (drunk driving, homelessness, herpes, smoking, drug abuse, gangs, teenage pregnancy, etc.) clutter the hyperreal landscape and are fueled by a sensationalist rhetoric designed to light brushfires of moral distress or, at minimum, capture the overloaded public attention long enough to motivate half-hearted policy experts to propose weak legislative correctives, which might, if adequately funded, prevent a few deaths or improve a few lives. For the most part, such panics are innocuous, having little or no affect on the lives of most people. However, some panics, rather than quickly dying out, turn into wildfire, especially when they are fed by popular resentments against marginalized groups or tap into the underground reservoir of insecurity that makes everyday life feel like a continuous emergency. Such situations, where panic becomes the motivation for political action and the foundation for long-term policy decisions capable of altering the basic institutional structure of society, are, by their nature, inherently volatile, making considered judgment—the essence of enlightened political thought—all but impossible. As Alan Blum notes in this regard:

Panic...constrains our relation to modernity by depriving us of an opportunity to collect ourselves with respect to the need to be imaginative about ephemerality, since reflection can only appear inconsequential at any ephemeral moment when measured by its perishability (1996, 695).

In the public discussion of the Five Oaks' defensible space plan, moral panic is clearly evident, providing both motivation and legitimation for the plan's supporters. For example, Newman has written:

Downtown Dayton still retains some of its finer old office and shopping buildings. Neighborhoods beautifully constructed in the 1920's border this downtown. Five Oaks is one of these, and it serves as a gateway between the downtown and the suburban residential communities to the north. It is encountered on a daily basis by those coming to the downtown area to work and shop. Five Oaks is a community symptomatic of the city's problems and aspirations. For this reason many in the city government felt that what happens to Five Oaks will happen to the rest of Dayton. *If Five Oaks fell, there would be a domino effect on the surrounding communities* (1996, 32, emphasis added).

If Five Oaks fell ...? Here, Newman raises the thorny matter of ethical consequentialism. What are the consequences of one's actions? Can we weigh them, even precisely calculate the probable outcomes of one course of action over another? Domino effect. To do nothing, to risk nothing in the short-term, is to not only lose the battle but the war as well. To decide to move to a new neighborhood, and perhaps watch as a city eventually decays from the inside out, or to stay and fight, to make good on a commitment, to stave-off conquest, to cordon-off disorder and suppress chaos: this is the moral question, the quandary, the conundrum, Newman would have us decide, elucidate, and decisively act toward.

In contrast, consider the world-embracing consciousness of Brenda Crank, a Five Oaks resident and defensible space critic: "It amazes me, we just took the Berlin Wall down in Europe, and now we're putting them up in Five Oaks" (Dayton Daily News, 1992, p. B3). And Curtis Print, described by *The New York Times* as a "black resident who works in a manufacturing plant," for whom the following connection made sense: "This is just like South Africa, caging people in like this" (*The New York Times* 1994, p. B1). Others spoke of feeling "caged in" as well, as though ensnared, trapped. This type of fear, it would seem, is consequential but must be contrasted to the fears motivating the plan proponents. Witness Dr. Patrick Donnelly's account:

> People were feeling hopeless. It was a time to either work together to solve the problems or put the 'For Sale' sign up (1994, p. 8).

Consider, too, other University of Dayton-connected points of view:

> "Things got very bad very fast," recalls Mike Means, associate professor of English and a resident for three decades in the neighborhood that sits about a mile north of downtown Dayton sandwiches between Main Street and Salem Avenue. While working in the front yard after dinner, Means would routinely see "men on the corner flagging down cars, offering to sell drugs."

And:

> Social worker Karen DeMasi-Risk, a two-time UD graduate, vividly remembers lying in bed, hearing gunfire and thinking, "I've got to get out of here."

And, again, with respect to the Donnellys' experience:

> For Patrick Donnelly, associate professor of sociology, the turning point came when he found a prostitute in the alley behind his house and condoms

in the neighborhood park where his children played T-ball on Saturday mornings.

Here, in remarks made within the covers of a University of Dayton publication (1994, p. 8)—and which, in part, suggest the significant participatory and legitimizing role of the local academic intelligentsia, which helped grease the path for defensible space ideas in the first place and who would later bolster the plan via research into the plan's effect on community solidarity and crime prevention—we find the same expression of everyday fears that one would expect from the stereotypical NIMBY middle-class participant-observers: fear of close proximity to moral perpetuity (vis-à-vis, as Alexander Liazos [1972] once wryly remarked, the "Nuts, Sluts, and Perverts" of traditional deviance studies), violence (again, and we stress, quite real), economic hardship (the ever-important home owner's property values, the middle class' capital), and simple parental concern for the innocence and safety of children. Plan proponents saw Five Oaks in a "state of siege," as "numerous drug houses opened in the neighborhood, speeding cars raced down residential streets, gunfire could be heard nightly throughout the area, and prostitutes and 'johns' began using the residential streets and alleys for their encounters" (Donnelly and Kimble 1997, p. 497). Plan critics saw the Five Oaks defensible space plan as evidence of atavistic retreat, with the middle-class portions of Five Oaks threatening low-intensity class/race warfare against the neighborhoods' growing proportions of African-American, working-class, impoverished, and renter residents. [1]

While two sets of fears confronted one another, they were separate and unequal: the overwhelming if also underlying and barely understood rationality of the order paradigm devalued "the opposition's" concerns. In Newman's world, the fears of the transcending, comparative/historical critic might as well be the ranting of the hysterical or pathetically naive, for in defensible space ideology, attention must first be paid to the time/space of the immediate, the here and now, the urgent demands of today. Mediated thought is, in contrast, suspect. Newman's own account of the conditions leading to his intervention in Five Oaks reveals the importance of alarmism as a justification for taking the decisive and perhaps even extreme steps of enclosing the usual cosmopolitan space of city life:

> During the year before the Defensible Space modifications were undertaken, violent crimes increased by 77 percent; robberies by 76 percent; vandalism by 38 percent; and overall crime by 16 percent. Not only was crime

increasing at a maddening pace, but drug dealers, pimps, and prostitutes had brazenly taken over the streets. Gun shots could be heard at all times of the day and night; blaring boomboxes meant to attract drug purchasers disturbed everyone's sleep; and speeding cars, the byproduct of these illicit activities, threatened people in their own streets. Children were virtually kept locked up in their homes. A 13-member police strike force hit the neighborhood round the clock every few months, but the results were only temporary (1996, p. 32).

The nose of the imaginary cosmopolitan critic, who would think of Berlin or South Africa in order to gain perspective on themselves and their place, must be rubbed in the shit, the dross, the detritus of *this* urban crime, *this* fear and malaise. If a police strike force cannot silence the blaring boomboxes—or, as Newman also writes, "flush out the bad elements" (1996, p. 58)—then something else has to happen, for the noise must be stopped, the cars slowed or rerouted, and the bad element flushed out as though via a sewage system. These are the only fears and the only consequences that register in the 1990's version of 1960's style liberal, gradualist, welfare state sociology preferred by Newman and that undergirds his self-congratulatory, traveling salesman rhetoric of helping the little people cope with "disorder."

If Human Society writ large is best conceived, following Durkheim and Newman, as at base a tenuous moral order, then it makes sense for sociologists and policy makers to attend to the phenomena of "deviance," which is the typical truncation of "deviance from conformity with a normative order." That is, the deviant moves outside the boundaries of the shared do's and don'ts of social life that regulate social relations. The conformist, in contrast, heeds these regulations, even takes them as his/her own. Social analysts concerned with the making and unmaking of social order are therefore drawn to name the various agents of disorder. They might adopt the perspective of the social system as a whole, as have Parsons, Coser, and Luhmann, or a relative position from within the social order, perhaps even purposely the perspective of those on the short-end of the stick, as Becker and Denzin have. Others work to integrate both perspectives, as does Habermas in the shifting perspectives of his lifeworld/system paradigm, or Giddens (1984) via his metaphors of the "duality of structure" and, ultimately, the "constitution of society." Regardless of the particular variant on this theme and despite the value of the order perspective in-itself, our point is that the problem of order, which is often these days rendered as the specific problem of the making of "community," or just as often, "civil society," always demands its deviants. The metatheoretical boundaries erected by the order paradigm imply also an ethics that is wed to order, the ratio of positivism *cum* social theory. Indeed, the legitimacy of Five Oaks' overarching "neighborhood stabilization plan," as its name suggests, derives from this set of well-established background assumptions (see Gouldner 1970). It is conceived, though perhaps not fully consciously so by its proponents, as an ethical response to a type of social disorder that can be empirically verified and measured and, presumably, corrected, namely by the elimination, displacement, or at least the containment of deviance.

But what if the assumption of a "moral order" is itself domination, the on-going production of historically specific power? We would then be forced to forever reflexively *historize*, and, recalling Foucault and more to the point, Soja, *spatialize* everything, even the problem of order, which in our time/space, "often involves a crisis in institutional arrangements, and often too ... what Marxists call 'contradictions' or 'antagonisms,'" to borrow again from Mills (1959, p. 9). And, adopting this vanishing vantage point that returns us to *our* lifeworld, we are compelled to problematize an ethics built on the illusion of a normative order whose justification is said to be redeemed in a universal, transcendent fashion, without recourse to the making of that order or without ultimate reference to power. This would apply to Habermas' discourse ethics as much to mystical or metaphysical reflection, whether the source of mystery be theological or the metaphysics buttressed by scientific research into linguistics, cognitive psychology, or the so-called stages of moral development. In other words, we ask: which ethical considerations would illuminate the dilemmas of a world that has internalized its "self," its identity, *as* mediation, a world where truly "all that is solid melts into air," including deviants and Otherness of all kinds?

In answering this question, we would posit an ethical space where "race," "ethnicity," "gender," "sexuality," "nationality," indeed, any essential marker of identity that would by its nature imply the possibility of escaping the historically specific determination, exists only for those who, for whatever reason—ignorance, fear, habit—persist in making it exist. Such an ethics would be appropriate to a world conceived sociologically, at least in Bauman's postmodern sense of a sociology without illusions, a sociology that is reflexive about its own historically and spatially specific concepts, including the old standbys of sociodemographic analysis noted above. This, of course, is our world, the world in which we live, and in it, too, there exists the Five Oaks Community Stabilization Plan.

At this point, the usual objection is based in a fear of social chaos, of a social disorder without boundaries or regulation, and in particular those fears that border on panic, given that they raise existential anxieties for the individual facing the prospects of living in such a world. Everything goes! Nihilism! Anomie! But also: Who am I, if not a White/Black/Yellow/Red/Brown/Man/Women/Virgin/Slut/Hetero/Homosexual/Good/Bad/Ameri can/Un-American? What am I? What are you? What must I be? The attempt to fix an essential identity is but the mirror of the positing of a social order, itself immune to historical process, and both are false. These binaries that undergird either/or responses and their various versions of the slippery slope of moralistic relativism are reactions unmediated by an awareness of the social processes that create identities. In other words, they are themselves part of the problem, having more to do with psychic splitting and infant psychology than dialectical reason, but there, too, revealing a truthful connection to the vulnerable, helpless, frail human body. The compelling problem is not, then, how to control the dialectic of self and society so as to exclude the inexorably historically and spatially specific nature of identity, perhaps by inscribing an impenetrable safe territory of permanence, predictability, and solidity—a home, neighborhood, city or nation, a haven in a heartless world—but rather how to live without these things, even as frail human bodies, for we must.

Not wishing to here rehearse the social-psychological arguments in Erich Fromm's *Escape from Freedom* much less explicate the "Grand Inquisitor" scene from Dostoyevsky's *Brothers Karamozov*, we would point to what we believe is a more efficient, if also, somewhat elliptical point of departure: Adorno's essay titled, simply, "Commitment," which takes Sartre's *What is Literature?* as its own stepping off point.

For Sartre, "one does not write for slaves" (1965, p. 59). This is an apparently simple statement that nevertheless says a lot about Sartre's understanding of language and his uncompromising political commitments. It is also an instance of his sobering general position on ethics, that one does not live outside of a moral/political order, and that therefore every act is, whether we like it or not, a moral and political act. Issuing from what he elsewhere calls "the most austere of doctrines," existentialism—where we are compelled to be forever and always responsible for our freedom, for we *are* freedom—Sartre more or less straightforwardly conceives of modern life as bound by an ethics of political commitment ([1957]1987, p. 12). To write, to read, to act in-the-world, is both to live our freedom as well as to engage the world-in-the-making as existentially free beings, which is to say, as radically undetermined beings, and to do so from within that world as it is constituted as both what is and what it could be. This means that meaningful action is choice, and that the where and the when and the how of our participation in society is always already participation in history-making. Commitment, to repeat, is the ethics of modern life, for it is as consistent with our incomplete ontology as it is with our distinguishing human faculty of language. Perhaps with the French Resistance in mind, anything less is, for Sartre, tantamount to collaboration with the merely existing order of things, which his Marxist analysis eventually found, to say the least, wanting.

Explicated this way, which is but an approximation of Sartre's complex rendering, the smell of the rat is pungent enough, we suppose. Political commitment is transformed from a principled, philosophically-based rejection of complacency and false dis-engagement to become a form of moral blackmail, itself, in a twist, disengaged from the contingencies and exigencies of history and spatiality. As Adorno points out:

> In Sartre the notion of choice—originally a Kierkegaardian category—is heir to the Christian doctrine 'He who is not with me is against me,' but now voided of any concrete theological content. What remains is merely the abstract authority of a choice enjoined, with no regard for the fact that the very possibility of choosing depends on what can be chosen (1977, p. 180).

The problem is that the "abstract authority" of Sartre's "most austere of doctrines" lacks dialectical attention to the content of the particular life-world of subjects, and there to "what can be chosen." As Adorno writes, "[w]ithin a predetermined reality, freedom becomes an empty claim ..." (1977, p. 180). Here, with his attention to "predetermined reality," the subject matter of sociology, or at least a phenomenologically sensitive sociology, Adorno prefigures what participation must mean in postmodern times.

We must not, Adorno states, accept the "flat objectivity" that is the product of objectivating positivism as much as it is the product of radically subjectivating Sartreian existentialism (1977, p. 181). We must, instead, recognize the entanglement of subject and object, with regard to which no either/or conceptualization can do justice. While this does not mean that our actions do not have political implications, or that judgements cannot be made against them, it does mean that their implications are relative to our social embeddness. In mass society, this means that we cannot control them, and that for most people, they will not add up to much, or rather, they will add up to nothing of consequence. Our actions and the minute consequences that derive from them are not straightforwardly our own, just as an art object is not the simple expression of the artist. Our actions and our responsibility "float," as Bauman suggests, even if our moral intention is to take responsibility for our responsibility. In this sense, the sociology of the postmodern situation is humbling, for there is no place in this world for the existential hero, who, in a notably masculine if not also a sectarian manner, asks, Are you with me or against me? In the face of such a challenge, Adorno concludes (and here quoting once again from *Minima Moralia*, which was composed some years before Sartre's *What is Literature?*):

> The best mode of conduct, in face of all this, still seems an uncommitted, suspended one: to lead a private life, as far as the social order and one's own needs will tolerate nothing else, but not to attach weight to it as to something still socially substantial and individually appropriate. "It is even part of my good fortune not to be a house-owner," Nietzsche already wrote in the *Gay Science*. Today we should have to add: it is part of morality not to be at home in one's home (1974, p. 39).

Like art, which must remain only in a negative relation to politics and philosophy lest it become politics and philosophy, or worse, propaganda, the conduct of life must remain free of the "flat objectivity" of sociologicalism, lest it become deaf to the truth of its own situation.

And what is this truth, especially with respect to something like the Five Oaks Defensible Space Plan? Five Oaks in the early 1990s was no Pruitt-Igoe in the tumultuous 1960s; the situation in the here and now is less dramatic. This strategic hamlet is fortified only by what even Newman describes as "not too elegant" gates, adorned with the Five Oaks neighborhood seal, a symbol of (mini-)community solidarity (1996, p. 50). Five Oaks is not a Great Society (Johnson, Moynnihan), perhaps, but a Good One (Bush, Bellah et al.). In an era of welfare state crisis, city government was forced to eliminate, among other things, the lights and special pedestrian gates that Newman had originally proposed, thus, according to Newman, saving on "replacement bulbs" and "wiring" (1996, p. 50). And so it is in such a marginal corner of the postmodern terrain that we can pay witness to what has become of the dust of Pruitt-Igoe and agree wholeheartedly with Stephen Crook's pithy synopsis of Adorno's analysis of the dialectic of rationality and irrationality:

> When social "reality" models itself after a paranoid system, paranoid thinking is an eminently "rational" response (1994, p. 18).

Moreover, there is no justice in Five Oaks, nor, by extension, true comfort and security for the individual who lives behind "enclosures" designed to repel, or merely re-route, as it were, the feared deviants. "Dwelling," Adorno asserts, "in the proper sense, is now impossible." "The house," he notes, "is past." "No individual," he stresses, "can resist this process" (1974, pp. 38, 39). The effort to do so—to resist, to attempt to secure one's existence and to offer for this act a moral veneer derived from a fictive normative order— is an affront to the empirical world that daily repels such morality by virtue of its seamless objectification of the subject as a mere flesh-ball of power-enacted. Such an effort is an ethically suspect act that carries one away from the "homelessness" that is the truth of the postmodern, for to build walls, to wish for the "stabilization" of middle-class neighborhood life (in a neighborhood that is not predominately middle class, no less), is tantamount to saying "I," to separating one's self from the phenomenological shit, the aimless wandering of a life lived without recourse to order. As Adorno observes in his aphorism titled "Refuge for the homeless," "each trait of comfort in them," that is, in "the traditional residences we grew up in," is "paid for with a betrayal of knowledge, each vestige of shelter with the musty pact of family interests" (1974, p. 38).

Finally, "the trick," writes Adorno,

> is to keep in view, and to express, the fact that private property no longer belongs to one, in the sense that consumer goods have become potentially so abundant that no individual has the right to cling to the principle of their limitation; but that one must nevertheless have possessions, if one is not to sink into that dependence and need which serves the blind perpetuation of property relations.

> But the thesis of this paradox leads to destruction, a loveless disregard for things which necessarily turns against people too; and the antithesis, no sooner uttered, is an ideology for those wishing with a bad conscience to keep what they have (1977, p. 39).

The trick, in other words, is to refrain from participating in a false moral order on the belief that one must, or even could, make a difference. The trick is to demur from subjective "commitment" in favor of the truth of contradiction, for this is the only way of surviving with anything like the homeless nonidentity foisted upon us by our necessary participation in the postmodern. To do otherwise is not simply to risk hubris in the face of disaster, to act macho before a rifle butt aimed at one's face, or to lay down before the roulette wheel of violence. To do otherwise is also to risk any hope there might be for an ethical life by undermining the very things to be protected. Just as Sartre, with plays filled with too many quotable quotes, and surely against his sincere wish, "became," as Adorno sadly notes, "acceptable to the culture industry" (1977, 182), so too does the erection of defended spaces on morally defined ground risk the integrity of the moral impulse itself vis-à-vis the order of things. Indeed, what greater risk is there than in using everyday fears to fortify the main drift a contradiction-ridden society bent on realizing, it would seem, Davis' satirical slogan, "Vietnam Here"?

CONCLUSION

In his *All That Is Solid Melts Into Air* (1982), Marshall Berman notes that Jane Jacobs' *Death and Life of Great American Cities* is a rare instance of a "women's view of the city," not simply because Jacobs is female, but due to her sensitivity to the flows and networks of everyday life. He writes as though in loving and nearly awe-filled tribute:

> She [Jacobs] knows her neighborhood in such precise twenty-four-hour detail because she has been around it all day, in ways that most women are normally around all day, especially when they become mothers, but hardly any men ever are, except when they become chronically unemployed. She knows the shopkeepers, and the vast informal social networks they maintain, because it is her responsibility to take care of her household affairs. She portrays the ecology and phenomenology of the sidewalks with uncanny fidelity and sensitivity, because she has spent years piloting children (first in carriages and strollers, then on roller skates and bikes) through these troubled waters, with balancing heavy shopping bags, talking to neighbors and trying to keep hold of her life. Much of her intellectual authority springs from her perfect grasp of the structures and processes of everyday life. She makes her readers feel that women know what it is like to live in cities, street by street, day by day, far better than the men who plan and build them (1982, pp. 150-151).

For all the melodrama of this description, or perhaps because of it, Berman is quick to add:

> [But] any careful reader of *The Death and Life of Great American Cities* will realize that Jacobs is celebrating the family and the block in distinctively modernist terms: her ideal street is full of strangers passing through, of people of many different classes, ethnic groups, ages, beliefs and life-styles; her ideal family is one in which women go out to work, men spend a great deal of time at home, both parents work in small and easily manageable units

close to home, so that children can discover and grow into a world where there are two sexes and where work plays a central role in everyday life. Jacobs' street and family are microcosms of all the diversity and fullness of the modern world as a whole (1982, pp. 151-152).

Finally, Berman asks the really pertinent question:

What is relevant and disturbing here is that ideologues of the New Right have more than once cited Jacobs as one of their patron saints. Is this connection entirely fraudulent? Or is there something in Jacobs that leaves her open to this misuse? (1982, pp. 151-152).

To which Berman states:

It seems to me that beneath her modernist text there is an anti-modernist subtext, a sort of undertow of nostalgia for a family and a neighborhood in which the self could be securely embedded, *ein'feste Burg*, a solid refuge against all the dangerous currents of freedom and ambiguity in which all modern men and women are caught up. (1982, pp. 151-152).

And adds:

There is another order of difficulty in Jacobs' perspective. Sometimes her vision seems positively pastoral: she insists, for instance, that in a vibrant neighborhood with a mixture of shops and residences, with constant activity on the sidewalks, with easy surveillance of the streets from within houses and stores, there will be no crime. As we read this, we wonder what planet Jacobs can possibly have been thinking of. If we look back a little skeptically at her vision of her block, we may see the trouble. The inventory of the people in her neighborhood has the aura of a WPA mural .... (1982, pp. 151-152).

With the key missing element thus being, and in pre-PC language:

[There are] no blacks on her block. This is what makes her neighborhood vision seem pastoral: it is the city before the blacks [sic] got there. Her world ranges from solid working-class whites at the bottom to professional middle-class whites at the top. There is nothing and no one above; what matters more here, however, is that there is nothing and no one below—there are no stepchildren in Jacobs' family of eyes (p. 153).

For Berman, then, Jacobs' legacy is mixed: both proto-feminist (if in a dated, merely liberal sense) as well as anti-modernist, cosmopolitan as well as naive, progressive and potentially liberatory, but also giving aid and comfort to racism and New Right reaction.

On this account, Oscar Newman's self-proclaimed debt to Jacobs would indeed seem substantial. Newman's advocacy of defensible-space "slash" community-building initiatives is rife with contradictions that he, so deeply invested in his own ideology, is barely aware of. So, too, is this true for those locals for whom fear for the safety of their children, but not the society of "stepchildren," much less for the general state of "homelessness," is paramount, and for whom, therefore, no short-term measure can be too extreme. Indeed, the prospect of panopticonism wrapped in the carceral surrounded by domination must be from this perspective little more than theoretical gibberish, that is, a riddle, an enigma, a mystery at best, not really worth the effort necessary to decode it. And so, the panic/cynicism of a paranoid, disempowered class, stirred with the ready legitimacy of pastoral tableaus there for the local intelligentsia's asking, catalyzed by the public money for a quick, technological fix, ends up in the mortar-and-bricks of "enclosures" and "gates," the salve of a postmodernity gone bad because it never started out good. And so it is that the Enlightenment's *weltburgerlich* attitude has come to this: people defending their space within a common terrain. Public policy has devolved to this: every block mobilizing for itself. From Simmel's merely ambivalent "Metropolis and Mental life" (see Kasinitz 1995) to today's fear and loathing in Ohio ("the heart of it all"), defensible space planning represents an all too salient manifestation of today's postmodern panic/cynicism.

On a recent pilgrimage to the former site of Pruitt-Igoe in St. Louis, we paid our respects to Newman's and postmodernity's ground zero by paying witness to the empty space—an overgrown field, actually—that remains. One adjacent structure, however, stood out from the surrounding flattened urban wasteland: the Gateway Middle School, sporting bright colors, textured, playful brickwork, and swooping, futuristic entryways; Gateway Middle School is postmodern architecture as though radiated by the luminous negativity of Pruitt-Igoe; Gateway Middle School, for the kids, is a testament, like Five Oaks, to what we postmoderns can do to ourselves, bereft of any "map" that would point us in another direction and of the nonparticipation and suspended commitment that would get us there.

Returning, in the end, to the level of highbrow philosophy, Hauke Brunkhorst reminds us that:

Whereas ... the "communitarianism" fashionable today in the West consists in a renewal of the expressive model of collective life developed from Herder to Hegel, for Adorno *all* freedom of modernity begins with criticism of that model's metaphysical character of compulsion ...(1997, p. 45, emphasis in original).

Thus, between panic and cynicism there lies two compulsions, one objective and terrifying, and another theoretical and melancholy. Everything depends on protecting the latter in the face of the former.

NOTES

1.   As Donnelly and Kimble document, Five Oaks is "one of the only racially and economically diverse neighborhoods" in Dayton.

In 1970, the population was 97% White and 3% minorities; by 1990, Five Oaks was 52% White and 46% African American. The percentage of residents in poverty increased from 15% in 1980 to 25% in 1990. Rates of home ownership declined, and landlords made minimal investments in their properties (1997, p. 497).

Donnelly and Majka provide additional empirical description of Five Oaks changing social demographics:

In 1989, the median household income for whites was $27,554 while for blacks it was $15,076. Fifteen percent of all white families were living in poverty while 40% of black families fell below the poverty line. The rate of home ownership declined from 34% in 1980 to 31% in 1990. The home ownership rate is artificially low due to the presence of a number of large apartment buildings and a significant number of doubles and duplexes. Whites owned 82% of all owner occupied housing units while blacks rented 62% of all renter occupied units (1998, p. 194).

Note also that the Five Oaks defensible space plan was part of a comprehensive "neighborhood stablization plan," which was supported by "fully 93% of the residents voting on the plan," and which included "coordination of community-based policing" and "programs to encourage home ownership and housing maintenance" in addition to the defensible space initiative. The defensible space part of the overall plan involved the closure of 35 streets and 26 alleys (Donnelly and Kimble 1997, pp. 497-498).

2. The critical analysis of "communitarianism" that best fits with the present study is certainly Timothy Bewes' excellent *Cynicism and Postmodernity* (1997). See especially pages 81-89, where Bewes notes, for example, with specific reference to Etzioni's version of communitarianism, that it is "envisaged as a (non-politicized) grass-roots political movement for the middle-brow bourgeois masses…" (p. 87), which, in its "fetishization of specificity," often tends toward a policy of "humiliation by workshop" (p. 88). Bewes continues:

> The Communitarian citizen…fills the gaps left by the skeletal legal framework, make "complete" a legislative structure which must refrain from explicitly adjustication on its own account. By maintaining instead a "hands-off" policy of *implicit* governance, Communitarianism proposes an ethos of unwritten rules of behavior, under the sign of "empowerment", which are not less powerful and effective because they are implicit. A society of unwritten—that is, not legally binding—laws is assumed to be free; in fact, as we can see, the tacit legislature of Communitarianism effects a far more thorough and indeed repressive policing of the individual. (p. 88, emphasis in original).

Five Oaks Neighborhood Sign, with Logo

Single Gate

Double Gates, Five Oaks Avenue and
Richmond Avenue

One Gate Viewed Through the Bars of Another; Wroe Avenue

Domino's Pizza Ad Featuring Five Oaks' Gates

Temporary Gate Dividing Mt. Vernon and
Santa Clara Neighborhoods; 100 Yards From Our House

Private Lane Installs a More Stylish Barricade; 300 Yards
From Our House, in Mt. Vernon Neighborhood

Gateway Middle School, St. Louis, MO; Entrance

Gateway Middle School, Featuring White Pod-like Structure

Gateway Middle School, Roadside Monument
with Background Dilapidation

Chapter 6

Dystopian Elements in Richard Rorty's Liberal Utopia

...the minimal public self works for ethics only as long as the demands of ethics are themselves both minimal and transparent—but as soon as that transparency is denied, as soon as we work towards descriptions of our relations to social contexts which we might describe as cruel but which seem not to have a transparent relation to our own identity, then we discover that it is precisely our identity which must be determined.
—Steven E. Cole, "Evading the Subject" (1994, pp. 48-49)

If we take care of freedom, truth can take care of itself.
—Richard Rorty, Contingency, Irony and Solidarity (1989, p. 176)

[It] looks like freedom but it feels like death. It's something in between, I guess.
—Leonard Cohen, "Closing Time" (1992)

I lift my glass to the Awful Truth, which you can't reveal to the ears of youth, except to say it isn't worth a dime.
—Leonard Cohen, "Closing Time" (1992)

If America has a leading public intellectual, it is surely Richard Rorty. No other contemporary thinker can combine the elements essential to such a title. That is, no other is so evidently the product of America's unique philosophical heritage: pragmatism. No other has issued such an intellectually challenging and original immanent critique of that tradition, pushing American pragmatism into direct and sustained dialogue with the most serious and pressing contemporary intellectual and social issues of the postmodern age. No other has so transcended the confines of academic discourse and the academic division of labor to speak regularly and with significant consequence to a wider public audience. And, finally, no other seems more to express our *zeitgeist*; no other is more in tune with the tendencies of the age. If Germany has its Habermas, America has its Rorty. Like Habermas, Rorty is both an intellectual as well as a political superstar, grounded in but also transcendent of the tradition of his intellectual homeland, flirting with the status of true historic greatness, such that school kids will someday, if they do not already, encounter his name in the same context and with the same frequency as they now come face-to-text with John Dewey.

Thus, in the spring of 1992, when we learned that Richard Rorty, the actual person, was to give a public lecture during a visit to Michigan State University, we knew that this was one of those rare opportunities to stare into the face of history: the *weltgeist* on horseback! And we were not disappointed. He wore his signature white suit which matches so well his white hair; he slumped over the podium before the packed lecture hall, conveying through his body language that what he had come to say was really rather ordinary, and although he was asked during the post-talk Q&A to espouse his nonfoundational anti-philosophy, he seemed to prefer discussion of the mundane if also pressing social problems that afflict contemporary American society. We don't need, said Rorty, all the grand ideas of philosophical systems to figure out what needs doing. Put aside Marx. Get out there and help solve today's specific problems. Act. Act in the public sphere and save your intellectualism for quiet nights by the fireplace. It was hard to tell what the assembled audience of intellectuals and wannabes thought of this message, but most seemed content just to get a look at him. That's why we were there.

As of this writing, Richard Rorty is 66 years old. At this point in his life, he seems a model of mature intellectual reflexivity and engaged practice. Indeed, Rorty's career has a telos from academic success to public significance that many of the younger generation of intellectuals envy, for they are the product of an era that Russell Jacoby, in his *The Last Intellectuals* (1987), calls the "age of academe," in which the young are not so much castigated for failing to overcome the structural impediments to such a vaunted status as they, and we, are simply pitied for our obscurity and historical irrelevance. The pitiful state of intellectuals today is surely a new type of intellectual default, one that causes profound moral ambivalence for the ambitious yet powerless proletarian professorate.

In this context, Rorty is exceptional. Like Habermas, Rorty's work directly speaks to intellectuals and, moreover, addresses the role of the intellectual class directly in terms of their potential involvement in the making and remaking of the society and culture. In particular, Rorty focuses on the problem of social legitimation and, in our time, the problem of what Habermas (1973), for one, calls legitimation crisis. In this respect, at least, Rorty *is* like Marx. He demands that today's intellectual reflexively account for their politics; that they weigh their political commitments as carefully as they assemble their journal articles and curry favor with their Deans.

In this chapter, we mean to take up the challenge thrown down by America's leading public intellectual by confronting the problematic significance of intellectual practice in today's post-literate culture. Our approach is both direct and circuitous. For example, we do not attempt to construct a sociology of the public intellectual, for that would involve a theory of the social structuring of intellectual culture. Instead, in Part One of the chapter, we consider but a single work which offers itself as a prescription for what ails today's aspiring intellectual. The work is Rorty's *Contingency, Irony, and Solidarity* (1989), the promotion of which, incidently, motivated Rorty to schlep his way to East Lansing and, we imagine, to countless other outposts of American academe. We approach this work phenomenologically, that is, as it appears to us *as a text*, limiting ourselves to explicating the text's meaning.

In Part Two, we narrow our attention even further by focusing on Rorty's reading of George Orwell's last and most famous work of fiction, the novel *Nineteen Eighty-Four* (1949). Among other things, this novel is perhaps the most widely recognized work of fiction written in the English language this century, or perhaps ever. It has certainly been part of *our* world since we were school kids. Here, and perhaps unexpectedly, we read Orwell *against* Rorty, arguing that Rorty's interpretation of the novel is fundamentally flawed. We argue that when read with Orwell's implicit theory of power in mind, *Nineteen Eighty-Four* raises basic questions concerning Rorty's proposals for the reformation of intellectual culture.

We seek not so much to place Rorty on his feet whereas before he walked upside down, for that would be farce. Instead, and put prosaically, we argue to our fellow would-be public intellectuals that Rorty is no good for us and no good for you, for we live under a volcano that is much worse than the confines of academe or the weight of foundational epistemology, and that, if left to churn and spew its bile, will surely be the end of us all.

Herein, for us, lies the post-ethics of mature intellectual practice: read well, lest ye ingest a "world" that will kill you; trust your own mind, lest ye be swayed by a white knight on horseback; remember fallen heros who risked everything in Spain, lest ye be left with heros all-too-comfortable posing for pictures in some garden on bright sunny days.

PART ONE. THE UNAVOIDABLE RICHARD RORTY

A complex book, Richard Rorty's *Contingency, Irony, and Solidarity* (1989) is written at the edges of philosophy and the liberal tradition of which it is a part. Rorty negotiates the boundaries between disciplines and fields of study, searching for continuities between such diverse topics as philosophy of science and political theory, metaphysics, and psychology. He seeks the point where established understandings wear thin, clear-cutting the last vestiges of a philosophical tradition that has outworn its utility. Having set for himself the task of leading philosophy into its new postmodern, post-metaphysical, but thoroughly bourgeois age, Rorty intends to show the practical implications of his positions for intellectual activity.

A central element of Rorty's *Contingency, Irony, and Solidarity* is his call to re-evaluate the status of narratively construed intellectual disciplines such as literature and ethnography relative to the foundationalist disciplines of philosophy and social theory. Specifically, Rorty claims that novels, poems, ethnography, journalism, comic books, and television programs can successfully provide for the development of popular normative commitments at the level of both the individual and the collective (1989, p. xvi). Such genres as these can produce the substance of a vibrant intellectual culture capable of meeting the needs for personal meaning and social or communal stability. Philosophy and its close relation, social theory, are thus demoted by Rorty to the status of a special interest: of no general public relevance and the concern of only the few who find them satisfying.

That this general position we have attributed to Rorty tends toward the conservative, as has been pointed out, for example, by Cornel West (1993), Nancy Fraser (1989), Richard J. Bernstein, (1987), Jo Burrows (1991), and Roy Bhaskar (1991), should not come as a surprise given that Rorty openly acknowledges that his unapologetic liberal political commitments shape his philosophical speculations. Indeed, an important strategy in Rorty's attempt to show the desirability of his articulation of post-metaphysical intellectual activity is to establish its consistency with existing liberal political institutions.

It is with this explicitly political intention in mind that we have organized our interpretation of Rorty's *Contingency, Irony, and Solidarity* around the theme of social legitimation, especially as it relates to intellectual practice. At stake in both the task of creating and supporting a sense of human solidarity and the task of social legitimation is the preservation of an institutionalized community in the face of challenges to its pre-given validity. Following Peter L. Berger, in his *The Sacred Canopy* (1967), we define social legitimation as "socially objectivated 'knowledge' that serves to explain and justify the social order. Put differently, legitimations are answers to any questions about the why of institutional arrangements" (1967, p. 29). The very possibility of asking about the 'whys' of institutions presupposes a break down in the pregiven order of the humanly constructed world such that the social order appears *as a construction*. The successful resolution of challenges concerning the whys of institutional arrangements involves actively restoring the naturalness or given-ness of the construction. Of course, this task is a perfect contradiction, the bearing of which requires the mobilization of intellectual resources necessary to the contradiction's maintenance.[1]

Placing Rorty's *Contingency, Irony, and Solidarity* in this broad context brings out the full complexity of his attempted reconciliation of irony and solidarity. Having long ago rejected theories of human nature, Rorty does not isolate a single characteristic common to all members of a post-metaphysical culture. Instead, Rorty addresses the problem of creating and supporting a sense of human solidarity from two perspectives, specifically, the perspective of those who question who they are and the social processes that create who they are and the perspective of those who do not. In other words, the primary social division relevant to the problem of human solidarity is that between the ironist intellectual and the commonsensical non-metaphysician.

This distinction between the ironist intellectual and the commonsensical non-metaphysician is premised on Rorty's discussion of a "final vocabulary" as the limit of language and thus the linguistically construed self. A final vocabulary is composed of words which, if questioned, cannot be defended argumentatively. Their defense can only be circular. Concretely, Rorty describes a final vocabulary as:

> a set of words which ... [people] ... employ to justify their actions, their
> beliefs, and their lives. These are the words in which we formulate praise of

our friends and contempt for our enemies, our long term projects, our deepest self-doubts and our highest hopes. They are the words in which we tell...the story of our lives (1989, p. 73).

One's final vocabulary effectively draws a circle around the core region of the self, the last resort of a differentiated identity. Within that circle is undifferentiated otherness.

The commonsensical non-metaphysician takes for granted the taken for granted nature of this vocabulary. As Rorty describes it, such a person would "unselfconsciously describe everything important in terms of the final vocabulary to which they and those around them are habituated" (1989, p. 73). While a commonsensical non-metaphysician might acknowledge a relation between social processes and their final vocabulary, they do not question the facticity of either this relation or the social processes themselves. Most people would not be concerned with such matters, for Rorty "cannot imagine a culture which socialized its youth in such a way as to make them continually dubious of their own processes of socialization" (1989, p. 87).

Some people, ironist intellectuals in particular, will harbor such doubts. Ironists take a reflexive attitude toward their final vocabularies. Having been impressed with other final vocabularies, the ironist understands that even this last resort of language is contingent on something other than itself. The ironist knows that while final vocabularies may be the last words on the matter, they are never the end of the matter. The ironist knows that there is always an element of arbitrariness to the terms through which individuals settle on their selves.

This distinction between ironists and commonsensical non-metaphysicians provides the backdrop for Rorty's articulation of the problem of social legitimation. At stake for Rorty is the question of grounding and justifying a sense of human solidarity without recourse to metaphysical concepts. Rorty claims in the first place that, "The idea that liberal societies are bound together by philosophical beliefs ... is ... ludicrous" (1989, p. 87). Instead, for Rorty, it is common vocabularies and common hopes that bind liberal societies together. The vocabularies are dependant on common hopes in so far as "... the principle function of the vocabularies is to tell stories about future outcomes which compensate for present sacrifices" (1989, p. 86). Such stories of social hope underwrite the commitment of most people to the liberal tradition; and, in "modern, literate, secular societies," they are political scenarios. Thus, Rorty writes:

To retain social hope, members of such a society need to be able to tell themselves a story about how things might get better, and to see no insuperable
obstacle to this story's coming true (1989, p. 85).

In general, then, Rorty contends that social solidarity is underwritten by a
shared belief in progress articulated through a common vocabulary and
narrative tradition.[2]

Rorty approaches the problem of legitimating such a belief in progress
in terms of different strategies appropriate to different segments of the
population. As a rule, the issue of social legitimation is hardly a dilemma
for the majority population of commonsensical non-metaphysicians.
Because Rorty defines commonsensical non-metaphysicians in terms of
their lack of reflexivity towards their final vocabularies, it is unlikely that
the issue of justifying one's sense of solidarity will ever be an issue for
most people. In Rorty's formulation, commonsensical non-metaphysicians
would not need such justification, if only because "... she was not raised to
play the language game in which one asks for and gets justifications for
that sort of belief" (1989, p. 87).

Moreover, popular political commitments and allegiances would not be
grounded philosophically through the exploration of principles and definitions, but, instead, would be grounded through the exploration of concrete
practical alternatives and programs (1989, p. 87). For example, Rorty
maintains in a different context that liberal political institutions would be
well served if relieved of the burden of philosophical justification. Appeal-
ing to the authority of such figures as John Dewey, Michael Oakeshott, and
John Rawls, Rorty writes, "... that a circular justification of our practices
which makes one feature of our culture look good by citing still another,
or comparing our culture invidiously with others with reference to our own
standards, is the only sort of justification we are going to get" (1989, p. 57).
In other words, legitimation issues can be resolved through the narrative
re-description of the concrete alternatives to liberal institutions which
make the alternatives look bad and the liberal institutions look good.

For the ironist, however, social legitimation *is* a problem, because the
ironist, by definition, questions the shared narrative tradition that would
otherwise establish as given a sense of human solidarity within a post-
metaphysical liberal society. It is with this group in mind that Rorty frames
the issue of social legitimation in terms of the problem of reconciling the
need for human solidarity or community with the ironic awareness of the
contingency of the same. This problem is not, for Rorty, irresolvable:
although irony and community may be contrary impulses, they need not be

thought of as contradictory or mutually exclusive. Thus, while Rorty is fully aware that irony can interfere with the taken for granted nature of community and is thus potentially dangerous to social stability, he also contends that intellectuals can choose to *not* make this a problem by simply privatizing such ironic tendencies.

This privatization of irony would characterize intellectual life in Rorty's post-metaphysical intellectual culture. Rorty contends that the privatization of irony contradicts neither the needs of liberal institutions nor the interests of a well-intentioned ironist. Intellectuals who understand the inter-relationship between liberal institutions and private freedom will voluntarily censor their ironic reflection. Moreover, this voluntary compliance with the requirements of liberalism is itself motivated by an awareness of contingency,[3] or irony. Rorty argues this position concerning the consistency of liberalism and ironism through a combined appeal to both the sympathy and self-interest of ironist intellectuals. We will now consider the details of this crucial aspect of his argument.

In his appeal to the sympathy of ironist intellectuals, Rorty contends that the liberal ironist's understanding of the power of re-description is the foundation for a sense of solidarity with the commonsensical non-metaphysician. This is because Rorty defines liberalism in terms of its primary publicly relevant end, "the elimination of cruelty" (1989, pp. 65, 68), and further asserts that a liberal is one for whom "cruelty" is the worst thing humans can do (1989, pp. xv, 74). In addition to the relatively unimportant phenomena of its physical manifestation, cruelty refers to "humiliation," a form of cruelty produced through re-description. Following Elaine Scarry (1985), Rorty writes:

> The best way to cause people long lasting pain is to humiliate them by making the things that seemed most important to them to look facile, obsolete, and powerless (1989, p. 89).

This is precisely what the intellectual does to the non-intellectual, for the intellectual's *modus operandi* is re-description and "re-description often humiliates" (1989, p. 90). While this tendency to humiliate is characteristic of both metaphysical and ironist intellectual activity, ironist intellectual activity is especially humiliating, given that it is informed by an "awareness of the power of re-description" itself (1989, p. 89). Because metaphysical re-description assumes a relationship between a particular re-description and some sort of truth, its humiliating tendencies are compensated for by promises of an increase in power, freedom, enlightenment, or some other similarly transcendent value. In other words, this is a type of humiliation attenuated by hope.

Ironists, however, make no such promises, for their heightened awareness of the arbitrary moment in all re-descriptive activity prevents this. Ironists thus humiliate without the ancillary claim that something good will come of it. The ironist understands the world-destroying power of words and hence the potentially cruel consequences of re-descriptive activity. Rorty (1989) writes of the liberal ironist:

> She thinks that what unites her with the rest of the species is not a common language but *just* susceptibility to pain, and in particular to that special sort of pain which the brutes do not share with the humans—humiliation (p. 92, emphasis in original);

and

> What matters for the liberal ironist is not finding such a reason [to care about suffering] but making sure that she *notices* suffering when it occurs. Her hope is that she will not be limited by her own final vocabulary when faced with the possibility of humiliating someone with a quite different final vocabulary (p. 93, emphasis in original).

According to Rorty, ironists who desire not to be cruel will, in public life, *act* like a metaphysician or hold their tongues, reserving their irony for the privacy of their own homes.[4] Of course, this can only be counted on in the liberal, one who, above all else, is dedicated to the elimination of cruelty. Rorty is aware that not all ironists are liberal.

It is perhaps the problem of the nonliberal ironist—the intellectual who does not care about caring—that causes Rorty to include within his attempt to establish the compatibility of liberalism and ironism the notion that it would be in the self-interest of ironists themselves to recognize the validity, or at least the utility, of his position.[5] Again, Rorty's definition of liberalism provides the basis for his argument. According to Rorty, the liberal desire to eliminate cruelty is related to the desire to expand private freedom in the interest of increasing opportunities for self-creation. Because cruelty deprives humans of their ability to use language and thus of their ability to create their selves, cruelty is contrary to this end (1989, p. 94). Because ironism is potentially humiliating and thus potentially cruel, it is inappropriate for political discourse and should be limited to the private sphere. Such a limitation might on the surface appear to contradict the end of expanding freedom, but, in Rorty's accounting, it does no such thing. This is because Rorty works with two understandings of freedom, one appropriate to public life and one appropriate to private life.

With regard to the former, Rorty resists defining political freedom in terms other than existing liberal political institutions, which, in his view, should be thought of as having been "designed to diminish cruelty, make possible government by consent of the governed, and permit as much domination-free communication as possible to take place" in order to optimize the "balance between leaving people's private life alone and preventing suffering" (1989, pp. 68, 63). Public or political freedoms, such as those which exist "when the press, the judiciary, the elections and the universities are free" are necessary to the liberal goal of maximizing opportunities for self-creation (1989, p. 84). Rorty writes:

> ... without the protection of something like the institutions of bourgeois liberal society, people will be less able to work out their private salvations, create their private self-images, reweave their webs of belief and desire in light of whatever new people and books they happen to encounter (1989, pp. 84-85).

Understood in this way, freedom in the public sphere is limited by the goal of maximizing freedom in the private sphere. It is here that Rorty's counsel that ironists should privatize "their attempts at authenticity and purity" lest they come "to think that there is some social goal more important than avoiding cruelty" can be seen as an appeal to the self-interests of ironists themselves (1989, p. 65).

As Rorty understands it, irony, an attitude oriented towards questioning that which is held in common by members of a community, especially the pre-given sense of human solidarity, is necessarily parasitic on and disruptive of common traditions and vocabularies. Additionally, and for this reason, irony involves a reflexive understanding of the contingent nature of communal institutions and is thus intimately aware of the fragility of those institutions. Even the liberal value of private freedom oriented towards self-creation is contingent on the lucky coincidence of various historical tendencies. Because of this, Rorty suggests that not only are liberal institutions contingent on such things as peace, wealth, universal literacy, and higher education, but that the ironist's freedom to question those institutions, and recreate their selves according to an alternative image of their own choosing, is equally contingent. In short, the freedom to pursue the project of private perfection is a liberal freedom dependant on the institutions characteristic of a liberal society. The implication of Rorty's claim is that the interest of the ironist and the interest of liberal institutions are the same: the ironist seeks private perfection and liberal institutions create and preserve the conditions wherein that search might be possible for the greatest number of people. The ironist should thus recognize the utility of keeping whatever doubts they may have about those institutions to themselves, lest they shake the ground of their own freedom. Thus, even if one is not instinctively repulsed by cruelty or if one is not quite taken by Rorty's equation of cruelty, humiliation, re-description, and intellectual activity, one might still be persuaded of the validity of the liberal cause by considerations of one's own self-interest in that cause, namely, that Rorty's liberalism promises to protect even the most difficult, recalcitrant, and uncaring ironist.

In general, then, Rorty's effective claim is that the legitimation of liberal traditions and institutions is only an issue for an elite population of intellectuals, who, by definition, understand the contingency and mutability of social institutions. This understanding would have a reflexive element in that it would include an awareness that the intellectual's own freedom to question the foundations of social institutions is itself dependant on liberal institutions. Due to this relationship, Rorty's implicit claim is that the interests of intellectuals and the interests of liberal institutions are the same. As we read Rorty, his recommendation is that intellectuals should adopt this self-understanding as their own and, as a result, voluntarily privatize their doubts about liberal institutions. Rorty is claiming that intellectuals should see the utility of keeping their ironic awareness of the fragility of institutions out of public discourse, lest their own institutionalized freedom be threatened.

It has been argued by Nancy Fraser (1989, pp. 100-102), Roy Bhaskar (1991, pp. 89-91), Charles Anderson (1991, p. 367), and others, that, if taken at face value, this reconciliation of the contrary tendencies of ironism and liberalism would seem to depend on the salience of Rorty's distinction between public and private spheres. This distinction is notoriously unstable in liberal political thought. Criticizing Rorty on this count, however, assumes that there ought to be a relation between the ideas expressed in *Contingency, Irony, and Solidarity* and non-discursive material practice. In essence, such criticisms assume that this work is best interpreted as a program for institutional change and that, therefore, questions of practical implementation are relevant issues.

That Rorty does often adopt the persona of a strident critic and reformer tirelessly dedicated to social causes—a postmodern Jane Addams—lends credence to this assumption. However, if one brackets these rhetorical devices and focuses on Rorty's stated commitment to a consistently maintained rejection of attempts to posit or assume a positive relation between linguistically construed artifacts and those which are not linguistically construed, the relevance of such questions is immediately brought into question. Having set aside the epistemological problematic as irretrievably metaphysical, Rorty also sets aside all issues revolving around the relation between language and that which is external to language. This includes the implementation of concrete programs for institutional reform as well as problems arising from actual attempts to practice his posited reconciliation of the pursuit of private perfection and the pursuit of human solidarity. That Rorty's stated intention is conservative with respect to existing social institutions implies that part of his aim is precisely to prevent the translation of ironic reflection on the contingency of institutions into a viable program for institutional change. When set in the context of the historical fact of the absence of revolution in liberal societies, it can be concluded that the public/private split has proven, in practice, to be quite stable. Rorty's own sophisticated, participatory self-understanding further renders as questionable the relevance of criticizing *Contingency, Irony, and Solidarity* on such grounds.

Post-metaphysical Intellectual Practice and Human Agency

Rorty fully intends to avoid entanglement in what he considers to be the irresolvable problems inherent in a conception of truth which posits truth to be a representation of "the world." These problems have been famously articulated in his earlier masterwork, *Philosophy and the Mirror of Nature* (1979). In *Contingency, Irony, and Solidarity*, Rorty assumes as given many of the positions worked out in *Philosophy and the Mirror of Nature*, applying them to new problems and contexts.[6] Indeed, we suspect that Rorty's interrogation of the problems inherent in conceptualizing "truth" as a straightforward representation or correspondence to reality outlined in *Philosophy and the Mirror of Nature*, has, by the time of *Contingency, Irony, and Solidarity*, been extended by Rorty to include any posited or assumed relation between language and something external to it. "Truth" is thus dispensed with as a regulative ideal. Our concern in this section is to explore some of the consequences of this, focusing on Rorty's tendency in *Contingency, Irony, and Solidarity* to treat language and the world as separate spheres. We argue that this separation, when combined with his textual practice of privileging the sphere of language, has a double result: it restricts the significance of language to its pragmatic utility in furthering the immediate concerns of the language user at the same time as it works to hypostatize the world as it exists.

Rorty's dismissal of a theory of truth that posits a connection between language and something which exists independently of language is evident in both his pragmatic understanding of language and his understanding of selfhood as a coping mechanism. In both cases, Rorty avoids defining his objects of analysis in terms of what they *are*, choosing instead to define them functionally, in terms of how they work in the human effort to deal with our contingency on other humans. From this perspective, language is a means to directly manipulate other people. A sense of self is, in its turn, the product of processes of indirect manipulation or imaginative re-descriptions of one's personal relationships in terms of one's own choosing.

In both cases, Rorty's focus is centered on the active agent or subject, while his emphasis is on empowerment. This empowerment, however, occurs in an objective context of powerlessness. The power of the objective world is, for Rorty, not

> the sort we can appropriate by adopting and then transforming its language, thereby becoming identical with the threatening power and subsuming it under our own more powerful selves. This latter strategy is appropriate only for coping with other persons ... (1989, p. 40).

As an instrument uniquely suited for overcoming the power of other humans, language is, as Rorty presents it, of no use for influencing the extra-linguistic environment. Thus, while "the world can blindly and inarticulately crush us; mute despair, intense mental pain can cause us to blot ourselves out," re-description is a poor defense against this sort of thing (1989, p. 40). The world which exists independent of its description is not vulnerable to the transformative power of language, nor is the body of the self so vulnerable, since it, too, exists independent of one's linguistically construed identity.[7] Rorty writes that "...our relationship to the world, to brute power and to naked pain, is not the sort of relation we have to persons," concluding that, "when faced with the non-human and the non-linguistic, we no longer have an ability to overcome contingency and pain" (1989, p. 40).

The general consequences of this view are indicated in Rorty's use of the metaphor "playfulness" to describe the culture anticipated in his re-description of intellectual activity.

According to Rorty, resignation in the face of the world and the non-linguistic self would allow for the development of a culture wherein projects of self-creation would be characterized by a "spirit of playfulness" (1989, pp. 39-40). Importantly, it is the recognition of contingency that underwrites this cultural freedom. Presumably, once reconciled to their own contingency, people would no longer feel responsible to the conditions of their existence and would no longer feel responsible for things they cannot change. Unconstrained by the objective demands of their situation and reconciled to their own powerlessness, they could afford to dispense with seriousness and pretension; they would be free to pursue diverse projects of self-creation. It seems only a slight exaggeration to summarize Rorty's notion of cultural freedom/playfulness as follows: the acceptance of the fact that the shape of each individual's consciousness is the product of random events, a crystalization of a seemingly infinite web of occurrences, includes within it the realization of the fact that no single individual is any more essential than any other. All can be free because no one matters. No one matters because, having only language with which to create their world, all are powerless in the face of the world. It is only within this greater unfreedom that cultural freedom finds its home.

What we wish to emphasize is that Rorty's reliance on a subject-centered view of language-use and the self as well as his re-description of intellectual culture in terms of play, together imply an objective state of effective powerlessness. Rorty's use of instrumentalist and gaming metaphors suggest that individuals can use language to further their own immediate ends or desires. However, Rorty's language users are powerless in the face of the objective context in which they use language. They may successfully maneuver within a particular language game, but the nature of the game itself, its rules and conditions, is beyond their control. Furthermore, Rorty's contention that an intellectual culture premised on the full appreciation of contingency and characterized by an experimental, non-binding approach to its artifacts suggests that members of such a culture would be free to choose their own narrative identities. They would, however, remain passive with respect to the conditions of their existence. In other words, their freedom would be of a compensatory, coping nature, and not expandable to material practice.

The consequences of this view can be seen most clearly in Rorty's contention that freedom is best understood in terms of the "recognition of contingency," which means that freedom is both founded on and limited by the experienced awareness of contingency (1989, pp. 46, 40). Rorty's privileging of the speaking subject does preserve a form of freedom;[8] however, Rorty's neglect of human agency—the power to affect the material conditions of one's existence and the existence of others through concrete practice—limits his articulation of the concept freedom to its most abstract, subjective form.

Moreover, combined with his abstract, negative rendering of contingency, this downgrading of agency obscures the self-directed, self-formative structuring of human behavior. Rorty's equation of contingency with randomness[9] closes off from analysis that upon which human behavior is contingent, suggesting, at times, that such analysis is the product of an only psychologically relevant, metaphysical approach to the world (1989, pp. 26-27). There would be no point to inquiring into the concrete determinants of human behavior if those determinants are already assumed to be randomly distributed. Agency is in this way rendered inexplicable and unanalyzable and thus free from critical evaluation.

This last move effectively unifies the concepts of contingency and freedom. Rorty's recognition that there is nothing universal governing human behavior implies further that human behavior is contingent upon unpredictable random events not subject to conscious control. When combined with Rorty's implied understanding of freedom in negative terms, as not being subject to conscious control, leads Rorty to conclude that contingency is the foundation for human freedom. An embracing of contingency is the best protection freedom can hope for.

At issue in Rorty's post-metaphysical account of intellectual activity is that his intention to avoid epistemological issues, combined with his neglect of agency, creates an unstable dualism in the face of the relation between intellectual and material phenomena. In the articulation of his positions, this dualism collapses into a monistic totality of discourse. Intellectual activity is in this way rendered by Rorty to be a self-contained, self-referential sphere, its objective significance limited to the immediate concerns of the language user. Finally, this results in the hypostatization of existing social institutions and institutional social power. This dynamic is consistent with Rorty's intention to develop a model of intellectual practice capable of meeting intellectual challenges to social institutions, for it occurs in a context where Rorty discounts the possibility that social and political institutions can be justified independent of the fact that they exist.[10] In short, Rorty's tendency to hypostatize the world independent of language helps to relieve social institutions of any burden of accountability, both theoretical and practical.

Social Legitimation Without Truth

Rorty's attempt to persuade intellectuals to relieve themselves of metaphysics revolves around his contention that the embracing of the contingency of community would be a step further in the progressive disenchantment of the world, a step which most liberal intellectuals have been unwilling to take. Rorty's claim is that liberal social institutions would not be endangered by a general appreciation of the fact and its implications that communities are not permanent self-subsisting entities but, rather, are dependent always on situations and conditions (1989, pp. 44, 57). Such an appreciation would aid in the development of a worldview consistent with the liberal values of individual freedom and tolerance, particularly in the domain of culture (1989, p. 52). This is because institutions would not (if they ever did) depend on philosophical justifications for their legitimacy (1989, p. 86). Intellectuals would thus be liberated to pursue the popular forms of literature and political rhetoric (1989, pp. 53-55). Furthermore, this shift away from epistemology and metaphysics would neutralize long-established ideological threats to existing institutions (1989, pp. 53, 69).

Rorty hints at the potential efficacy of his position in his recognition that, if widely accepted, it would be necessary to give up

> the idea that liberalism could be justified, and Nazi and Marxist enemies refuted, by driving the latter up against an argumentative brick wall ... [for] ... any attempt to drive one's opponent up against a wall in this way fails when the wall against which he is driven comes to be seen as one more vocabulary, one more way of describing things (1989, p. 53).

This is only a minor problem, however, for while it does undermine the possibility of meeting social criticism with arguments, it also neutralizes the effect of those criticisms. An intellectual culture that viewed all positions as artifacts and that seeks a multiplicity of vocabularies and perspectives could tolerate even highly critical perspectives so long as they were considered just examples of many possible perspectives. For example, in *The Gulf War Did Not Take Place* (1995), Jean Baudrillard refers to this logic as the "paradox of deterrence." Referring to the deterrent effect of the proliferation of weapons, Baudrillard writes: "It is like information, culture or other material and spiritual goods: only their profusion renders them indifferent and neutralizes their negative perverse effects. Multiply vices in order to ensure the collective good" (1995, p. 70).

It seems that Rorty's suggestion is that liberal institutions would be strengthened if their justifications were always dependent on the institutions being legitimated. Such circularity, when accepted as valid, would render the intellect an ineffective weapon against social institutions and established powers. This would, in turn, create the conditions for the generalization of intellectual freedom: no longer able to do much damage, intellectuals could also provide a positive legitimating function both in the practice of that freedom and its product. In other words, the product of a liberated intellect would not be restricted to negative, de-legitimating practices, but would still prove useful to attempts to generate positive legitimacy.

This claim refers to the significance of "stories of social hope" described earlier. According to Rorty, such stories underwrite the commitment of the general population to liberal social institutions. Providing these stories is a literary project and therefore, according to Rorty, is not a job for philosophers or even social theorists. Rather, this important task is ceded to novelists, ethnographers, and others who produce thick descriptions of everyday life. As Rorty presents it, the focus of such descriptions would be on private, inarticulate suffering, thereby giving this suffering a linguistic and thus potentially public form.[11] In this process, writers contribute to creating the conditions for solidarity with victims.[12] Summarizing this position, Rorty writes:

> Within an ironist culture,....it is the disciplines which specialize in thick descriptions of the private and idiosyncratic which are assigned this job of [of creating human solidarity]. In particular, novels and ethnographies which sensitize one to the pain of those who do not speak our language must do the job which demonstrations of a common human nature were supposed to do. Solidarity has to be created out of little pieces ... (1989, p. 94).

In the above discussion, we have explored some of the implications of Rorty's proposed compromise with intellectuals in which he urges the limitation of philosophy and social theory to the private sphere which, in his rendering, effectively subordinates public discourse to the task of maintaining social institutions. His acknowledged goals are political: he describes his intentions concerning ironist theory in terms of how, through privatization, ironism can be prevented from "becoming a threat to political liberalism" (1989, pp. 190, 197). Assuming a liberal world as the best possible world, Rorty devotes himself to the project of developing an understanding of intellectual practice which would not and could not come into conflict with liberal social institutions. The extremes to which he is willing to go—illustrated in his ban on truth whereby he cuts language, and thus thought, off from the world, transforming it into a self-contained sphere capable of referring only to the idiosyncratic needs of individuals— is suggestive of the tenacity of his commitment to the status quo.[13] Even so, that Rorty is willing to go to such extremes in the project of disabling the intellect implies that an unfettered intellect must be very powerful indeed. Alternatively, but equally to the point, Rorty's restriction of all intellectual practice to a very narrow sphere indicates, as much as anything else, that the customs and institutions he intends to defend rest on very shaky ground.

PART TWO. RE-DESCRIBING *NINETEEN EIGHTY-FOUR*

We turn now to Richard Rorty's treatment of George Orwell's *Nineteen Eighty-Four* as a concrete model of a post-metaphysical intellectual practice which, in addition to furthering the specific claims made in *Contingency, Irony, and Solidarity*, exemplifies Rorty's intellectual ideals. In general, Rorty appeals to Orwell's legacy[14] in his effort to support his claim that literature and related genres can do the job of developing a normative framework consistent with the liberal goal of preventing cruelty and furthering human solidarity that has been traditionally reserved for foundationalist disciplines such as philosophy (1989, pp. 95, 185-6, 190).

After briefly considering Rorty's reading of *Nineteen Eighty-Four* as it relates to this issue, we argue that Rorty's interpretation obscures Orwell's interrogation of the position of the intellectual relative to the reproduction of institutionalized social power. Specifically, we propose that in *Nineteen Eighty-Four* Orwell articulates, through the character Winston Smith, one danger facing intellectuals who, by virtue of their profession, contribute to the reproduction of their own domination, domination which, alas, they only partially understand. This is significant because an interpretation of *Nineteen Eighty-Four* which adopts this perspective as its organizing theme is not only more true to the text in question, but also suggests an analogy between the resistance of Winston Smith to the Party's power and

Rorty's use of the idea of irony as underwriting social legitimation in liberal societies. Just as Rorty claims that irony, as the experienced awareness of contingency, both undermines and reestablishes the primacy of liberal institutions, Winston's half-articulated recognition of the arbitrariness of the Party's power was the foundation for establishing a thorough-going identification with that power. More to the point, Rorty's irony and Winston's alienation have the same latent function of establishing the primacy of institutionalized social power. As a result, we argue, contra Rorty, that the primary danger presented in *Nineteen Eighty-Four* is not cruelty or humiliation, but the failure of intellectuals to place their own selves in their objective context and incorporate into their self-understanding their own powerlessness. We also draw out the analogy between Winston's alienation and Rorty's ironism, effectively redescribing Winston Smith as an ironic intellectual.

Orwell's Contribution to the Self-Understanding of Contemporary Liberals

Rorty's interpretation of *Nineteen Eighty-Four* revolves around Orwell's contribution to the self-understanding of intellectuals in a climate threatened by a loss of liberal hope, where it seems that liberal ideals have little chance of realization. George Orwell has proved useful to Richard Rorty's liberalism if only because, as a dystopian novelist, Orwell has provided contemporary intellectuals with a compelling narrative that renders attractive even Rorty's minimalist utopia. In general, Rorty interprets Orwell's positive achievement in the writing of *Nineteen Eighty-Four* as a sort of object lesson, invoking it as a thinly veiled threat: in the absence of liberal hope, intellectuals are in danger of becoming sadistic torturers. Accordingly, for Rorty, the character O'Brien is Orwell's answer to the question of how intellectuals "might conceive of themselves, once it had become clear that liberal ideals had no relation to a possible human future" (1989, p. 171). The lesson of O'Brien is particularly urgent given that Rorty does "not think that we liberals *can* now imagine a future of 'human dignity, freedom and peace'" (1989, pp. 181-182, emphasis in original). In Rorty's view, our current situation is one that is likely to favor the emergence of intellectuals like O'Brien, whose only pleasure in life is the spectacle of other people's pain.

The plausibility of this interpretation depends on Rorty's decision to treat the last part of *Nineteen Eighty-Four* as being *about* O'Brien and not about Winston Smith. Involved in this decision is Rorty's contention that the third part of the novel is fundamentally different from the first two parts. He implies, in other words, that Part III of *Nineteen Eighty-Four* can be read as an independent whole, without reference to the entirety of the novel. Rorty writes:

> ... In the last third of *1984* we get something different—something not topical, prospective rather than descriptive. After Winston and Julia go to O'Brien's apartment, *1984* becomes a book about O'Brien ... (1989, pp. 171, 175).

Rorty's focus on O'Brien, to the neglect of Winston Smith, overlooks Orwell's consistent and uninterrupted employment of the third person singular perspective through which the story of *Nineteen Eighty-Four* is limited by Winston's own perceptions.[15]

These interpretive decisions are significant in as much as they result in a reading of Orwell's last novel that is difficult to reconcile with the text.[16] Treating *Nineteen Eighty-Four* as a unified whole with the character Winston Smith at its center, a reading which is consistent with the book Orwell presumably wrote, discloses that Winston's resistance related directly to his position as a Party intellectual. Placing Winston's rebellion, arrest, torture, and subsequent love of Big Brother in the context of the material operation and logic of power illuminates the origins of Winston's rebellion in his employment by the Party at the Ministry of Truth. Of equal importance, Winston's failure to understand his experience of alienation in the context of objective social processes was constitutive of the organizing logic of Oceanic society. In other words, both Winston's alienation—his sense of himself as a self distinct from other selves—and his failure to understand the causes of that alienation, were both consistent with the demands of social reproduction within Oceania.

On the surface, the interpretation we propose would seem irreconcilable with the third part of *Nineteen Eighty-Four*, the part that addresses Winston's imprisonment in the Ministry of Love, at least if that imprisonment is understood, as it usually is, as a reprogramming or a brainwashing. If, as we are suggesting, Winston was already a functional member of his society and an integral part of the reproduction of power, why torture him?

Richard Rorty's answer that the Party engaged in torture for its own sake, as a form of pleasure, is only minimally consistent with the reading of *Nineteen Eighty-Four* that we propose (1989, p. 179). Its consistency lies in the fact that Rorty directs attention away from what Winston does or does not do, thinks or does not think, as the explanation for Winston's torture. However, this position is decidedly out of sync with the text in two important ways. First, there is no textual evidence that O'Brien enjoyed torturing Winston, at least not in the sense alluded to in Rorty's description of a "rich, complicated, delicate absorbing spectacle of mental pain" (1989, p. 179). While it is clear that O'Brien was challenged by the problem posed by Winston, there is no indication of sadistic pleasure. Instead, there is in O'Brien an enthusiastic dedication to the task at hand, a tiredness combined with lunatic intensity (Orwell [1949]1983, pp. 202, 209, 216, 217). That Orwell's descriptions of O'Brien at work echo his descriptions of Winston at work suggests that the crucial operating emotional dynamic is not a transgressive sadism but the far more mundane dynamic of worker satisfaction ([1949]1983, pp. 39, 151).[17]

Second, Rorty's understanding of torture as a means of increasing the pleasure of Party members, and as "the only art form and the only intellectual discipline available to sensitive intellectuals in a post-totalitarian culture," is contrary to the totalizing telos of the Party (1989, p. 180). Pleasure, even that produced through torture, would necessitate a differentiation between the Party as a hegemonic collective and the individual Party member. Torturing for the sake of enjoyment would be as foreign to the logic of this power, which is a total power, as making love for the sake of enjoyment. Both pleasure and pain presuppose an existence external to the Party. For these reasons, Rorty's understanding of the function of torture is plainly insufficient to the text of *Nineteen Eighty-Four*, failing to attend to Orwell's complex conceptualization of power and the position of Winston Smith, as an intellectual, in the reproduction of that power.

The Alienation of Winston Smith: The Division of Labor

The crucial question in understanding the significance of torture in *Nineteen Eighty-Four* is whether or not Winston could have avoided imprisonment and Room 101. The first clue to answering of this question involves various hints in the text that Winston's resistance was created by O'Brien in his work as a functionary of the Party. For example, O'Brien explained to Winston:

> This drama I have played out with you during seven years will be played out over and over again, generation after generation, always in subtler forms ([1949]1983, pp. 221, 201).

216 / A Wrong Life

Here, O'Brien claimed agency for himself, if not in actually creating Winston's rebellion, then in shaping it, encouraging it, and cultivating it.

Furthermore and significantly, Winston's specifically unorthodox feelings and actions appear always to be initiated by external occurrences that were, in principle, outside his control.[18] For example, the geography of his room, in conjunction with the young ladies keepsake album that he had bought, suggested to him that he start a diary. That a photograph of three former Party elites who had by then become "unpersons" mysteriously appeared among other work-a-day documents suggested to Winston the possibility of documenting that Party histories were lies. A piece of paper, passed to him in full view of the telescreen with the words "I love you" on it, suggested to Winston that he not only engage in adultery, but that he also fall in love with a woman for whom he had previously felt only hatred and rage. On the basis of these clues it is conceivable that Winston's resistance may well have been little more than an entrapment and Winston but a hapless puppet on a string.

Though such a scenario seems consistent with the text and tenor of *Nineteen Eighty-Four*, the extent to which Winston's resistance was the product of a conspiracy is never conclusively determined, nor is there any real need for such a settlement. It could have gone either way. All that really mattered was that if Winston's resistance did not exist, it could have been and probably would have been created. Power is as power does, and what power does is overcome opposition. Opposition, real or concocted, is essential to power's movement ([1949]1983, p. 221).[19]

The important secondary character, Parsons, a conformist in thought and deed, further illustrates the claim we are making. Having been turned in by his daughter for talking in his sleep, Parsons was no more successful in escaping the Thought Police than was Winston. While Parsons was not conscious of having committed thoughtcrime, he did not question the integrity of his daughter as an informant nor did he doubt his own guilt. The mere fact of his arrest proved his guilt, for it was unfathomable that the Party arrest an innocent man ([1949]1983, pp. 192-193). Of course, Parsons was right in assuming his culpability, for the only issue at stake was that he think of himself as a thought criminal so that his Party loyalty could be recreated as a product of the Party's doing rather than his own. Even the most conforming of souls must be reworked, lest they take credit for their subservience and in so doing challenge the Party's omnipotence. Parsons, too, must feel the wrath of the Party, if only because he was too happy to obey its demands. In other words, Parsons was no rebel, yet he was arrested. This corroborates by analogy the suspicion that Winston's defiance was not the determining factor in his arrest.

Why, then, was Winston arrested? Could he have done anything to avoid imprisonment? Recall that on the sixth day of Hate Week, when the general delirium inspired by the ceremonies reached its peak, it became known to the citizens of Oceania that the country "... was not, after all, at war with Eurasia. Oceania was at war with Eastasia. Eurasia was an ally" ([1949]1983, p. 148). Although the Hate Week continued "exactly as before, except that the target had been changed," this change meant a great deal of work for Winston and his colleagues at the Ministry of Truth (p. 150). As a matter of course and without any external motivation, Winston reported to his post as soon as the demonstrations were over. The history of the previous five years required rewriting and Winston and his colleagues at the Ministry of Truth were responsible for the task. Less than a day after their work was complete, Winston was arrested.

This coincidence of events seems hardly accidental, for it is in keeping with the principles of doublethink, as the organizing logic of Oceania, that the process through which reality is continuously remade according to the demands of the moment be relegated to the same oblivion as the inconvenient details of that reality ([1949]1983, pp. 176-177).[20] Winston was as culpable in his conformity as he was in his deviance given that his very existence as a worker in the Ministry of Truth was evidence of the fallibility of the Party. Only through a remaking of Winston himself and presumably his colleagues, too, could the Party remake itself as total. On these grounds, the tension between conformity and deviance, submission and resistance, obedience and rebellion, simply implodes. As an employee of the Ministry of Truth, Winston was doomed regardless of anything he did or did not do.[21]

We have placed Winston's arrest in the context of his work for the Party, arguing that this work explains Winston's arrest. In other words, it was his very conformity to Party expectations which made him suspect. Attention to the inherent contradictions of maintaining a class hierarchy in a highly differentiated, complex society helps to clarify this point.

A highly differentiated society such as Oceania cannot help but allow to exist a certain degree of individuation, if only that which results from the jagged combination of the division of labor[22] necessary to the maintenance of a complex society, on the one hand, with the human species' diverse biological inheritance on the other. A form of social organization requiring poets and proletarians, housewives and prostitutes, historians and soldiers, intellectuals and machinists, will inevitably give rise to people who act and feel like poets and proletarians, housewives and prostitutes, historians and soldiers, intellectuals and machinists.

In addition to this social division of labor characteristic of Oceanic society was a detailed division of labor organized according to assembly line processes of industrialized production in which no single individual makes more than a minute contribution to any given whole. In and through these divisions of labor are those differentiating characteristics which are related to human biology: the differences between males and females, associated with the necessaries of reproduction; the differences between those newly born into the species and those who have been around for sometime; the differences which result from the fragility of the biological body, creating the potential for illness and disability and leading inevitably toward death. And then there is that irreducible, indivisible fact that each of the species is its own body, enduring its own pain, and enjoying its own pleasure. Since no two bodies can occupy the same space, each body lives out its life span in a unique fashion and from its own perspective.

Winston's individuation, his alienation, his sense of his self distinct from the collective, were all functional, a consequence of his social position and the intelligence required of him in his duties to the Party. He could not have rewritten history with sufficient precision had he not developed a sophisticated historical sense, had he not pondered the metaphysics of history. Moreover, because his task required more than an arbitrary rewriting— because it required that his creations were consistent with Party aims and doctrines intellectually upholding the Party in its power—his political consciousness also needed to be highly developed. This job requirement called for the expansion and simultaneous contraction of Winston's historical consciousness. Understanding the nature of power and the relation of power to history was essential to his work.

Winston Smith was, therefore, a walking, talking version of a highly differentiated member of a complex society, ruled by an apparently all powerful elite that was fiercely dedicated to the goal of maintaining its position. The individual was both necessary and dangerous to the maintenance of the hierarchical structure of Oceanic society. The Party's intent to put an end to class struggle, to stop history in its tracks, was first and foremost a practical problem, namely, the problem of what to do with surplus individuation ([1949]1983, pp. 170-171).[23]

Summarizing these considerations, attention to the social structure of Oceania reveals that Winston's rebellion and alienation were more an occupational hazard and a function of his position as an intellectual than a autonomous product of Winston's independent consciousness. A complex society like Oceania requires a degree of individuation, if only that it might continue as a going concern. That Winston's alienation can be explained this way does not invalidate his experiences, but it does provide a context for understanding them. That Winston himself did not understand his own self as a product of his place in the social and detailed division of labor, and that he was unaware of the consistency between his own consciousness and the institutionalized power of the Party, are two of the more interesting features of *Nineteen Eighty Four*. They establish the primacy of the intellectual dynamic Orwell famously named "doublethink" as the organizing logic of both Winston's consciousness and Party power.

The Alienation of Winston Smith: Doublethink

It is truly one of literature's little ironies that Winston Smith's attempt to maintain a tension between his utopian wishes for a life worth living and the dreary futility of his everyday existence required of him a habit of thinking indistinguishable from doublethink. All the key features of that habit of thinking were involved in Winston's intellectual consciousness:

> To know and not know, to be conscious of complete truthfulness while telling carefully constructed lies, to hold consciously two opinions which cancelled out, knowing them to be contradictory and believing in both of them, to use logic against logic, to repudiate morality while laying claim to it ([1949]1983, p. 32).

At the extreme, Winston's faith in the concept of resistance in the name of abstract ideas, to which he never gave concrete determination, led him to assent to the commission of all manner of atrocities in the employ of the "Brotherhood." Winston, it must be recalled, promised "to do *anything* which is likely to cause demoralization and weaken the power of the Party" ([1949]1983, p. 142, emphasis added).

This suggests that, for Winston, resistance had become an end-in-itself, as continuous and all-embracing as the perpetual war engaged in by *Nineteen Eighty-Four*'s three superpowers. Mirroring the unity of war and peace, freedom and slavery, and ignorance and strength, Winston's resistance, once totalized, became its opposite. It therefore involved a submission indistinguishable from that demanded by the Party.

More than a literary curiosity, recognizing that Winston Smith was no amateur practitioner of doublethink[24] provides the key to understanding the full complexity of George Orwell's *Nineteen Eighty-Four*. Doublethink was the intellectual means through which the Party maintained itself as the ruling elite of Oceania, because it was through this logic that the Party was able to preserve the myth of itself as an omnipotent totality. Doublethink was the governing logic of the Party's power, but it was more than a habit of thinking imposed on a passive literati by an all powerful elite. In *Nineteen Eighty-Four*, Orwell portrayed doublethink to be a fully ambiguous, emergent phenomena, rooted in the division of labor and the irrational social structure of Oceania. Even a cursory, denotative examination is suggestive of this claim. According to the principles of Newspeak, supplied by Orwell in his famous appendix, doublethink means "very thoughtful." This can be understood as the practice of thinking taken to its extremes, where thought turns back on itself and is transformed into its opposite. Doublethink thus means both thoughtful and not thoughtful at the same time, and is descriptive of thought taken to be absolute. Of course, thought is not and cannot be absolute. Thought is always conditioned, hence brutality is necessary to force the issue even as such brutality admits its own lie by constituting *itself* as thought's first cause. This may very well be Orwell's point.

Winston's devotion to his work for the Party in conjunction with his continuing indignation at the Party's systematic distortion of truth and history is particularly useful in illustrating the normal workings of Winston's doublethinkful existence. This is due to the structural role that this value complex has in establishing the unity of Winston's subjective consciousness with objective social processes.

When it came to his employment at the Ministry of Truth, Winston was no slacker, having internalized a work ethic worthy of any dedicated professional:

> Winston's greatest pleasure in life was in his work. Most of it was a tedious routine, but included in it were also jobs so difficult and intricate that you could loose yourself in them ... delicate pieces of forgery in which you had nothing to guide you except your estimate of what the Party wanted you to say. Winston was good at that kind of thing ([1949]1983, p. 39).

This commitment to his work devoted to the rectification of printed matter in accordance with the everchanging needs of the Party coexisted with Winston's outrage and fright concerning the metaphysical significance of the Party's practice of propaganda. Importantly, this commitment to his job—a job wholly devoted to the re-writing of history—did not waiver even after he pledged himself, in the name of history, to the resistance ([1949]1983, p. 146). Thus, shortly after his meeting with O'Brien concerning his entry into the Brotherhood, Winston and his colleagues at the Ministry of Truth were charged with the task of rectifying most of the political literature of five years past, which, due to a change in Oceania's wartime alliance, had become obsolete. While the work was demanding and necessitated the utmost exertion and dedication, Winston was not philosophically or morally bothered by it:

> It was like struggling with some crushing physical task which one had the right to refuse and which one was never the less neurotically anxious to accomplish. In so far as he had time to remember it, he was not troubled by the fact that every word he murmured into the speakwrite, every stroke of his inkpencil was a deliberate lie. He was as anxious as anyone else in the department that the forgery be perfect ([1949]1983, p. 151).

In the heat of the moment, Winston was not concerned with the rectification's implications; he attended dutifully to the job at hand. Clearly, this ability to forget his internal rebellion against the Party as he dedicated his entire being to its arbitrary purposes illuminates both the degree and nature of Winston's submission to that habit of mind called doublethink.

If Winston's resistance is illustrative of the contradictory nature of Winston's thought-process at the extremes, his attitude toward his work illustrates the extent to which Winston lived up to the demands of Party conformity in his everyday activity. His relations with other humans were no less affected. For example, Winston took minor comfort in his conviction that, "If there was hope, *it must* lie in the Proles;" this conviction haunted him as "a mystical truth and a palatable absurdity" ([1949]1983, pp. 60, 70, emphasis in original). The great expectations he placed on the proles were inversely related to the contempt with which he regarded them. Thus, Winston's estimation that the proles were without intelligence or general ideas did not deter him from imposing on them the burden of utopia or the responsibility of realizing his revolution (pp. 60-61).

This contradiction is captured in Winston's thought that "... the proles, if only they could somehow become conscious of their own strength, would have no need to conspire. They need only rise up and shake themselves like a horse shaking off flies" (p. 60). Winston's view is that if the proles had insight into their own strategic position within Oceanic society, they would comprehend their own raw power and could generate the force necessary to the revolution. The analogy with the horse suggests that such an event would require nothing more than a reflexive aversion response; thus, even in their triumph, the proles would remain mindless. His insight boiled down to the dubious conclusion that if the proles could become conscious, they would have no need for consciousness.

As Winston saw it, the proles would provide the raw power necessary to the overthrow of the Party while intellectuals such as himself would provide the ideas. In addition to merely replicating a value system rooted in Party doctrine and the exploitative social structure of Oceania, Winston's evaluation of the relation between intellectuals and the masses is exaggerated to the point where its core lunacy emerges. Thus, just before his and Julia's arrest, Winston contemplates a prole woman while she hangs the laundry, pondering the world-historical significance of her female form. He thinks:

> ... everywhere stood the same solid unconquerable figure, made monstrous by work and childbearing, toiling from birth to death and still singing. Out of those mighty loins a race of conscious beings must one day come. You were the dead, theirs was the future. But you could share in that future if you kept alive the mind as they kept alive the body, and passed on the secret doctrine that two plus two make four (p. 182).

This scenario imagined by Winston is as preposterous as any provided by the Party: A child's arithmetic problem is transformed into "a secret doctrine" containing an insight of utmost importance destined to save the great masses of humankind. A woman tending to her household chores is exaggerated in the same way, first reduced to her physical body, the strength of her arms and the productivity of her womb, that body then grows enormous, a monster enveloping all of history.

These examples are intended to illustrate Winston's adoption of a ludicrous doctrine vis-à-vis the proles. His attitudes towards his colleagues at the records department, his obsessive categorizing of individuals according to his conclusions about their Party loyalty and intelligence, suggests further that Winston had internalized the demands of the thoughtpolice vis-à-vis his peers. Winston assumed that, in principle, there is always external evidence of one's inner life. He maintains this attitude despite the fact that he took great pains to conceal his own feelings from casual observation, arranging his face into an appropriate expression, managing his presentation of self so as not to disclose his heretical leanings. Julia provides a contrast to this attitude in her and Winston's discussion of the Party's sexual education efforts. She said, "I dare say it works in a lot of cases. But, of course, you can never tell; people are such hypocrites" (p. 110). Her assertion that people are hypocrites assumes a difference between a person's inner-life and outer appearance, thus implying the need for a certain amount of skepticism. Of course, Winston's powers of perception were consistently undermined by events, in the end with disastrous consequences. Julia was not a member of the thoughtpolice, nor was she saddled with any thorough-going orthodoxy. Parsons was as vulnerable to thoughtcrime as anybody else. Charrington, the shopkeeper in the prole quarter, *was* in the employ of the thoughtpolice and, of course, O'Brien was not a revolutionary. Still, Winston never questioned the principle that one could tell, or even that it mattered.

The above discussion is intended to show the skill with which Winston practiced doublethink. There was no necessary connection between his thoughts and his actions nor, indeed, was there even a basic consistency within his internal, reflexive thought-process. Obsessed with visions of resistance, Winston was ignorant of his own complicity. Convinced of the profundity of trivia, insight slipped through Winston's fingers. Unable to implicate himself in his own thought-process, Winston's essential identity with the Party remained intact, as obvious as the blue overalls of his Party uniform were to the proles (p. 71).

Moreover, it becomes clear that, for Orwell, doublethink is more than just a form of consciousness, abstracted from social processes, but refers directly to the concrete means through which the ruling elite maintained the myth of its absolute power. That the Party was required to actively maintain this myth through material practice necessitated a performative concession that its power was, in fact, limited. This relates directly to the problem of social legitimation earlier defined in terms of the requirement that the institutions being legitimated can maintain their given-ness in the face of the recognition that they are humanly constructed. Both the challenge to given-ness and the mobilization of resources necessary to the resolution of the challenge point to the contradiction inherent in the requirement that this given-ness of institutions must be justified at all. Applying this to the situation of Oceania, it can be said that the Party's desire to constitute its own past required a tremendous expenditure of resources, as did the Party's insistence on controlling its own members. The Party's willingness to thus exert itself involved entangling itself in a core contradiction, namely, the recognition of its own limited power. The

Party insisted on the myth of its omnipotence precisely because it was not, in fact, omnipotent. In other words, even the ruling elite of a closed society was forced to settle. These considerations relate directly to the meaning of Winston's imprisonment, and thus to the question of the function of torture in *Nineteen Eighty-Four*.

First, a brief return to the analysis of Oceanic society is warranted. Oceania was a hierarchical society composed of three strata. As is clearly stated in the theoretical treatise within the larger novel titled *The Theory and Practice of Oligarchic Collectivism*, the Inner Party's intention to remain in permanent control could only be achieved through continuously safeguarding the mental attitude of the top two tiers of Oceanic society—the Inner and Outer Party—which, together, comprised roughly 15 percent of the population:

> The only genuine dangers are the splitting off of able, underemployed, power hungry people, and the growth of liberalism and skepticism in their own ranks. The problem, that is to say, is educational. It is a problem of continuously molding the consciousness both of the directing group and of the larger group that lies immediately below it. The consciousness of the masses need only to be influenced in a negative way ([1949]1983, p. 171).

In other words, the Party's totalizing telos was restricted to the Party itself. Accordingly, even totalitarianism was not total, but merely a means to the all-encompassing goal of maintaining the existing social structure of Oceania and the Party's hegemony. At issue was "the persistence of a certain world view and a certain way of life imposed by the dead upon the living" (1989, p. 173). The maintenance of Party power required that the Party existed as a felt presence in its members. Its reality was to be not only assumed but directly intuited, perceived, and experienced ([1949]1983, pp. 217-218). This is because the Party was an "adoptive organization," and consequently, its preservation depended first and foremost on the willingness of the upper two tiers of society to *voluntarily* maintain their identification with it ([1949]1983, p. 173). The issue, then, is one of social legitimation. It is here that the meaning of Winston's imprisonment emerges, for it is now possible to develop a concrete understanding of precisely what happened to Winston under the tutelage of O'Brien.

On the surface nothing seems to have happened other than a gratuitous infliction of pain. This was made explicit to Winston, who was repeatedly reminded by O'Brien that he already knew what was wrong with him, that he, Winston Smith, knew what he was to do. And it was indeed true that

O'Brien did not present Winston with any intellectual argument or insight that Winston had not already stumbled over.

Even more to the point, Winston had encountered O'Brien's arguments and positions twice, first in the stream of his own thought-process as he conducted his business (described in Part I of the novel), and second as Winston refined his understanding of the world he lived in, contrasting the bleakness of his existence with the utopian experience of his relationship with Julia, culminating in the affirmation of his sanity via his reading of *The Theory and Practice of Oligarchic Collectivism* (described in Part II). Thus, when O'Brien informed Winston that, "There are three stages to your reintegration ... there is learning, there is understanding, and there is acceptance," this statement also applied to Winston's own *dis*integration as documented in the first two parts of the novel ([1949]1983, p. 215). And, to complete this dialectic, the final stage of Winston's disintegration merges with the beginning of his reintegration. His arrest was the peak of his alienation from his society at the same time as it was the foundation for the restoration of an identity between himself and the Party as a collective.

Winston's arrest, then, was an individuation through which he came into unmediated conflict with the Party. Alone, he was to defend himself against the apparatus of power, standing up against its truth in the name of his own. Locked in its prison and the victim of its violence, the Party ceased to be an abstraction, concretizing itself in the pain of Winston's body. In this context, Winston was forced to feel his own weakness, the frailty of his body and his mind, as his hopes and dreams, his memories and reminiscences, were absorbed in the infinite present of the prison cell. The first lesson Winston learned was, "In the face of pain, there are no heros" ([1949]1983 , p. 197).

Consequently, it was only in prison that Winston was able to combine his intellectual knowledge of how the Party maintained its power and the emotional understanding of what the power of the Party meant with the embodied experience of that power. In other words, Winston was forced in prison to incorporate his knowledge of the mechanics of social organization and his understanding of its significance for the conduct of life with the experience of his own body in pain. With O'Brien as his guide, he relived the process of his disintegration so that he could come to identify with himself as an unimportant Party functionary, capable of the lowest deeds, worthy of only scorn, and thus willing to transfer his sense of himself as a "self" onto the Party. O'Brien's task was thus to penetrate the haze of doublethink for but an instant and make Winston see himself as he was, not as he imagined or wished himself to be.

The success of this program of establishing Winston's identification with the Party was based on the carefully regulated infliction of pain on Winston's body. O'Brien, speaking on behalf of the Party, explains to Winston:

... power is power over human beings. Over the body—but above all, over the mind. Power over matter—external reality as you would call it— is not important. Already our control over matter is absolute .... We control matter because we control the mind. Reality is inside the skull ([1949]1983, p. 218).

Dialogically establishing this truth, however, required that O'Brien and Winston together agree to discount the significance of the fact of power over the material body. Physical brutality was necessary to Winston's acceptance of the Party's power. The efficacy of O'Brien's effort to reform Winston depended on the fact that Winston was willing to overlook his status as a prisoner and a victim of an agent whose control over him was total.

Thus, Winston searched his mind in vain for arguments which would demonstrate the fallacy of O'Brien's position that "nothing exists outside your own mind" ([1949]1983, p. 219). That he felt the need to provide such an argument suggests that he was in a basic agreement with O'Brien without being fully conscious of it. This, of course, is perfectly consistent with the internalized practice of doublethink. Had he not been so skilled at doublethink, the absurdity of his efforts would have been apparent to him. Winston *was* in agreement with O'Brien's position that the significance of the objective world was secondary to that of his own personal subjective experience. This is established earlier in the novel where Winston insisted that, "Nothing was your own except the few cubic centimeters inside your skull" ([1949]1983, p. 26). Winston took refuge in these sorts of convictions even though he knew them to be futile in the sense that he knew that his own personal thoughts and feelings would have no objective consequences.

Winston, whose rebellion could only be the most secret of affairs, established an identity distinct from the Party through his subjective opposition. This was his only claim to power, and he understood it as such: "If you can feel that staying human is worthwhile, even when it can't have any result whatever, you've beaten them" ([1949]1983, p. 138). Aside from the fact that this is perfectly contradictory (as are so many of Winston's convictions), it also points to the degree to which Winston had subordinated all values—even his essential humanity—to opposing the Party's power. In this way, he attempted to compensate for the Party's having robbed him of "all power over the material world" by insisting on the primacy of his own thoughts and feelings as the source of his opposition to the Party's power ([1949]1983, p. 136).

More essential to the core of Winston's self than his opinion of rats was his inability to directly confront and accept his own powerlessness (1983 [1949], pp. 233-234). That Winston felt intellectually inferior to O'Brien and could not meet O'Brien's arguments with his own, yet still remained convinced of the mind's superiority, rendered it acceptable to Winston that he transfer his identity onto O'Brien and through O'Brien onto Big Brother. Winston's inability to reconcile himself to his own limitations, his unwillingness to accept the undeniable fact of his own powerlessness and leave it at that, constituted the foundation for the identification between Winston's individual self-consciousness and the objective logic of power. Not that it mattered; even Winston knew his resistance to be hardly more than a desperate act of vanity, the effects of which only prolonged his own pain, got him a raise in pay and, ultimately, a reserved table at the Chestnut Tree Cafe.

We have set Winston's imprisonment in the broad context of the social organization of Oceania and the requirements of maintaining the hegemonic power of the Party in that society. Objectively, the problem appeared in the form of a necessary but potentially destabilizing surplus individuation. Subjectively, it took the form of creating and preserving the identification of each Party member with the Party as a collective. Unfortunately for Winston, the Party was able to manage these crises tendencies by systematically turning surplus individuation against itself, exploiting its vulnerabilities and weaknesses for its own purposes, and in so doing, maintained itself as a going concern in the minds of its members. Winston's alienation from the Party was thoroughly conditioned by his objective dependance on the Party. It was O'Brien's challenge to demonstrate this to Winston, to show him he was no different. In this way, Winston's subjective identification with the Party was solidified, allowing the Party to constitute its own reality.

At this point, it is possible to draw an analogy between Rorty's liberal ironist characteristic of a post-metaphysical culture and Winston Smith. Like Rorty's ironist, Winston was an intellectual who was subject to doubts concerning the nature of his work devoted to the production of propaganda for mass consumption. Just as Rorty's ironist is not troubled by epistemological doubts, Winston understood well the epistemological status of his intellectual activity: he knew knowledge to be a sham based on his own participation in the systematic production of lies within the Ministry of Truth. And, just as Rorty's ironists stoically accept their political commitments as given by existing institutions, swallowing their doubts about the foundations of those institutions, Winston also knew politics to be a sham as well, even in the face of its penetration into every aspect of existence. Of course, Winston also knew better than to publicly articulate his political doubts. The question that continued to riddle Winston and the question which Rorty dismisses as both inappropriate to a post-metaphysical ironist culture and irrelevant to the understanding of *Nineteen Eighty-Four*—referring to it as a "red herring" (1989, p. 182)—concerned the metaphysical implications of the Party's power to alter history. In other words, it was the systematic dislocation of reality itself—"the power of re-description," to use Rorty's phrase—which Winston felt to be the final and most disturbing consequence of the Party's practice of propaganda in the interests of preserving its hegemonic position. Thus, Winston writes in his diary, "I understand HOW: I do not understand WHY" ([1949]1983, p. 68). It is this question, both a question of ultimate motive and purpose as well as a question of social legitimation, that Rorty dismisses as unanswerable in a post-metaphysical culture. Unfortunately, it was also Winston's inability or unwillingness to answer this question that establishes his ultimate complicity with Party power.

Applying this analogy to Winston's practice of doublethink, Winston's ability to re-write history was crucial to his ability to successfully maneuver within his society, yet stood in sharp contrast to his having been deprived of any control over the conditions of his existence. Just as, in Rorty's view, linguistic re-description is a form of empowerment, Winston's intellectual skills were essential to his short-term survival but did not have any real effect on his life. Moreover, just as members of Rorty's post-metaphysical utopia would approach their identity and cultural productions with a spirit of playfulness, Winston was forced, in the interests of coping and compensation, to take a nonbinding approach to his own intellectual and emotional commitments. Winston's ability to shift his commitments at will and in accordance with the external demands of his situation suggests both the extent of his ability to manipulate his own mind as well as replicates the dynamic implicit in the expectation that Party members shift their political allegiances at will according to the demands of the moment and without experiencing any conflict. Just as the liberal ironist is encouraged in Rorty's text to privilege a discursive reality amenable to the transformative power of language, Winston created for himself a fantastic world where he imagined himself destined to save the masses of humankind and preserve the human spirit. In so doing, Winston occupied a dual universe of fantasy and reality, experiencing his fantasies as more real than reality. Even so, Winston never failed conform to the demands of reality.

Finally, as Rorty promises the liberal ironist an expansion of private freedom in return for their conformity, Winston, too, gained his freedom. Winston's freedom—an abstract, negative freedom which had no implications outside his own mind—was premised on his recognition and acceptance of his contingency on the power of the Party. Thus, having already faced in Room 101 the worst thing in the world, a confrontation which established his identity with the Party through the lived experience of his own powerlessness, Winston finds himself sitting in the Chestnut Tree Cafe: drinking oily gin, flavored with saccharine and cloves, Winston was free. He was free to meet and speak with Julia, for, "He knew it as though instinctively that they now took almost no interest in his doings" ([1949]1983, p. 239). He was free to recall a happy memory from childhood, for he knew it to be a false memory and false memories "did not matter, so long as one knew them for what they were" ([1949]1983, p. 243). He was free to let his mind wander wherever it chose, and, presumably, to give voice to those wanderings if he wished to do so. No longer compelled to negotiate the contradiction between his inner world of resistance and his outer world of conformity, Winston's existence became one of indifference.

In the above discussion, we have considered the extent of Rorty's redescription of George Orwell's *Nineteen Eighty-Four* through the presentation of an alternative reading that we feel better accounts for the text. Specifically, we argue that Rorty's reading fails to account for Orwell's presentation of the role of the intellectual in the reproduction of institutionalized social power in a complex society. Our posited analogy between Rorty's ironic intellectual and the character Winston Smith is oriented towards showing that, in both texts, it is a reflexive understanding of the arbitrariness of social institutions combined with a thoroughgoing powerlessness which solidifies the commitment of intellectuals to those institutions. This dynamic in the fictional world of *Nineteen Eighty-Four* is rooted in the institutionalized division of labor and the intent by the Party to deny that division's individuating and destabilizing consequences, this, combined with the inability or unwillingness of individuals to incorporate into their self-consciousness their own powerlessness. In *Contingency, Irony, and Solidarity*, the case is not so clear, given Rorty's unwillingness to resort to such theoretical constructions as the division of labor. But, at the risk of engaging in metaphysics, we think it safe to point out that Rorty's distinction between the ironic intellectual and the commonsensical non-metaphysician would seem to imply something along the lines of a division of labor, if only because it assumes that some people engage in intellectual activity and some people do not. The next question, and the question Rorty will not pose, is "why?"

The possibility of an analogy between Rorty's utopian vision and Orwell's decidedly dystopian vision suggests that Rorty's proposals for the reform of intellectual culture (wherein ironic reflexivity is privatized) might not be as consistent with the interests of intellectuals as Rorty claims. At issue in both texts is the possibility and function of theory, broadly conceived as the attempt to understand one's experience in relation to one's social context. Rorty thinks that a liberal postmodern bourgeois culture can do without such theoretical efforts. He is probably right and Orwell may well have agreed with him. The question that remains open concerns the consequences of doing without self-reflection for individuals living within such a society. Rorty's implicit claim is that the privatization of philosophy and social theory, both of which would seem necessary to a reflexive understanding of one's place in the order of things, will not endanger those who engage in intellectual activity and will enable the preservation of social hope crucial to the legitimation of liberal social institutions. The validity of this claim would seem to depend on the nature of the institutions in question. This is, at base, a sociological issue, one that Rorty cannot confront within the confines of his position.

Orwell, however, in his concern to articulate the details of a life lived mindlessly, constructs a tale wherein knowing the truth of one's experience, however desperate, is somehow better than a self-indulgent ignorance. It is unlikely that Winston's fate would have been any different if he had been prepared to intellectually confront his situation. Given the structural determinants of his situation, Winston still would have been arrested and still would have been tortured. No theory would have changed this. At issue, then, is not the instrumental value of self-knowledge in furthering one's own interest but the value of self-knowledge for its own sake.

CONCLUSION

We would like to conclude by considering the possibilities for resistance under the desperate conditions stipulated by Orwell. At issue is the possibility for resisting the world's process in the absence of any means of certifying claims to difference from that process. In other words, if it is necessary to transcend the social-historical context in order to question it, and if humans prove incapable of such transcendence, must they then resign themselves to the way things are?

This question relates directly to the practical efficacy of the views outlined in Rorty's *Contingency, Irony, and Solidarity*, for his underlying assumption seems to be that challenges to social institutions depend for their articulation on the ability to transcend or envision qualitative alternatives to those institutions. Thus, Rorty both subtly and effectively invokes the dependency of ironic intellectuals on the very institutions about which they wax ironic, as if this knowledge alone will solidify their commitment to and thus the legitimacy of those institutions.

We think it is to Orwell's credit that his last novel provides an inquiry into the idea of difference, alienation, and subjective otherness, tracing it back to its origins in recognizable social forms. As we have attempted to show, Winston Smith was a conformist through and through, his rebellious inclinations effectively determined by his environment. Does this undermine the validity of Winston's feelings of resistance? Was Winston merely a pretender?

In answering this, an analogy may be drawn with Winston's irritation at the proles for having the power but not the sense to realize his utopia, as if supplying the labor power for an entire society under the most exploitative conditions short of abject slavery was not enough to keep one class busy. A comment by a prole woman overheard by Winston provides a simple corrective:

> But if you'd been in my place, you'd of done the same as what I done. It's easy to criticize ... but you ain't got the same problems as what I got (p. 71).

The suggestion here is that such judgements are always dubious, a product of arrogance more than understanding.

Applying this to Winston's situation requires that one attend not to his evident intellectual shortcomings but to his lifetime of emotional and material deprivation, which rendered a self-indulgent ignorance functional. The vicissitudes of his emotional and intellectual life cannot be understood without reference to his dreary existence of bread crusts and victory gin and the fact that, above all else, he was a very unhappy person. It is true that he was no better than the proles he denigrates, hoarding razor blades with the same spirit of pettiness that they fought over cheap tin pots, and that he took the same satisfaction in the illusory promise of love provided in his relationship with Julia that the proles took in the illusory promise of wealth provided by the lottery (pp. 43-44, 53, 60-61, 73, 124).

Nor was Winston much different than O'Brien or any of the other characters in the novel. This is indicated after his arrest, in his first meeting with O'Brien, when in lieu of a greeting, he cried "They got you too!" O'Brien responded, "They got me a long time ago," hinting that all have been gotten, and as such, all have been had (p. 197). Members of the Inner Party, too, were obliged to operate under the sign of the irrational, behaving according to the laws of individual survival. In a society like Oceania, where there was no effective agency, no possibility for doing what one would choose if things were otherwise, all were on a moral plane determined by necessity. Successful adaptation and simple prudence replaces morality as the logic governing individual behavior.

Thus, there is intimated in the novel a deep universality where all were equal in their misery and no one could be said to benefit from the organization of power in Oceanic Society. There were differences in status and there were differences in consumption habits, yet these were minor compared to the pervasive sameness extending through the hierarchy. An essential equality existed through the hierarchy, an equality which required brutal torture and manifest irrationality for its suppression. That is, it was precisely because the inhabitants of Oceania were essentially the same that unfreedom and repression were necessary to the maintenance of the hierarchy. It was precisely because the institutional arrangements of Oceania had no rational connection to the way humans were, even in that society, that widespread irrationality was necessary.

This, then, is the basis for resistance provided by Orwell in his novel *Nineteen Eighty-Four*. That Winston's resistance was the product of the very social institutions he resisted provides the ground of its truth. That his rebellion was an expression of a greater conformity, that even his alienation was not his own—facts which made torture and repression integral to the operation of the system—provides the basic reason for revolution.

Finally, Winston's fatal flaw was not his inability to transcend his immediate situation or his inability to ground his utopian hopes in something immune from social processes, but rather, his having bought into the mystification that he should have. When, under the guidance of O'Brien, he was forced to identify with himself as he was and not as he wished to be, he could not recover. His betrayal of Julia, despite the fact that it occurred under the most extreme of circumstances and had no practical consequences, destroyed his belief in himself as somehow different. The sad irony is that he fell before the same harsh, though faulty, judgment that he employed against the proles: he felt himself to be less than human for not being superhuman.[25]

NOTES

1. Rorty does not use the term "social legitimation." Our framing of the various ideas contained in *Contingency, Irony, and Solidarity* in terms of this problematic is thus an interpretive act. For a full consideration of the relation between the problem of social legitimation and the problem of knowledge, see Peter L. Berger and Thomas Luckman's *The Social Construction of Reality* (1966). Jurgen Habermas, in *Legitimation Crisis* ([1973]1975) provides a technical discussion of the problem of legitimation in contemporary capitalist societies.

2. Keith Toppler (1995) provides an account of the role of narrative in the maintenance of liberal democracy.

3. In his "Richard Rorty, Liberalism and the Politics of Re-description," Toppler analyses Rorty's use of the concept of "contingency," focusing on Rorty's use of the concept in two opposing ways. Rorty's tendencey to equivocate vis-à-vis contingency is, as we hope to make apparent, one of the more interesting and disturbing features of *Contingency, Irony, and Solidarity*.

4. Rorty's appeal to the sympathy of liberal ironists is a variant of an appeal to self-interest because, in his presentation, liberals define themselves in terms of their desire to avoid and diminish cruelty. Their willingness to subordinate their intellectual practice to the ends of preventing cruelty would thus be motivated by the desire to maintain the coherence of their identities.

5. Rorty's appeal to the self-interest of intellecturals generally occurs at the periphery of his presentation. We are thus actively and insistently reconstructing an argument which occurs at the subtextual level.

6. Charles Anderson, in "Pragmatism & Liberalism, Rationalism & Irrationalism: A Response to Richard Rorty," describes *Contingency, Irony, and Solidarity* as "Rorty's first systematic effort to link his 'foundationless' philosophy to political theory" (1991, p. 358). Anderson is suggesting that with this book, Rorty ceases to address an audience primarily composed of professional philosophers focused on technical questions and thus subjects his work to the judgment of "a new community of inquiry and against new standards" (1991, pp. 358-359).

7.   Rorty tends to treat "the world" as an undifferentiated totality referring to everything and anything which does not take a linguistic form. The implicit contrast is with "our world," or the specifically human world which always takes a discursive form.

8.   Roy Bhaskar, in his *Rorty, Realism, and the Idea of Freedom* (1990, pp. 225-230), provides a technical discussion of Rorty's treatment of "freedom."

9.   See Bhaskar (1991, p. 97).

10.   Goodheart, in commenting on this aspect of Rorty's work, suggests Rorty's acceptance of the fact that his liberalism is indefensible and is rooted in Rorty's complacency concerning the prospects of liberal democracy (1996, p. 234).

11.   Toppler discusses "re-description" as a vechicle for political change (1995, pp. 962-964).

12.   See Anderson (1991, pp. 369-370).

13.   Anderson observes that a tendency toward closure is a general characteristic of liberalism (1991, p. 366).

14.   In the literature on Orwell and his literary and political writings, there is an unusually high degree of self-consciousness concerning the tendency for thinkers of widely divergent political and intellectual persuasions to claim Orwell's legacy as their own. For example, Harold Bloom contends that Orwell and *Nineteen Eighty-Four* have been absorbed into the culture industry (1987, p. 4). John Rodden, in *The Politics of Literary Reputation* (1989), provides a detailed analysis of the history of commenting on George Orwell.

15.   Sue Lonoff, in "Composing *Nineteen Eighty-Four*: The Art of Nightmare," points out that Orwell's use of this perspective filters the reader's perceptions of Oceania and the events of the novel (1991, p. 35).

16.   Others have questioned Rorty's practice of textual interpretation. For example, Goodheart (1996) argues that Rorty equates interpretation with appropriation, an equation which tends to be coercive (1996, pp. 228-229). Richard J. Bernstein comments on Rorty's tendency to project his own concerns into his readings of others (1989, pp. 545-546). Also relevant here is the point made by David Hall, a commentator more sympathetic to Rorty than those just mentioned, concerning Rorty's endorsement of Harold Bloom's notion of a "strong misreading" (1994, p. 5). For Rorty's own understanding of this idea of a strong misreading, see his "Nineteenth-Century Idealism and Twentieth-Century Textualism" (1982, pp. 151-152).

17.   Our interpretation here is very different from that of many commentators, even different from the general tendency of Orwell's own writings. Orwell, particularly in his polemics against left-leaning intellectuals, frequently relied on metaphors derived from, what were in his view, deviant sexual practices, including sadism, homosexuality, vegetarianism, and that horrible pox on the visage of humanity, wearing sandals. Of the devices used in *Nineteen Eighty-Four* to create distance between the perspective of Winston Smith, as not quite credible, and that of the reader, is Orwell's attributing to him a masculinity which—within the

framework of the novel—is degraded or distorted, as indicated by, for example, Winston's homoerotic attraction toward O'Brien and the suggestion that Winston was impotent within officially sanctioned relations and, perhaps, infertile (although this latter point may be an interpretive stretch on our part).

18. Daniel Kies, in "Fourteen Types of Passivity: Suppressing Agency in *Nineteen Eighty-Four*," analyzes the various techniques Orwell uses to deprive Winston of agency, conveying the futility of Winston's existence and his essential powerlessness (1992, p. 48).

19. Orwell seems to be relying on a conception of power similar to Max Weber's, who defined power, famously, as "... the probabilty that one actor within a social relationship will be in a position to carry out his own will despite resistance, regardless of the basis on which this probability rests" (1978, p. 53).

20. Orwell's reliance on temporal imagary, which echo the origins myth in the *Book of Genesis*, is suggestive of the claim that we are making.

21. The character Winston is thus anticipated by Boxer, the horse in Orwell's earlier work, *Animal Farm*. Boxer's loyalty and commitment to the revolution, in whose name he labored tirelessly and (unlike Winston) without question, led him straight to the glue factory.

22. While a detailed discussin of Orwell's characterology is beyond the scope of this chapter, it suggests all of these divisions. Orwell gave considerable attention to the social structure of Oceania, including gender relationships, class relations, the geo-political situation, the structuring of work, and so forth. Still, he never, to our knowledge, uses the term "division of labor" in *Nineteen Eighty-Four*. Our employment of the concept is thus an interpretive act. Harry Braverman, in *Labor and Monopoly Capital* (1974), provides a thorough theoretical treatment of the divsion of labor in late capitalist society. See also Berger and Luckmann for a consideration of the relationship between social complexity, the division of labor, and legitimation problems (1966, pp. 92-116).

23. Orwell does not use this term.

24. This aspect of *Nineteen Eighty-Four* is consistently overlooked in the commentary on the novel, Rorty's included. For example, in the context of considering whether or not O'Brien was an ironist, Rorty writes, "O'Brien has mastered doublethink, and is not troubled by doubts about himself or the Party" (1989, p. 185). Rorty concludes from this that O'Brien was not an ironist. The question that Rorty does not consider, a neglect which is consistent with his general tendency to de-emphasize the character Winston, is whether or not *Winston* had mastered the practice of doublethink.

25. We are leaning heavily on, and distorting, Richard Ree's criticisms contained in his 1962 essay, "All or Nothing," where Ree suggests that Winston's and Julia's (and thus Orwell's) real trouble was that "they could not forgive themselves for not being superhumanly brave" (1984, p. 217)

Chapter 7

Mass Death: Exterminism, Extinction, Execution, Excrement, Et Cetera at the Fin de Siecle

Hamm:	*Nature has forgotten us.*
Clov:	*There's no more nature.*
Hamm:	*No more nature! You exaggerate.*
Clov:	*In the vicinity.*
Hamm:	*But we breathe, we change! We lose our hair, our teeth! Our bloom! Our ideals!*
Clov:	*Then she hasn't forgotten us.*
Hamm:	*But you say there is none.*
Clov (sadly):	*No one that ever lived ever thought so crooked as we.*
Hamm:	*We do what we can.*
Clov:	*We shouldn't. (pause.)*

—Samuel Beckett, End-Game (1958, p. 11)

There is no end to death, it seems. And every attempt to write words about the reality of mass death is forever condemned as untimely (see Foucault [1976]1980, especially "Right of Death and Power Over Life," pp. 135-159).

Baudrillard, for his part, lived past the modern to see a new desert landscape forming: a space of identity, located in its most exaggerated form in postwar America, where "identity is untenable: it *is* death, since it fails to inscribe its own death" ([1976]1993b, p. 4). For Baudrillard, America is, in this sense, the land of mass death.

The theoretical tradition of Adorno and Benjamin is naturally behind Baudrillard's thesis of the American desert as "the only remaining primitive society" precisely because it "lacks a past through which to reflect ..." (1988a, p. 7). For example, in Eva Geulen's words, Adorno also "perceived ... [that] the United States has no relation to tradition, and nothing could be more natural and thus more naturally traditional than the lack of a conscious relationship to tradition" (1997, p. 188). As for Benjamin, Baudrillard positions his written reflections in what is perhaps his most important work, *Symbolic Exchange and Death* ([1976]1993b), with reference to one of this century's most tragic suicide victims:

> Today, we have made the vertigo of politics that Benjamin denounces in fascism, its perverse aesthetic enjoyment, into the experience of production at the level of the general system. We produce the experience of a de-politicised, de-ideologicalised vertigo of the rational administration of things, of endlessly exploding finalities ([1976]1993b, p. 186).

From this, again echoing Adorno's vertigo and the silent body of Benjamin lying before the border with the postmodern that Baudrillard himself has successfully transgressed, he concludes that:

> Strictly speaking, nothing remains for us to base anything on. All that remains for us is theoretical violence—speculation to the death, whose only method is the radicalisation of hypotheses ([1976]1993b, p. 5).

Gathering up these thoughts, it seems to us that the Adorno/Benjamin "method" of negative dialectics (see Buck-Morss 1977) is a form of theoretical violence that calls for the strict radicalization of investigative hypotheses. In *Negative Dialectics*, Adorno himself makes this point:

> If negative dialectics calls for the self-reflection of thinking, the tangible implication is that if thinking is to be true—if it is to be true today, in any case—it must also be a thinking against itself. If thought is not measured by the extremity that eludes the concept, it is from the outset in the nature of the musical accompaniment with which the SS liked to drown out the screams of its victims (1966, p. 365).

While this method issued from Adorno's philosophical thesis, parallel to Baudrillard's some years later, that "throughout history, identity thinking has been something deathly, something that devours everything" ([1964]1973, p. 139), we must not take from this the misapprehension that "identity thinking" is deathly only *in abstracto*. In Adorno, "history" is not empty time, for we remember that it was "*Auschwitz* [which] confirmed the philosopheme of pure identity as death" (p. 362, emphasis added). Adorno continues:

> The most far out dictum from Beckett's End *Game*, that there really is not so much to be feared any more, reacts to a practice whose first sample was given the concentration camps, and in whose concept—venerable once upon a time—the destruction of nonidentity is ideologically lurking. Absolute negativity is in plain sight and has ceased to surprise anyone. Fear used to be tied to the *principium individuationis* of self-preservation, and that principle, by its own consistency, abolishes itself. What the sadists in the camps foretold their victims, "Tomorrow you'll be wiggling skyward as smoke from this chimney," bespeaks the indifference of each individual life that is the direction of history. Even in his formal freedom, the individual is as fungible and replaceable as he will be under the liquidators' boots (1966, p. 362).

In the present moment, in *our* totalitarian American desert world, we cannot be more aware of anything than the manifold presence of death. It surrounds us completely. Our consciousness is identical with it even as our bodies labor on. Death is the essence of everything before us and everything after us. Our concept, of course, has nothing to do with an idiosyncratic superficial morbidity and everything to do with an inescapable empirical facticity. Following the pied piper that is Baudrillard, death is the nothing that we have to base ourselves on, and therein lies the foundation of our lifeworld-grounded critical theory.

Our theoretical map is thus a cemetery guidebook, directing us, for example, to Herbert Spencer's eternal location directly across from Karl Marx's British Communist Big Head at London's Highgate cemetery (see Kivisto [1998, p. 14] for a photograph of Marx's headstone). There is nothing new or shocking in this metaphor. In an odd and apparently traditional gesture, Bauman (1989) has made all too explicit the identity between the Holocaust and modernity, which is the generalized sociological hypothesis of our world. For his own part, Foucault is content to blithely note:

> If genocide is indeed the dream of modern powers, this is not because of a recent return of the ancient right to kill; it is because power is situated and exercised at the level of life, the species, the race, and the large-scale phenomena of population ([1976]1980, p. 137).

The analysis of modernity's social structure is, in the last analysis, the study of concentrated power and thus the study of mass death, even if most run-of-the-mill analysts of social structure *sui generis* (Durkheim comes to mind) have always been ghostly unaware of this (until the death of Durkheim's beloved son in the Great War, perhaps?). Still, the sociology of social structure is the study of domination, where, following Adorno, "death" is understood as "the *Telos* of all domination" ([1970]1984, p. 357, emphasis in original). Mass death under a macro-scope is sociology's enduring subject-matter; it is a disciplinary raison d'être that emerges from the classic tradition; it is the same problem faced all along, since Max Weber sought the limits of "what he could stand," to Michel Foucault's having found them too soon (see Bendix 1962; Eribon 1991; Miller 1993).

History, too, is death: murder, actually. This is particularly the case when viewed from the point of view of the latest generation of First Worlders. Leonard Cohen, for one, has "seen the future, baby," and no doubt he is right, "it is murder." In this and in so many other ways, quantity has become identical with quality; value is liquidated. In the entwinment of, for example, Rwanda, our collective, world-historical dispassionate gaze at genocide in Rwanda, our ignorance of its particulars, and the enshrinement, therein, of "Rwanda," yet another case of genocide, history as an actuality dies. As a critical concept, then, history must become the rejection of its own concept. Everyone who is alive today, it seems, is silent before the termination of historical progress, the death of history. Among the affluent young, especially, few, it seems, are truly intellectually alive, and for this we must credit the culture industry. We may pretend to be turned on by change, by difference, like Jesus Jones, who sings "there's no place I'd rather be, right here, right now, watching the world wake up from history." We may sing along with REM's ironic "Shiny Happy People," try to follow their advice to "stand in the place where you are, think about direction, wonder why you haven't before," or ponder REM's touching tribute to "A Wrong Child," who is "not supposed to be like this, but it's okay." Or, we may prefer to identify with the melancholy longings voiced by the lead singer of Collective Soul, on-high, at the edge of <u>his</u> world, "and I laugh to myself as the tears roll down, because it's the world I know, it's the world I know." Or we can purchase, because the record company wants us to, the Smashing Pumpkins' really big 1996 smash hit, *Mellon Collie and the Infinite Sadness*, and so on and on. But run-on socialization in hyperreality cannot help but buttress the business of affirmative culture; music videos kill more than radio stars. As Adorno once noted: "to recommend ... rock- and-roll over Beethoven does nothing to dismantle the affirmative lie of culture" ([1970]1984, p. 441).

Finally, at the terminus, the level of the biographical corpse, there can be no equivalences anymore, no conceptual register that accounts for the numbers dead (whole species next to loved ones riddled with cancer, warehouses full of Muslim men, death-row inmates, and fellow-travelers lost in space), nor is there is a conceptual framework that heals the still-living-on (T.S. Elliot's "living, living, and partly living"), much less re-members them or consecrates the cemetery experience of persistent fragmented, split-subjectivity (as though Lincoln, for example, was really the demi-God that he is, in Ken Burns' American semi-school, made out to have-been). The sociological imagination today requires a rigid, inflexible, hyper-melancholy side, for there can be no positing of an actual "hope," not even, as in Ronald Aronson's *Dialectics of Disaster* (1988), a "preface to hope," because, for us, panic/cynicism implodes and drags us down. There are no more functionally undamaged lives, if there ever were.

The remainder of this chapter aims to side-step the actuality of our death as authors, and it is therefore, at base, fictional. In Part One, we go through the motions of a lifeless phenomenology of our excremental American culture, a true after-life experience in which we pass through hospital death at home, abortion protests in the streets, a meeting with Sister Helen Prejean outside of the death chamber at Louisiana's Angola State Prison, the second and the more interesting phase of the Cold War, and, finally, our ultimate surrender before the Dayton Peace Accords. What is left after this passage-work is the remainder of the remainder, which, as Part Two, is dedicated to the non-identity of the sociological imagination in-itself and for-itself.

If there is a traditional reason for going past this point, it is suggested, perhaps, by Max Horkheimer's oft-quoted remark from his essay "The Authoritarian State," that:

For the revolutionary, the world has always been ripe. What in retrospect appears as a preliminary stage or premature situation was once for a revolutionary a last chance for change. A revolutionary is with the desperate people for whom everything is on the line, not with those who have time ([1940]1982, pp. 95-117, 106).

If it is still in the urgent interest of truth, critical theory's traditional conceptual master, that the world must still be ripe especially when the world is positively rotten to the core, there is no choice, then, but to muster the conscientious objection to the discipline necessary to play-out in our minds the end-game that we did not originally choose but which is nonetheless and unavoidably given to us, even if on every reflexive theoretical, ethical, and aesthetic ground, we can't, we shouldn't, indeed, we couldn't promise anything actually redemptive by it. Since the Messianic power of *our* words is something less than weak, but our writing is something greater than degree zero, we are therefore forced to write from the zone of the life-support system and risk sharing more of our oxygen than we should.

PART ONE. A QUICK TOUR OF DEATH'S OTHER KINGDOM

Over the course of our 30-odd years, we have known first-hand many people who have died, but only once have we truly experienced the death of a dying man, his hand in our own. John S. Dandaneau, age 70, died of the effects of bladder, brain, and lung cancer on September 29, 1995, at his home in Flint, Michigan. Uncle John and his wife, my Aunt Helen, age 72 at her own death on October 15, 1997, were my parents (and legal guardians) since the death of my own biological parents in 1970, at which time I was nearly seven years old. That Uncle John was allowed to die in his own bed under the auspices of Hospice (*not* in a hospital room under the direct authority of medical science) is an actuality directly tied to the reform movements of the 1960s and 1970 that sought a new understanding of death and dying, a new social contract for the terminally ill and chronically infirm, and a new set of rights and opportunities for those facing the last years and days of their mortal existence (see Keleman 1974; Kubler-Ross 1969; Levine 1982; also, for critical analysis of the death industry and Western attitudes toward death, see Aries 1974; Mitford 1963; Newman 1997). Uncle John's "home death" is also, however, a product of the twenty-year crisis of the American welfare state economy, where cost-consciousness among various public and private officials charged with subsidizing the life and the death of various state- clients and customer-beneficiaries has worked to grease the skids for Hospice-like reforms for the terminally ill. If they prefer to die at home, and it is cheaper, then who is to stand in the way? By 1994, home health agencies numbered nearly 10,000, and hospice agencies totalled 1,100. In this same year, home health agencies served some 52,722,000 client-patients and hospices "discharged" roughly 328,000 client-patients. The vast majority of latter population received both medicare (87.6%) and medicaid (85.3%), as was the case with Uncle John. [1]

At about the same time as Uncle John was slowly learning of his "terminal" condition (more on this below), another person I knew, Professor Morris S. Schwartz, age 79, a Brandeis University sociologist and, in this capacity, a former teacher, was doing something unusual: he was publicly discussing his impending death from ALS, which is popularly known as Lou Gehrig's disease. In fact, Morrie was discussing his dying in such prominent venues as a series of three segments of Ted Koppel's *Nightline* program. Even though I did not know Professor Schwartz for very long or very well, I was not in the least surprised to find him and his supportive family and colleagues brilliant in the presentation of a straightforward, honest, and compelling wrestling match with dying. Morrie meant to speak plainly, human-to-human, as was his usual manner, and to accept the challenge of thinking through his dying (figuratively, and, given the nature of ALS, literally). His most basic reason for appearing on *Nightline* and accepting, even relishing, the fact of wide publicity was to help others, as many others as possible, learn from his dying experience. Some of these lessons are recorded in a published set of reflections, Morrie's last book, *Letting Go: Morrie's Reflections on Living While Dying* (1996). Other lessons live on in those who knew Professor Schwartz, even those who knew him only from a distance.

The coincidence of these two dying experiences provided for us an experimental moment. Could Morrie Schwartz's reflections travel from Boston to Flint and still remain intact? Could Morrie's candid self-and-sociological analysis prove therapeutic for someone like Uncle John, whose "encounters" with intellectuals were mostly limited to a few sparse moments like the Brandeis graduation ceremony marking the completion of my own sociology doctorate? After some "feeling him out" on this issue, I placed into Uncle John's VCR the first *Nightline* segment as well as an interview Schwartz conducted with Paul Solomon of Boston's WGBH and PBS's *Lerher News Hour*, and another former Schwartz student. Uncle John watched his big-screen TV, which usually featured golf and football. He was attentive, and, ultimately, he liked these programs. But I think that his response had more to do with the fact that he took pride in my knowing someone whose dying was worthy of television reality over against any substantive appreciation of Morrie's specific ideas about dying. In other words, as far as I could tell Uncle John never adopted

244 / A Wrong Life

Morrie's humanistic advice toward himself, despite even the unusual fact of my presence as a sort of long-distance teaching assistant. Instead, Uncle John's dying seemed more a function of lifeless inertia, a drift pushed along by a simple institutional logic and greatly facilitated by loads of morphine patches gladly prescribed by absent doctors and supplied by his Hospice nursing contingent. In this particular battle between the mundane result of so much countercultural sound and fury on the one hand, and the hegemonic dominance of pharmo-capitalist medicine on the other, the latter, we report, won hands-down.

As noted, Uncle John's last, difficult hours were experienced through massive doses of morphine-based painkillers. On the orders of his Hospice staff, an extremely warm and congenial group as a whole, he had also been denied all liquids. No IV, nothing. This fact alone, of course, determined the timing of his death. Uncle John, not surprisingly, had trouble breathing and swallowing, even as he lay unconscious and still. A handy Hospice pamphlet described the last hours before death. It was left for the benefit of those of us who would witness the last moments, especially so that we could determine death's actual occurrence, after which we were under orders to immediately call the Hospice staff so they could stop by and make things official. According to this how-to-tell-if-your-[insert name of loved one]-is-dead pamphlet, Uncle John's heavy breathing—his "death rattle"—was to be expected. It was the middle of the night, and around Uncle John had gathered a few of his younger relatives, including myself. As we talked about nothing, this situation having drug-on now for days, Uncle John, my father figure, suddenly lurched up, his eyes open, and in this state of apparent shock, he clenched my hand and took a last heavy breath before lying back, his eyes still open, but now filled with a milky gray hue. My "dad" was dead. A corpse. Later, the crew from the funeral home would thump his postoperative bald head on the doorjamb as they struggled to cart his naked body, which they had carefully wrapped in a black, flexible stretcher, out of the house. It was late morning. I did not immediately call the Hospice staff, per their instructions, and instead waited until after my Uncle's daughter could arrive, to see her dad as he died, at home.

However much it pains me to admit it, Uncle John's was a hospital death in the home; it was an instance of mass death and no more. While efforts were made to effect a profoundly different eventuality, that is, a real death of a real live human being, a dying that was part of one man's living, it is simply the case that a few well-meaning individuals cannot meaningfully, that is, objectively, weigh-in against a social structure hell-bent on erasing individuality right up until the end. In this single instance of a single man's death, the dying man was, over a seven month period, never directly told of his terminal condition by a single medical authority. Even persistent questioning by others, including myself, produced only vague statements and looks askance. For example, Uncle John's brain tumor surgeon, a good man, reported the removal of his brain tumor a success, even though he also knew, as I learned later in a chance phone conversation with a radiologist only tangentially related to my Uncle's care, that the sheer fact of a malignant brain tumor meant that Uncle John had about one year to live, on average. As it turned it out, this had been an optimistic estimate. Even the appearance of Hospice workers did not seal in my Uncle's mind the end of life quickly approaching, and, in lock-step, these home health aids and nurses and ministers did nothing to dispel his illusionary hopefulness, which is also true of Uncle John's chemotherapists, his family physician, and, for the most part, his family, too. [2] Morrie Schwartz may have been a solace, but only, it seemed, because he was on TV. We may have been a solace, too, but only because we demurred from insisting on shattering the cloak of irreality surrounding these events.

To be truthful, we didn't fully appreciate what was happening either, and maybe we still don't. We had trouble at the time, for example, assimilating the meaning of the no-liquid order which determined that my dearest Uncle would be desiccated to death in a state of medicated unconsciousness (to end his suffering, presumably). As an authority figure, too, in an essentially working-class family, it is difficult to override a parent's apparent wish to remain adrift in the dominant hyperreal culture as opposed to go suddenly head-under in the depths of the counterculture, a new sea for most. This is certainly the way it is in a place like Flint, in a brick house on the east side, near the old AC Sparkplug assembly lines.

Regardless, in the end, instead of a humanistic passage through the stages of dying, instead of a transformation of the spirit, Uncle John began and ended in "denial." And instead of blaming the victim for his own recalcitrance before mortality, let us say that this atomistic, unceremonial demise, this denial of death, was made infinitely easier by the willful participation in this false definition of the situation by an irresponsible medical profession that doesn't want to talk about, much less to, people dying, the simple religion-like charm of hyperreality (if we only were on television after we died, now that would be heaven), and, last but not least, the mind-numbing effects of morphine-based pain killers (and here, we think more of their effect on those who are complicitous with their administration than on the administered body itself). All of this, of course, is perfectly consonant with traditional hospital death in astral America. In fact, one of Uncle John's few stated regrets was his repeated and only half-jestful remark that he wasn't going to be around for the OJ verdict. He wasn't. Nor was Uncle John around to see Mitch Albom, the Detroit area sports writer and another former Morrie student, serialize his book, *Tuesdays With Morrie: An Old Man, A Young Man, and The Last Great Lesson* (1997), in the pages of the *Detroit Free Press* (September 7-11, 1997). Nor did Uncle John hang in there long enough to catch Mitch's appearance on the *Oprah show*, which would have looked real good on his big screen TV, just as the movie deal that is in the works will no doubt, someday, really light up the even bigger screen.

In contrast to Uncle John's all-too-real death, we are surrounded at other times by more ethereal reminders of death. There's the ubiquitous tobacco billboards, cemeteries, and funeral possessions, of course, but more interesting was the scene at a recent visitation upon Dayton of a cross-country contingent of the infamous anti-abortion group known as Operation Rescue. Operation Rescue had come to Dayton, in part, in order to ritualistically encircle a women's health clinic located near our house with their usual graphic images of aborted fetuses. Notably, a good many, perhaps the majority, of protesters were children. In their hands were the photographs of the partial bodies of apparently aborted fetuses and, in one especially eye-catching image, the remains of a small pre-human head grasped by forceps. These are the standard Operation Rescue signs used anywhere and everywhere as they enact their particular brand of street theater. These signs are meant, we presume, to convey the basic notion that abortion is a grizzly and unwarranted procedure, if for no other reason than it results in such gruesome eventualities for the fetus aborted. If one is disturbed by a dead baby's head in forceps, in other words, then one should oppose legal abortion—that's the message.

Such representations are an interesting blend of classical propaganda techniques (see Jackell 1995) and present an opportunity to reflect upon the relationship between stereotypical thinking and the death of the social. In Operation Rescue's tableau of dead fetuses, there is the appeal to emotions, of course, but also a brilliant blend of glittering generalities, card-stacking, transfer, and bandwagon methods of propaganda. On the surface, it is no great intellectual feat to note that Operation Rescue is a "pro-life" organization, where the concept of life is deployed as a presumably universal value, like freedom and justice. Pro-life is thus a form of glittering generality in that it roots itself in a widely unobjectional value position, while simultaneously it implies that its opposition is anti-life and, *ipso facto*, beyond-the-pale of reason and compassion.

Beyond this surface reading, however, we observe that dead-baby propaganda is also emotional card-stacking, in the sense that the response to the displayed images is pre-given: disgust and horror, or, at minimum, even for the politically sophisticated, disquiet. The outcome of the communication is thus determined by the terms of its enactment; it's stacked. The form precedes and contains the content, which is rendered a means to the desired ends. In addition, that children often carry these signs is itself an act of propaganda, meant, surely, to transmute the image of a fetus into that of a born and grown human child and thus to transfer easily evoked positive feelings toward the child-protester to the "unborn child" depicted in the warped images. Finally, the Operation Rescue contingent is itself something many people crave: a community of people freely and cooperatively engaged in what is for them a profoundly meaningful, indeed, sacred mission in life. They are acting toward the world and on the world, and doing so on behalf of widely cherished values. They do so in the form of cross-country vacation/crusade, and it must look like to many a victim of anomie a superior lifestyle when implicitly compared to a humdrum nine-to-five, if that, existence. The carnivalesque comportment of Operation Rescue is itself, therefore, a form of bandwagoning, as if to say, "Come join in; it's a righteous movement."

In this way, the mind is assaulted by well-honed techniques of manipulation. Systematically distorted communication walks the streets. It is difficult for most people to see this because propaganda is nothing if not a ubiquitous feature of contemporary American life. Indeed, the extreme nature of Operation Rescue's propaganda is undoubtedly a response to the general and prevailing state of manipulation, requiring ever more shrill representations in order to successfully compete in the general system of reality distortion. They, too, are struggling with the code, and their success is hardly guaranteed. Most passers-by were surely like us, more attuned to the unexpected traffic delays and re-routings, the general hub-bub caused by police barricades and anti-protesters, and, perhaps, too, the seemingly unreal possibility of open political conflict in the streets of America. In other words, above and beyond the level of traditional propaganda analysis is the level of Baudrillard's "code," which in this case means that the sheer spectacle of the mass is more powerful than the specific, jumbled psychosocial content of the ideological message. What appears a protest on behalf of life is thus, perhaps, but a lifeless articulation of the death of the social.

The children are, of course, the most innocent and immediate victims, their having little choice but to adopt the pathologies of their parents' personality. But the society as whole shares in this death: we are forced to submit to the perpetual virtual recycling of the human carrion produced by the bio-medicalized truncation of procreation, as though we adults actually lived inside the dead-babies-in-a-blender-jokes that circulated among us as semi-perceptive children. We are therein diverted from historical projects oriented toward creating and sustaining a pacified life worth not aborting.

Historical projects? Theorists like us are typically accused of exaggerating the power of social structure at the expense of human agency; we are too quick to dismiss the potential for social change. But when we consider the efforts of the most entrepreneurial, the most sincere, the most clever "change agents," we find them successful, but thoroughly ineffective in their confrontation with "reality." The two characteristics—success as a change agent and political impotence—are neither mutually exclusive nor uncommon; indeed, they are mutually supportive and ubiquitous. The containment of dissent is as powerful a force in our world as it ever was, so much so that "dissent" itself seems to have an ever shorter half-life.

Consider the case of Sister Helen Prejean, the 58-year-old nun, who, with the publication of her exquisite, Pulitzer Prize-nominated *Dead Man Walking* (1993) and its subsequent movie adaptation by leftist filmmaker, Tim Robbins, has emerged as the preeminent public leader in the fight to abolish the death penalty in America. Today, Sister Helen is, indeed, a prominent public figure: a bestselling author and much-sought after speaker, the true-life heroine portrayed by Academy Award-winning actress, Susan Sarandon, and herself the subject of more than one television documentary, including a special *Frontline* segment dedicated solely to critically evaluating *Dead Man Walking*. Sister Helen Prejean has also served as the Chairperson of the Board of Directors of the National Coalition to Abolish the Death Penalty and is a member of Amnesty International. This humble nun, born, bred, and all her life a citizen of the lowly State of Louisiana, has received numerous awards and accolades, done more than most people ever dream of doing to combat the scourge of capital punishment, and attained an amazing public purchase.

But when Sister Helen visited the University of Dayton in the spring of 1994 as part of its Distinguished Speakers Series, things were different. There was no movie. In fact, it was only during her visit to Dayton that Sister Helen learned from Robbins that the film project had secured the necessary funding. "They ran the numbers," she happily reported, meaning that the projected revenues were sufficient to justify the cost of production. But even though her book was out and selling well, and a movie was now in the works, Sister Helen was mostly as yet unknown to the wider American public. We, too, admit that we had not heard of her or her work before UD's Dr. Patrick Donnelly brought her to our and everyone else's attention. Still, originally, my, the sociologist's, ignorance of her work made for a somewhat awkward phone call to her home to explore her interest in visiting Dayton. I had never even heard of Louisiana's "Angola" state prison, where, in the State of Louisiana, execution by lethal injection is performed, much less had I any knowledge of Patrick Sonnier and Robert Lee Willie and their innocent victims. As it turned out, though, Sister Helen gladly accepted the pittance that the University was willing to offer her, and she brought with her on that trip a set of stories, a set of experiences, and a philosophy of life connected to them, that left her audience and everyone around her that day in a state of respectful admiration, even as they naturally dismissed her simple policy proposal: The state must stop putting human beings to death.

Our experience is limited to but a day of intermittently chaperoning the good Sister from here to there, including dinner with a dozen or so other folks, and so forth. But we were able to witness in even this brief first-hand interaction an extraordinary energy and intelligence finely honed-in on the factious arguments in support of capital punishment. Sister Helen Prejean was a one-person antidehumanization machine. She explained that she maintained her energy by sneaking in short, "Ghandian naps." She had evidently set course on a peaceful, although nonetheless revolutionary, and, of course, effectively unattainable, mission, the abolition of capital punishment in the United States, and she was more than happy to sacrifice herself for its attainment.

Dead Man Walking is, we have noted, an exquisite book, and no one could say that Sister Helen's personal crusade is anything but successful. What more could she do? But there was never a possibility that her work would result in the abolition of the death penalty, for, by her own analysis, this would entail a series of cultural and social developments on a revolutionary scale, and not just in the usual, modern sense of an overturning of social institutions and a fundamental reformation of culture, but in a postmodern sense, too, in the destablization of the code itself. This would include, but is not limited to, the elimination of poverty, or at the very least, the elimination of the profound positive causal relationship between the economic statuses of the convicted and the distribution of equality before the law. In Sister Helen's modernist analysis of modern irrationality:

... race, poverty, and geography determine who gets the death penalty—if the victim is white, if the defendant is poor, and whether or not the local D.A. is willing to plea-bargain (1993, p. 50).

There must also be the mass transcendence of the social-psychological basis for a disciplinary society and its prison system, which even Foucault could barely imagine, and which would entail the mass internalization of the moral teaching that "every human is better than the worst thing they have done," a statement Sister Helen repeated in her talk at the University of Dayton. Here, Sister Helen joins with legions of religious thinkers before her who seek to use the masses' surface allegiance to existing irrational dogma (the fact of their religious affiliation, belief in god, self-righteousness, church attendance, etc.) to inspire, through moral exhortation, a mass movement of enlightened social action that would establish a system of moral rectitude on earth and in this life (we think also of Mohandas Gandhi, Martin Luther King, Jr., and even Baptist Bill Moyers). We might add the necessity of a mass recognition of the fictitious existence of "race," which undergirds its progeny, attitudinal and institutional racism, and which, entwined, have long been a pillar supporting America's peculiar, primitive mass allegiance to capital punishment (see Bruck [1983]1988). And we might add that the mass, the half-educated, obviously thrives on the live, local, and late-breaking news reports from outside of "Angola," which simultaneously quells and feeds their ubiquitous hyper-paranoia, even if providing them, of course, no real respite from fear, no real pacification of their fearful existence, and no true reconciliation for the victims' families or the society that identifies with them.

The mass of postmodern America is wired to the death penalty, beholden to it, and no book, no movie, is going to change that. Americans are in love with the death penalty; it seduces us. To systematically do what we know to be wrong, and to not care about the consequences: Wow!, what a thrilling transgression, what an obscene moment of post-ethical indulgence, for which the rest of the country surely thanks, and is a bit jealous of, Texas, Louisiana, Florida ("the death belt"), and the rest of its most primitive regions, for the gift of these treasured, mindless, hyperreal executions (see Hitchens 1998). Sister Helen and her ilk simply aid in making these execution gifts into what Jackie Orr might call "ambivalent gifts," though no less emotive, and, as such, all the more attractive and desired. Where, after all, would The Academy be without films "with a heart." It is really no irony that Tim Robbins is the same filmmaker who created the brilliant *Bob Roberts*, a movie about postmodern American fascism, as well as stared in *The Player*, a film about Hollywood's corruption, which even features a critique of the hyperreality of capital punishment. Tim Robbins and Oliver Stone, and their peers, are simply good at what they do. They spoon-feed us what we want, which are images of our own extermination.

Concern with extermination is a given for us, the generation who came of age politically, not under the aegis of Adorno's melancholy "Stars Down to Earth," but under the spell of Reagan's straightforwardly obscene "Star Wars." The popular book of the decade of the 80s might well have been Jonathan Schell's *The Fate of the Earth* (1982), which gave us a formative sense, among other things, for "the death of death." The popular movie of that "peacekeeper" decade was, perhaps, "The Atomic Cafe" (1982), which we first learned of, appropriately, when it was seriously discussed on "The Tonight Show" with Johnny Carson. And, of course, we watched "The Day After" (1983) like everyone else, and were impressed by the serious, humane discussion segment that followed it, featuring among other commentators we cannot remember, Carl Sagan, E.L. Doctorow, and Kurt Vonnegut, the author of *Slaughterhouse Five* (which begins with the observation that Dresden circa 1967 "looked a lot like Dayton, Ohio" [1969, p. 1]). Kurt Vonnegut has even recently shown up on the tube as an ad-man for the Discover Card. Baudrillard's theory of "virtual catastrophe," in other words, *is* our lifeworld (1991). E.P. Thompson's (1982) lonely poetry and his uncompromising theory of "exterminism" are always already circulating in our skulls. But the mass mobilizations in Europe, the millions who there filled the squares of those very old cities in protest of "medium range" nuclear missiles and the like: they might as well be among the stars themselves, replaced as they now have been by the throngs mourning the sudden death of the world's first truly hyperreal Princess.

A real public history of the development, use, and strategic deployment of nuclear weapons is probably forever lost to us. If the Enola Gay can be prevented from making its debut as a museum piece by a pack of Legionnaires from Indianapolis, then there is little hope in recovering the fine details of the origins of the Cold War itself, and its on-again-off-again enactment. In place of a history, only a genealogy of the Cold War may be possible, which would begin with the fact of our perpetual extermination

252 / A Wrong Life

potential, perhaps the greatest achievement of modernity, and read backwards from this no-place in search of a connection to the wrong(ed) children of Massachusetts' Fernald School "Science Club," which the U.S. Department of Energy recently revealed was one of many sites of top-secret domestic radiation experimentation. It is though we are to be forever awash in the water drained from Ronald Reagan's bruised, alzheimer-infected brain. That old man, that fictitious Cold War warrior, will never die until somewhere, someplace above ground, in our midst, a nuclear weapon is again detonated, and countless thousands of human beings are vaporized and burnt to death. In other words, Reagan cannot die until America has regained the power that in Baudrillard's reading it has lost; at *that* time, history will begin again.

In contrast, genocide has proven insufficient to the task of jump-starting the failed engines of world-historical movement. This is perhaps no more evident than from the vantage of "Dayton," where reflection upon the unspeakable "atrocities" undertaken in post-Cold War Yugoslavia attains its zenith absurdity. We shall never forget sitting paralyzed before news-images of the righteous Christian-Serb-Bosnia General Mladic spoon-feeding candy to the Bosnian-Muslim women and children of Serbinezca, a United Nations "safe haven." As everyone recognized, he was really spoon-feeding hyperreal propaganda to the worldwide television audience of on-lookers, less aghast, no doubt, than "interested." We imagine them/us knowing all along that at the same time the good General's loyal troops were taking the husbands, fathers, and sons of this community to be machine-gunned to bits in a far-off warehouse, the blood splattered on the high, gray cement ceiling evidence enough of what transpired. We imagine that anyone who knew anything, who had either "intelligence" or just intelligence, knew that this was happening, and that this real-live-knowledge, this recognition of an ongoing reality, did not lead to anything like a genuine attempt to prevent the realization of this slaughter. The only thing worse than this was later learning that Dayton's Wright-Patterson Air Force Base had been chosen to host to the utterly untimely "peace conference" meant primarily to put an end to these nightly news reports, and, secondarily, perhaps, to put a lid on the unseemly disorder churning in the underbelly of Europe.[3] This was a breath-taking eventuality, an epiphany of panic/cynicism. The actuality of the worse than the worst was going to be so horrible because the real meaningless of it all was pregiven and predetermined; all that was left to do was the enactment of a post-mortem circus. Predictably, like a dancing bear, Dayton has played right along.

It is impossible to understand the Bosnian Holocaust in Bosnia; for this, one must come to Dayton. In Dayton, the same Serbian president whose responsibility for the calamity in his homeland is well-known, and who spurned the peace talks location with the ironic flip, "I'm not a priest, you know?," also did an off-base photo-op, a walk-through of an upscale Dayton area shopping mall, The Mall at Fairfield Commons. In Dayton, the progressive, ecumenical religious community spent many nights outside of Wright-Patterson AFB, clutching their candles, praying for peace. In Dayton, the mayor and a bevy of others from the worlds of local business and academia, have worked hard to transmute the reality of the original location-decision, which was based on Dayton's media and cultural marginality, the fact of its sizable and secure air-war installation, and its comfortable proximity, at least by flight-time measures, to Washington, DC (a real place). The anticipated transmutation is, to say the least, ambitious: to turn this original reality into its opposite. Here, Dayton is positioning itself to become a culturally central location via its linguistic insinuation into the "Dayton Peace Accords" (don't forget that Paris wanted this honor, but, after a struggle, was denied it), and its use, now, as a term of diplomacy (as in, 'we may need to do a "Dayton" in order to resolve this conflict'). Dayton is also calling itself "The Peace City," which may be an appropriate moniker in the wake of the thousands of military-industrial complex jobs lost here. And, finally, Dayton is busy compressing the time/space between the Balkans and the Midwest with regular business and academic "friendship" junkets back-&-forth across the oceans that divide the two. Dayton is going global, becoming worldly, riding the coattails of genocide and chance: it's happily joining the brave new postmodern world order, with scarcely a murmur of protest much less embarrassment. Herein may lie the American postmodern truth of the mass death in Bosnia: it was not real enough for us; we want more.

As we were sitting down to draft this chapter, a small but newsworthy event took place in Arles, France, which is still famous even today as a result of its association with the wandering Dutch painter who could put a scream on canvas by applying himself to very heavy globs of colorful paints. In Arles, Madame Jeanne Calment, the official oldest living human being in the world, died at the age of 121 years old; she was born in 1875, before the invention of the light-bulb and the telephone, seven years before the death of Karl Marx, and a full 45 years before Max Weber finally couldn't stand anymore. She was a young adult at age 28 when Dayton's Orville and Wilber Wright flew their plane less than the distance of a Boeing 747's wingspan over the oceanside sands of Kitty Hawk, North Carolina, the home state of Senate Foreign Relations Committee Chairman, Jesse Helms, a political ally of the oldest U.S. Senator in history, Strom Thurmond, who my Uncle John once criticized as an idiot because of his remark during the televised Thomas/Hill hearings, when Senator Thurmond called on the witness to move "that machine," meaning the microphone, closer to his/her mouth. Senator Thurmond represents the state of South Carolina, where Susan Smith, an average looking American mom, drove her two young children strapped into their car-seats into a pond, drowning them, and then tried unsuccessfully to blame the crime on "black men," before confessing her crime and being represented by a superb, knowledgeable anti-death penalty attorney, who we have had occasion to cite in the preceding pages. Susan Smith and her K-Mart photography children live on in the obscene imagines of hyperreality that fill our minds, like the walk-through Madaline Albright did of the mass graves of Bosnia, the success of which may have been partly responsible for her ascendancy from U.N. Ambassador to her current position as the first female U.S. Secretary of State. This occurred over the failed candidacy of "Dayton's" Richard Holbrooke, whose main advocate for the job, Undersecretary of State and former *Time Magazine* employee, Strobe Talbot, was actually born in Dayton.

PART TWO. LET DEAD DOGS LIE

C. Wright Mills' several biographers are surprisingly silent on the facts surrounding his untimely death. If it is discussed at all, the usual, and it is safe to say, official, account, is to note that on March 20, 1962, C. Wright Mills died of a heart attack which overcame him, some say, while he was riding his motorcycle near his home in upstate New York. The assimilation of this account is made easy by the fact that Mills, though notoriously virile and only 46 years old at the time of his death, had a documented history of heart ailments. For example, Mills had a heart attack in December 1960, as he was laboring under the unusual stress of preparing for a much- anticipated nationally televised debate on NBC against former Undersecretary of State, Adolf Berle, and on no less of a topic than of U.S. foreign policy toward postrevolutionary Cuba. In this story, Mills effectively drove himself to his own death, spurred on by his own narcissistic longing for public and historical relevance. He had to withdraw from the debate in 1960, but he never gave up the self-righteous, grandiose, and futile effort to alter the course of history. In this reading, it was not Parsons or Lazarsfeld or Trilling, nor all the many other intellectual foils that Mills set upon with such ferocity, who truly embodied his worst enemy. Instead, it is suggested that Mills was his own worst enemy, or in Norman K. Denzin's phrase, that he was a "tarnished hero" (1990, p. 5; see also Horowitz 1983).

Perhaps, then, it is John F. Kennedy who is really Mills' alter ego, and not the effete intellectuals of Columbia University and the various Luce publications. JFK and Mills were the same age, and they died only 18 months apart. Mills, it is reported, detested Kennedy, in spite of, or perhaps because of, the fact that he shared with the President of the United States a number of essential qualities, among them, brilliance, an openly stated desire to speak intelligently to publics and to effect the course of history, womanizing and sexual bravado, a keen sense of the new, glitzy postmodern politics, an overriding interest in the workings of a new American power elite, and, implied in the above, cock-sure self-confidence, this, despite the fact of physical ailments (JFK's back, Mills' heart). Mills, for his part, expressed this aspect of his self in his oft-repeated advice to "take it big" (see Wakefield 1971). Then-Senator Kennedy made clear the scope of his ambition in his 1960 presidential campaign, in which he repeatedly stated that he wanted to be elected President because, in so many words, "that's where the action is."

The differences are notable also. Mills hailed from humble beginnings in Waco, Texas (Kennedy's beginnings were not humble). Mills went to high school in Dallas (Kennedy went to his death in Dallas). Mills considered becoming an insurance salesman before deciding to enter the graduate program in sociology at the University of Wisconsin (Kennedy dabbled in journalism, went to Harvard, and never had need of graduate school). Mills married three times and had three children (Kennedy married only once but still managed three offspring, one of whom died soon after birth). But despite obvious divergences with the obscenely well-known biography of Jack Kennedy, perhaps Mills was to Kennedy in the same way that, as DeGaulle is reported to have once conceded, Sartre was to France.

At any rate, it is interesting that the four figures just mentioned—Mills, Kennedy, Sartre, DeGaulle—were either brutally assassinated, survived attempted assassination, or were actively afraid of assassination at the end of their lives. The last, of course, refers to Mills' experience. As told in the records of the U.S. Federal Bureau of Investigation, Mills had received "an anonymous letter informing him that an American agent disguised as a South American would assassinate him on his next visit to Cuba" (FBI

Document 1, December 15, 1960, p. 14). It is reported in this same document that Mills was not surprised by this reported threat against his life, and that, in fact, he was thinking of "purchasing a gun for self-protection." In France, during *les temps moderne*, a public intellectual with the grandeur of Sartre could be the target of lethal political intrigue, including the bombing of his Paris apartment. This was the world of *Z* starring Yves Montogne, a film for macho, homophobic, modernist simpletons. In America, just coming into its postmodern, astral own, Sartre's wild-one, easy-rider contemporary avoided death in Cuba, at the margins of a new world order, by choking on his own fumes while out for a spin through the Empire State.

Of course, Mills did do his best to invite the ire of the power elite, for he did much more than simply name them, and therein expose them, in his widely acclaimed *The Power Elite* (1956). He followed this with *The Causes of World War III* (1958), which underscored the preponderant significance of the military in the Cold War period, and worse, he did so in a style that was generally accessible, if not for a mass public, then at least for a half-educated public, which represented a fair proportion of the citizenry. Finally, and, of course, worst of all, was Mills' *Listen Yankee!* (1961). It was bad enough that this book pushed the pamphleteering style to a new level of accessibility (a repeatedly stated concern in the FBI files). Indeed, so real was this threat that Mills' words teetered on the brink of spilling from the pages of *Harper's*, where a condensed version of the book was reprinted in December 1960, and on to the live surface of America's television screens that same month. But that the book also squarely addressed the problem of Cuba, the most delicate point of conflict in an on-going, largely secret, military struggle between nuclear superpowers, and did so in direct and open sympathy with the pro- Castro American community (Mills, unlike Oswald, was a *prominent* member of the Fair Play for Cuba Committee) and, indeed, in open collaboration with none other than Fidel Castro himself (Mills maintained direct contact with Castro, and came close to teaching a class in Cuba to Castro's revolutionary lieutenants), now this, this!, must have been seen, in the basement ruminations of the Mongoose Group and around the table at Alpha 66 meetings, as an act of utter treason.

Certainly, the infamous Director of the FBI, J. Edgar Hoover, was aware of this book and of Mills. In fact, Hoover personally ordered an investigation of Mills on November 29, 1960 (FBI Document 2). On December 1, 1960, Alan H. Belmont, a top FBI official, noted that one of his memoranda on Mills "was made available to Mr. DeLoach [Cartha "Deke" DeLoach, another topmost FBI official] for his use in connection with our counterintelligence operations against communism and Mr. DeLoach so utilized the data" (FBI Document 3, December 1, 1960, p. 1). According to FBI files, Mills was the subject of surveillance and scrutiny for the last 18 months of his life. This included numerous background checks, the use of about a dozen secret informants, surveillance of Mills' West Nyack, New York residence, and steady attention to his overseas travel, particularly to the Soviet Union and Cuba.

But, we report, that after several years of waiting for our Freedom of Information Act request to be fulfilled, we have obtained no documents from the FBI or CIA (and, to a lesser extent, from the Department of State and United States Information Agency) that, upon careful analysis of their content, disclose any information that indicates that Mills was either the target of an assassination plot, as he feared, nor the target of a "COINTEL-PRO" operation, the infamous FBI counterintelligence program begun in 1956 and that later targeted such victims as Martin Luther King, Jr. and Illinois Black Panther Party Chairman, Fred Hampton. Even though Mills had, as we noted, met more than once with Castro (in New York City *and* in Cuba), was a member of the Fair Play for Cuba Committee, was perhaps America's leading spokesperson in sympathy with the Castro-led revolution, had travelled to the Soviet Union, and had even declared while in London in May, 1961, in an interview with a Spanish language newspaper, *Prensa Latina*, that, "if it were physically possible, I would be fighting at the side of Fidel Castro," C. Wright Mills' CIA file consisted of a single index card with his name on it. In contrast, Mills' FBI file is some two-hundred pages dating mostly from 1960 onward, and includes a special "advance" copy of the *Harper's* reprinting of *Listen Yankee!*. The FBI file closes with obituaries from newspapers, which seems innocent enough, since these document that it is no longer necessary to keep track of C. Wright Mills. Mills' last book, *The Marxists* (1962), in which, among other things, he declares himself a "plain Marxist," was published a few months after his death.

We are left, then, to ponder the significance of Mills' "sociological imagination," which he asserted most directly amidst these other events in his life -that is, in his 1959 publication, *The Sociological Imagination*, and one year later, in his reader collecting the best theory of the "classic tradition," *Images of Man* (1960). In light of these untimely untheoretical reflections on the sheer fact of one sociologist's biographical death, is

there in Mills' work a still-valuable, still- viable connection between the
conceptualization of biography, history, and social structure that could
bring us closer to a postethical, sociological point of view vis-à-vis the
phantom of "mass death"?

Perhaps, like Kennedy's death in *America*, Mills' death "radiates out
over present-day" American sociology, preventing it from connecting
with its past, leaving it, like the rest of "astral America," primitive, without history, and destined for nothing but eternal recurrence. It is not that
American sociology is actually dying, far from it. That undergraduate
enrollments and majors have waned precipitously in the wake of 60's
enthusiasm for the discipline, that there exists a paucity of employment
opportunities for new Ph.D.s, that once-proud departments of sociology
have been eliminated, that newspapers and newsmagazine seem to regularly announce its demise, that its leading lights, such as Stanley
Aronowitz and Fredric Jameson, can be made in the popular *and* academic press to play the fool, or that Mills' own leading biographer, Irving Louis Horowitz, sees the discipline as "decomposing" (Horowitz
1993; also see Lemert 1997), these facts have not in the least, for example, spoiled the party at American sociology's annual meetings, which
are better attended than ever and are overflowing with communitarian
spirit and verve. Sociology is not dead; it's just desert-like and holed-up
in Big City hotels.

In this sense, sociology has apparently freed itself from its classical
object, which, as we have asserted, is mass death; in so doing, it has
attained a kind of free-floating utopia in which anything goes because
nothing matters. In this utopia, there is no risk, not even in the theory of
risk (Beck); the juggernaut may be careening toward its much-anticipated
crash, but flashy textbooks are still in demand (Giddens); and McWeber,
of course, is still wildly popular (Ritzer). In this utopia, all is right with the
centered, ever-same, fictitious world of the sociological imaginary: the
same course offerings, the same liberal disapproval of too much poverty,
racism, and sexism; too much queer theory, and yet not enough nonradical
feminists; not enough methodological rigor, yet too much unreadable theoretical acumen; and so forth and so on. Fissures, in other words, are
allowed and, indeed, are necessary and productive of the illusion that
something is at stake, lest we smell the stench of our own racket. Where,
indeed, would sociology be without its multi-paradigmatic squabbles
among always already legitimate factions, as in the conflict between
theorists of "conflict" and those for whom "order" is most problematic,

and between those who prefer working with data sets and those who prefer face-to-face interactions (see Agger 1989b)? All that's left that might cause real friction is "reflexive sociology" or a strike by Big City hotel workers (see Gouldner 1970; Lemert 1997).

Let's try reflexive sociology. Mills doesn't really exist, but that is, for sociologists, probably for the best. Let this dead dog lie. Let him tell us, through our textbook portraits, that the sociological imagination is *really* identical with a generalized sociological perspective, where "social facts" distinguish sociology from biology and from psychology. Let Mills be the big *man* he so wanted to be, so that we post-feminists can get on with our paradigm-shifts. Let Mills stand for his own nostalgia for "the classic tradition," lest that tradition get loosed upon *our* world. Let "the power elite" become the answer to the questions, "Who rules ... ?" or "Who *now* rules America?," for that is much safer than asking why or how. And let this "plain Marxist" sleep with the fishes, because sociology has no use for a Church Committee, unless we mean by this *Bellah et al.*

For, honestly, if we were really to go about with our sociological imaginations intact, then we would be compelled to self-consciously risk self-annihilation as the analysts of mass death, risk, that is, being overcome by our objects. More attractive, no doubt, is fading away like old soldiers since MacArthur are supposed to do, via the soft devolution of sociology into cultural studies, women studies, African-American studies, communications, gay/lesbian studies, literary theory, postcontemporary theory, and similar tiny openings in the decomposing corpus of sociology, where primacy still goes to the object. Too bad, though, that once in this way dissipated, there is little hope of again "taking it big" (see Dandaneau 1994).

An alternative would be to return to the scene of the crime, circa 1962, in search of clues for a new beginning, but that is not really possible by means of conventional (modernist, empirical) sociology, even of Mills' sort. One can carefully seek documentation that would support causal analysis until the cows come home, but you're better off just reading Don Dellio's *Libra* or his *Underworld* and then getting on with the work of healing, feeling, reeling, while we bide our time waiting, not so much for a rebirth of wonder (with apologies to Mr. Ferlinghetti), as for the much-needed nuclear blast.

CONCLUSION

We have made no pretense of documenting the actuality of mass death in this world, for postethical reasons. That project is too much for us; it exceeds our capabilities and is best left to those for whom statistics are self-referential. In this regard, we are reminded of a moment at an excellent interdisciplinary conference on "State Organized Terror: The Case of Violent Internal Repression" that we attended some ten years ago (see Bushnell et al. 1991). The principle speaker at the time was Professor Stephen G. Wheatcroft, a demographer and an expert on the subject of various twentieth-century instances of state-organized mass death. After the presentation of his paper, "The Scale and Significance of the Terror in the USSR in the 1930's," a heated conflict arose concerning his estimate of the number of Russians dead as a result of Stalin's reign of terror. Professor Wheatcroft, visibly agitated, declared that "he had wrote the book" on this subject, that the numbers being bandied about by others at the conference were exaggerations, and that, in part, he knew this because bodies in certain mass graves (the details escape us) were wearing "Lithuanian galoshes," thus implying that the bodies therein entombed could not be of Russian nationals. "Professor Wheatcroft"— our remembrance of him, that is—is our ideal typical expert on the empirical dimensions of mass death. We do not pose ourselves as in his league.

Nor, in the opposite direction, do we claim to know much about individual dying and particular deaths. As we have noted, our experience is limited in this regard. We are not like war correspondents or emergency medical personnel, for whom death is a daily occurrence; death is not something with which we are truly on familiar much less intimate terms. For the most part, individual death, like mass death, is for us a mediated experience. When we imagine ourselves addressing this subject, then, it is with considerable trepidation, for we risk being laughed at, which has actually happened. Having felt compelled to criticize the absence of risk, there is little that we can do now except eschew a mature risk-management repose.

Consider, then, by way of conclusion, two personal/political documents (i.e., excrement) plucked from our shared lifeworld, both authored by the older of us, who is perhaps closer to death, in consultation with the younger, who is hardly naive to its finality. This, then, is our last, fatal strategy.

A EULOGY IN FIVE STORIES, AND AN EPILOGUE

FOR

JOHN S. DANDANEAU, JR.

(1925-1995)

A Preface

John S. Dandaneau, Jr. was born May 23, 1925, in Beverly, Massachusetts, the fourth child of John and Corrine Dandaneau, and died early Friday Morning, September 29, 1995, after a seven-month struggle with cancer, at the age of 70, survived by Helen, his wife of nearly 50 years, and his two children, Michael and Nancy.

In addition to his having grown up in Depression-era Flint, gone off at the age of 17 to serve as a Marine in the Pacific Theater;

in addition to his having married his wartime sweetheart, Helen Henson, and with her, parenting their two children;

in addition to his having worked steadily and successfully as a manager in the retail grocery business, often transcending the formal managerial role to become "Johnny," a fixture in the East Court Street community for over 26 years, as elsewhere;

in addition to his late in life, with Helen, accepting parenting responsibility for the three young children of his late brother;

in addition to these things, and more, Uncle John was one who told me a lot of important stories.

As the youngest of the nephews mentioned just previously, I listened for 24 years as Uncle John spun his many tales of poverty, war, and human relations; his parables about honesty, comportment, and the eternal high value of education; his gentle and nurturing remembrances of my own deceased mother and father, Lucille and Leonard Dandaneau; his reflections on childhood, public life, and, for the entire time of our intimate relationship, intelligent thoughts about death and the meaning of life as seen from the standpoint of a careful consideration of one's own mortality. Generally, then, Uncle John's transmission of events, lessons, and images, otherwise for me unknown, through the venerable and widely practiced cultural tradition of recurring, ritual storytelling, was for me a formative experience.

And I propose, then, at this time, in a mostly personal tribute to him, and upon his own request, to share with you snippets from just five such stories of the 5,000 or so that I think I remember, this, by way of reflection upon the storyteller before us but no longer with us.

STORIES

"Solving the Potato Chips Problem"

Seems that Uncle John's Marine platoon would often, while lying around their training tent on the hills of New Zealand, cajole their exceptionally young commanding corporal for some chips please from his freshly opened bag. Solution? Uncle John would proudly tell me of how he decided to "buy everyone their own bag," and, poking himself in his chest with his stiffened index finger, he continued, "so I could have my bag to myself," as though somehow demonstrating his having cleverly outwitted his subordinates, when, of course, as he also knew, this was really a parable about leadership as shared sacrifice.

"Ma Gave Me $10 Bucks When I Left Home at Seventeen"

Even after accounting for inflation, ten bucks isn't exactly venture capital. But Uncle John's story of his leaving home in 1942 with just a ten spot in his pocket wasn't the cliched and invidious "and with that ten bucks and a lot of hard work I made a million/pull yourself up by the bootstraps," kind of story. Rather, always with a twinkle in his eye, he went on to tell me of how, with the help of some dice, he not only enlarged the original ten bucks considerably before the troop train ever made it to California, but how also in New Zealand in preparation for war he won so much gambling that when an older sergeant made him send it home instead of spending it on a giant party for the guys, his Mother, seeing enough loot arriving in the mail to then buy a house, worried that Uncle John had robbed a bank. Money was important, and scarce; but was never for Uncle John an end in itself. His occasional joy and notable success with gambling was, for example, more of an ironic reproach of money's power than anything like its false idolization.

"Egghead, and the Letter Never Sent"

As you might imagine, Uncle John told a good many "war stories." One that I always liked concerned a young Japanese boy who adopted Uncle John and who Uncle John in turn affectionately called Tomago, which was Japanese for "egghead." Often Uncle John would criticize the way American troops behaved toward the Japanese civilians during the immediate postwar occupation—sometimes they were disrespectful, sometimes violent and disgusting, he would say. He told of how he tried to prevent such abuses; he spoke about the fascination he had with the amazing cultural differences between feudal Imperial Japan and the United States at that time; and he never forgot a little bit of the Japanese that learned while there, which every once and awhile he would unexpectedly spring on you, when he was feeling good. But apparently when Tomago wrote Uncle John after his discharge and his return to Flint, Uncle John never wrote Tomago back. He wished he had, though. And that's probably why when little Georgy who lives next door asked Uncle John last year to come see him play in a little league football game, Uncle John, on second thought, decided to go.

"Lennie, Lou, and the Tape Recorder"

My wife Maude reminded me of this one, because, she said, for a long time whenever we stayed in Uncle John and Aunt Helen's basement bedroom, she worried our private conversations might be tape-recorded. Why? Well, Uncle John often told a story about the time he and Aunt Helen went to my mom and dad's for a social visit—I believe it was Christmas. They sat alone in the front room waiting, as Uncle John would say, for Lucille to "make her appearance." This kind of lightly disparaging talk went on for a while until, as Uncle John told it, Lenny popped into the room with the cheery announcement, "Well, I've been taping you with this new recorder I got for Christmas," which he produced from behind the sofa. Previous stories had established that (a) my dad was a real character, and (b) my mother had a vibrant temper, so it was apparently a great relief to Uncle John and Aunt Helen to find that (c) Lennie wasn't much of a spy, for his tape machine had malfunctioned and nothing was recorded. Uncle John usually added at this point a histrionic "Oh my god were we relieved" to stress what a near catastrophe had thus been avoided. While the apparent lesson here is: If you don't have anything good to say, make sure you're not being tape-recorded, I think also that Uncle John meant to underscore the power of errant and unwisely chosen words, the fragility of family relationships, and how tough it is a lesson to consistently practice.

"My Brother Bob's Amazing Shirt Collars"

Uncle John looked up to or admired many, many people: his first real boss, Mr. Vern Comber; his friend Art Miller; even establishment Flint figures which he had some contact with, like Mr. Art Sarvis and Mr. James Welch; but it was his big brother Robert Dandaneau who Uncle John most reminisced about, and, perhaps, most admired.

One such story was about the care Bob took with his appearance. He looked "sharp," Uncle John would say. Uncle John was particularly enamored with the "starched collars" on Bob's white shirts, more so, perhaps, because Bob once bought him some of these shirts as a gift. Uncle John's big brother was killed in the Philippines at about the same time that he was wounded on Iwo Jima. In addition to the tiny bits of shrapnel that continually surfaced in his skin, stiff white collars kept Uncle John's head on straight for many years thereafter.

In his later years when I knew him best, storytelling was for Uncle John a way of life. He liked to know people and to remember people and to place them in their times. In storytelling, Uncle John brought past and divergence experiences into order and assigned them meanings. These stories were thus Uncle John's philosophy; his studied reflections upon an ongoing life. Whatever the value of their content, they say of Uncle John that he was a reflective man; a man who remembered; who was invested in and who cared for others; and a man who was generous enough to share his remembrances, parables, and tales—for whatever their worth—with the Tomagos of the world, who would care to listen. Of course, it was ironic that another one of Uncle John's stories concerned how he had always to fight nodding-off as Helen's dad, Frank Pruder, regaled him with sometimes less than scintillating narrative, but Uncle John hung in there, and listened, and he felt better off for the experience, as very much do I.

AN EPILOGUE

As I mentioned, in the last weeks of his life, Uncle John explicitly asked me to eulogize him; I told him I would have had it no other way.

He so trusted my deeply loving and affectionate feelings toward him not to even attempt to proscribe the anticipated content of my remarks about him, but he did ask of me one other thing.

He asked me to tell the people who gathered for his funeral that, although he had too often, as he put it, been a "horse's ass," that he hoped for their sake as well as for his own that those us gathered here today would remember him, not for his faults, but for his genuine and many efforts to be decent guy, a good husband, father, grandpa, brother, and uncle; a good boss, a good neighbor, a friend; in the end, a simple fallible human being trying to live a difficult life as rightly as is possible.

[S.P.D., read on October 2, 1995 at Brown's Funeral Home, Flint, Michigan]

[Letter that appeared in the *Dayton Daily News* in a slightly modified form (Sunday, December 8, 1996, p. B15].

Dear Editor:

In step with the venerable albeit disturbing customs of American boosterism, which, among other things, make it almost mandatory that a local paper cheerlead for the community that it services, the *Dayton Daily News* has in the past weeks repeatedly used its editorial pages to unabashedly trumpet the potential local benefits to be had from exploitation of the notoriety which happened to attached itself to this city as a consequence of the Dayton Peace Accords. From discussion of area image-enhancement to business opportunities abroad and even to anticipating the effect on upcoming local political races, the *Dayton Daily News* has shown itself more than willing to engage in a predictably cynical form of self-interested, insensitive analysis. I would argue, however, that the long-term effect of this discourse will likely be the converse of what its purveyors anticipate. Instead of teetering on the edge of a glorious "Peace City" status, Dayton is in danger of becoming a world-class laughing stock; the epitome of a small-minded, provincial America.

Consider evidence in support of my charge of cynicism. *Dayton Daily News* editor Max Jennings took the time this past week to confess to a moment of "anger" he experienced during the anniversary conference (see "Anniversary Has Uplifting Effect," 11/24/96, p. B18). Jennings, it seems, was momentarily incensed by a Bosnian diplomat's apparent ingratitude toward the fact of U.S. assistance in the region. Although this was not enough to spoil what for Jennings was the overall "uplifting effect" of the conference proceedings, the Bosnian diplomate's invocation of a compelling "moral imperative" to stop genocide in this world, and specifically in the former Yugoslavia, caused Jennings only to think of the "billions of our tax dollars" spent "to stop them from fighting and help them rebuild their nation." If only Malik Skaljic, deputy chief of mission of the Embassy of Bosnia and Herzegovina, would have "been a bit more gracious about recognizing that it was those dollars that put an end to the horrible slaughter," ponders the generous and not at all provincial editor. I would suggest that editor Jennings perhaps request thank yous from the should-be-grateful people of Bosnia during his anticipated "walk in the aftermath of the war" next month, during which he and other Daytonians will "share the homes of those who have experienced it." I suggest but a variation on Jennings' own words: "Hi y'all, 'we are all brothers on this Earth,' but this brother wants a thank you."

Elsewhere on the same page, the *Dayton Daily News* editorial staff collectively mulls over how best for Dayton area business to "take advantage" of the "magic of the word 'Dayton'" ("Dayton-Bosnia Link Is Not Just Talk," 11/24/96, p. B18). There are substantial stumbling blocks; as the editors warn, "the going will be rough." For example: "As for Bosnia, officials were frank to say Thursday that it will not really be a ripe market [!] for another three or four years." What is causing the Bosnian market to be less than "ripe"? Oh, "the place is a war-torn hell hole," write the editors. Darn. And all those bodies buried everywhere, and all that suffering, and all the never-ending nightmares and pain, and all the children without their parents, and all the war criminals without their shame; all very inconvenient for the much-anticipated smooth flow of dollars, you know. But never fear: "Dayton has a built-in edge"; "It is organized to take advantage of its advantages," the editors reassure. It is too bad, I think, that we in Dayton do not make earth-moving equipment, toothbrushes, or sanitary body-bags, which are in demand, I expect, in a country busy exhuming the thousands of innocent people that Daytonians and the rest of the world stood by and watched systematically butchered night after night on their evening news.

Finally, consider the example of Martin Gottlieb's speculation that Mayor Mike Turner's re- election prospects have perked-up as a result of his role in promoting the anniversary conference, especially the notion that Turner's deft shilling for local business has netted him both "exposure" and "contacts with well-heeled potential contributors" ("Turner Gets a Peace Dividend," 11/27/96, p. A10). The suggestion is that the Mayor of the City of Dayton can expect big campaign bucks in what amounts to kick-backs (all legal, of course) from local vested-interest vultures circling a still-fresh holocaust of mind-numbing proportions. I would hope the Mayor would have no use for such an uplifting effect; that he would publicly denounce Gottlieb's cynical cheerleading.

But let me conclude on a conciliatory note. The *Dayton Daily News* editorial staff has no monopoly on cynicism. Cynicism of this sort is not unique to this paper, to Dayton's conference-sponsoring institutions, nor to America as a whole, nor, of course, is it absent in the former Yugoslavia. Still, in this instance, going with the flow is tantamount to selling ourselves down the river. If Dayton wants to measure up to the challenge posed by coincidence of history—if it wants to proudly join such hamlets as Runnymeade, Ghent, and Masterich in the history of "agreement-making" in off-the-beaten-track locations (I hesitate to use the word "peace" for what obtains in Bosnia, let alone for my historical allusions)—better first that we here resolve to meditate on the significance of ubiquitous mass death in particular and the uncertain future of humankind in general at the close of this, our American Century. After such an eventuality, we would be in a better position to play host to the worst that our world has to offer. We might even have something more than shallow boosterism to offer in return.

Yours Sincerely,

Steven P. Dandaneau, Ph.D.

Assistant Professor of Sociology

NOTES

1. See U.S. Bureau of the Census (1996, Table No. 203, 135). *Note:* Discharges from home health agencies may double count persons who have had more than one episode of care during the year.

2. We hasten to underscore our genuine appreciation for Hospice workers, including those who attended Uncle John. We were only mildly surprised when, for example, Uncle John's Hospice minister appeared at Aunt Helen's memorial service some two years after his work with Uncle John. In a modern world characterized by a high degree of impersonalism and instrumentality, this gesture is a truly uncommon act of commitment and attentiveness.

3. Perhaps the single best source that addresses the politics of the Bosnian civil war, including especially *American* politics and policy, is Peter Maass, *Love Thy Neighbor: A Story of War* (1996). See especially his chapter on "The Appeasers," which includes a contemptuous analysis of President Clinton and his glorious Dayton Peace Accords. We have consulted other sources as well, including

Cohen (1993), Vulliamy (1994), and Mestrovic (1997) as well as documents and fieldnotes kindly provided to us by Erin M. Dougherty, which she gathered during her August 17- 26, 1997, visit to Sarajevo, Bosnia-Herzegovina, as part of the 1997 University of Dayton Honors Systems Design Seminar research project, "Reaching To Bosnia."

Chapter 8

Epilogue: Why Theorize?

... the created world is radically evil, and its negation is the chance of another world that is not yet. As long as the world is as it is, all pictures of reconciliation, peace, and quiet resemble the picture of death. The slightest difference between nothingness and coming to rest would be the haven of hope, the no man's land between the border posts of being and nothingness. Rather than overcome that zone, consciousness would have to extricate from it what is not in the power of the alternative. The true nihilists are the ones who oppose nihilism with their more and more faded positives, the ones who are thus conspiring with all extant malice, and eventually with the destructive principle itself. Thought honors itself by defending what is damned as nihilism.
—Theodor W. Adorno, *Negative Dialectics* ([1966]1987, p. 381)

... it is only in the right society that chances for the right life will arise. The present society still tells us lies about death not having to be feared, and it sabotages any reflection upon it.
—Theodor W. Adorno, *Negative Dialectics* ([1966]1987, p. 396)

The mere thought of hope is a transgression against it, an act of working against it.
—Theodor W. Adorno, *Negative Dialectics* ([1966]1987, p. 402)

Dialectics is the self-consciousness of the objective context of delusion; it does not mean to have escaped from that context. Its objective goal is to break out of the context from within.
—Theodor W. Adorno, *Negative Dialectics* ([1966]1987, p. 406)

We are embarrassed to admit it, but we have engaged in our share of political activism. This may come as a surprise to the reader and may seem to contradict our stated thesis. We have, for example, worked as the local Flint, Michigan, coordinators for the Brown for President campaign in 1992, where we helped to arrange several visits to that city by the former Governor of California, who, at the time, was calling for "a second American Revolution." Our hundreds of hours of labor ultimately translated into the election of two of six possible area delegates to the Democratic National Convention, at which Jerry Brown was, indeed, allowed to speak. Democracy.

In Dayton, we have organized a "Progressive Dayton" coalition. Flint's most famous filmmaker, Michael Moore of *Roger & Me* (1989) fame, catalyzed this effort with an October 1996 appearance in Dayton, which has since become a segment in his latest film, *The Big One* (1997). We held on that day an "Activist Cafe," a "March for Justice in Dayton and the Nation" around a local General Motors' facility, and Moore addressed a variety of public and university audiences and received standing ovations. The Progressive Dayton group has met several times since, and supported various causes, such as a proposed "living wage" ordinance spearheaded by progressive Dayton City Commissioner, Dean A. Lovelace. A splinter group of Progressive Dayton members supported a pop-up candidate for city commission. In May 1996, this candidate, our friend Logan Martinez, received less than two percent of the primary vote, and, as of this writing, the living wage ordinance is still in city commission limbo. Of course, even if this city ordinance is eventually passed into law, and even if our friend had been elected City Commissioner, such efforts do not substantially effect the life-chances of today's would-be postmodern citizen. These are largely symbolic gestures, like our last Progressive Dayton meeting, which was oriented around Ralph Nader's 1997 University of Dayton Law School commencement address, and which was safe at any speed.

We also serve on a variety of task forces and organize various groups. For example, as a member of the City of Dayton Poverty Reduction Task Force, I, the sociologist, facilitated an Urban Poverty Symposium at which the distinguished Dr. William Julius Wilson presides as the keynote speaker. As an involved and apparently competent parent, I, Patrick's mother, organize a support group for parents with disabled children and serve as a parent representative on the Montgomery County Early Intervention Consortium. I, the sociologist, volunteer for a United Way "outcome team" on "economic self-sufficiency," while I, the stay-at-home citizen-scholar, bake bread and make spaghetti sauce to entice local progressives to talk about Dayton's social problems, which are not just economic in nature, as they enjoy a free meal.

We write letters to the editor, letters to our Congressman, letters to *Harper's*. We dabble in Green Party, New Party, Labor Party, and Democratic Party politics. I, the sociologist, join Michael Moore and others on a panel in Flint that addresses that city's evident woes. There are the television and radio interviews, of course, and the audiences that flocks to see Michael, the celebrity. I, the citizen-scholar, address parent workshops in the Dayton Public School system designed to encourage parental involvement in the only free educational system around, but no one attends. We also encourage students to "get involved," both on campus and off. They are remarkably entrepreneurial. They have created Students for Progressive Action (SPA), which has hosted a "Meet the Candidates Night," registered voters, collected signatures, campaigned, and tutored city kids. Once, a SPA representative even went toe-to-toe with the Mayor of Dayton, in public, no less, during a televised City Commission meeting over a local issue that involved the stench of homophobia. We've joined Dayton Peace Action, raised money from labor unions, wrote letters recommending young activists for positions of responsibility, inveighed on behalf of left programming on the local public radio station, organized and supported forums on racism, sexism, and homophobia, and provided political advice to office holders when asked and sometimes even when they don't. And so on and so forth.

We have engaged in activism, then, but we are most certainly not activists. An activist is one who thinks that they are doing something of consequence, and we have never—never—viewed these types of acts as of any consequence. If we organize, educate, and agitate, we do so without the thought that these things will make a difference. Indeed, we are as certain about this as anything: our activism is historically meaningless, it is spatially nothing. At best, it is a mode of living in which one can make acquaintance with some decent folks, help some specific people at specific points of time and space, and get out of the house every once and awhile. Politically, however, it is nothing because meaningful, historical politics is the result of macro-power, and all we have is micro-power. There is, therefore, no contradiction between our thesis and our lives: both are wrong.

We are not activists, but we do try to be theorists. Theory, for us, *is* consequential. It is furthermore essential. We couldn't get along without it. We live it. The mundane particulars of day-to-day existence notwithstanding, there is little else.

In this regard, we must admit that Habermas is certainly right about one thing. In what is perhaps his most famous and widely read analysis of *Dialectic of Enlightenment* (1947), Habermas concludes that it is impossible to hold to the position therein articulated unless "one makes it at least minimally plausible that there is *no way out*" ([1985]1987, p. 128, emphasis added). Habermas, of course, thinks that there *is* a way out. He is, in Charles Lemert's (1997, p. xii) technical usage, "brilliant," and he uses his theoretical acumen to make a strong case for his posited alternative. He thinks we should finish what modernity started. It is the only reasonable thing to do.

These series of interrelated studies, however, are meant as empirical counter-evidence that would establish, contra Habermas, and from the point of view of actually living people, the minimal plausibility of a society that is in fact radically evil and unworthy of further development, and in which there is, as a result, no straightforward way out. So much depends, in other words, on one's experience in-the-world and the final assessment about possibility that one derives from this experience. For us, critical theory begins in 1947 with the assessment that there is no way out. There is yet no reason to overcome this starting point. This is a post-ethical position.

If sociology is, as we have suggested, the documentation of dialectic of enlightenment, then theory—critical reason, dialectical reason, the sociological imagination, whatever terminology one prefers—is but the truth-content of actually existing total falsity. From such a position, one does not engage in wishful thinking. One does not seek hope where there is none. One does not posit, one does not name, one does not aspire. One does not, in other words, collapse the tension between that which (still) exists and its (not yet existing) alternatives. Thus it is, we think, that the truth of postmodern ethics lies in what Foucault might have called the permanent critique of ethics. We must live our contradictions, and there is, in principle, no theoretical constellation that is going to change that. Theory is, therefore, ethical only when it knows this; it is forever unethical because it cannot by itself do anything to change this context, except remain truthful to itself, an act of meaningless micro-resistance, which is all that is left to us.

While we share J.M. Bernstein's (1995) desire to "recover ethical life," we know, like Bernstein, that this is not a matter for positive Hegelian dialectics much less Kantian boundary maintenance. Habermas, for his part, wants to avoid "the performative contradiction inherent in an ideology critique that outstrips itself" by setting "the normative foundations of critical social theory so deep that ... [it would not be] ... disturbed by the decomposition of bourgeois culture" ([1985]1987, pp. 127, 129). For our part and, again, contra Habermas, we state the obvious: we live in that decomposing culture of which he writes; we are of it. And we cannot imagine talking our way out of it, nor do we have faith that theory in-itself will extricate us. If critique must be sunk so deep that reality does not disturb it, then, we ask, what good is it?

Still, Habermas may have a point. There is something productive in sublimating what can only kill you if you face it squarely. There is something liberating in sinking critique so deep that the everyday is not the only thing. We do not, of course, mean to simply set aside mediation or to spurn theory itself, for the act of conceptualization not only portends the truth of our existence, it also effects a difference between that existence and our all-too-predictable future. As we have argued and attempted to demonstrate over the course of these studies, it is theory that is our chosen medium for our world; it is theory that is, for us, the stand-in for what even in an alternative society would never come to rest in-itself: a life worth living. We need, following Ernst Bloch ([1961]1986, p. 316), this "memory of future times." It is the only thing that stands between us and our fate.

In contrast to a linguistic turn, we have in mind for critical theory a turn toward the body and the earth, and the healing of both. This is what sinking theory deep means for us. In this sense, we theorize because theory points beyond itself to what is ultimately in actual life determining: life and death and the desert expanse between them. From the point of view that is sociology *as* ethics, we cannot allow the prevailing calamities that will never be undone to sabotage our reflexive fidelity to the truth, just like we cannot allow wishful thinking to allow us a cool breath of imaginary fresh air. As Max Horkheimer states in his essay, "On the Problem of Truth," "It is a utopian illusion to expect that the strength to live with sober truth will become general until the causes of untruth are removed" ([1935]1982, p. 443). We, at any rate, cannot escape our always already suffocating context. Until it finally determines us, we must act within it the way anyone would who understood it, that is, in its contradiction and in its confusion, in awe of its power, in sadness for its harm.

A damaged life demands a melancholy science as surely as postmodern society today demands a postmodern sociological imagination. As Fredric Jameson has noted:

> Even after the "end of history," there has seemed to persist some historical curiosity of a generally systemic—rather than a merely anecdotal—kind: not merely to know what will happen next, but as a more general anxiety about the larger fate or destiny of our system or mode of production as

such—about which individual experience (of a postmodern kind) tells us that it must be eternal, while our intelligence suggests this feeling to be most improbable indeed, without coming up with plausible scenarios as to its disintegration or replacement. It seems to be easier for us today to imagine the thoroughgoing deterioration of the earth and of nature than the breakdown of late capitalism; perhaps that is due to some weakness in our imaginations. I have come to think that the word *postmodern* ought to be reserved for thoughts of this kind (1994, pp. xi-xii, emphasis in original).

In the end, the task of a postmodern critical theory remains the same: to work from within the anxiety that Jameson points to in order to map this delusion, lest this delusion eclipse the last vestiges of self-consciousness, of imagination, and critical theory reign like a orange-clad deer hunter from Hunter S. Thompson's Phoenix, who, just for kicks, has the Owl of Minerva square in his sights and dead to rights.

Bibliography

Abrams, A., and D. Lipsky. 1994. *Late Bloomers: The Declining Prospects of the Twenty Something Generation.* New York: Times Books.

Adams, A.E. 1994. *Reproducing the Womb.* Ithaca, NY: Cornell University Press.

Adorno, T.W. 1994 [1952-53]. *The Stars Down to Earth and Other Essays on the Irrational in Culture,* edited by S. Crook. New York: Routledge.

————. 1984 [1970]. *Aesthetic Theory.* New York: Routledge & Kegan Paul.

————. 1987 [1966]. *Negative Dialectics.* New York: Continuum.

————. 1984 [1958]. "The Essay as Form." *New German Critique* 32 (Spring-Summer): 151-171.

————. 1977 [1965]. "Commitment." Pp. 177-195 in *Aesthetics and Politics,* edited by R. Taylor. Afterword by F. Jameson. London: Verso.

————. 1974 [1951]. *Minima Moralia: Reflections from Damaged Life.* New York: Verso.

————. 1973 [1964]. *The Jargon of Authenticity.* Evanston, IL: Northwestern University Press.

Agger, Bn. 1998. *Critical Social Theories: An Introduction.* Boulder. CO: Westview Press.

————. 1992a. *Cultural Studies as Critical Theory.* London: Falmer Press.

————. 1992b. *The Discourse of Domination.* Evanston, IL: Northwestern University Press.

————. 1991. *A Critical Theory of Public Life.* London: Falmer Press.

————. 1989a. *Fast Capitalism: A Critical Theory of Significance.* Urbana: University of Illinois Press.

————. 1989b. *Socio(onto)logy: A Disciplinary Reading.* Urbana: University of Illinois Press.

Albom, M. 1997. *Tuesdays with Morrie.* New York: Doubleday.

Anderson, C.W. 1991. "Pragmatism & Liberalism, Rationalism & Irrationalism: A Response to Richard Rorty." *Polity* 3: 357-371.

Arato, A., and E. Gerhardt, eds. 1982. *The Essential Frankfurt School Reader.* New York: Continuum.

Arendt, H. 1976 [1964]. *Eichmann in Jerusalem: A Report on the Banality of Evil.* New York: Penguin.

Aries, P. 1974. *Western Attitudes Towards Death.* Baltimore, MD: The Johns Hopkins University Press.

Arms, S. 1975. *Immaculate Deception*. Boston: Houghton Mifflin.

Aronson, R. 1983. *Dialectics of Disaster: A Preface to Hope*. London: Verso.

Baudrillard, J. 1996 [1990]. *Cool Memories, II*. Durham, NC: Duke University Press.

———. 1995 [1991]. *The Gulf War Did Not Take Place*. Bloomington: Indiana University Press.

———. 1993a [1990]. *The Transparency of Evil: Essays on Extreme Phenomena*. London: Verso.

———. 1993b [1976]. *Symbolic Exchange and Death*. Thousand Oaks, CA: Sage.

———. 1993c. *Baudrillard Live: Selected Interviews*, edited by M. Gane. London: Routledge.

———. 1991. "Panic Crash!" Pp. 64-67 in *The Panic Encyclopedia*, edited by A. Kroker, M. Kroker, and D. Cook. New York: St. Martin's Press.

———. 1988a [1986]. *America*. London: Verso.

———. 1988b. *Jean Baudrillard: Selected Writings*, edited by M. Poster. Stanford, CA: Stanford University Press.

Bauman, Z. 1995. *Life in Fragments: Essays in Postmodern Morality*. Cambridge, MA: Blackwell.

———. 1993. *Postmodern Ethics*. Cambridge, MA: Blackwell.

———. 1989. *Modernity and the Holocaust*. Ithaca, NY: Cornell University Press.

———. 1988. "Is There a Post-Modern Sociology?" *Theory, Culture, & Society* 5: 217-237.

Beckett, S. 1958. *The End Game*. New York: Grove Press.

Bedau, H.A., ed. 1982. *The Death Penalty in America*, 3rd ed. Oxford: Oxford University Press.

Bendix, R. 1962 [1960]. *Max Weber: An Intellectual Portrait*. Berkeley: University of California Press.

Bengtson, V.L., and W.A. Achenbaum, eds. 1993. *The Changing Contract Across Generations*. New York: Aldine De Gruyter.

Benjamin, Walter. 1969. *Illuminations*. New York: Schocken.

Berger, P.L. 1967. *The Sacred Canopy: Elements of a Sociological Theory of Religion*. Garden City, NY: Doubleday.

———. 1963. *Invitation to Sociology*. Garden City, NY: Doubleday.

Berger, P.L., and T. Luckmann. 1966. *The Social Construction of Reality*. Garden City, NY: Anchor.

Berman, M. 1982. *All That Is Solid Melts Into Air*. New York: Penguin.

Bernstein, J.M. 1995. *Recovering Ethical Life*. New York: Routledge.

Bernstein, R.J. 1991. *The New Constellation*. Cambridge, MA: MIT Press.

———. 1987. "One Step Forward, Two Steps Backward: Richard Rorty on Liberal Democracy and Philosophy." *Political Theory* 15: 538-563.

Bérubé, M. 1996. *Life As We Know It*. New York: Pantheon.

————. 1994. "Life As We Know It." *Harper's Magazine* (December): 41-51.

Bewes, T. 1997. *Cynicism and Postmodernity*. London: Verso.

Bhaskar, R. 1991a. "Rorty, Realism, and the Idea of Freedom." Pp. 198-232 in *Reading Rorty,* edited by Alan Malachowski and Jo Burrows. Cambridge, MA: Blackwell.

————. 1991b. *Philosophy and the Idea of Freedom*. Cambridge, MA: Blackwell.

Billig, M. 1993. "Nationalism and Richard Rorty: The Text as a Flag for *Pax Americana*." *New Left Review* 202: 69-84.

Block, E. 1986 [1961]. *Natural Law and Human Dignity*. Cambridge, MA: MIT Press.

Bloom, H., ed. 1987a. *George Orwell*. New York: Chelsea House Publishers.

————. 1987b. *1984*. New York: Chelsea House Publishers.

Blum, A. 1996. "Panic and Fear: On the Phenomenology of Desperation." *The Sociological Quarterly* 37 (4): 673-698.

Bokina, J. 1994. "Marcuse Revisited." Pp. 1-24 in *Marcuse: From New Left to Next Left,* edited by J. Bokina and T.J. Lukes. Lawrence: University Press of Kansas.

Bokina, J., and T.J. Lukes, eds. 1994. *Marcuse: From New Left to Next Left*. Lawrence: University Press of Kansas.

Bradley, R.A. 1965. *Husband-Coached Childbirth*. New York: Harper & Row.

Braverman, H. 1974. *Labor and Monopoly Capital: The Degradation of Work in the Twentieth Century*. New York: Monthly Review Press.

Breines, P. 1994. "Revisiting Marcuse with Foucault," Pp. 41-56 in *Marcuse: From the New Left to the Next Left,* edited by J. Bokina and T.J. Lukes. Lawrence: University Press of Kansas.

Bruck, D. 1988 [1983]. "Decisions of Death." Pp. 496-508 in *Crisis in American Institutions,* 7th ed., edited by J.H. Skolnick and E. Currie. Boston: Scott, Foresman and Co.

Brunkhorst, H. 1996. "Theodor W. Adorno: Aesthetic Constructivism and a Negative Ethic of the Non-forfeited Life." Pp. 305-322 in *The Handbook of Critical Theory,* edited by D.M. Rasmussen. New York: Blackwell.

Buck-Morss, S. 1977. *The Origin of Negative Dialectics*. New York: The Free Press.

Bulter, J. *Gender Trouble: Feminism and the Subversion of Sexuality*. New York: Routledge.

Burrows, J. 1990. "Conversational Politics: Rorty's Pragmatist Apology for Liberalism." Pp. 322-338 in *Reading Rorty,* edited by A. Malachowski and J. Burrows. Cambridge, MA: Blackwell.

Bushnell, P.T., V. Shlapentokh, C.K. Vanderpool, and J. Sandram, eds. 1991. *State Organized Terror: The Case of Violent Internal Repression*. Boulder, CO: Westview Press.

Cahill, S.E., and R. Eggleston. 1995. "Reconsidering the Stigma of Physical Disability: Wheelchair Use and Public Kindness." *The Sociological Quarterly* 36 (4): 681-698.

Cisneros, H. 1995. *Defensible Space: Deterring Crime and Building Community.* Washington, DC: U.S. Department of Housing and Urban Development.

Cohen, A. 1993. "Me and My Zeitgeist." *The Nation* (July): 96-100.

Cohen, J., and M. Krugman. 1994. *Generation Ecch!* New York: Simon & Schuster.

Cohen, L.J. 1993. *Broken Bonds: The Disintegration of Yugoslavia.* Boulder, CO: Westview Press.

Cohen, M.L. 1993. *The Twenty Something American Dream.* New York: Dalton.

Cole, S.E. 1994. "Evading the Subject." Pp. 38-57 in *After Postmodernism: Reconstructing Ideology Critique*, edited by H.W. Simons and M. Billig. Thousand Oaks, CA: Sage.

Corea, G. 1985. *The Mother Machine.* New York: Harper & Row.

Cosslett, T. 1994. *Women Writing Childbirth: Modern Discourses of Motherhood.* New York: Manchester University Press.

Coupland, D. 1991. *Generation X: Tales from an Accelerated Culture.* New York: St. Martin's Press.

Crook, S. 1994. "Introduction: Adorno and Authoritarian Irrationalism." Pp. 1-33 in*The Stars Down to Earth and Other Essays on the Irrational in Culture*, edited byTheodor W. Adorno. New York: Routledge.

Daly, M. 1978. *Gynecology.* Boston: Beacon Press.

Dandaneau, S.P. 1998. "Critical Theory, Legitimation Crisis, and the Deindustrialization of Flint, Michigan." Pp. 151-182 in *Illuminating Social Life*, edited by Peter Kivisto. Thousand Oaks, CA: Pine Forge Press.

———. 1996. *A Town Abandoned: Flint, Michigan, Confronts Deindustrialization.* Albany: State University of New York Press.

———. 1994. "'Minimalist' Sociology Versus 'Taking It Big.'" Pp. 213-239 in *Current Perspectives in Social Theory, Volume 14*, edited by Ben Agger. Greenwich, CT: JAI Press.

Davis, L.J. 1997. "Constructing Normalcy." Pp. 9-28 in *The Disability Studies Reader*, edited by L.J. Davis. New York: Routledge.

Davis, M. 1992. "Beyond Blade Runner: Urban Control: The Ecology of Fear." *Open Magazine Pamphlet Series* 23: 1-21.

———. 1990. *City of Quartz.* New York: Vintage.

Denzin, N.K. 1991. *Images of Postmodern Society.* Newbury Park, CA: Sage.

———. 1990. "The Sociological Imagination Revisited." *The Sociological Quarterly* 31 (1): 1-22.

Donnelly, P.G. 1988. "Individual and Neighborhood Influences on Fear of Crime." *Sociological Focus* 22 (1): 69-85.

Donnelly, P.G., and T.J. Majka. 1998. "Residents' Efforts at Neighborhood Stabilization: Facing the Challenges of Inner City Neighborhoods." *Sociological Forum* 13(2): 189-213.

———. 1996. "Change, Cohesion, and Commitment in a Diverse Urban Neighborhood." *Journal of Urban Affairs* 18(3): 269-284.

Donnelly, P.G., and C.E. Kimble. 1997. "Community Organizing, Environmental Change and Neighborhood Crime." *Crime and Delinquency* 43(4): 493-511.

Dunn, S. 1994. *The Official Slacker Handbook*. New York: Warner Books.

Eribon, D. 1991. *Michel Foucault*. Cambridge, MA: Harvard University Press.

Forester, J., ed. 1985. *Critical Theory of Public Life*. Cambridge, MA: MIT Press.

Foucault, M. 1984. "What is Enlightenment?" Pp. 32-50 in *The Foucault Reader*, edited by P. Rabinow. New York: Pantheon.

———. 1980 [1976]. *The History of Sexuality, Volume I*. New York: Vintage.

Fraser, N. 1989. *Unruly Practices*. Minneapolis: University of Minnesota Press.

Friedan, B. 1963. *The Feminine Mystique*. New York: Norton.

Gelbspan, R. 1995. "The Heat Is On." *Harper's Magazine* (December): 31-37.

Geulen, E. 1997. "Theodor Adorno on Tradition." Pp. 183-193 in *The Actuality of Adorno* edited by Max Pensky. Albany: State University of New York Press.

Giddens, A. 1984. *The Constitution of Society*. Cambridge: Polity Press.

———. 1982. "Historical Materialism Today: An Interview with Anthony Giddens." *Theory, Culture & Society* 1: 63-113.

Giles, J. 1994. "Generations X." *Newsweek Magazine* (June 6): 66-72.

Goode, E., and N. Ben-Yehuda. 1994. *Moral Panics: The Social Construction of Deviance*. Cambridge, MA: Blackwell.

Goodheart, E. 1996. "The Postmodern Liberalism of Richard Rorty." *Partisan Review* 2: 223-235.

Goodman, P. 1960 [1956]. *Growing Up Absurd*. New York: Random House.

Gouldner, A.W. 1970. *The Coming Crisis of Western Sociology*. New York: Basic Books.

Gross, D.M., and S. Scott. 1990. "A Step At a Time." *Time Magazine* (July 16): 36-39.

Habermas, J. 1987a. *The Philosophical Discourses of Modernity*. Cambridge, MA: MIT Press.

———. 1987b [1981]. *The Theory of Communicative Action, Volume II*. Boston: Beacon Press.

———. 1986. "The New Obscurity: The Crisis of the Welfare State and the Exhaustion of Utopian Energies." *Philosophy and Social Criticism* 2 (11): 1-18.

———. 1984 [1981]. *The Theory of Communicative Action, Volume I*. Boston: Beacon Press.

———. 1975 [1973]. *Legitimation Crisis*. Boston: Beacon Press.

Hall, D.L. 1994. *Richard Rorty: Prophet and Poet of the Pragmatism.* Albany: State University of New York Press.

Hayim, G.J. 1980. *The Existential Sociology of Jean-Paul Sartre.* Amherst: University of Massachusetts Press.

Harvey, D. 1996. *Justice, Nature and the Geography of Difference.* Cambridge, MA: Blackwell.

——. 1989. *The Condition of Postmodernity.* Oxford: Basil Blackwell.

Hegel, G.W.F. 1977 [1807]. *Phenomenology of Spirit.* New York: Oxford University Press.

Hernstein, R.T., and C. Murray. 1994. *The Bell Curve: Intelligence and Class Structure in American Life.* New York: The Free Press.

Hitchens, C. 1998. "Scenes from an Execution." *Vanity Fair* 449 (January): 30-42.

Hollis, M. 1990. "The Poetics of Personhood." Pp. 244-256 in *Reading Rorty,* edited by A. Malachowski and J. Burrows. Cambridge, MA: Blackwell.

Holmstrom, David. 1995. "Gates in Dayton Fortress a Diverse Neighborhood." *Christian Science Monitor* (Monday, July 31): 12.

Horkheimer, M. 1987 [1947]. *Eclipse of Reason.* New York: Continumm.

——. 1987 [1947]. "The Revolt of Nature." Pp. 92-127 in *Eclipse of Reason.* New York: Continumm.

——. 1982 [1940]. "The Authoritarian State." Pp. 95-117 in *The Essential Frankfurt School Reader,* edited by A. Arato and E. Gerhardt. New York: Continuum.

——. 1982 [1935]. "On the Problem of Truth." Pp. 407-443 in *The Essential Frankfurt School Reader,* edited by A. Arato and E. Gerhardt. New York: Continuum.

Horkheimer, M., and T.W. Adorno. 1972 [1947]. *Dialectic of Enlightenment.* New York: Herder and Herder.

Hornblower, M. 1997. "Great Xpectations." *Time Magazine* (June 9): 58-68.

Horowitz, I.L. 1993. *The Decomposition of Sociology.* New York: Oxford University Press.

——. 1983. *C. Wright Mills: An American Utopian.* New York: The Free Press.

Howe, I. 1970. *Decline of the New.* New York: Harcourt Brace & World.

Howe, N., and B. Strauss. 1993. *13th Gen.* New York: Vintage.

——. 1992. "The New Generation Gap." *The Atlantic Monthly* (December): 67-89.

Hultkrans, A. 1994. "The Slacker Factor." Pp. 297-303 in *The GexX Reader,* edited by D. Rushkoff. New York: Ballantine Books.

Huyssen, A. 1990 [1984]. "Mapping the Postmodern." Pp. 234-277 in *Feminism/ Postmodernism,* edited by L. Nicholson. New York: Routledge.

——. 1983. "Foreword: The Return of Diogenes as Postmodern Intellectual." Pp. ix-xxv in *Critique of Cynical Reason,* by Peter Sloterdijk. Minneapolis: University of Minnesota Press.

Jackell, R., ed. 1995. *Propaganda*. New York: New York University Press.

Jacobs, J. 1961. *The Death and Life of the American City*. New York: Random House.

Jacoby, R. 1987. *The Last Intellectuals*. New York: Basic Books.

Jameson, F. 1994. *The Seeds of Time*. New York: Columbia University Press.

———. 1991. *Postmodernism, or, The Cultural Logic of Late Capitalism*. Durham, NC: Duke University Press.

———. 1990. *Late Marxism: Adorno, or, The Persistence of the Dialectic*. London: Verso.

———. 1984. "Postmodernism, or, The Cultural Logic of Late Capitalism." *New Left Review* 146: 53-93.

Jay, M. 1984a. *Adorno*. Cambridge, MA: Harvard University Press.

———. 1984b. *Marxism & Totality*. Berkeley: University of California Press.

———. 1973. *The Dialectical Imagination*. Boston: Little Brown and Company.

Karlen, N. 1994. "The Woodstock Nation." *New York Times* (August 5): A11.

Kasinitz, P., ed. 1995. *Metropolis: Center and Symbol of Our Time*. New York: New York University Press.

Katz-Rothman, B. 1989. *Recreating Motherhood: Ideology and Technology in a Patriarchal Society*. New York: W.W. Norton & Co.

Keleman, S. 1983 [1974]. *Living Your Dying*. Berkeley, CA: Center Press.

Kelly, M., ed. 1990. *Hermeneutics and Critical Theory in Ethics and Politics*. Cambridge, MA: MIT Press.

Kies, D. 1991. "Fourteen Types of Passivity: Suppressing Agency in *Nineteen Eighty-Four*. Pp. 47-60 in *The Revised Orwell*, edited by J. Rose. East Lansing: Michigan State University Press.

Kivisto, P. 1998. *Key Ideas in Sociology*. Thousand Oaks. CA: Pine Forge Press.

Kroker, A., M. Kroker, and D. Cook, eds. 1989. *Panic Encyclopedia*. New York: St. Martin's Press.

Kubler-Ross, E. 1969. *On Death and Dying*. New York: Macmillian.

Kunen, J.S. 1997. "It Ain't Us, Babe." *Time Magazine* (September 1): 66-67.

Lemert, C. 1997. *Postmodernism is Not What You Think*. Cambridge, MA: Blackwell.

Levine, S. 1982. *Who Dies?* Garden City, NY: Anchor Press.

Leavitt, J.W. 1986. *Brought to Bed*. New York: Oxford University Press.

Liazos, A. 1972. "The Poverty of the Sociology of Deviance: Nuts, Sluts, and Perverts." *Social Problems* 20 (1): 103-120.

Liu, E. 1994. *Next: Young American Writers on the New Generation*. New York: W.W. Norton.

Lonoff, S. 1991. "Composing *Nineteen Eighty-Four*: The Art of Nightmare." Pp. 25-45 in *The Revised Orwell*, edited by J. Rose. East Lansing: Michigan State University Press.

Lorde, A. 1984. *Sister Outsider*. Freedom, CA: Crossing Press.

Lyman, S.M. 1997. *Postmoderism and a Sociology of the Absurd.* Fayetteville: University of Arkansas Press.

Lyotard, F. 1984. *The Postmodern Condition.* Minneapolis: University of Minnesota Press.

Maass, P. 1996. *Love Thy Neighbor: A Story of War.* New York: Knopf.

Majka, T.J., and P.G. Donnelly. 1988. "Cohesiveness Within a Heterogenous Urban Neighborhood: Implications for Community in a Diverse Setting." *Journal of Urban Affairs* 10: 141-159.

Malachowski, A., and J. Burrows, eds. 1990. *Reading Rorty.* Cambridge, MA: Blackwell.

Mannheim, K. 1952. "The Problem of Generations." Pp. 276-322 in Karl Mannheim, *Essays on the Sociology of Knowledge*, edited by P. Kecskemeti. London: Routledge & Kegan Paul.

Marcus, G.E., and M.M. J. Fischer. 1986. *Anthropology As Cultural Critique.* Chicago: University of Chicago Press.

Marcuse, H. 1972. *Counter-Revolution and Revolt.* Boston: Beacon Press.

———. 1969. *An Essay on Liberation.* Boston: Beacon Press.

———. 1966 [1955]. *Eros and Civilization.* Boston: Beacon Press.

———. 1964. *One-Dimensional Man.* Boston: Beacon Press.

Martin, D. 1993. "The Whiny Generation." *Newsweek Magazine* (November 1): 10.

Marx, K. 1977 [1867]. *Capital, Volume I*, edited by E. Mandel. New York: Vintage.

———. 1963 [1852]. *The Eighteenth Brumaire of Louis Bonaparte.* New York: International Publishers.

Marx, K., and F. Engels. 1977 [1846]. *The German Ideology*, edited by C. J. Arthur. London: Lawrence & Wishart.

Merchant, C. 1980. *The Death of Nature.* New York: Harper & Row.

Mestrovic, S.G. 1997. *Postemotional Society.* Foreword by David Riesman. Thousand Oaks, CA: Sage.

Miller, J. 1993. *The Passion of Michel Foucault.* New York: Simon & Schuster.

Mills, C.W. 1970 [1960]. "Letter to the New Left." Pp. 338-347 in *American Radical Thought,* edited by H.J. Silverman. Lexington, MA: D. C. Heath and Company.

———. 1962. *The Marxists.* New York: Ballantine.

———. 1960a. *Listen Yankee!.* New York: McGraw-Hill Books.

———. 1960b. *Images of Man.* New York: George Braziller.

———. 1959. *The Sociological Imagination.* Oxford: Oxford University Press.

———. 1958. *The Causes of World War III.* New York: Simon & Schuster.

———. 1956. *The Power Elite.* Oxford: Oxford University Press.

Mitford, J. 1993. *The American Way of Birth.* New York: Plume.

———. 1963. *The American Way of Death.* Greenwich CT: Fawcett-Crest.

Nash, M.J. 1997. "Fertile Minds." *Time Magazine* (February 3): 48-56.

Nelson, R., and J. Cowan. 1994. *Revolution X: A Survival Guide for Our Generation*. London: Penguin.

Newman, J. 1997. "At Your Disposal: The Funeral Industry Prepares for Boon Times." *Harper's Magazine* (November): 61-71.

Newman, O. 1996. *Creating Defensible Space*. Washington, DC: U.S. Department of Housing and Urban development, Office of Policy Development and Research.

———. 1973 [1971]. *Architectural Design for Crime Prevention*. Washington, DC: National Institute of Law Enforcement and Criminal Justice.

———. 1972. *Defensible Space*. New York: Macmillian.

Nicholsen, S.W. 1994. "The Persistence of Passionate Subjectivity." Pp. 149-169 in *Marcuse: From New Left to Next Left*, edited by J. Bokina and T.J. Lukes. Lawrence: University Press of Kansas.

Offe, C. 1984. *Contradictions of the Welfare State*. Cambridge, MA: MIT Press.

Orr, J. 1990. "Theory on the Market: Panic, Incorporating." *Social Problems* 37 (4): 460-484.

Orwell, G. 1990 [1945]. *Animal Farm*. San Diego, CA: Harcourt Brace Jovanovich.

———. 1983 [1949]. *Nineteen Eighty-Four*. New York: The New American Library.

Pensky, M., ed. 1997. *The Actuality of Adorno*. Albany: State University of New York Press.

Pfuefer-Kahn, R. 1995. *Bearing Meaning*. Urbana: University of Illinois Press.

Prejean, Sister Helen. 1993. *Dead Man Walking*. New York: Random House.

Ratan, S. 1993. "Why Busters Hate Boomers." *Fortune Magazine* (October 4): 56-70.

Raymond, J.G. 1993. *Women as Wombs*. New York: HarperCollins.

Rees, R. 1984. "All or Nothing." Pp. 201-223 in *Nineteen Eighty-Four to 1984*, edited by C. J. Kuppig. New York: Carroll & Graf Publisher.

Rich, A. 1986 [1976]. *Of Women Born*. New York: W.W. Norton & Co.

Rizvi, T. 1994. "Taking Back the Streets." *University of Dayton Quarterly* (Autumn): 8-9.

Rodden, J. 1989. *The Politics of Literary Reputation: The Making and Claiming of 'St. George' Orwell*. Oxford: Oxford University Press.

Rorty, R. 1995. "Two Cheers for Elitism." *The New Yorker* (January 30): 86-89.

———. 1992. "For a More Banal Politics." *Harper's Magazine* (May): 16-21.

———. 1989. *Contingency, Irony, and Solidarity*. Cambridge: Cambridge University Press.

———. 1985. "Habermas and Lyotard on Postmodernity." Pp. 161-175 in *Habermas and Modernity* edited by Richard J. Bernstein. Cambridge, MA: MIT Press.

———. 1982. *Consequences of Pragmatism*. Minneapolis: University of Minnesota Press.

————. 1979. *Philosophy and the Mirror of Nature*. Princeton, NJ: Princeton University Press.

Rose, J., ed. 1992. *The Revised Rorty*. East Lansing: Michigan State University Press.

Royce, E. 1996. "The Public Intellectual Reconsidered." *Humanity and Society* 20(1): 3-17.

Rushkoff, D., ed. 1994. *The GenX Reader*. New York: Ballantine.

Sanera, M., and J.S. Shaw. 1997. "Facts, Not Fear: Make Sure Your Child Has a Balanced View of the Environment." *Focus on the Family* 21 (8): 10-11.

Sartre, J.-P. 1987 [1957]. *Existentialism and Human Emotions*. Secaucus, NJ: Citadel Press.

————. 1978 [1965]. *What is Literature?* Gloucester: Peter Smith.

————. 1966 [1943]. *Being and Nothingness*. New York: Washington Square Press.

Scarry, E. 1985. *The Body in Pain: The Making and Unmaking of the World*. Oxford: Oxford University Press.

Schell, J. 1982. *The Fate of the Earth*. New York: Avon.

Schwartz, M.S. 1996. *Letting Go: Morrie's Reflections on Dying*. New York: Walker and Company.

Shapiro, J. 1993. "Just Fix It!" *U.S. News & World Report* (February 22): 50-56.

Shapiro, M. et al. 1994. "Don't Call Me Slacker." *Rolling Stone Magazine* (March 24): 85-89.

Simon, D.R., and J.H. Henderson. 1997. *Private Troubles and Public Issues: Social Problems in the Postmodern Era*. Fort Worth, TX: Harcourt Brace.

Sloterdijk, P. 1987 [1983]. *Critique of Cynical Reason*. Minneapolis: University of Minnesota Press.

Soja, E. 1989. *Postmodern Geographies: The Reassertion of Space in Critical Social Theory*. London: Verso.

Star, A. 1993. "The Twentysomething Myth." *The New Republic* (January 4 & 11): 22-25.

Star, J. 1994. "Poor, poor Generation X." Newspaper Enterprise Association (August 29).

Stein, M.R. 1963. "The Poetic Metaphors of Sociology." Pp. 173-182 in *Sociology on Trial,* edited by M.R. Stein and A. J. Vidich. Englewood Cliffs, NJ: Prentice-Hall.

Stephanson, A. 1989. "Regarding Postmodernism: A Conversation with Fredric Jameson." Pp. 43-74 in *Postmodernism, Jameson, Critique*, edited by Douglas Kellner. Washington, DC: Maisonneuve Press.

Strong, D. 1994. "Generation Hex." *New York Times* (OP-ED, Saturday, October 1): 15.

Taylor, C. 1990. "Rorty in the Epistemological Tradition." Pp. 257-265 in *Reading Rorty,* edited by A. Malachowski and J. Burrows. Cambridge, MA: Blackwell.

Terkel, S. 1984. *The Good War*. New York: Pantheon.

Thompson, E.P. 1982. *Notes on Exterminism*. London: Verso.

Thompson, H.S. 1988. *Generation of Swine*. New York: Summit Books.

Toppler, K. 1995. "Richard Rorty, Liberalism, and the Politics of Redescription." *The American Political Science Review* 4: 954-965.

Van Maanen, J. 1988. *Tales of the Field*. Chicago: University of Chicago Press.

Vonnegut, K. 1988 [1968]. Slaughterhouse 5, or *The Children's Crusade: A Duty-Dance with Death*. New York: Dell.

Vulliamy, E. 1994. *Seasons in Hell: Understanding Bosnia's War*. New York: St. Martin's Press.

Wakefield, D. 1971. "Taking It Big: A Memoir of C. Wright Mills." *The Atlantic Monthly* 228 (3): 65-71.

Weber, L.E. 1962. *Between Us Women*. Garden City, NY: Doubleday.

Weber, M. 1978. *Economy and Society*, edited by G. Roth and C. Wittich. Berkeley: University of California Press.

Wertz, R.W., and D.C. Wertz. 1977. *Lying-In*. New York: The Free Press.

West, C. 1993. *Keeping Faith*. New York: Routledge.

———. 1989. *The American Evasion of Philosophy: A Genealogy of Pragmatism*. Madison: University of Wisconsin Press.

Wilson, W.J. 1996. *When Work Disappears: The World of the New Urban Poor*. New York: Knopf.

INDEX

abortion, 246-248
Abrams, Alexander, 148n
Adams, Alice E., 46-48
administered society, 72, 93, 96-97
administration, public, xiii
Adorno, Theodor W., xvii n, xviii, 25n,
    71, 113, 114, 160, 251
  and the administered society, 11
  on astrology, 13, 88-89, 97-100
  and Baudrillard, 238
  on Beethoven, 108
  on commitment, 180-182
  on critical reason, 72
  and critical theory, xvi, 14, 16, 22-
    23
  on culture, 241
  on death, 239, 269
  on domination, 240
  and enlightenment, 1, 27-30
  and ethics, xi, xii, 161-162
  Habermas on, 95
  and history, 21, 61
  on homelessness, 183
  legacy of, 145-146
  and Marcuse, 111
  on Marx, 107
  method of, 6
  on normality, 105
  on Sartre, 184

  and sociological imagination, 2
  theoretical writing of, 3
agency, 13, 235n
  absence of, 139
  and birth, 41, 54, 63-64
  and ethics, xiv
  in *Nineteen Eighty-Four*, 216, 232
  and Rorty, 209
  and social structure, 248
Agger, Ben, xi, xvii n, 3-4, 13, 15, 97,
    259
Albom, Mitch, 246
Albright, Madeline, 254
alienation, 55, 213
  and birth, 41, 46, 54
  and lifeworld, 165
  in *Nineteen Eighty-Four*, 214, 218,
    225, 227, 231, 232
  and resistance, 143
American sociology, 258
Amnesty International, 248
Anderson, Charles, 205, 233n, 234n
Aries, 242
Arms, Suzanne, 50
Aronowitz, Stanley, 258
Aronson, Ronald, 241
astrology, 88-9, 97-100, 102
authority, 29, 44, 56, 66, 104

Pruitt-Igoe, 167, 170, 174, 182, 186
public intellectual, 197, 221
  and biography, 18
  in Dayton, 13
  and defensible space, 152
  demands on, 160
public life, 155
public policy, 104, 163-169, 175, 186
public sphere, 13, 204, 205

racism, 52-53
Rainwater, Lee, 170
Ratan, Suneel, 148n
rationality, psuedo, 88
Raymond, Janice, 57, 69n
Reagan, President Ronald W., 251, 252
Ree, Richard, 235n
reflexive sociology, 259
REM, 240
reproduction, 123
reproductive technology, 42-53, 45, 61,
  69n
resistance, and theory, 272
Rich, Adrienne, 29
Ritzer, George, 258
Rivera, Gelraldo, 130
Robbins, Tim, 248-249, 251
Rock, Chris, 159
Rodden, John, 234n
Rorty, Richard, and
  agency, 209
  R.J. Bernstein on, 24n
  commonsensical non-metaphysi-
    cian, 199, 200-202, 230
  contingency, 202-209, 233
  cruelty, 204-205
  division of labor, 230
  freedom, 204, 208-209, 234n
  home, social, 200
  humiliation, 202-203, 205
  identity, 195, 207, 208, 233
  institutions, social and political,
    202, 204-212, 230

  intellectual, ironic, 199-202, 227-
    230
  intellectual practice, 196-197, 207,
    212, 230
  irony, 197, 201-205, 213
  language, 207
  liberalism, 198, 201-205
  Orwell, 213-215, 229
  philosophy, 198, 211
  playfulness, 208
  politics, 22
  public/private spheres, 204-206
  social legitimation, 197, 200-201,
    209-213, 230, 231, 233
  solidarity, 199-202, 204, 206
  theory, 198, 211, 230
  truth, 206-207, 212
Royce, Edward, 152
Rushkoff, Douglas, 118
Rwanda, 240

Sagan, Carl, 251
Sarandon, Susan, 248
Sartre, John-Paul, xv, 7, 24n, 72, 255,
  256
  on commitment, 180-182
  and the culture industry, 184
Scarry, Elaine, 202
Schell, Jonathan, 251
Schutz, Alfred, 115
Schwartz, Morris, 243-244, 245
science, 43
  and birth, 50, 60, 65
  and death, 242
  and enlightenment, 28-30, 72
  and history, 61-64
  and irrationality, 89
Scott, Sophronia, 148n
Shapiro, Joseph, 148n
Simmel, Georg, 186
Slacker, 114-121
Sloterdijk, Peter, 25n, 66
  and postmodernity, 15-17
Smashing Pumpkins, 240